Using Evidence in

Social
Work
Practice

Also available from Lyceum Books, Inc.

INTRODUCTION TO SOCIAL WORK: THE PEOPLE'S PROFESSION, 2E,
by Ira Colby and Sophia Dziegielewski

SOCIAL POLICY ANALYSIS AND PRACTICE,
by Thomas M. Meenaghan, Keith M. Kilty, and John G. McNutt

CASE MANAGEMENT: AN INTRODUCTION TO CONCEPTS AND SKILLS, 2E,
by Arthur Frankel and Sheldon Gelman

SOCIAL WORK WITH FAMILIES: CONTENT AND PROCESS,
by Robert Constable and Daniel B. Lee

NAVIGATING HUMAN SERVICE ORGANIZATIONS,
by Margaret Gibelman

ENDINGS IN CLINICAL PRACTICE: EFFECTIVE CLOSURE IN DIVERSE SETTINGS,
by Joseph Walsh

RAISE UP A CHILD,
by Edith V. P. Hudley, Wendy Haight, and Peggy Miller

ADVOCACY, ACTIVISM, AND THE INTERNET,
by Steven F. Hick and John G. McNutt

GENERALIST PRACTICE IN LARGER SETTINGS: KNOWLEDGE AND
SKILL CONCEPTS,
by Thomas M. Meenaghan and W. Eugene Gibbons

TEAMWORK IN MULTIPROFESSIONAL CARE,
by Malcolm Payne, foreword by Thomas M. Meenaghan

MODERN SOCIAL WORK THEORY: A CRITICAL INTRODUCTION, 2E,
by Malcolm Payne, foreword by Stephen C. Anderson

CROSS-CULTURAL PRACTICE: SOCIAL WORK WITH DIVERSE POPULATIONS,
by Karen V. Harper and Jim Lantz

WORKING WITH CHILDREN AND THEIR FAMILIES, 3E,
by Martin Herbert and Karen V. Harper-Dorton

SCHOOL SOCIAL WORK: PRACTICE, POLICY, AND
RESEARCH PERSPECTIVES, 5E,
by Robert Constable, Shirley McDonald, and John P. Flynn

Using Evidence in

Social
Work
Practice

Behavioral Perspectives

EDITED BY

Harold E. Briggs   *and*   Tina L. Rzepnicki
Portland State University   University of Chicago

LYCEUM
BOOKS, INC.
5758 South Blackstone Avenue
Chicago, Illinois 60637

© Lyceum Books, Inc., 2004

Published by
LYCEUM BOOKS, INC.
5758 S. Blackstone Ave.
Chicago, Illinois 60637
(773) 643-1902 (phone)
(773) 643-1903 (fax)
lyceum@lyceumbooks.com
http://www.lyceumbooks.com

Library of Congress Cataloging-in-Publication Data

Using evidence in social work practice : behavioral perspectives / [edited] by Harold E. Briggs and Tina L. Rzepnicki
    p. cm.
Includes bibliographical references.
ISBN 0-925065-44-7
    1. Social service—Decision making. 2. Critical thinking. 3. Social service—Evaluation. I. Briggs, Harold E. II. Rzepnicki, Tina L.
HV41.U73 2004
361.3'2—dc22

                                      2004001722

CONTENTS

FOREWORD

The chapters in this book comprise findings from original research, arguments from theoretical papers, and thoughts on the current and future directions of social work practice. They were written by colleagues and former students of Professor Elsie M. Pinkston to commemorate her retirement from the University of Chicago School of Social Service Administration (SSA). During her twenty-nine years at the University of Chicago, Elsie demonstrated in her research and teaching the themes reflected in this book—an evidence-based approach to learning and discovery, adherence to reliable scientific methods, and the pursuit of socially relevant applications to extend practitioner knowledge within a cogent and consistent theoretical framework. The range of topics considered in this book parallels Elsie's varied interests and spans the developmental spectrum, from parent training to work with the elderly, and touches on a wide array of social issues.

Elsie's career began at the University of Kansas, where she earned undergraduate and advanced degrees in human development and child psychology from the Department of Human Development and Family Life. She was awarded fellowships from the National Institute of Mental Health and the National Institute of Child Health and Human Development in support of her research on the effectiveness of parent training procedures. After earning her doctorate in 1973, she joined the SSA faculty as cochair of the new Behavior Analysis Sequence and was instrumental in developing new fieldwork sites in mental health, school, and gerontology settings. This early focus on setting an innovative direction for training and service characterizes her career contributions to the field of clinical social work practice.

Elsie divided her time between teaching at the master's and doctoral levels and applied clinical research with families, children, and the elderly. Her contributions to the development of the SSA curriculum in direct practice focused on expanding the applications of behavioral treatment methods to specialized populations and using empirical methods to assess treatment effectiveness. Her research, supported by various federal, state, and private grants and often pursued in collaboration with doctoral students, resulted in several significant publications. She is the primary author of two books. The first, *Effective Social Work Practice*, demonstrates the integration of behavioral methods with social work applications. The second, *Care of the Elderly: A Family Approach*, outlines innovative techniques of working with the elderly. She is also coeditor of *Environment and Behavior*, and her collaborative service with the Office of the Inspector General of the Illinois Department of Children and Family Services resulted in the development of an ethics manual, *Ethical Child Welfare Practice, Volume 1: Clinical Issues*, published by the Child Welfare League of America. Elsie's recent research involves an evaluation of the system variables and the ensuing consequences involved in using "sexual aggression" as a category for treatment of children who are wards of the state.

Elsie's care toward, respect for, and nurturing of her students cannot be directly conveyed by these chapters, which were developed independently as examples of scholarship at the invitation of the editors. She has been an informal mentor for countless doctoral students and a direct supervisor for more than thirty doctoral dissertations. This volume as a whole stands as a testament to the inspiration she has given to those who have gone on to become accomplished social work professionals.

On April 4, 2003, SSA hosted a public research symposium, "Bridging the Gap between Research and Practice," in honor of Elsie's retirement. Many of the contributors to this book joined SSA faculty members and other social work professionals in a discussion of the implications of the work presented here on current and future social work practices. It is our hope that these chapters will extend Elsie's vision and inspire continuing debate and progress in the field of social work.

Ben Friedman

INTRODUCTION

USING EVIDENCE IN YOUR PRACTICE

Tina L. Rzepnicki and
Harold E. Briggs

This book focuses on the art and science of using evidence to help people change. It provides a framework for considering the relationship of ethics, evidence, and theory to behavioral social work practice, a discussion of some of the technical aspects of implementation, and illustrations of evidence-based behavioral practice in a range of settings and with a variety of client problems. As an anthology, it is not meant to be comprehensive. Instead, the chapters in part 1 raise questions and provoke discussion about ethics, the nature of evidence, and the role of theory. The chapters in part 2 serve as models for developing practice to address particular problems and client populations on the basis of empirical evidence and behavioral theory. The chapters in part 3 raise practical issues in implementation.

Compiling these chapters has given me cause to remember my time as a graduate student; I was a little nervous about what I was plunging into but very excited about having the opportunity to learn about the field and profession of social work in a challenging academic environment with world-class professors.[1] I tried to remember, as best I could (it was a long time ago), what my initial reasons were for wanting a master's degree in social work. In fact, the memory is quite vivid because my reason for seeking a professional education continues to be one of my driving goals today as an educator and a researcher.

Prior to enrolling in graduate school, I worked for several years at the House of the Good Shepherd, a residential treatment center in Chicago for abused, neglected, and dependent teenage girls. The job came with a lot of responsibility. I had a caseload of twenty girls. My charge was to help them get along better in their placement, at school, and with their families. I wanted to do well by them, but, having majored in sociology as an undergraduate, I had taken on professional social work duties without the requisite credentials and with very little knowledge or skills. I was constantly frustrated by not knowing if I was really being helpful to my clients; even when they said I was, I was doubtful. And although I recognized that the impact of my work was rarely dramatic, I simply did not have the skills to know if small but important changes were occurring in my clients' lives.

The House of the Good Shepherd had two consultants, both of whom were

---

1. This vignette reflects the experience of the first author.

very dynamic individuals with impressive reputations. One was a psychiatrist who brought a strong psychoanalytic perspective to the table and wrote prescriptions for the girls. The other was a behavioral psychologist who encouraged the use of behavioral contracts and the rearrangement of environmental contingencies. I had no basis on which to select the guidance of one over that of the other. And because their theoretical frameworks were so different, it was nearly impossible to integrate their advice.

I visited the library and the bookstores searching for material that would teach me how to do my job more effectively, without really knowing or even questioning whether the theories and strategies I found were scientifically sound or not. I believed that the books and articles written by experts would certainly clarify the best ways of proceeding. But, in truth, I really had no way to evaluate the knowledge contained in those publications.

My frustrations led me to graduate school with an explicit set of goals in mind: to be exposed to current knowledge relevant to social work; to learn ways of thinking that would enable me to use this knowledge wisely (effectively) in professional decision making; and, most important, to learn how to assess the value of information by evaluating its relevance, integrity, and usefulness. These goals may be different from yours, but they are primary objectives of professional education. They represent elements of critical thinking. They are also core elements of evidence-based practice, and their application will help you become a competent professional.

PANNING FOR GOLD

Neil Browne and Stuart Keeley, in their book *Asking the Right Questions: A Guide to Critical Thinking* (2001), apply two noteworthy metaphors to describe approaches to learning. The first is a sponge metaphor, which represents the process of absorbing as much information as possible, without judging its worth. This is a rather passive approach based on the assumption that the more information you acquire, the more capable you are of understanding its complexities. A disadvantage is that there is no method for deciding which information and opinions to believe and which to reject. The sponge approach requires good concentration and memory. Although the approach is useful in the initial stages of knowledge acquisition, eventually one needs a way to sort information. The second metaphor they use is "panning for gold." The panning-for-gold approach to learning is much more active than the sponge approach. It involves some level of interaction between the speaker and the listener (or the author and the reader). It requires ways to figure out what information is gold and what is gravel. Panning strategies include asking the right questions to identify deficiencies in the information. As Browne and Keeley state, "The two approaches complement each other. To pan for intellectual gold, there must be something in your pan to evaluate. To evaluate arguments, you must possess knowledge" (p. 4).

This book is meant to highlight the importance of knowing how to "pan for gold," emphasizing the use of critical thinking skills for evaluating and using knowledge for practice. The chapters, written by prominent social work scholars and practitioners, embrace four principles related to this emphasis:

1. Critical thinking is essential to your development as a social work professional.
2. Social work practice should be guided by the best available evidence.
3. Social work practitioners have an obligation to monitor client progress.
4. Social work practitioners build their own practice models based on their experience and the experience of others.

CRITICAL THINKING FOR THE SOCIAL WORK PROFESSIONAL

In chapter 1, Eileen Gambrill states, "Critical thinking involves the careful appraisal of beliefs and actions to arrive at well-reasoned ones that maximize the likelihood of helping clients and avoiding harm. . . . It requires clarity of expression, critical appraisal of evidence and reasons, and consideration of well-argued alternative points of view" (p. 3). Two basic assumptions of critical thinking are that not all knowledge is equally useful and that even knowledge that has a firm empirical basis is tentative and subject to revision. If we attempt to engage in helping on the basis of bad information, our judgments about client needs and interventions will be wrong and our actions ineffective or, worse, harmful. We need critical-thinking skills to sort through what is useful knowledge and what is not. Skepticism, which stands squarely between gullibility at one extreme and cynicism at the other, is essential to the thinking process.

In the world of social science knowledge, and in social work education in particular, searching for right answers causes students a great deal of frustration. When dealing with questions of human behavior, particularly the causes of behavior, key variables and relationships among them are so complex that it is difficult to apply rigorous standards of evidence. In fact, we usually cannot do more than make intelligent guesses. In most instances our answers will be probabilistic—they will lack the degree of certainty that would provide comfort and increase confidence that we are on the right track in understanding and predicting behavior or events (Browne & Keeley, 2001).

As you are introduced to various theories, you will be wise to become familiar with the level of empirical support for each, as well as the limits and the overall integrity of that support, and to remember the tentativeness of knowledge generally. This will aid in keeping you vigilant, reduce your temptation to become overly confident, and encourage you to seek out multiple sources of information, as well as conflicting views, in order to make reasonable choices for yourself. Eight guiding questions to ask as you invoke critical thinking (adapted from Browne & Keeley, 2001) are

1. What is the issue or claim being made, in simple and direct language?
2. Are there any ambiguities or a lack of clarity in the claim?

3. What are the underlying value and theory assumptions?
4. Is there indication of any misleading beliefs or faulty reasoning?
5. How good is the evidence presented?
6. Is any important information missing?
7. Is consideration given to alternative explanations?
8. Are the conclusions reasonable?

Possession of relevant knowledge and skills should reduce some of your uncertainty about human behavior and how to intervene effectively to reduce problems in living. You are embarking on an educational experience that includes classroom instruction meant to increase your understanding of the contributions of the biological and social sciences to the broad field of social work. You are also learning to apply this knowledge through the development of professional skills in your fieldwork. Even though formal theories and supporting research are not perfect or complete, they do help fill in missing pieces of a picture, so that you can be more confident in taking particular actions.

Critical thinking is important in another aspect of learning as well. Evidence-based practice, an approach that is gaining prominence in social work curricula, depends on critical thinking to identify empirically validated methods for helping clients. Although the term "evidence-based practice" has emerged in social work only in the past five years or so, its principles continue social work's long tradition in social work of using scientific methods in practice. Although objective criteria for determining whether an approach is empirically validated are lacking, research-based interventions seem to offer some of the best information for selecting intervention strategies (Witkin, 1991; Klein & Bloom, 1995, cited in Reid, 2002). Critical thinking will help you assess the quality of information you obtain not only from the literature but also from your clients directly. Critical thinking will help you choose the best information sources to inform your practice decision making, whether you are problem solving with clients, managing staff, or designing new programs.

As a professional social worker, use of critical thinking skills will increase the likelihood that you will stay current with the developing knowledge base and be able to avoid ineffective or harmful practices. This is precisely why an education that gives you merely a handy toolbox is not good enough for a professional lifetime of use. Some social work techniques and strategies currently in use will soon become obsolete because of the rapidly developing scientific foundation of practice. If a toolbox were all that was required for competent practice, then in-service training, not professional education, would address your learning needs. Graduation is not the time to put away good habits of the mind. Indeed, it is a launching into the very arena in which you will need them most. After you complete your education, there are likely to be many continuing-education opportunities available to you. In the workplace, you may be inundated with new information and feel pressured to conform to agency culture and norms. You may be understandably reluctant to question too much at the outset, but you can use that time to assess the extent to which thoughtful employees and well-informed practice are valued. Seek out resources that support you in your work: the library, colleagues whose analytic skills can be called on to supplement your own, and professional organizations that promote well-informed practice. But also seek out professional literature and colleagues whose perspectives conflict with yours, for they can help you challenge your customary views and preferred approaches.

To summarize, critical thinking is an essential part of your professional development. It requires asking the right questions to determine, for you, the value of what you see and hear in the classroom and in the field. Obviously, you will not be able to scrutinize fully every piece of information thrown your way. You will have to decide which pieces are worth the effort and which will have the biggest consequences if they are incorrect. In any case, recognize that you will make errors but that you can learn from them. Identify what you do not know but need to learn that is relevant to your coursework and field experience. Go after that knowledge aggressively on your own and look for opportunities to pan for gold wherever and whenever you can. We hope that this book will give you some nuggets to ponder.

USING EVIDENCE TO GUIDE SOCIAL WORK PRACTICE

All social workers form a perspective about the clients and systems they serve. That perspective includes a definition of problems in need of resolution, desirable outcomes, and ways to proceed with intervention. The targets of practice (selected problems and goals) open the door for the practitioner to use theory that explains them as a guide for intervention planning and as the focus for evaluating change. Ideally, the target serves as a thread that binds theories of human behavior to intervention method and evaluation schemes as if they were joined as links in a chain. Theory provides the conceptual blueprint of what needs attention, what can be done about it, and how the practitioner will know when the situation has been resolved.

Practitioners who work in theory-based practices and have techniques that are not derived from empirical findings or accompanied by scientific methods are faced with a significant challenge. When practitioners do not document their intervention process using reliable and valid methods of assessment, including tracking procedures, they do not have a database to inform case decision making or to determine outcomes. Knowledge that can be derived from their experience cannot be easily discerned and then added to a knowledge base for continued use. It becomes impossible to know which strategies are helpful and which should be discarded. If practitioners cannot demonstrate that what they do is beneficial to clients, then they will not be able to replicate their success when helping other clients.

Evidence-based social work practice has been described in this way: "Placing the client's benefits first, evidence-based practitioners adopt a process of lifelong learning that involves continually posing specific questions of direct practical importance to clients, searching objectively and efficiently for the current best evidence relative to each question, and taking appropriate action guided by evidence" (Gibbs, 2003, p. 6). Taking appropriate action guided by evidence includes ensuring that data on intervention and case progress are systematically collected and used to make decisions on whether to continue, revise, or discontinue the problem-solving effort. Important practice principles identified by Reid (2002) include informing clients "about the evidence supporting interventions so that they can make informed decisions about the kind of services they will choose to receive" and replacing the practitioner's authority "with openly shared knowledge about the efficacy of the interventions at the practitioner's disposal" (p. 12). As can be seen from these conceptualizations, an evidence-based approach integrates three aspects of practice: the client's preferences, the practitioner's individual expertise, and the best external evidence available (Gibbs, 2003; Sackett, Strauss, Richardson, Rosenberg, & Haynes, 2000). Their importance is reflected in the National Association of Social Workers' Code of Ethics (National Association of Social Workers, 1999). Specific sections of the code that apply (Gibbs, 2003, p. 16) are

- "Social workers' primary responsibility is to promote the well-being of clients" (section 1.01).

- "Social workers respect and promote the right of clients to self-determination and assist clients in their efforts to identify and clarify their goals [with notable exceptions regarding harm to self and to others]" (section 1.02: Self-Determination).

- "Social workers practice within their areas of competence and develop and enhance their professional expertise" (section 1.04: Competence).

- "Social workers should critically examine and keep current with emerging knowledge relevant to social work and fully use evaluation and research evidence in their professional practice" (section 5.02: Evaluation and Research).

We acknowledge, however, that at present there are enormous gaps in the empirical knowledge base and that, for many decisions, practitioners will find it "insufficient for guiding practice" (Berlin & Marsh, 1993, p. 15; Marsh, chapter 2, this volume). How, then, can we blend theory and empirical findings to inform practice? There are many social workers who choose to use methods derived from science and practitioners who use science as a part of their community organizing practice (e.g., the works of Friesen and colleagues on family support in children's mental health (Friesen, 1993). The chapters in part 2 of this volume present many applications of applied behavior analysis and other scientifically derived interventions that highlight the integration of empirical and theoretical knowledge as a basis for framing practitioner hunches, guesses, and critical perspectives. Given the definition of problem targets, the practitioner develops a set

of hypotheses or hunches that describe what should be done for successful problem reduction or goal attainment. In the best of worlds, practice hunches are derived from a literature review that includes empirical evidence suggesting best
practices in order to address a particular issue as well as from a firm understanding of the limits of current knowledge regarding the efficacy and effectiveness of possible solutions. You will have to decide for yourself if evidence-based
practice represents a true shift in emphasis or "old wine in new bottles," as Thyer
suggests (chapter 5, this volume).

Objections

Opposition to evidence-based practice has been raised on several grounds,
many of which have their origins in its application to medical practice but also
have been identified as pertaining to social work. Major objections (italicized) are
briefly described below. You are encouraged to seek out additional discussion of
these points and consider others that may be raised as you read this book and in
your practice.

Evidence-based practice limits professional autonomy. Those raising this
objection are perhaps reluctant to give up their reliance on traditional authority
structures and presumed expertise (e.g., that of a supervisor) in favor of practice
informed by the most current social science knowledge (Reynolds, 2000). This
leads to the next objection.

*Evidence-based practice relies on a biased and partial version of science that
depends heavily on randomized experiments as the only legitimate source of evidence (Reynolds, 2000).* It is widely believed that evidence-based practice is
only concerned with randomized clinical trials that do not answer clinical questions and cannot be applied to complex personal, social, and organizational environments in which both clients and practitioners operate (Geddes, 2000;
Trinder, 2000). If that were the case, then there would be very little acceptable
evidence for use in social work practice. But that perspective does not allow for
the rich body of research that makes use of a variety of designs (including qualitative methods) and methodological compromises. It does not recognize the
value of single-case methods as most appropriate in developing new interventions and programs. Furthermore, it does not recognize that other, less rigorous
research can contribute important insights into practice that are superior to approaches that do not make use of any empirical evidence. Fortune and Reid
(1999) refer to this as relying on the "best available knowledge" and Klein and
Bloom (1995), the "best available information" (Kirk & Reid, 2002, p. 199).

*Evidence-based practice is nothing new; it merely represents what good prac-
titioners do anyway* (Geddes, 2000). That is, for years social work education has
taught practitioners to draw on the professional knowledge base to inform their
practice, and, presumably, good practitioners do so. Yet, routine use of social science knowledge does not seem to happen. Why?

Obstacles that Reynolds (2000) mentions include the difficulties that a practitioner is likely to experience when attempting to identify clinical research questions that are relevant to the client's situation and can inform professional decisions. Although social work education teaches the four domains of inquiry— the cause of the problem, diagnosis/assessment procedures, intervention options, and appropriate outcomes against which specific actions can be tested— practitioners may not be skilled at articulating their specific information needs at a particular decision point. Even if an appropriate question is identified, finding the evidence related to the specific question may be problematic. There are far too many sources of useful information (professional journals, books, and research reports) for the average practitioner to search effectively, especially within strict time constraints. Fortunately, guidelines have been developed to help professionals conduct thorough and efficient computer searches and to assist them in evaluating the quality of the evidence they find (e.g., Gibbs, 2003).

THE OBLIGATION TO MONITOR CLIENT PROGRESS

The main reasons for tracking client progress are to inform case decision making, to demonstrate to stakeholders (e.g., the client and his or her significant others, other authorities in the client's life, the practitioner, supervisors, agency funding sources) the results of problem-solving efforts, and to build knowledge for practice. Strategies to monitor client progress exist on a continuum of informal to formal and rigorous case evaluation. Most practitioners track changes at least informally. Systematic measurements to track progress and guide decision making can help you be a more effective helper by providing less biased indications of progress and feedback to help you know when you need to change your approach and by allowing clients to attribute changes in the problem situation to their own efforts. In addition, the collection of evaluative data from multiple sources potentially provides corroboration, which increases confidence in the results obtained. The practitioner who relies primarily on instincts and subjective judgments is like the lost sea captain in a large vessel, sailing alone in the fog without the proper support of navigation equipment, visual aids, or time to steer the ship free of dangerous waters.

As with any profession, social work's credibility relies on the ability to monitor and regulate the activities of its members. Practitioners have an overarching ethical responsibility to their clients to provide the most effective assessment, treatment, and referral, and this requires an ongoing critical examination of practice. Consistent with the National Association of Social Workers' Code of Ethics (National Association of Social Workers, 1999), "Social workers should monitor and evaluate policies, the implementation of programs, and practice interventions" (section 5.02).

Why, then, do practitioners resist careful examination of their practices? Often, social workers have little or no professional incentive to examine their practices, and they view requests to do so as intrusive. Reasons for lack of motivation are likely due to collegial mistrust, logistical realities, and philosophical differences (Galassi & Gersh, 1993; Levy, 1996; Wong, 1996). Use of data requires that practitioners take the time to track patterns of change, make decisions based on the data, and continue to monitor client reactions to intervention. Documentation of these activities increases vulnerability to third-party scrutiny by supervisors, funders, and collateral resources. Additional scrutiny may threaten the practitioner's sense of autonomy.

Participating in knowledge development exposes practitioners and their practices to the scrutiny of their colleagues and clients. To be fair, this may be a scary proposition, but, in fact, it is exactly what social workers ask of their clients. Practitioners develop and nurture trusting relationships with their clients as a matter of course, for without this trust, very little can be accomplished. Practitioners foster this trust by responding to their clients with courtesy, respect, and reassurance; this same kind of trusting relationship needs to be developed between the practitioner and his or her professional colleagues. Through the establishment of supportive work environments, individual practitioners can be encouraged to participate in knowledge development and to expect considered, respectful responses from their colleagues. Mistakes and missteps in practice are viewed as indications of exploration and developing knowledge; if there are no mistakes, no misunderstandings, then there is probably no significant learning going on. Practitioners must learn to value themselves as worthwhile participants in the development of their profession; what they know, what they do, and how they do it constitute the very substance of social work.

Lack of funding and understaffing continually strain scarce resources and create logistical concerns. Chief among these concerns is a lack of adequate time to accomplish necessary tasks. How is a practitioner to fit more work into an already overtaxed schedule? This is a legitimate concern because, with few exceptions, social service providers operate under tight time constraints, and it is difficult for them to imagine adding more tasks. Practitioners may need to rethink how they use their time in practice in order to avoid acting impulsively and with too much subjectivity.

Finally, some practitioners may have philosophical objections to systematic tracking of case progress. They may fear that collecting data eventually leads to forming theories, theories that then contribute principles to more definitive practice models. Some practitioners fear that theory leads to a one-size-fits-all practice approach that carries little meaning at the individual level. Polarizing theory-based and theory-free practice and casting them as adversaries completely dismisses a more useful and more realistic relationship that exists between the two; namely, theory and practice inform and modify each other. The relationship between the two is not linear, not cause and effect, but rather recursive and mutually interactive. Case evaluation is not simply an important component to this recursive activity; it is essential. Marsh significantly extends this discussion in chapter 2, which focuses on the utility and benefits of theory-based practice and research.

As practitioners employ theoretically based practices, the practices become tempered and modified by experience and intuition. This trial and error is not without merit—experience and intuition are powerful sources of knowledge; nevertheless, practitioners are often confused when sometimes an approach works, yet other times it does not. The crucial point to note here is that often there is no way to know or to understand why this happens. To be sure, much data exist in client files, agency reports, and client information databases, but these data are rarely compiled and analyzed in any comprehensive manner beyond providing statistics for funding sources. In recent years there has been an increased push for agencies to focus on outcomes as a basis for management decisions, but rarely have client outcomes been used to guide supervision or alter practice at the level of direct line staff. This may be because the data collected are not necessarily the data that would best inform intervention activities. The outcomes selected may not be particularly relevant at the individual case level. For example, data collected on out-of-home placement of a child may provide evidence of program failure at an administrative level, if the goal of the program is to keep children safe in their own homes. However, it may not represent a failure for a particular family whose child could be protected only through placement in foster care. Data, systematically collected on key dimensions of a case and its interventions, constitute a potentially rich source of information for program evaluation and for ultimately providing the best services available to individual families.

In general, evaluation efforts focus on phenomena that are observable and thus can be recorded. However, there are phenomena that, although they are not observable, can nonetheless be recorded, compiled, categorized, analyzed, evaluated, and used as a basis for case decision making and program evaluation (e.g., practitioners' and clients' beliefs, attitudes, expectations, and intuitions). Social work practitioners and their clients represent rich sources of data for both client and program evaluation. The information they posses must be collected systematically in order for it to be useful for individual case or program monitoring and development. These data can also become the grist for the mills of theory as helping knowledge.

BUILDING PRACTICE MODELS BASED ON EXPERIENCE AND WHAT CAN BE LEARNED FROM OTHERS

Now we have come full circle. From our experiences in applying critical thinking to theory and empirical evidence, in monitoring and evaluating client progress to get a sense of what, in our own experience, works best for whom, we build knowledge for practice—for ourselves and potentially for others. The National Association of Social Workers' Code of Ethics (National Association of Social Workers, 1999) puts forth the following principle: "Social workers should contribute to the knowledge base of social work and share with colleagues their knowledge related to practice, research, and ethics. Social workers should seek to contribute to the profession's literature and to share their knowledge at professional meetings and conferences" (section 5.01).

The purpose of this particular standard is, at the very least, to encourage the social work practitioner to systematically build a personal repertoire of skills—a personal model of practice (Mullen, 1994). However, without an *exchange* of these ideas, strategies, and approaches, social work practice risks becoming stagnant, ineffectual, and even dangerous.

Drawing on the work of Rothman and Thomas (1994) and Mullen (1994), one can say that the process of building intervention knowledge involves converting research findings into social interventions for particular clients or target populations. Practitioners can design interventions, develop practice guidelines, and test and refine those guidelines over time in their own practice. Building knowledge for personal use does not require the use of sophisticated research design. In fact, focusing on a single case can provide rich information that is useful for tailoring intervention strategies to clients' needs in a way that group designs do not permit. Several social work scholars have emphasized the utility of pilot testing using single cases or groups as a means of determining whether an intervention is on the right track with respect to the initial stages of building helping knowledge (e.g., Fawcett, Suarez-Balcazar, Balcazar, White, Paine, Blanchard, & Embree, 1994; Kirk & Reid, 2002; Rothman & Tumblin, 1994; Thomas, 1984). Questions to be answered at this early stage of development include, Can the intervention be successfully implemented and, if so, can it achieve desired outcomes? In chapter 9, Shibano provides an illustration of the design and development paradigm applied to a parent-training program in Japan.

Intervention knowledge is also reflected in practice wisdom learned over repeated trials. It can be found in the body of evidence gathered from permanent products, such as information routinely recorded in agency files. It includes data that points to the client's responses to treatment, lessons learned from practice, and unintended consequences observed during intervention, as well as specific design, development, and testing of particular intervention strategies. Thus, intervention knowledge is that class of information that represents what we currently know about how to help. It is the codification, classification, and functional analysis of human systems and their responses to social work intervention.

SUMMARY AND CONCLUSION

This introduction highlighted the importance of knowing how to "pan for gold," emphasizing the use of critical-thinking skills for evaluating and using knowledge for practice. We addressed four principles related to this emphasis:

1. Critical thinking is essential to your development as a social work professional.
2. Social work practice should be guided by the best available evidence.
3. Social work practitioners have an obligation to monitor client progress.
4. Social work practitioners build their own practice models based on their experience and the experience of others.

Although these principles form a foundation for the rest of the book, it is important to recognize that there are important benefits, as well as challenges, to using evidence in social work practice.

Benefits

Evidence-based practice helps you link what your client wants (regardless of whether your client is an individual, a family, an organization, or a community) with your professional expertise and the best evidence available to inform your work together. It has the potential to enhance your credibility, the therapeutic alliance, and client outcomes (Sackett et al., 2000).

Evidence-based practice is consistent with professional standards of practice as expressed in the National Association of Social Workers' Code of Ethics (National Association of Social Workers, 1997). In chapter 1, Gambrill discusses the ways in which evidence-based practice assists the practitioner in meeting these ethical responsibilities. Thyer (chapter 5) offers suggestions for expanding the Code of Ethics to more directly support evidence-based practice.

Searching for the best available evidence to inform your practice will provide direct exposure to critical thinking and knowledge use. It will shape a critical approach to the investigative process that combines problem analysis, problem solving, and scientific methods. It enables you to generate informed theoretical assumptions and sound operational hypotheses that can guide practice and research alike (Marsh, chapter 2, this volume).

Compared to time-consuming manual searches, electronic searches may actually reduce the amount of time it takes to locate good and useful information without sacrificing quality. In fact, new strategies for more efficient searching may also enhance the quality of the information found (Gibbs, 1991; for electronic search guidelines, see Gibbs, 2003).

Application of critical thinking and research tools enables you to track intervention effectiveness. When you do this, you directly experience well-grounded lessons on the synergy and important links between research and practice and a set of tools for you to use routinely in practice. The tools range from simple tracking mechanisms to more rigorous evaluation methods of single-subject or program-evaluation designs. Practitioners can pick and choose those that are most suitable to their clients and the service environment. In chapter 19, Briggs, Feyerham, and Gingerich discuss the application of single-subject designs in practice.

Use of evidence in practice is a knowledge development process. The best available evidence (including external social science knowledge and professional expertise), as well as client interests and the problem situation, informs selection of particular intervention strategies. Practitioners track intervention strategies and measure relevant outcomes to provide evidence of their effectiveness, rather than relying on claims alone. Use of evidence in these different ways enhances the quality of work by ensuring that data continuously inform practice decisions, which enables the practitioner to revise and refine interventions and maximize the likelihood of obtaining desired outcomes. This knowledge also contributes to the development of the social worker's personal repertoire of skills and techniques that can be called on in the future and in similar situations.

Finally, using evidence in your practice replaces notions of practice intuition as the primary means for judging outcomes and implementation processes. This is simultaneously a benefit and a challenge.

Challenges

By understanding the barriers to evidence-based practice (see earlier discussion), we can identify some of the challenges social work faces in achieving its widespread adoption. Many chapters in parts 1 and 3 of this volume address these issues in detail. Additional challenges are identified below.

First, social science knowledge must be more readily available and accessible to practitioners. Better dissemination and communication of research findings to practitioners remains a major hurdle, as do organizational barriers.

Motivation to engage in evidence-based practice can be increased through leadership and example, which requires support at supervisory and higher administrative levels. McCracken and Corrigan address this issue in depth in their chapter on staff development in mental health (chapter 14). Let it be said here that practitioners must have sufficient time to engage in the activities required by this approach. Additional resources may be necessary to revise data-collection strategies and documentation forms to better fit with practice needs. Administrative databases may need to be revamped and made more accessible to practitioners to provide information useful for case decision making. Enhanced support may also require resources for additional staff and training.

The development of staff competencies related to evidence-based practice will likely be necessary. In-service training should focus on skills for identifying relevant clinical questions to guide the search for useful evidence, for appraising different research methods and the quality of evidence, and for evaluating one's practice. Some of these competencies are discussed by Green and Washington (chapter 11), McCracken and Corrigan (chapter 14), Rzepnicki (chapter 16), and Briggs et al. (chapter 19). Practitioners would also greatly benefit from the development of computer search skills that can help them quickly access useful information without time-consuming library visits and inefficient, hit or miss manual search strategies.

Teachers of social work practice will need to work with field instructors to gain a better understanding of constraints and figure out ways to adapt empirically supported strategies to the realities of practice. At the same time, as advocates for evidence-based practice methods, they can contribute to the retooling of field instructors to better serve students. This can only happen, of course, if participants are willing to learn from one another in a negotiated process with compromises and adaptation by each along the way. An approach to the accomplishment of a successful partnership is through linking schools of social work and the administrators and field staff of social service agencies for joint curriculum planning and implementation in both the classroom and field. Such efforts may discourage continued reliance on practice intuition as the popular barometer of practice effectiveness (Gerdes, Edmonds, Haslam, & McCartney, 1996).

Overcoming the structural, skill, and attitudinal challenges to implement evidence-based practice requires the establishment of a culture in which the values and practices discussed here are embraced. Other steps may also be necessary. With that in mind, we hope this book stimulates your thinking about the potential of evidence-based practice to improve the quality of social work interventions and to produce better outcomes for clients.

REFERENCES

Berlin, S. B., & Marsh, J. C. (1993). *Informing practice decisions.* New York: Macmillan.

Browne, N., & Keeley, S. (2001). *Asking the right questions: A guide to critical thinking.* Upper Saddle River, NJ: Prentice Hall.

Fawcett, S. B., Suarez-Balcazar, Y., Balcazar, F. E., White, G. W., Paine, A. L., Blanchard, K. A., & Embree, M. G. (1994). Conducting intervention research—the design and development process. In J. Rothman & E. J. Thomas (Eds.), *Intervention research: Design and development for human service.* (pp. 25– 56). New York: Haworth Press.

Fortune, A. E., & Reid, W. J. (1999). *Research in social work,* 3rd ed. New York: Columbia University Press.

Friesen, B. J. (1993). *Advances in child mental health in the 1990's: Curricula for graduate and undergraduate professional education.* Rockville, MD: U.S. Department of Health and Human Services.

Galassi, J. P., & Gersh, T. L. (1993). Myths, misconceptions, and missed opportunity: Single case designs and counseling psychology. *Journal of Counseling Psychology, 40*(4), 525–531.

Geddes, J. (2000). Evidence-based practice in mental health. In L. Trinder & S. Reynolds (Eds.), *Evidence-based practice: A critical appraisal* (pp. 66–88). Malden, MA: Blackwell Science.

Gerdes, K. E., Edmonds, R. M., Haslam, D. R., & McCartney, T. L. (1996). Clinical social work use of practice evaluation procedures. *Research On Social Work Practice, 6*(1), 27–39.

Gibbs, L. E. (1991). *Scientific reasoning for social workers: Bridging the gap between research and practice.* New York: Macmillan.

Gibbs, L. E. (2003). *Evidence-based practice for the helping professions.* Pacific Grove, CA: Brooks/Cole-Thomson Learning.

Kirk, S. A., & Reid, W. J. (2002). *Science and social work: A critical appraisal.* New York: Columbia University Press.

Klein, W. C., & Bloom, M. (1995). Practice wisdom. *Social Work, 40*(3), 799–807.

Levy, R. L. (1996). Data analysis problems in single case evaluation: Much ado about nothing. *Research On Social Work Practice, 6*(1), 66–71.

Mullen, E. J. (1994). Design of social intervention. In J. Rothman & E. J. Thomas (Eds.), *Intervention research: Design and development for human service* (pp. 163–194). New York: Haworth Press.

National Association of Social Workers. (1997). *Code of ethics.* Silver Spring, MD: NASW Press.

National Association of Social Workers. (1999). *Code of ethics.* Retrieved on August 12, 2003, from http://www.socialworkers.org/pubs/code/code.asp

Reid, W. J. (2002) Knowledge for direct social work practice: An analysis of trends. *Social Service Review, 76,* 6–33.

Reynolds, S. (2000). The anatomy of evidence-based practice: Principles and methods. In L. Trinder & S. Reynolds (Eds.), *Evidence-based practice: A critical appraisal.* (pp. 17–34). Malden, MA: Blackwell Science.

Rothman, J., & Tumblin, A. (1994). Pilot testing and early development of a model of case management intervention. In J. Rothman & E. J. Thomas, (Eds.), *Intervention research: Design and development for human service.* (pp. 215–244). New York: Haworth Press.

Sackett, D. L., Strauss, S. E., Richardson, W. S., Rosenberg, W., & Haynes, R. B. (2000). *Evidence-based medicine: How to practice and teach EBM.* Edinburgh, UK: Harcourt Publishers Limited.

Thomas, E. J. (1984). *Designing interventions for the helping professions.* Beverly Hills, CA: Sage.

Trinder, L. (2000). Evidence-based practice in social work and probation. In L. Trinder & S. Reynolds (Eds.), *Evidence-based practice: A critical appraisal* (pp. 138–162). Malden, MA: Blackwell Science.

Witkin, S. (1991) Empirical clinical practice: A critical analysis. *Social Work, 36*(2), 158–163.

Wong, S. E. (1996). Single case evaluation on trial: Broken promise or new scapegoat? *Research On Social Work Practice, 6*(1), 72–76.

PART ONE

PERSPECTIVES

The conceptual foundation that is the basis for the rest of the volume is presented in this section, which encourages the use of critical thinking and evidence in the development and evaluation of social work interventions. These important tools are used to aid social workers in developing informed approaches to relieve human suffering and in promoting client functioning. The chapters in part 1 contribute extensive support to practitioners seeking to be grounded in the use of theory and evidence from a behavioral perspective. They provide an ethically and empirically based rationale for application of the scientific method in promoting changes in human interactions. In this context, the practitioner is able to explore the interrelationships among theory, ethics, and science as an organizing framework for the development, delivery, and ongoing assessment of client progress and intervention outcomes. These chapters are intended to raise questions and provide substantial discussion about the roles of ethics, the nature of evidence, theory, and science in social work practice.

Eileen Gambrill (chapter 1) makes the case that evidence and critical thinking in practice are the means to social workers' fulfillment of ethical obligations to clients. She describes their significance and overlapping elements and offers a convincing rationale for the application of critical thinking and evidence-based knowledge in practice decision making. Jeanne Marsh (chapter 2) presents a dynamic view of the roles of theory and theory-free perspectives in social work practice and argues that theory-driven rather than theory-free research is likely to provide the most benefit to practitioners and to the ongoing development of social work knowledge. The following two chapters, by William Reid (chapter 3) and Mark Mattaini and Sarah Moore (chapter 4), address the role of behavioral theory in social work practice. Reid examines the historical contributions of operant theory and its potential for influencing practice and research in the future, highlighting advancements in the care of the elderly and their families. Mattaini and Moore describe the marriage between behavioral theory and the theoretical framework of ecological systems that is used in social work. They present an eco-behavioral view of human behavior for use in practice and review empirical support for its applicability at all levels of intervention. In the final chapter of this section, Bruce Thyer (chapter 5) discusses the history and evolution of the role of science in shaping social work practice and as a foundation for evidence-based social work methods. He emphasizes ways to incorporate the advances reported in the literature as information to critically evaluate and consider when seeking ways to provide clients access to the most effective interventions.

CHAPTER 1

Contributions of Critical Thinking and Evidence-Based Practice to the Fulfillment of the Ethical Obligations of Professionals

Eileen Gambrill

Professionals are required to be familiar with and to honor the code of ethics of their profession. Examples of obligations described in such codes include drawing on practice- and policy-related research, accurately informing clients about the risks and benefits of recommended procedures and alternatives, taking steps when incompetence is suspected in fellow staff, empowering clients, treating them with respect, and acting with integrity. Research regarding the extent to which helpers honor such obligations shows that the rhetoric in such codes does not match reality. For example, many helpers do not honor requirements for informed consent (e.g., Braddock, Edwards, Hasenberg, Laidley, & Levinson, 1999) and do not draw on practice-related research findings to inform practice decisions (see, e.g., Rosen, Proctor, Morrow-Howell, & Staudt, 1995). Not keeping up with practice-related research findings makes it impossible to honor informed-consent obligations and may result in decisions that harm rather than help clients (e.g., Jacobson, Mulick, & Schwartz, 1995). This chapter discusses the role of critical thinking in honoring ethical obligations and its relation to evidence-based practice.

CRITICAL THINKING

Critical thinking involves the careful appraisal of beliefs and actions to arrive at well-reasoned ones that maximize the likelihood of helping clients and avoiding harm. It involves reasonable and reflective thinking focused on deciding what to believe or do (Ennis, 1987). Viewed broadly, the process is part of problem solving—for example, providing strategies to check intuitive assumptions (Hogarth, 2001). Critical thinking involves more than the mere possession of related knowledge and skills; it requires using them in everyday situations and acting on the results (Paul, 1993). It requires clarity of expression, critical appraisal of evidence and reasons, and consideration of well-argued alternative points of view. Critical thinkers question what others take for granted. They ask questions such as the following: Could I be wrong? Have there been any critical tests of this claim? If so, what are the results? How representative were the samples used? Were studies relatively free of bias? Are the presented facts correct? Has counterevidence been presented? Are weak appeals used, such as to emotion or to special interests? Critical thinking involves the *accurate* presentation of alternative perspectives and attention to the process of reasoning, not just the product. Critical thinking and scientific reasoning are closely related. Both value clarity and the critical appraisal of claims. Only by thinking critically about practice- and policy-related claims can we maximize the services that are effective in achieving outcomes that clients value and minimize ineffective and harmful ones. Basing decisions on incomplete or inaccurate accounts may result in the use of ineffective or harmful methods.

Research shows that a variety of biases come into play that dilute the quality of decisions (e.g., Gambrill, 1990; Hastie & Dawes, 2001). Examples include the *fundamental attribution error* (the tendency to attribute the cause of behaviors to personal characteristics of people and to overlook environmental factors) and the *confirmation bias* (the tendency to search for data that support favored positions and to ignore data that do not). Practitioners are influenced by the availability of material such as vivid case examples that may be misleading rather than informative. Such biases have been found not only in the helping professions but in a wide range of other contexts as well (e.g., Dawes, 2001). Confirmation biases may result in overlooking contradictory data (Nickerson, 1998). Failure to ask, Is there a better alternative? and What are problems with my view? encourages justification of favored views and ignoring of alternative accounts that may be more accurate. The emphasis on gathering evidence in support of a favored position rather than exploring alternative views may hinder the discovery of valuable options. Base-rate data are often ignored. A social worker who sees many parents who sexually abuse their children may "overdiagnose" this event because of his or her unique situation; the social worker may overestimate the true prevalence of sexual abuse. Resemblance criteria—that is, the extent to which a characteristic seems to resemble or be similar to another characteristic—can also lead helpers astray (e.g., Nisbett & Ross, 1980). The social worker may assume that effects resemble their causes when, in fact, causes and effects may bear little or no resemblance to each other.

Errors in judgment may result in incorrect assumptions about the causes of problems and inaccurate predictions about suicidal potential, need for hospitalization, future recurrence of violent acts, or the results of a new service policy. Only if social workers are aware of common biases and fallacies and develop skills and related values to counter them, such as questioning their assumptions, may biases be minimized (see, e.g., Skrabanek & Mc Cormick, 1998). It could thus be argued that professional helpers have an ethical obligation to do so, given that not doing so may compromise ethical, effective, efficient services. Critical-thinking knowledge, skills, and values can help professionals critically appraise claims and arguments, use language clearly, recognize affective influences on decisions, avoid cognitive biases that interfere with sound decision making, and spot pseudoscience and quackery and thus help avoid their influence. Critical-

thinking skills are of value in avoiding reliance on questionable grounds for ac-
cepting claims about what may be true or false, such as authority, popularity, or
tradition (Gambrill & Gibbs, 1999). Although intuition is an invaluable source of
ideas, it is not a sound guide for testing beliefs.

There is an unacknowledged subtext of problem definition and explanation
in helping professions such as social work, psychology, and psychiatry that is often unquestioned but questionable (e.g., Szasz, 1987). A professional who assumes that problems have a biochemical or genetic cause overlooks well-argued
critiques (see, e.g., Leo & Cohen, 2003) that are often ignored in the professional
literature. Critical thinking encourages conceptual critiques. It encourages deep
rather than superficial appraisal. It can be of value in spotting and avoiding informal fallacies (such as straw-man arguments and ad hominem appeals) and in
discovering methodological and conceptual problems related to common assertions. It is an antidote to mystification that may harm clients, such as assuming un-
critically that an entity called schizophrenia is responsible for a variety of troubling
behaviors when there may be no evidence for this (Boyle, 2002). The history of
the mental health industry reveals a long list of false causes for personal troubles
and social problems, as well as harmful interventions to cure "mental illnesses"
(e.g., Ofshe & Watters, 1994; Valenstein, 1986). Thinking critically about basic assumptions—for example, about the assumed biochemical bases for mental disorders or about the very term *mental disorder*—can help professionals avoid actions and beliefs that may diminish opportunities to help clients, such as relying
on the DSM to categorize clients in spite of the lack of reliability and validity of its
classifications and in spite of its focus on pathology and neglect of client assets
and environmental factors (e.g., Houts, 2002; Kutchins & Kirk, 1997). A key implication of critical thinking and evidence-based practice is an openness to and a
welcoming of criticism. Feedback that facilitates learning is vital. A critical attitude,
which Karl Popper (1972) defines as a willingness and commitment to open up
favored views to severe scrutiny, is basic to science, which distinguishes it from
pseudoscience. A culture in which criticism flourishes can be contrasted with one
in which false knowledge reigns. False knowledge refers to beliefs that are not
true and that are not questioned (Munz, 1985). No one has attempted to calculate the overall costs and benefits to different parties of the premature acceptance
of questionable definitions of personal and social problems and assumed causes
of related behaviors and circumstances or how they can be changed. These include creating a victim mentality (Dineen, 1996), creating false hope, masking
value judgments as scientific (e.g., Skrabanek, 1994), neglecting promising alternatives, and wasting money on ineffective and harmful services at the cost of not
fully funding programs found to be effective.

EVIDENCE-BASED PRACTICE

Evidence-based practice arose as an alternative to authority-based practice in
which decisions are based on criteria such as consensus, anecdotal experience,

and tradition (see, e.g., Chalmers, 1983; Sackett, Richardson, Rosenberg, & Haynes, 1997). Although evidence-based practice's philosophical roots are old, its blooming as a process attending to evidentiary, ethical, and application issues in all professional venues (education practice and policy as well as research) is fairly recent—facilitated by the Internet revolution. It is designed to break down the division between research, practice, and policy—emphasizing the importance of attention to ethical issues. Codes of ethics call on professionals to consider practice-related research findings and to inform clients about them. Evidence-based practice involves "the conscientious, explicit and judicious use of current best evidence in making decisions about the care of individual [clients]" (Sackett et al., 1997, p. 2). *Best available external clinical evidence* refers to practice-related research on the accuracy and precision of assessment, risk measures and descriptive data, and the efficacy and safety of treatment and preventive services. "Without clinical expertise, practice risks becoming tyrannized by evidence, for even excellent external evidence may be inapplicable to or inappropriate for an individual [client]. Without current best evidence, practice risks becoming rapidly out-of-date, to the detriment of [clients]" (Sackett et al., 1997, p. 2).

Evidence-based practice is an evolving process designed to attend to interrelated evidentiary, ethical, and implementation concerns. It "is the integration of best research evidence with clinical expertise and [client] values" (Sackett, Straus, Richardson, Rosenberg, & Haynes, 2000, p. 1). It describes a philosophy and process designed to forward effective use of professional judgment in the integration of information about each client's unique characteristics, circumstances, preferences, and actions with external research findings. "It is a guide for thinking about how decisions should be made" (Haynes, Devereaux, & Guyatt, 2002). Although the term *evidence-based practice* can be mistaken to mean only that the decisions made are based on evidence of their effectiveness, its use does call attention to the fact that available evidence may not be used or the current state of ignorance in the field may not be shared with clients. It is hoped that professionals who consider related research findings regarding decisions and inform clients about them will provide more effective and ethical care than those who rely on criteria such as anecdotal experience, available resources, or popularity.

Evidence-based practice requires professionals to search for research findings related to important practice and policy decisions and to share what is found (including nothing) with clients. It highlights the uncertainty involved in helping clients, and it attempts to give helpers the knowledge and skills they need to handle this constructively and to help clients handle it. Evidence-based practice is designed to break down the division between research and practice, for example, by emphasizing the importance of clinicians' critical appraisals of research reviews and by developing a technology to help them to do so: "the leading figures in EBM . . . emphasized that clinicians had to use their scientific training and their judgment to interpret [guidelines] and individualize care accordingly" (Gray, 2001a, p. 26). Clinical expertise includes the use of effective relationship skills and the experience of individual helpers to rapidly identify each client's unique

circumstances, characteristics, and "their individual risks and benefits of potential interventions and their personal values and expectations" (p. 1). It is drawn
on to integrate information from these various sources (Haynes, Devereaux, &
Guyatt, 2002). Client values refer to "the unique preferences, concerns and expectations each [client] brings to an . . . encounter and which must be integrated
into . . . decisions if they are to serve the [client]" (p. 1). Steps in evidence-based
practice include the following:

1. Converting information needs related to practice decisions into answerable
   questions

2. Tracking down, with maximum efficiency, the best evidence with which to
   answer questions

3. Critically appraising the evidence for its validity, impact (size of effect), and
   applicability (usefulness in practice)

4. Applying the results of this appraisal to practice and policy decisions. (This
   involves deciding whether evidence found [if any] applies to the decision at
   hand [e.g., Is a client similar to those studied? Is there access to services described?] and considering client values and preferences, as well as other applicability concerns, in making decisions.)

5. Evaluating the effectiveness and efficiency in carrying out steps 1–4 and
   seeking ways to improve them in the future (Sackett et al., 2000, pp. 3–4).

Evidence-based practice draws on the results of systematic, rigorous, critical
appraisal of research related to important practice questions such as, Is this assessment measure valid? and Does this intervention do more good than harm?
(see, e.g., Sackett et al., 1997). Such rigorous searches and appraisals decrease the
likelihood that professionals pose as "false prophets" (Popper, 1992, p. 128). Different questions require different kinds of tests to critically appraise them (see,
e.g., Gray, 2001b; Greenhalgh, 2000; Sackett et al., 2000). Each method is subject
to certain biases. The Cochrane Collaboration has developed guidelines for locating and critically appraising research related to specific questions. Reviews are
based on a hand search for all material, both published and unpublished and in
all languages, related to a question (see, e.g., Bero & Rennie, 1995).

Evidence-based practice and health care originated in medicine in part because of variations in services offered and their outcomes (Wennberg, 2002). In
discussing the origins of evidence-based practice, Gray (2001a) notes the increasing lack of confidence in data of potential use to clinicians: peer review, which
he refers to as "feet of clay," and flaws in books, editorials, and journal articles.
Examples include submission bias, publication bias, methodological bias, abstract
bias, and framing bias. This remains a problem (Altman, 2002). There are biased
estimates of the prevalence of concerns in the professional literature; there is
often propagandistic advocacy in place of careful weighing of evidence and reporting of related facts and figures (e.g., Sarnoff, 2001). For example, recommendations regarding practice guidelines may not be sound. In place of critical,

systematic reviews of research, there are often fragmented, uncritical ones (e.g., Oxman & Guyatt, 1993). Books with titles such as *What Works* (without a question mark) may not describe search procedures used or criteria used to critically appraise research (Kluger, Alexander, & Curtis, 2001).

CRITICAL THINKING, EVIDENCE-BASED PRACTICE, AND ETHICAL OBLIGATIONS

There are many interrelated contributions of critical thinking and evidence-based practice in attending to ethical obligations to clients.

Encouraging Transparency

Respect, integrity, and self-determination called for in professional codes of ethics require being honest with clients—for example, sharing the evidentiary status of services (which is often none). Both critical thinking and EPB encourage clear description of what is done to what effect, including mistakes and errors. This contributes to the discovery of ways to improve services and to judicious distribution of scarce resources. Increased transparency of services and outcomes allows for pointed criticism, as do research methods that can critically test questions and rigorous reviews of research related to a claim. Currently, gaps between what research suggests is effective and what services are provided are hidden. For example, rarely does a professional compare services offered by an agency, such as parent-training programs, with what research suggests is effective and then disseminate that information to all involved parties, including clients. Clients are typically not informed that recommended services have no evidentiary base or have been found to be ineffective or harmful. Whenever services of unknown effect receive funding, there is less money for services that have been critically tested and found to help clients. Transparency by means of clear writing and description allows for critical appraisal of arguments and related evidence. Such transparency may help practitioners avoid inflated claims of knowledge that mislead clients (impede informed consent) and hinder the growth of knowledge. Terms such as *well established,* and *validated* convey a certainty that is not possible (see Popper, 1972).

A Comprehensive Approach to Providing Ethical, Effective, Efficient Services

Evidence-based practice involves a systemic approach for improving quality of services, including attending to the education of professionals who are lifelong learners, involving clients as informed participants in decision making, attending to management practices and policies that influence practice, and considering the implications of scarce resources on services purchased (e.g., Gray, 2001a; Sackett et al., 2000). This includes identifying and helping practitioners acquire the knowledge, skills, and tools required to deliver services to clients within a helping framework in which related research findings are actively sought and critically appraised. Quality of services is unlikely to improve in a fragmented approach, that is, without attending to *all* links in the system of service provision. Only by considering the interlinked contingencies related to a problem can a professional accurately define it and estimate the degree to which it is solvable and, if so, how. Many problems confronting clients are not solvable by social workers (e.g., lack of well-paying unskilled jobs, poor-quality education, lack of health care for all residents). An understanding of interlinked contingencies among different levels (e.g., how a public policy affects personal options) may be needed to identify constraints to and opportunities for helping clients. Critical thinking encourages professionals to think contextually, to consider the big picture, and to connect personal troubles to social issues. The National Association of Social Workers' Code of Ethics states that "Fundamental to social work is attention to the environmental forces that create, contribute to, and address problems-in-living" (National Association of Social Workers, 1996, preamble). This requires social workers to be aware of methodological and conceptual problems associated with the framing of problems such as depression and social anxiety as biologically based with no attention to related psychological and environmental circumstances.

Helping Practitioners Integrate Research Findings Related to Practice and Policy Decisions

The National Association of Social Workers' Code of Ethics calls for workers to "critically examine and keep current with emerging knowledge relevant to social work" and "fully utilize evaluation and research evidence in their professional practice" (5.02). Ignoring practice- and policy-related research findings or forwarding bogus claims of effectiveness violates workers' ethical obligation to provide informed consent and may result in wasting money on ineffective services, harming clients in the name of helping them, and decreasing clients' chances of attaining hoped-for outcomes. Reasons practitioners do not draw on practice-related research findings include difficulties in accessing them and a lack of time to critically review and integrate findings. An extensive literature in evidence-based practice addresses challenges of integrating research findings and practice decisions, including descriptions of tools of value in locating relevant research and critical appraisal of these tools, such as valuable Web sites and systematic reviews. A major contribution of evidence-based practice is that it encourages preparation of systematic research reviews based on an exhaustive search for research findings related to specific practice and policy questions and rigorous critical appraisal of each study located (e.g., Egger, Smith, & Altman, 2001). Evidence-based practice is closely tied to the Cochrane Collaboration, a worldwide network of centers designed to prepare, maintain, and disseminate high-quality reviews of the effects of health care. The Campbell Collaboration has been formed to prepare and disseminate reviews in the areas of social welfare, crime and justice, and education. Critical appraisal may reveal that programs that are now widely disseminated are not effective (e.g., Gomory, 1999). Preparing fragmented (incomplete), uncritical research reviews regarding practice and policy questions may result in inflated claims of effectiveness that provide misleading conclusions.

A key focus in evidence-based practice is helping practitioners develop the skills required to critically appraise research findings related to practice and policy questions, including the adequacy of research reviews (e.g., Geddes, Tomlin, & Price, 1999; Greenhalgh, 2000). In addition, there is a focus on helping clients develop skills in the critical appraisal of practice-related research findings and on giving them access to related material. Practitioners are encouraged to develop and use critical-appraisal skills to review practice-related findings and not to depend on the prescriptions of authorities who may pretend to knowledge that does not exist. Keep in mind that misleading claims in the professional literature on the part of academics and researchers was a key reason for the development of evidence-based practice (Gray, 2001b). Both critical thinking and evidence-based practice encourage knowledge flow by promoting accurate descriptions of the evidentiary status of services, for example, via the diffusion and dissemination of critical appraisals of practice- and policy-related research findings and by offering programs designed to enhance the critical appraisal skills of both clients and professionals. The flow of knowledge and ignorance is becoming more democratized, and organizations such as the National Health Service in the United Kingdom encourage this free-market economy of knowledge. Sources such as *Bandolier* produce a steady stream of material that reviews the effectiveness of common practices and highlights common errors in practice-related research. Censorship of competing views and critiques of preferred views misleads rather than informs. It prevents discovery of promising alternatives.

Evidence-based practice encourages the purchase of services on the basis of evidentiary criteria. Concerns about social justice constrain professionals to allocate scarce resources wisely. Offering ineffective services to some clients may deprive others of effective services. Burton Gummer (1997) argues that the National Association of Social Workers' Code of Ethics is silent on the hard decisions that social workers must make about how to distribute scarce resources. Evidence-based practice encourages the purchase of services on the basis of their acceptability to clients and their documented record of success. It encourages clear description (transparency) of variations in services and related outcomes and gaps between services provided and what information is available (if any) describing what is needed to attain outcomes. It encourages consideration of populations and individuals. Resources are limited; saving money by not paying for ineffective service allows for more money to provide services that have been found to be effective at a level that maximizes the likelihood of valued outcomes.

Considering Individual Differences

Decisions must be made, together with the client, about whether research findings apply to a particular client, considering the client's values and expectations. Different clients may weigh potential risks and benefits differently. "Expertise [proficiency and judgment that individual practitioners acquire through experience and practice] is reflected in many ways, but especially in more effective and efficient [assessment] and in the more thoughtful identification and compassionate use of individual [clients'] predicaments, rights, and preferences in making . . . decisions about their care" (Sackett, et al., 1997). Evidence-based practitioners are encouraged to transform information needs related to decisions about a particular client into four-part answerable questions that apply to particular clients and that guide an efficient literature search (Gibbs, 2003; Sackett et al., 2000).

Encouraging Self-Determination and Empowerment

Self-determination refers to a belief that people should be allowed to arrange their lives in accordance with their preferences. Self-determination and empowerment involve giving clients real (rather than perceived) influence over the quality of their lives and including clients in making decisions that affect them. They require a focus on outcomes that clients value (whenever they do not compromise the rights of others) and a candid recognition and discussion of any coercive aspects of contact between social workers and clients. Considering client values and expectations and involving clients as informed participants in decision making are hallmarks of evidence-based practice, as envisioned by its originators. Clearly describing goals and methods (including their risks and benefits as well as alternative options) and any coercive aspects of meetings (including unapparent negative consequences dependent on the amount of participation), provide a degree of self-determination that contrasts with the pursuit of vague goals and vaguely described methods. A perennial concern in the helping professions is a disregard for or a drift away from addressing outcomes that clients value (e.g., Sharpe & Faden, 1998). Consumers have access to Cochrane Collaboration Internet communication networks (www.cochraneconsumer.com) on which they can raise questions and give comments (e.g., they can identify outcomes researchers fail to consider that they believe are important) and seek information. Consumer involvement may reveal that outcomes of clients' concern are not addressed. Professionals sometimes assume that people labeled "mentally ill" cannot make any decisions for themselves, an assumption that is likely to result in coercive interventions. Such clients may be coerced into using certain services even when there is no evidence that they are effective (e.g., Gomory, 1999). This assumption of "lack of agency" (the inability to make decisions) lies behind the intrusive methods that have been used in psychiatry since the beginning of this profession's history.

In the public social services, conflicts between individual and state rights (as reflected in legislation and public policies) limit the self-determination of both social workers and clients. The National Association of Social Workers' Code of Ethics states the following: "social workers' responsibility to the larger society or specific legal obligations may on limited occasions [actually there are many occasions] supersede loyalty owed clients, and clients should be so advised" (1.01).

The code also contains the statement, "Social workers may limit clients' right to self-determination when, in the social workers' professional judgment, clients' actions or potential actions pose a serious, foreseeable, and imminent risk to themselves or others" (1.02). Mark Hardin (1990) argues that professional ethics in public agencies are "the ethics of the role holders in institutions" (p. 528), not the ethics emphasized in the National Association of Social Workers' Code of Ethics, which primarily concern the individual relationship between clients and social workers. Social workers who work in public agencies are agents of the state, not clients' agents. They are mediators between clients' interests and constraints imposed by agency policies and funding patterns. For instance, social workers may invade clients' privacy and interfere in family life (e.g., remove children from the care of their parents) and confine people against their will for psychiatric evaluation. The law views these intrusions as necessary on the grounds that they further interests of social importance, such as by protecting children from neglect or abuse (Leever, DeCiani, Mulaney, & Hasslinger, 2002). Hiding coercive elements may result in professionals misleading both themselves and clients about what they can offer and how effective it is likely to be. There are many opportunities to honor components of informed consent even in nonautonomous (coercive) situations (Faden & Beauchamp, 1986). For example, staff could be required to give clients a written description of the evidentiary status of recommended services, the agency's record of success in achieving related outcomes, and the record of success of the staff member who will offer the service (Entwistle, Sheldon, Sowden, & Watt, 1998).

Professionals should explore different formats and their consequences for involving clients in decisions as informed participants, including interactive computer programs that allow clients to control the information they obtain (e.g., Edwards & Elwyn, 2001; O'Conner, 2001). Data regarding the record of success of each agency in a community could be stored on databases, available at community centers, that clients could consult. Another important way to involve clients is to establish accessible, accountable, timely complaint (and compliment) procedures, audit their implementation, and make use of findings to improve services. Ongoing monitoring of valid progress indicators allows for timely, informed decisions and keeps clients informed about degree of progress. The National Association of Social Workers' Code of Ethics calls for social workers to "monitor and evaluate policies, the implementation of programs and practice interventions" (section 5.02). (It does not, but should, call for social workers to share this information with clients.)

Helpers cannot empower clients if they are not empowered themselves (e.g., are not informed about research findings related to practice and policy decisions that must be made or do not have the knowledge or resources needed). Social workers cannot inform clients about the risks and benefits of recommended methods (including assessment, intervention, and evaluation) unless they are well informed (i.e., unless they have searched for research findings about questions that arise in practice, critically appraise what is found (if anything), consider whether findings (if any) apply to clients, share what is found (if anything) with clients, and consider clients' values and preferences when making decisions. The degree to which social workers "empower" clients thus depends partly on the extent to which their knowledge, skills, and other resources match what is needed to help clients attain outcomes they value. Accurately estimating this match is an important way that social workers take responsibility for their decisions.

Minimize Harm in the Name of Helping

Some procedures designed to help or protect people may have the opposite effect. Harm includes removing valued opportunities that do not harm others, stigmatizing people by applying negative diagnostic labels of dubious value in understanding or minimizing problems, and not fully informing clients with the result that they make decisions they otherwise would not make. The history of the helping professions reveals the frequency of harm in the name of helping (e.g., Sharpe & Faden, 1998; Valenstein, 1986). Blenkner, Bloom, and Nielson (1971) found that intensive case management *increased* mortality for older clients. Common practices believed to help people were found to harm them. Consider the blinding of 10,000 children because of the use of oxygen at birth (Silverman, 1998) and the death of a child by "rebirthing" therapy. Professionals should fully inform clients about the risks and benefits of recommended services. Underplaying potential negative effects does not honor obligations to fully inform clients and may result in irreversible harm, such as tardive dyskinesia. Both critical thinking and evidence-based practice encourage questions such as, Has this method been critically tested and does it do more good than harm? How many people will receive unnecessary treatment and perhaps be harmed to help one client?

Identifying and minimizing errors, accidents, and mistakes will decrease harm. There is remarkably little systemic study of errors, accidents, and mistakes in social work (for an example, see Munro, 1996). If, indeed, professionals learn through their mistakes, they are forgoing many opportunities to learn. By trying to solve a problem and failing, they may learn a little more about clients' problem (problems–theories–criticisms–new problems) (Popper, 1994, p. 159). A careful review of the circumstances related to mistakes allows professionals to plan how to minimize avoidable ones. Research regarding errors in medicine shows that latent causes (e.g., quality of staff training, agency policy) contribute to mistakes and errors (Reason, 2001). Evidence-based practice encourages programmatic research regarding error, both avoidable and unavoidable; its causes and consequences for clients and other involved parties; and exploration of methods designed to minimize avoidable errors, including agencywide risk management programs (e.g., Gambrill & Shlonsky, 2001). Each agency should have a system for identifying, tracking, and reporting errors; identifying their causes and consequences; and using the information gained to minimize avoidable errors that diminish quality of services. Familiarity with common errors that occur in practice and their causes (as far as is known), as well as acquiring skills and providing tools (e.g., interactive decision programs) to minimize errors, may contribute to a decrease in avoidable errors. Many errors occur because of reliance on questionable criteria, such as anecdotal experience, to evaluate the accuracy of claims. Only through critical inquiry can professionals avoid errors they are prone to make, no matter their intelligence.

Blowing the Whistle on Pseudoscience, Propaganda, Quackery, and Fraud

Transparency of what is done to what effect, critical appraisal of claims, and honoring ethical obligations to clients call for blowing the whistle on pseudoscience, fraud, quackery, and propaganda in professional contexts. Propaganda is designed to encourage beliefs and actions with the least thought possible (Ellul, 1965). Common propaganda methods include suppression of well-argued alternative views and glittering generalizations, including inflated claims of effectiveness. Some medical schools now include courses designed to alert students to propaganda methods that pharmaceutical companies use to promote drugs (Wilkes & Hoffman, 2001). Pseudoscience (material with the trappings of science without the substance), quackery, and fraud take advantage of propaganda methods. Quackery refers to the for-profit promotion and marketing of untested, often worthless, and sometimes dangerous health products and procedures, by either professionals or others (Young, 1992). Indicators include the use of anecdotes and testimonials to support claims and secrecy (claims are not open to objective scrutiny). Fraud is the intentional misrepresentation of the effect of certain actions to persuade people to part with something of value (e.g., money). Fraudulent claims (often appealing to the trappings of science) may result in overlooking effective methods or being harmed by remedies that are supposed to help. Agencies and professions may try to block attempts to explore the exact nature of services by claiming that confidential client information would be revealed. For years the State of New Jersey Department of Youth and Family Services appealed to concerns about confidentiality in refusing to open their records for inspection. They were finally forced to do so as a result of lawsuits. An examination of the records revealed alarming lapses (DePanfilis, 2003). It may be assumed that loyalty to one's profession requires hiding one's "dirty linen." But the following question must be asked: What are our ethical obligations to clients? They are not to hide serious problems that negatively affect clients but to identify and remedy them as quickly as possible.

OBSTACLES

Obstacles to the use of evidence-based practice and critical thinking to honor ethical obligations to clients include personal and environmental ones. Both critical thinking and evidence-based practice encourage critical appraisal of beliefs and arguments. Such appraisal may not be valued. Professionals may use different standards to make personal decisions and decisions regarding clients (Gambrill & Gibbs, 2002). The history of the helping professions shows that many professionals prefer to rely on status and authority to promote claims about what is "true" and that many squelch rather than welcome critical appraisal of their arguments and related evidence. Clients' interests in maintaining hope and seeking certainty may contribute to professionals' overestimates of what is "known." Environmental obstacles include authoritarian cultures in which professionals rely on status and authority rather than critical appraisal of arguments for practices and policies. Misunderstandings and misrepresentations of evidence-based practice (e.g., that it ignores client values and expectations, that it attends only to randomized controlled trials or ignores clinical expertise; Gibbs & Gambrill, 2002), obstruct the recognition and addressing of real challenges to evidence-based practice, such as integrating clinical expertise and external research findings, acquiring new skills, and developing an agency culture in which critical appraisal is valued. Narrow definitions such as "EBP means using effective interventions" omit attention to ethical and application concerns (Gambrill, 2003). A lack of resources pose constraints. High caseloads, insufficient resources, and inadequate training and supervision increase the likelihood of inadequate handling of cases, the results of which are sometimes described in daily newspapers. (see, e.g., Roche, 2000). Perhaps in no other profession than social work is there a greater contrast between the loftiness of service ideals and the stark realities of daily practice in the limited help that can be offered. Social workers must try daily to resolve problems whose fundamental causes lie outside social work. Unless helpers develop skills to honestly cope with mismatches between ideals and realities, they may fall into habits that harm clients, such as pretending that they are competent to offer certain services when they are not, denying that they make decisions, congratulating themselves for success even when they have had none, offering clients empty promises, and applying rules and regulations in a rigid manner that disregards clients' unique characteristics and circumstances. They may deny rather than examine dilemmas created by conflicting loyalties (Leever, 2003). They may overlook coercive aspects of practice. Pursuit of outcomes that clients and their significant others value as well as avoidance of harm, critically reviewing assumptions of one's own as well as those of others, and taking responsibility for decisions should promote ethical decisions. Clearly describing desired outcomes and related contingencies will contribute to accurate estimates of what can be accomplished given current constraints and resources and to avoidance of unrealistic paths.

SUMMARY

The history of the helping professions illustrates the need for limits on professional discretion in choosing objectives, service plans, and evaluation methods. The potential for professional abuse of power highlights the importance of professional codes of ethics and practices and policies that forward their implementation. Critical thinking and evidence-based practice are suggested as guides for making ethical decisions. Both encourage basing decisions on well-reasoned judgments in which the interests of all parties are considered. Advantages of both with respect to ethical practice include an emphasis on the transparency of what is done to what effect and the encouragement of the integration of research and practice. Sources such as the Cochrane and Campbell collaborations and other avenues for diffusion, together with helping practitioners and clients to acquire critical appraisal skills, will make it increasingly difficult to mislead people about "what we know." It will be more difficult to ignore questions and alternative views, lack of evidence regarding services used, and harm done in the name of helping. It may be easier to locate programs that have been critically tested and found to help clients with particular problems. Only by being soft-hearted (compassionate and caring) as well as hardheaded (clarifying and critically evaluating assumptions) and competent (in possession of knowledge and skills required to address problems), do professionals have the best chance of helping clients and avoiding harm. Ask: Would I be satisfied with compassion alone on the part of my physician? Does the answer reflect a double standard—art for my clients and science for me? Taking responsibility for decisions is a hallmark of professionals and is essential to ethical practice. Acceptance of this responsibility is a burden, but it is also a freedom—a freedom to exercise discretion in the best interests of clients. Not taking responsibility leaves helpers unaccountable to clients and unlikely to recognize social control aims masked as "doing good."

REFERENCES

Altman, D. G. (2002). Poor-quality medical research. What can journals do? *Journal of the American Medical Association, 287,* 2765–2767.

Bero, L., & Rennie, D. (1995). The Cochrane Collaboration: Preparing, maintaining, and disseminating systematic reviews of the effects of health care. *Journal of the American Medical Association, 274*(24), 1935–1938.

Blenkner, M., Bloom, M., & Nielson, M. (1971). A research and demonstration of protective services. *Social Casework, 52*(8), 483–499.

Boyle, M. (2002). *Schizophrenia: A scientific delusion?* (2nd ed.). London: Routledge.

Braddock, C. H., Edwards, K. A., Hasenberg, N. M., Laidley, T. L., & Levinson, W. (1999). Informed decision making in outpatient practice: Time to get back to basics. *Journal of the American Medical Association, 282*(24), 2313–2320.

Chalmers, I. (1983). Scientific inquiry and authoritarianism in perinatal care and education. *Birth, 10*(3), 151–155.

Dawes, R. M. (2001). *Everyday irrationality: How pseudo-scientists, lunatics and the rest of us systematically fail to think rationally.* Boulder, CO: Westview Press.

DePanfilis, D. (2003). *Review of IAIU investigations of suspected child abuse and neglect in DYFS out-of-home care settings in New Jersey* (Final Report). Baltimore, MD: School of Social Work, University of Maryland.

Dineen, T. (1996). *Manufacturing victims: What the psychology industry is doing to people* (2nd ed.). Montreal: Robert Davies Multimedia Pub.

Edwards, A., & Elwyn, G. (Eds.) (2001). *Evidence-based patient choice: Inevitable or impossible?* New York: Oxford University Press.

Egger, M., Smith, G. D., & Altman, D. G. (Eds.). (2001). *Systematic reviews in health care: Meta-analysis in context* (2nd ed.). London: BMJ Books.

Ellul, J. (1965). *Propaganda: The formation of men's attitudes.* New York: Vintage.

Ennis, R. H. (1987). A taxonomy of critical thinking dispositions and abilities. In J. B. Baron & R. J. Sternberg (Eds.), *Teaching thinking skills: Theory and practice* (pp. 9–26). New York: W.H. Freeman.

Entwistle, V. A., Sheldon, T. A., Sowden, A. J., & Watt, I. A. (1998). Evidence-informed patient choice. *International Journal of Technology Assessment in Health Care, 14,* 212–215.

Faden, R. R., & Beauchamp, T. L. (with King, N. M. P.). (1986). *A history and theory of informed consent.* Oxford: Oxford University Press.

Gambrill, E. (1990). *Critical thinking in clinical practice: Improving the accuracy of judgments and decisions about clients.* San Francisco: Jossey-Bass.

Gambrill, E. (2003). Evidence-based practice: Sea change or the emperor's new clothes? *Journal of Social Work Education, 39,* 3–23.

Gambrill, E., & Gibbs, L. (2002). Making practice decisions: Is what's good for the goose good for the gander? *Ethical Human Sciences and Services, 4,* 31–46.

Gambrill, E., & Shlonsky, A. (2001). The need for comprehensive risk management systems in child welfare. *Children and Youth Services Review, 23,* 79–107.

Geddes, J., Tomlin, A., & Price, J. (1999). *Practicing evidence-based mental health.* Abingdon, Oxon, UK: Radcliffe Medical Press.

Gibbs, L. E. (2003). *Evidence-based practice for the helping professions.* Pacific Grove, CA: Thompson/Brooks/Cole.

Gibbs, L., & Gambrill, E. (2002). Evidence-based practice: Counterarguments to objections. *Research on Social Work Practice, 12,* 452–476.

Gomory, T. (1999). Programs of Assertive Community Treatment (PACT): A critical review. *Ethical Human Sciences and Services, 1,* 147–163.

Gray, J. A. M. (2001a). *Evidence-based health care: How to make health policy and management decisions* (2nd ed.). New York: Churchill Livingstone.

Gray, J. A. M. (2001b). The origin of evidence-based practice. In A. Edwards & G. Elywn (Eds.), *Evidence-informed client choice* (pp. 19–33). New York: Oxford.

Greenhalgh, T. (2000). *How to read a paper: The basis of evidence-based medicine* (2nd ed.). London: BMJ.

Gummer, B. (1997). Is the Code of Ethics as applicable to agency executives as it is to direct service practitioners? NO. In E. Gambrill & R. Pruger (Eds.), *Controversial issues in social work ethics, values and obligations* (pp. 143–148). Boston: Allyn & Bacon.

Hardin, R. (1990). The artificial duties of contemporary professionals. *Social Service Review, 64,* 528–541.

Hastie, R., & Dawes, R. M. (2001). *Rational choice in an uncertain world* (2nd ed.). Thousand Oaks, CA: Sage.

Haynes, R. B., Devereaux, P. J., & Guyatt, G. H. (2002). Clinical expertise in the era of evidence-based medicine and patient choice [Editorial]. *ACP Journal Club,* March/April, 136:A11, pp. 1–7.

Hogarth, R. (2001). *Educating intuition.* Chicago: University of Chicago Press.

Houts, A. (2002). Discovery, invention, and the expansion of the modern diagnostic and statistical manuals of mental disorders. In L. E. Beutler & M. L. Malik (Eds.), *Rethinking the DSM: A psychological perspective* (pp. 17–65). Washington, DC: American Psychological Association.

Jacobson, J. W., Mulick, J. A., & Schwartz, A. A. (1995). A history of facilitated communication: Science, pseudoscience, and antiscience [Science Working Group on Facilitated Communication]. *American Psychologist, 50*(9), 750–765.

Kluger, M. P., Alexander, G., & Curtis, P. A. (Eds.). (2001). *What works in child welfare*. Washington, DC: CWLA Press.

Kutchins, H., & Kirk, S. A. (1997). *Making us crazy: DSM: The psychiatric bible and creation of mental illness*. New York: Free Press.

Leever, M. G. (2003). Conflicts of interest in the privatization of child welfare. *Philosophy in the Contemporary World, 10*, 55–60.

Leever, M. G., DeCiani, G., Mulaney, E., & Hasslinger, H. (2002). *Ethical child welfare practice*. Washington, DC: CWLA Press.

Leo, J., & Cohen, D. (2003). Broken brains or flawed studies? A critical review of ADHD neuroimaging research. *Journal of Mind and Behavior, 24*, 29–55.

Munro, E. (1996). Avoidable and unavoidable mistakes in child protection work. *British Journal of Social Work, 26*, 793–808.

Munz, P. (1985). *Our knowledge of the growth of knowledge: Popper or Wittgenstein*. London: Routledge & Kegan Paul.

National Association of Social Workers. (1996). *Code of ethics*. Silver Spring, MD: NASW Press.

Nickerson, R. S. (1998). Confirmation biases: Ambiguous phenomenon in many guises. *Review of General Psychology, 2*, 175–220.

Nisbett, R., & Ross, L. (1980). *Human inference: Strategies and shortcomings of social judgement*. Englewood Cliffs, NJ: Prentice-Hall.

O'Conner, A. M., Stacey, D., Rovner, D., Holmes-Rovner, M., Tetroe, J., Llewellyn-Thomas, H., et al. (2002). Decision aids for people facing health treatment or screening decisions [Cochrane Review]. *The Cochrane Library Issue 2*. Oxford: Update Software.

Ofshe, R., & Watters, E. (1994). *Making monsters: False memories, psychotherapy, and sexual hysteria*. New York: Charles Scribner's Sons.

Oxman, A. D., & Guyatt, G. H. (1993). The science of reviewing research. In K. S. Warren & F. Mosteller (Eds.), *Doing more good than harm: The evaluation of health care interventions* (pp. 125–133). New York: New York Academy of Sciences.

Paul, R. (1993). *Critical thinking: What every person needs to survive in a rapidly changing world* (3rd ed.). Sonoma, CA: Foundation for Critical Thinking.

Popper, K. R. (1972). *Conjectures and refutations: The growth of scientific knowledge* (4th ed.). London: Routledge & Kegan Paul.

Popper, K. R. (1992). *In search of a better world: Lectures and essays from thirty years*. New York: Routledge.

Popper, K. R. (1994). *The myth of the framework: In defense of science and rationality*. New York: Routledge.

Reason, J. (2001). Understanding adverse events: The human factor. In C. Vincent (Ed.), *Clinical risk management* (2nd ed., pp. 9–20). London: BMJ Press.

Roche, T. (2000, Nov. 13). The crisis in foster care. *Time, 156*, p. 74.

Rosen, A., Proctor, E. E., Morrow-Howell, N., & Staudt, M. (1995). Rationales for practice decisions: Variations in knowledge use by decision task and social work service. *Research on Social Work Practice, 15*(4), 501–523.

Sackett, D. L., Richardson, W. S., Rosenberg, W., & Haynes, R. B. (1997). *Evidence-based medicine: How to practice and teach EBM.* New York: Churchill Livingstone.

Sackett, D. L., Straus, S. E., Richardson, W. S., Rosenberg, W., & Haynes, R. D. (2000). *Evidence-based medicine: How to practice & teach EBM* (2nd ed.). New York: Churchill Livingstone.

Sarnoff, S. K. (2001). *Sanctified snake oil: The effects of junk science and public policy.* Westport, CT: Praeger.

Sharpe, V. A., & Faden, A. I. (1998). *Medical harm: Historical, conceptual, and ethical dimensions of iatrogenic illness.* New York: Cambridge University Press.

Silverman, W. A. (1998). *Where's the evidence?: Controversies in modern medicine.* Oxford: Oxford University Press.

Skrabanek, P. (1994). *The death of humane medicine and the rise of coercive healthism.* Bury St. Edmunds, Suffolk, UK: St. Edmundsbury Press.

Skrabanek, P., & McCormick, J. (1998). *Follies and fallacies in medicine* (3rd ed.). Glencaple, Dumfries, UK: Beaufort Press.

Szasz, T. (1987). *Insanity: The idea and its consequences.* New York: John Wiley & Sons.

Valenstein, E. S. (1986). *Great and desperate cures: The rise and decline of psychosurgery and other medical treatments for mental illness.* New York: Basic Books.

Wennberg, J. E. (2002). Unwarranted variations in healthcare delivery: Implications for academic medical centres. *British Medical Journal, 325,* 961–964.

Wilkes, M. S., & Hoffman, J. R. (2001). An innovative approach to educating medical students about pharmaceutical promotion. *Academic Medicine, 76,* 1271–1277.

Young, J. H. (1992). *American health quackery.* Princeton: Princeton University Press.

CHAPTER 2

THEORY-DRIVEN VERSUS THEORY-FREE RESEARCH IN EMPIRICAL SOCIAL WORK PRACTICE

Jeanne C. Marsh

The role of theory in empirical practice research has received limited attention. Empirical practice research in social work has focused primarily on the identification and development of research methodologies amenable to practice settings. Theoretical discussions often have been restricted to claims that social work practice relies too heavily on theory—especially psychodynamic theory—to the exclusion of research evidence. Increasingly, however, empirical practice advocates argue for both the utility of multiple theoretical frameworks and the enhancement of practice effectiveness through the use of evidence *plus* theory *plus* practice experience. It is the purpose of this chapter to expand the discussion of empirical practice by examining the role of theory and arguing for theory-driven, rather than theory-free (or methods-driven), evaluations in empirical social work practice. This chapter will take the position that theory-free practice research is impossible and research and practice are enhanced when the theory underlying the definition of the problem and the intervention are articulated.

HISTORICAL BACKGROUND

Reid's (1994) analysis of the empirical practice movement provides an important perspective on the role of theory in social work practice research. As he notes, the scientific method has served as a model for the analysis of social work practice since the beginning of the profession. In Mary Richmond's *Social Diagnosis*, published in 1917, case analyses required the use of facts and theory to formulate hypotheses that could be tested with the application of additional evidence. In these early days, the psychoanalytic movement was the primary source of theories and interventions to be tested. The scientific paradigm that Richmond used called for practice to be systematic and rational, but it lacked the specific procedures found in contemporary empirical practice. For example, Richmond's paradigm did not include goal specification, progress and outcome monitoring, or the use of research instruments—all of which are fundamental elements of contemporary social work practice research.

Reid (1994) observes that these early perspectives came under scrutiny in the 1950s and 1960s, when doctoral programs in social work began turning out significant numbers of doctorate-level faculty who would ultimately assume academic leadership positions in social work training programs. Most of the future faculty members had been trained in psychodynamic approaches to practice. Reid notes that in the program at Columbia, "the inadequacy of existing casework method and the need for a 'new wave', one that would have a stronger base in research, was a recurring topic of discussion among the students. Yet neither faculty nor student research posed any direct challenges to the psychodynamic model or developed alternatives to it. The program prepared students for a different approach to intervention but fell short of helping them develop it" (p. 168). Although doctoral training at Columbia did not provide alternatives to the psychodynamic perspective, it did "reinforce [students'] research-mindedness, expose them to developments in the social sciences, and equip them with tools to study practice" (p. 167).

Another major doctoral program, the University of Michigan School of Social Work, was specifically organized to emphasize the utility of the social science theory for social work. The joint degree program in social work and the social sciences required students to complete course work and qualifying examinations in both social work and a social science discipline—sociology, psychology, political science, or economics. Preparation in this program required students to have exposure to the social sciences, to master theoretical frameworks and methodologies of a particular discipline, and to find social work problems and issues to which they could usefully apply these theories and methods. This program provided students with multiple theoretical frameworks from the social science disciplines (i.e., many alternatives to psychoanalytic theory) to guide their work.

A significant application of social science theory to social work practice emerged when University of Michigan professor Ed Thomas and some doctoral students began working with ideas derived from social learning theory that had been developing in psychology and psychiatry. Thomas had been systematically examining the broad relevance of social psychology for social work in *Role Theory: Concepts and Research* (with B. J. Biddle, 1966), *Behavioral Science for Social Workers* (1967), *The Socio-Behavioral Approach and Applications for Social Work* (1967). In 1967, he and his students introduced the "socio-behavioral approach" to social work. The approach was grounded in well-tested principles of learning theory, used specific measures of treatment and outcome, and, most significantly, identified a rigorous methodology for evaluating interventions with a single case (Reid, 1994). This was the first application of behavioral theory and methods to social work practice.

As students left Michigan, they spread respect for the utility of social science theory generally and behavioral theory more specifically. Behavioral approaches began to spread and to influence the development of empirical practice at other institutions. Sheldon Rose left the University of Michigan to develop behavioral group work at the University of Wisconsin-Madison; Eileen Gambrill left Michigan for University of California at Berkeley; and William Butterfield left Michigan to develop behavioral methods at Washington University in St. Louis. At the same time, a group of students from Columbia University began to contribute to the behavioral movement occurring at other institutions. Richard Stuart, Tony Tripodi, and Irwin Epstein went to Michigan from Columbia to contribute to the development of empirical practice. The Columbia graduate Arthur Schwartz organized a behavioral program at the University of Chicago's School of Social Service Administration and recruited the University of Kansas developmental psychologist Elsie Pinkston. At Chicago, Pinkston joined forces with William Reid and Laura Epstein, who were then developing the empirically oriented, task-centered model. Soon behavioral theory provided the leading alternative to psychoanalytic theory in the development of clinical interventions in social work.

Behavioral theory became a leading perspective for the development of social work interventions created for diverse service populations in a variety of settings. Elsie Pinkston's work exemplified the use of behavioral theory for the development of social work interventions. With her colleagues and students at Chicago, she used operant conditioning and social learning theories to develop and test service models addressing individuals and families, with a range of problems, in both homes and institutions (Pinkston, Levitt, Green, Linsk, & Rzepnicki, 1982). A significant portion of her work has focused on the development and testing of models for working with impaired elderly people living at home (Green, Linsk, & Pinkston, 1986; Linsk, Pinkston, & Green, 1982; Pinkston & Linsk, 1984a, 1984b; Pinkston, Linsk, & Young, 1988). Another focus of her work has been the effectiveness of behavioral parent training (Pinkston, 1984; Pinkston, Budd, & Baer, 1989; Pinkston, Friedman, & Polster, 1981; Pinkston & Smith, 1998). Pinkston's work is a leading exemplar of the contributions of behavioral theory to empirical social work practice.

It is clear that behavioral theory has been important to the development of effective models of service delivery. It is equally clear that the methodology of behaviorism, single-case methodology, has been a significant influence on the development of empirical practice. Again, as Reid (1994) notes, "a more general conception of empirical practice began to emerge. This conception was built around the methods of assessment, case monitoring, and outcome evaluation that were used in the single-system studies of behavioral approaches. It was assumed that these methods could be applied to any form of direct social work practice. They could not only guide practice in individual cases but also could be used in more rigorous forms by practitioner-researchers to test the effectiveness of practice models" (p. 169).

During this period, several other social work theories were under development but were only tangentially related to empirical practice. Germain (1970, 1983) reviews the development of theories in social work and describes their evolution as increasingly structured, scientifically defensible thought. She describes the growth and interconnection of the main theoretical frameworks that have guided social work practice since the Charity Organization and Settlement House movements. Payne (1997) also identifies the multiple theoretical perspectives guiding practice today as well as their assumptions and practice prescriptions;

these perspectives include psychodynamics, crisis intervention and task-centered models, cognitive-behavioral theories, systems and ecological perspectives, social psychological and communication models, humanism and existentialism, social and community development, radical and Marxist perspectives, antidiscrimination and antioppression, and empowerment and advocacy. Overall, these theoretical reviews reveal that although it was the methods of behavioral theory that shaped empirical practice, empirical practice methods eventually were described as relevant to the development and testing of any theoretical framework.

DEFINITION OF THEORY

Achieving agreement on a definition for *theory* is not as straightforward as one might expect (Gomory, 2001; Payne, 1995; Thyer, 2001). In their book providing a framework for conducting empirical practice, Berlin and Marsh (1993) describe theories as a type of knowledge structure that practitioners bring to bear in practice decision making. Schemas, or the relatively informal condensations of personal and practice experience, shape professional development and provide one kind of knowledge structure; theories provide another. Berlin and Marsh describe practice theories as the "schema of experts," that is, "experts' organized ideas about how people develop, how problems occur, how problems and people change" (p. 11). A textbook definition of theories is that they are comprehensive, precise, testable propositions that serve to explain and predict phenomena (Kerlinger, 1973). Berlin and Marsh (1993) argue for a "generic use of the term that includes a wide range of explicit explanatory or predictive propositions as well: models, perspectives, approaches and frameworks" (p. 11). Payne (1997) similarly supports a broad definition of theory; he suggests that in social work, theories are used to provide values and views and to describe ordered patterns of activity, not simply to deduce hypotheses. As a result, it is practical to use a broader definition of theory. He observes that writers who insist that theories must be testable often restrict the function of theories to hypothesis generation in order to enhance the legitimacy and validity of their ideas by requiring scientific proof.

An ever-expanding number of theories has led to appeals for theoretical ecumenism in the form of either theoretical pluralism or theoretical integration. Many social work scholars have argued for theoretical integration under the rubric of "eclectic practice" (Fischer, 1978; Tolson, 1988). Others make a distinction between theoretical integration and theoretical pluralism (Berlin and Marsh, 1993; Walsh and Peterson, 1985). They suggest that the integration of theoretical constructs without explicit consideration of strengths and weaknesses of each framework, as required in theoretical pluralism, can lead to conceptual confusion and intellectually flabby frameworks. Berlin and Marsh (1993) suggest that theoretical pluralism that incorporates critical analysis of each framework "emphasizes the importance of clarity about the merits of specific approaches and explicitly encourages the clinician to develop a repertoire of perspectives and skills in order to identify those that best fit the circumstances at hand" (p. 13).

The primary theoretical debate in the literature has not pertained to the distinctiveness or utility of these emerging theories. Instead, as Payne (1997) describes it, the debate has been between positivist and postmodern views of theory in social work practice. Simply stated, a positivist view defines knowledge as limited to that which can be observed or experienced and views the scientific method as the only appropriate means for acquiring it. In contrast, postmodernism recognizes that humans interpret and bring meaning to observation and experience and consider knowledge a representation, rather than a concrete reflection, of reality. Since it is not possible to simply observe the world and report accordingly from a postmodernist perspective, the theories and paradigms one brings to the analysis have a significant impact on the findings from that analysis (Gergen, 2001)

Positivist perspectives in social work have been articulated by Fischer (1978) when he declared social casework to be ineffective and argued for its replacement with empirically tested practice. Thyer (1993) has also expressed positivist views: "The methods of scientific inquiry derived from logical positivism have a demonstrated value in the development of validated knowledge of value to social work practice" (p. 8). Thyer (2001) also makes clear that from a positivist perspective, theory is "neither essential or necessarily desirable for research on social work practice" (p. 22). Witkin (1989; Witkin & Gottschalk 1988) has reflected the postmodern perspective in his questioning of the validity of fundamental positivist assumptions about the objectivity of data and human information processing. He concludes his 1991 critique of the positivist perspectives embodied in empirical clinical practice by rejecting empirical practice altogether. He states that the development of an empirical foundation "is largely illusory and a questionable base for social work practice" (p. 161). At the same time, he promotes the use of theory as "a step toward the development of a social science consistent with social work's mission and goals" (p. 221). Thus, social work scholars operating from a positivist perspective (as interpreted by Thyer) have espoused little need for theory and those coming from a postmodernist perspective (as represented by Witkin) eschew empirical methods as a base for developing social work practice.

Several other social work researchers acknowledge the limits of positivist perspectives while remaining committed to empirical practice. For example, Berlin and Marsh (1993) state that despite the importance of empirical knowledge, it is "insufficient as a practice base" (p. 230). They and others emphasize that clear conceptual frameworks, commitments and values, spontaneous improvisation, intuitive hunches, empathic understanding, and empirically derived data are appropriate bases for empirical practice. Thus, discussions of the use of theory in social work practice have been embedded in philosophical debates between scholars adhering to positivist and postmodernist perspectives of knowledge development. Increasingly, researchers and practitioners have sought to move beyond issues of the philosophy of science to identify pragmatic strategies for using theory to advance knowledge about effective social work practice.

LEVELS OF THEORY

In determining the role of theory in empirical practice, it is useful to consider possible levels of theory. The sociologist Robert Merton makes a valuable distinction among various levels of theory in his classic paper "On Sociological Theories of the Middle Range" (1967). He argues for the development and use of middle-range theories that fall between unified theories seeking to encompass all social behavior and the necessary working hypotheses that evolve as researchers seek to solve problems through research. He suggests that middle-range theories help negotiate the conflicts between the general and the specific, that is, between broad philosophical statements and specific relations to be understood. Targeting the development and use of middle-range theories is relevant to empirical practice because these theories are useful for guiding empirical inquiry. Middle-range theories are the basis for hypotheses that can be empirically tested. They enable us to organize our understanding of key concepts and the relations among them and to consolidate our understanding in ways that go beyond either loose descriptions or empirical generalizations.

The use of theory in empirical practice is sometimes rejected with the claim that extant social science theory has a focus or level of abstraction that lacks relevance for the problems that concern social work researchers. To support this claim, Thyer (2001) provides an example of a social work dissertation that analyzes alumni of a Florida orphanage. For the dissertation, the doctoral candidate was required to review the literature on "some theory related to the topic." The level of the theory or its relevance to the research question was apparently not important to the dissertation committee. The student used attachment theory and risk and resilience theory as guideposts for understanding the findings. Thyer uses the fact that the discussion of theory was not included in the published article as weak proof that the theory may have been at the wrong level of abstraction. In this case, a careful articulation of the research questions might have led to a more appropriate choice and level of theory, enhancing the design and overall contribution of the study.

IMPLICIT AND EXPLICIT THEORY

Occasionally, theories of a problem or theories of a program are well articulated, especially when the original design of a program is based on an explicit social science theory. For example, Pinkston and her colleagues have developed a model of practice for working with the elderly based on operant conditioning and social learning theory (Pinkston, Green, Linsk, & Young, 2001). Similarly, Fraser, Nash, Galinsky, and Darwin (2001) developed an approach to teaching social problem-solving to young children based on theories of risk and resilience and cognitive-behavioral theory. The theoretical foundations of the approach are carefully outlined in the treatment manual. More often, programs are developed in practice settings, and the theory that drives the practice remains implicit or tacit (Rossi, Freeman, & Lipsky, 1999; Weiss, 1997). For example, Thyer (2001) cites an example of a social work doctoral student who developed and tested an intervention for mothers who failed to comply with pediatricians' prescription for regular use of a home apnea monitor. The student used a "case management model and some simple behavioral prompting strategies" to design the intervention, but her dissertation committee required that she incorporate the "health belief model" into her dissertation. The example suggests that the student may have developed the intervention on the basis of an implicit model guided by social learning theory (emphasizing stimulus control through instruction and prompting) but failed to make the model explicit for the dissertation committee.

In cases in which the program theory is implicit, it is the responsibility of the practitioner-researcher to make the implicit explicit through literature reviews, interviews with practitioners, observation of program operation, and reviews of program documents (Alter & Egan, 1997; Rossi, Freeman, & Lipsky, 1999). This process has been variously labeled as expressing program theory, concept mapping, and logic modeling. The process requires practitioners and researchers to work together to review relevant research and ongoing program operations in order to articulate the theory embodied in program structure and operation (Alter & Egan, 1997; Chen & Rossi, 1983). Rossi, Freeman, and Lipsky (1999) describe program theory as a "detailed description of the relationships between program resources, program activities, and program outcomes that shows how the program is supposed to work and, in particular, how it is supposed to bring about the intended outcomes" (p. 160). In addition, Finney and Moos (1992) suggest that "the critical issues are whether a theory (a) is relevant in its content to the intervention being applied; (b) is specified at a high enough level of abstraction to have generality; and (c) identifies intervening processes or mechanisms that link program activities and ultimate outcomes" (p. 21). They indicate that "theories of experts" or social science theories are more likely to have the latter two properties, but implicit theories derived through work with practitioners and program staff may be more relevant for identifying the active ingredients of treatment.

Formal procedures for making the implicit explicit, such as logic modeling and concept mapping, are increasingly well developed (Alter & Egan, 1997; Trochim, 1985). Alter and Egan (1997) promote logic modeling as a method that facilitates making theoretical connection between "unconscious theories in action" and proposed interventions. They note that logic modeling promotes thinking about "the clinical experience as a whole and how the component parts contribute to achieving a desired outcome" (p. 103). Practitioners and researchers who argue for the use of these procedures point to the logical impossibility of theory-free evaluations. Although program theories may be implicit and remain implicit for lack of specification by researchers and practitioners, all programs are based on some idea about which mechanisms cause change and why. By failing to make these ideas explicit, theory-free evaluators risk misspecification of measured constructs, the chance to contribute to treatment and service knowledge development, and the opportunity to develop more effective programs overall.

According to Berlin and Marsh (1993), theory-free evaluators risk losing "an expanded sense of how to understand and to act" (p. 11).

TYPES OF THEORY: PROBLEM, SERVICE, AND PROBLEM-SERVICE MATCHING THEORY

Most discussions of theory in social work practice discuss theory as it relates to treatment process or programmatic intervention. Certainly, the early "theory wars" between psychodynamic and behavioral theory focused on the effectiveness of intervention from these two different perspectives. However, recent work in program evaluation points to the value of identifying different types of theory (Finney & Moos, 1992; Rossi, Freeman, & Lipsky, 1999; Shadish, Cook, & Leviton, 1991). The types or categories of theories that have emerged in program evaluation are relevant to the fundamental questions addressed by evaluation, questions such as the following: What are the problems this program is addressing? How are clients selected into the program? How are particular clients matched with particular treatments? Does the program work? What and whose values are operating to determine whether the program works? What methods should be used to evaluate the program? How can the results be used to improve the program? For each of these questions relevant to program evaluation, there is a body of knowledge that helps organize, describe, predict, and understand the answers to these questions. In other words, for each of these questions there are explicit or implicit theoretical frameworks that are employed in answering the questions. Shadish, Cook, and Leviton (1991) identify five fundamental issues that undergird program evaluation: (1) social programming, (2) knowledge construction, (3) valuing, (4) knowledge use, and (5) evaluation practice. They describe and discuss the theory or knowledge bases that are employed in each of these areas in their book *Foundations of Program Evaluation: Theories of Practice* (1991).

Empirical practice research in social work is concerned with many of the same questions with which program evaluation is concerned, such as defining problems, intervening effectively, selecting research methods appropriate for evaluating interventions, and maximizing the utility of research. Although discussions of empirical practice have focused predominantly on the question of methods (e.g., the best way to implement single-case designs in practice settings or overall utility of qualitative versus quantitative methods), empirical practice researchers are also necessarily concerned with issues of problem definition, intervention design, and research utilization. For purposes of this discussion of empirical practice in social work, it is useful to distinguish among problem theory, treatment or service theory, and problem-service matching theory. Problem theory pertains to theories relevant to explaining the etiology and expression of a personal or social problem. For example, social workers are concerned with substance abuse as a personal and social problem. They have identified several explanations for causes of substance abuse that are based in theory, including neurological theories, stress and coping theories, and deviance theories. Problem theory is relevant to designing interventions in that it puts a problem in context and identifies specific aspects or dimensions of the problem that might be amenable to change or intervention. For example, recent evidence that substance users come into treatment with a number of co-occurring disorders has resulted in treatment programs that incorporate a range of ancillary health and social services (McLellan, et al., 1997). Treatment or service theory, in contrast, refers to specific resources and activities related to achieving specific goals. Theory relevant to social work practice, that is also relevant to bringing about change, is treatment or service theory. Reid and Epstein's task-centered model (1972) or Berlin's cognitive-integrative perspective (2002) are examples of some social work treatment theories. Problem-service matching theories specify the interaction of specific problems and other client characteristics and specific service models or treatment characteristics. Problem-service matching theories begin to take into account differential treatment planning, or the need to tailor treatments and services to client needs and characteristics (Marsh & Berlin, 1983). Smith and Marsh (2002) discuss an approach to problem-service matching in substance-abuse treatment for women with children.

ROLE OF THEORY

Theory has both conceptual and instrumental roles to play in social work research. On a conceptual level, social workers look to theories as guides for thinking about problems and specifying interventions in response to them. Theoretical understanding comes from identifying mechanisms related to the development of problems, dismantling problems into constituent parts, and determining patterns of relations among interdependent parts. We are interested in the component parts as antecedents, consequences, correlates, and causal factors. Behavioral theory is particularly informative in social work research in the delineation of the characteristics of problems and their controlling conditions, the antecedents and consequences (Pinkston et al., 1982). All theories highlight particular component parts and can, in fact, be differentiated in terms of the components they emphasize. Behavioral theories focus on behaviors, psychodynamic theories on feelings, cognitive theories on beliefs, and family on interpersonal relations. A number of authors have suggested that the differential emphasis of theories contributes to their differential utility in understanding different types of problems (Beutler & Clarkin, 1990; Marsh & Berlin, 1993).

In empirical practice, theories help articulate constituent parts of problems and their interrelations primarily to enable better specification of a plan of action (i.e., an intervention). Kazdin (1997) suggests that in clinical research, researchers use theory frequently to understand the problem but less frequently to design interventions. Too often there is a detailed construction of the problem addressed with only general treatment approaches that have wide applicability across problems. He suggests that researchers fail to use their theoretical understandings of the problem to specify and refine treatment. He advocates for treatment that has "conceptual underpinnings—that is, explicit views about what treatment is designed to accomplish and through what processes" (p. 118). Kazdin is advocating implicitly for the use of logic models in clinical research. To the extent that practitioners specify their theory of intervention and use logic models to break out the relevant component parts, they are explicitly drawing on theory to specify treatment resources and processes that will result in expected outcomes. An important, instrumental role for theory is, therefore, that of guiding the specification of variables representing the problem, the intervention, the outcome, and the control variables. Use of theory to identify control variables is especially important for theory. A clear conceptualization of the problem provides an understanding of extraneous factors that, in addition to the intervention, influence the outcome and need to be controlled in order to gain a clear understanding of intervention effects. For example, research on women and substance use has, to date, failed to control for the parenting role in influencing the impact of substance-abuse treatment for women. Much of the research to date has assumed that women are parents. Role theory has had limited application in the design and evaluation of treatment programs for women substance abusers, despite its obvious utility (Colten & Marsh, 1983). Thus, theory-driven evaluations require specification of the problem and the intervention in order to provide guidance for targeted and comprehensive "operationalization" of those theories.

Theories are also useful for linking results back to the frameworks that guide empirical practice and the questions that practice research seeks to address. Fundamentally, knowledge building is an incremental process. Each study answers a relatively constrained question or solves a particular problem. Even if it remains implicit or vague, every study is influenced by some conceptualizations of the problem and the intervention. To the extent that these can be made explicit, findings from the study can be used to inform, elaborate, or refine this larger framework. For example, if the utility of client contracting can be studied within a larger framework of services research, then findings on the effectiveness of client contracting have relevance to models of service delivery in a variety of settings, compared with answering a particular practice question of program efficacy in a particular agency.

Finally, when the goal of the research is theory testing, then theories are the basis for developing the specific hypotheses to be tested. The formal process of hypothesis testing is designed to provide a means for formal theory development. As I have noted, theory development or knowledge development more generally is only one of the roles of theory in empirical practice.

THEORIES OF THE PROBLEM

Problem theories are concerned with topography or characteristics of problems, the factors and conditions that shape and constrain them, and the ways that they change in response to those factors and conditions. Problem theories can focus on genetic predispositions, acquired physiological abnormalities, learned behavioral problems, expressions of underlying psychiatric or physical problems, or lack of family and community support for appropriate functioning. For example, when psychodynamic perspectives are employed to understand the factors that shape the development of a problem, there is an emphasis on the expression of the problem and its underlying causes, which are identified in terms of both the physical or social environment and the stress of internal conflicts, which are often developmental in nature. Psychodynamic theories of substance abuse suggest that individuals who are lacking emotional and social supports in childhood turn to substances to fulfill these basic needs. In contrast, stress and coping theories suggest that substance abuse results from current stressful life events or conditions such as insufficient emotional or economic resources. Finney and Moos (1992) describe a substance-abuse study that used stress and coping theory to explain the nature of substance abuse as a problem. The stress and coping perspective of the problem led them to examine the role of life context (both stressors and social resources) as well as coping factors with respect to treatment outcome. They found that life context and coping factors doubled the variance in outcome that could be explained when taking account of patient characteristics and treatment factors alone.

The relevance of problem theories in the evaluation of social work intervention might be questioned because their focus is not on the intervention itself. As Finney and Moos (1992) note, theories of the problem put the intervention in context, emphasizing that the intervention is only one factor affecting an individual's functioning. To the extent that problem theory can identify factors other than the intervention that may influence functioning, they provide guidance for revising or enhancing a less-than-optimum intervention. Theories of problems can provide more comprehensive ideas of predictive and explanatory factors of the problem that can be used to design and evaluate the intervention.

THEORIES OF THE TREATMENT OR SERVICE

Theories of treatment or service specify the resources and activities deployed to achieve desired outcomes. Treatment theories also can indicate the process of change expected to take place and the specific variables or processes of treatment that may mediate treatment effects. Treatment theory based on psychodynamic perspectives emphasizes the establishment of a corrective relationship and the expression of feeling as therapeutic activities that lead to the achievement of treatment goals. In contrast, cognitive-behavioral approaches focus on restructuring beliefs and supporting and reinforcing specific behaviors, such as abstinence, as active ingredients in treatment. Marlatt and Gordon's (1985) cognitive-behavioral approach to relapse prevention provides an example of an approach focused on shifting the thoughts and behaviors associated with "slips" from abstinence.

THEORIES OF PROBLEM-SERVICE MATCHING

Problem-treatment matching theories address the interaction between clients and interventions. The testing of emerging treatment theories requires their proceduralization or manualization. To test the effectiveness of particular theory, it must be operationalized in the form of treatment or practice guidelines. The development of practice guidelines in social work, psychology, and other professions is well documented (Howard & Jenson, in press) The existence of practice guidelines leads immediately to the question of how to match treatments to clients, that is, how to determine which problems or clients should receive a certain treatment.

The substance-abuse field is one in which theories of problem-service matching have been examined (McLellan & McKay, 1998). Approximately twenty years of research studies based on diverse matching theories have been conducted. The most common approach has attempted to identify client characteristics that predict the best response to different forms of treatment (Marsh & Miller, 1985; McLellan & McKay, 1998). In general, studies attempting to determine appropriate treatment on the basis of client characteristics (e.g., gender, cognitive style, level of impairment) have yielded little (Finney & Moos, 1986; Marsh & Miller, 1985; McLellan & McKay, 1995). Among the more promising approaches are those that assess the severity of clients' problems in a range of areas (e.g., health, mental health, family conflict) and then to match services to the identified service needs. These approaches are consistent with the emphasis in social work practice on a thorough assessment as the basis for a tailored approach to service provision. In the substance-abuse literature, this has been called problem-service matching. McLellan and colleagues (1997) and Smith and Marsh (2002) have shown that matching services to client-reported needs results in significant reductions in substance use. Both studies point to advantages of employing problem-service matching in services research. Overall, problem-service matching theories expand the scope of explanatory frameworks by taking into account client characteristics and life contexts and their interactions with specific service models.

CONCLUSIONS

History reveals that the use of theory in empirical practice research in social work has benefited significantly from the development and use of behavioral theory and methods. Behavioral theory has provided an important and influential framework for several important interventions. More significantly perhaps, behavioral research methods of assessment, case monitoring, and outcome evaluation have been used to develop and test interventions that derive from a range of theoretical perspectives. Unfortunately, discussions of the role of theory in empirical practice has been limited, for the most part, to the assertion that empirical practice research methods are independent of behavioral theory; that is, they are relevant to a broad range of theoretical perspectives.

Understanding the role of theory in empirical practice benefits from recognition of the function of theory in social work more generally. In the past twenty-five years, social work has experienced a significant expansion in the number of theories that are recognized as relevant to social work practice. This expansion has led to the need for both flexibility and integrity with respect to the use of theory. As the number of theoretical perspectives—or ways to think about problems and interventions—has grown, practitioners and researchers have recognized the value of clarity about the merits and limitations of specific perspectives. They have identified the importance of having a repertoire of perspectives and skills that can be matched with the circumstances at hand.

The expansion of theoretical perspectives has also led to the recognition that although a variety of theoretical perspectives may influence the understanding of a problem or the development of an intervention, too often these perspectives remain implicit or unspecified. Sometimes when guiding theoretical perspectives are made explicit, they are misspecified or misunderstood. As a result, social work researchers and practitioners increasingly rely on tools such as logic modeling to determine problem definition and to explicate the theory embodied in program structure and operation. Logic-modeling tools are especially useful for enabling researchers to specify the appropriate level of theory that helps organize understanding of important concepts and relationships among them and that helps guide empirical inquiry.

Theory plays both a conceptual and an instrumental role in social work practice research. On a conceptual level, theories provide guidance for thinking about problems and designing interventions to respond to them. On an instrumental level, theories enable articulation of the component parts of problems and interventions and their relation to one another, explicit testing of specific hypotheses derived from the theory, linking of our research questions to larger issues in the field, and ultimately design of more effective interventions.

Recognizing different types of theory in empirical practice increases the understanding of the role that theory can play. At least three types of theories are relevant to empirical practice research: theories of the problem, theories of treatment or service, and theories of problem-service matching. Theories of problems are related to the characteristics of problems and the factors that shape and constrain their expression. Theories of treatment or services describe the resources, activities, and processes related to the achievement of specific outcomes. Problem-service matching theories begin to identify factors relevant to differential treatment planning, that is, to tailoring or matching the treatments or services to clients or client problems in order to achieve the most effective results.

Elucidation of specific types of theory and uses for theory in empirical practice research forces recognition of the potentially significant role for theory in expanding understanding of problems and alternative interventions and ultimately for increasing practice effectiveness. Whether theory is implicit or explicit, it defines the understanding of problems and approaches to resolving them. Practice and research may fail to acknowledge or specify the ideas that shape the activity, but it is not possible for practice activities to be developed free of some motivating or organizing ideas or frameworks. Thus, although research and practice may have theory that remains unspecified, they cannot remain theory-free. Both research and practice are well served by a theory-driven approach that emphasizes the value of articulating the theory underlying the problem, the intervention, and the relation of the problem to services received.

REFERENCES

Alter, C., & Egan, M. (1997). Logic modeling: A tool for teaching practice evaluation. *Journal of Social Work Education, 33*(1), 103–118.

Berlin, S. (2002). *Clinical social work practice: A cognitive-integrative perspective.* New York: Oxford University Press.

Berlin, S., & Marsh, J. C. (1993). *Informing practice decisions.* New York: Macmillan.

Beutler, L. E., & Clarkin, J. F. (1990). *Systematic treatment selection.* New York: Brunner/Mazel.

Biddle, B. J., & Thomas, E. J. (1966). *Role theory: Concepts and research.* New York: John Wiley & Sons.

Chen, H. T., & Rossi, P. H. (1983). Evaluating with sense: The theory-driven approach. *Evaluation Review, 7,* 283–302.

Colten, M. E., & Marsh, J. C. (1983). A sex roles perspective on drug and alcohol use by women. In C. S. Widom (Ed.), *Sex roles and psychopathology* (pp. 219–248). New York: Plenum.

Finney, J. W., & Moos, R. H. (1992). Four types of theory that can guide treatment evaluations. In H. Chen & P. H. Rossi (Eds.), *Using theory to improve program and policy evaluations* (pp. 15–27). New York: Greenwood Press.

Fischer, J. (1978). *Effective casework practice: An eclectic approach.* New York: McGraw-Hill.

Fraser, M. W., Nash, J. K., Galinsky, M. J., & Darwin, K. E. (2001). *Making choices: Social problem-solving for children.* Washington, DC: NASW Press.

Gergen, K. J. (2001). Psychological science in a postmodern context. *American Psychologist, 56*(10), 803–813.

Germain, C. B. (1970). Casework and science: A historical encounter. In R. W. Roberts & R. H. Nee (Eds.), *Theories of social casework* (pp. 26–57). Chicago: University of Chicago Press.

Germain, C. B. (1983). Technological advances. In A. Rosenblatt & D. Waldfogel (Eds.), *Handbook of clinical social work.* San Francisco: Jossey-Bass.

Gomory, T. (2001). A fallibilistic response to Thyer's theory of theory-free empirical research in social work practice. *Journal of Social Work Education, 37*(1), 26–50.

Green, G. R., Linsk, N. L., & Pinkston, E. M. (1986). The modification of verbal behavior of the impaired elderly. *Journal of Applied Behavior Analysis, 19,* 329–336.

Howard, M. O., & Jensen, J. M. (in press). *Clinical guidelines and evidence-based practice in medicine, psychology, and allied professions.* In E. Procter & A. Rosen (Eds.), *Developing practice guidelines for social work interventions: Issues, methods, and research agenda.* New York: Columbia University Press.

Kazdin, A. E. (1997). A model for developing effective treatments: Progression and interplay of theory, research, and practice. *Journal of Clinical and Child Psychology, 26*(2), 114–129.

Kerlinger, F. N. (1973). *Foundations of behavioral research.* New York: Holt, Rinehart and Winston.

Linsk, N. L., Pinkston, E. M., & Green, G. R. (1982). Home-based behavioral social work with the elderly. In E. M. Pinkston, J. L. Levitt, G. R. Green, N. L. Linsk, & T. L. Rzepnicki (Eds.), *Effective social work practice*. San Francisco: Jossey-Bass.

Marlatt, A. G., & Gordon, J. R. (1985). *Relapse prevention: Maintenance strategies in addictive behavior change*. New York: Guilford Press.

Marsh, J. C., & Miller, N. A. (1985). Female clients in substance abuse treatment. *International Journal of the Addictions, 20*(6 & 7), 995–1019.

McLellan, A. T., Grissom, G. R., Zanis, D., Randall, M., Brill, P. & O'Brien, C. P. (1997). Problem-service matching in addiction treatment: A prospective study in four programs. *Archives of General Psychiatry, 54*, 730–735.

McLellan, A. T., & McKay, J. R. (1998). The treatment of addiction: What can research offer practice? In S. Lamb., M. R. Greenlick, & D. McCarty (Eds.), *Bridging the gap between practice and research: Forging partnerships with community-based drug and alcohol treatment* (147–186). Washington, DC: National Academy Press.

Merton, R. K. (1967). On sociological theories of the middle range. *On theoretical sociology*. New York: Free Press.

Payne, M. (1997). *Modern Social Work Theory* (2nd ed.). Chicago: Lyceum Books.

Pinkston, E. M. (1984). Individualized behavioral intervention for home and school. In R. F. Dangel & R. A. Polster (Eds.), *Parent training: Foundations of research and practice*. New York: Guilford Press.

Pinkston, E. M. (1997). A supportive environment for old age. In D. M. Baer & E. M. Pinkston (Eds.), *Environment and behavior*. Boulder, CO: Westview Press.

Pinkston, E. M., Budd, K. S., & Baer, D. M. (1989). Evaluation of modeling as a parent training procedure. In B. A. Thyer (Ed.), *Behavioral family therapy*. Springfield, IL: Charles Thomas.

Pinkston, E. M., Friedman, B. S., & Polster, R. A. (1981). Parents as agents for behavior change. In S. P. Schinke (Ed.), *Behavioral methods in social welfare: Helping children, adults and families in community settings* (29–40). New York: Aldine.

Pinkston, E. M., Levitt, J. L., Green, G. R., Linsk, N. L., & Rzepnicki, T. L. (1982). *Effective social work practice: Advanced techniques for behavioral intervention with individuals, families and institutional staff*. San Francisco: Jossey-Bass.

Pinkston, E. M., & Linsk, N. L. (1984a). Behavioral family intervention with the impaired elderly. *The Gerontologist, 24*, 576–583.

Pinkston, E. M., & Linsk, N. L. (1984b). *Care of the elderly: A family approach*. New York: Pergamon Press.

Pinkston, E. M., Linsk, N. L., & Young, R. N. (1988). Home-based behavioral family treatment of the impaired elderly through stimulus control. *Journal of Applied Behavior Analysis, 19*, 331–344.

Pinkston, E. M., & Smith, M. D. (1988). Contributions of parent training to child welfare: Early history and current thought. In J. R. Lutzker (Ed.), *Handbook of child abuse research and treatment*. New York: Plenum Press.

Reid, W. J. (1994). The empirical practice movement. *Social Service Review, 68*(2), 165–184.

Reid, W. J., & Epstein, L. (1972). *Task-centered casework*. New York: Columbia University Press.

Richmond, M. (1917). *Social diagnosis*. New York: Russell Sage Foundation.

Rossi, P. H., Freeman, H. E., & Lipsky, M. W. (1999). *Evaluation: A systematic approach*. Thousand Oaks: Sage.

Smith, B. D., and Marsh, J. C. (2002). Client-service matching in substance abuse treatment for women with children. *Journal of Substance Abuse Treatment, 22,* 161–168.

Thomas, E. J. (1967a). *Behavioral science for social workers.* New York: Free Press.

Thomas, E. J. (1967b). *The socio-behavioral approach and applications to social work.* New York: Council on Social Work Education.

Thyer, B. A. (1993). Social work theory and practice research: The approach of logical positivism. *Social Work and Social Sciences Review, 4*(1), 5–26.

Thyer, B. A. (2001). What is the role of theory in research on social work practice? *Journal of Social Work Education, 37*(1), 9–25.

Tolson, E. R. (1988). *The metamodel and clinical social work.* New York: Columbia University Press.

Trochim, W. M. K. (1985). Pattern matching, validity and conceptualization in program evaluation. *Evaluation Review, 9,* 575–604.

Walsh, B. W., & Peterson, L. E. (1985). Philosophical foundations of psychological theories: The use of synthesis. *Psychotherapy: Theory, Research and Practice, 22,* 145–53.

Weiss, C. H. (1997). How can theory-based evaluation make greater headway? *Evaluation Review, 21*(4), 501–524.

Witkin, S. L. (1989). Towards a scientific social work. *Journal of Social Service Research, 12*(2), 83–98.

Witkin, S. L. (1991). Empirical clinical practice: A critical analysis. *Social Work, 36*(2), 158–163.

Witkin, S. L., & Gottschalk, S. S. (1988). Alternative criteria for theory evaluation. *Social Service Review, 62*(2), 211–224.

CHAPTER 3

CONTRIBUTION OF OPERANT THEORY TO SOCIAL WORK PRACTICE AND RESEARCH

William J. Reid

We are all very much aware that our actions are profoundly affected by what follows them. We work because of the rewards that ensue—money, grades, the approval of others, or feelings of accomplishment. We conform to various social norms because of what might happen if we do not—disapproval, rejection, or incarceration. Such connections between behavior and its consequences form the central concerns of operant theory. The theory is of particular importance in evidence-based social work practice, because it is one of the few theories used in social work that is firmly based in empirical research.

Contemporary operant theory evolved largely from the work of Skinner and his colleagues (1974), who were interested in developing a science of behavior, referred to as behavior analysis. Experimental behavior analysis was concerned with establishing principles of behavior primarily through laboratory research. Applied behavior analysis was directed at the application of operant theory and research in natural settings (Baer, Wolf, & Risley, 1968). Operant theory, together with theories of respondent (Pavlovian) conditioning and learning through imitation or modeling, formed what is known as learning theory, the foundation of behavior therapy.

In this chapter, I will first present an overview of operant theory. This will be followed by a brief historical sketch of its entry into social work. I will then examine its influence on social work practice and research. Finally, I will consider operant theory's potential for future contributions.

OPERANT THEORY

Operant theory incorporates both a theory of human behavior (the nature and causes of behavior) and a theory of practice (how one can assess and change behavior.) Both types of theory are reflected in the subsequent summary.

Operant Theory as a Theory of Behavior

The principal tenet of operant theory is that individuals learn from the consequences of their behavior, which "consists of everything a person *does* [including] . . . private events, such as thoughts and feelings" (Thyer & Myers, 2001, p 201). Consequences are classified in terms of the behavior changes that follow them. If a consequence is followed by an increase in the behavior, the behavior is said to have been reinforced (Milan, 1990). A distinction is made between *positive reinforcement,* in which a stimulus or condition is added and *negative reinforcement,* in which a stimulus or condition is withdrawn. Parents commonly use positive reinforcement, such as approval, to reward a child for behavior they regard as desirable. They may use negative reinforcement if they stop nagging a child to behave in a certain way when the child finally complies with their wishes. If the consequence of a behavior results in a decrease in that behavior, the consequence is defined as punishment.

Contingent relationships between events and consequences are then formed through either reinforcement or punishment. These relationships may be terminated through the process of *extinction,* which occurs when "previously reinforced responses are no longer followed by reinforcing events and previously punished responses are no longer followed by punishing responses" (Milan, 1990, p. 76). Thus, if a child's "silly" behavior is reinforced by parental attention to it, it may diminish (become extinguished) when the parents consistently ignore it.

An important principle in operant theory is that consequences may affect behavior through prior experience with them or knowledge of what they are likely to lead to. This principle emerges through two key notions. One concerns the effect of antecedent conditions. When individuals learn that certain stimuli are likely to lead to certain consequences, their behavior may be affected by the stimuli themselves. When this occurs, the behavior is said to be under stimulus or antecedent control. An "inviting" smile from a woman may signal to a man that approaching her is likely to be reinforced, and so he starts a conversation.

Another expression of the principle is "rule-governed behavior," which relates to behavior that is responsive to descriptions of consequences (Hayes, 1989; Mattaini, 1996; Thyer, 1996). Descriptions may be spelled out, as in the rules of the road; learned by word of mouth; or derived from observation; among other possibilities. Thus, a boy, for example, interacting with his peers might observe that certain remarks are likely to result in aggressive responses. His perception of this rule may influence his own behavior as if he had experienced the consequences himself.

Operant Theory as a Practice Theory

In its application to human problems, operant theory provides both assessment and intervention strategies for work with individuals, families, groups, communities, and organizations. Its primary mode of assessment is analysis of contingencies apparently controlling behaviors of interest (Thyer, 1987). An effort is made to determine connections between the antecedents of a behavior, the behavior itself, and its consequences. Through such analysis of behavior and its antecedents and consequences—referred to as functional or contingency analysis—the social worker can form hypotheses about contingencies maintaining problem behaviors and seek to alter these contingencies.

In addition to applications to individuals, families, and groups, contingency analysis can also be used in study of social problems and policies as well as of communities and other macro systems. For example, Mattaini et al. (1996) analyze the functions of reinforcement and punishment in youth violence as a societal problem. Briggs and Paulson (1996) use a multiple contingency framework to examine issues in implementation of affirmative action. Such studies can lead to the design of intervention programs to reshape contingencies toward more functional ends.

Operant theory has generated a rich variety of approaches to produce behavior change. Space permits only a brief review of some of the more commonly used methods in clinical work. *Positive reinforcement* is used by practitioners to encourage constructive client behaviors and to help caregivers learn to promote such behaviors in those they care for. Clients can be taught to supply their own reinforcers through the process of *self-reinforcement,* which requires that they both evaluate their own behaviors and reward themselves. Mild and controlled forms of punishment, such as time out for children, are used to replace harsh, inconsistent disciplinary practices.

In *contingency management,* parents, teachers, or others in control of reinforcement contingencies are taught to use *differential reinforcement* to influence behavior. For example, parents consistently reward (reinforce) their children for appropriate behavior. Inappropriate behavior is ignored, if possible, or punished through such consequences as loss of privileges or time out.

In many applications of operant theory, individuals work out contingencies of reinforcement between individuals through *contingency contracting,* or, as Pinkston et al. (1982) state, "the mutual agreement between two or more persons as to the consequences of particular behaviors" (p. 27). For example, a parent may agree to provide a reward to a child in the form of a privilege or tangibles, contingent on the child performing a given task (e.g., the child can watch an extra half-hour of television after chores are finished).

The notion of stimulus control occurs in many practice contexts. For example, in work with substance abusers, practitioners attempt to identify controlling stimuli or triggers that elicit drug-using behavior (Kirby, Lamb, & Iguchi, 1997).

Operant ideas also play an important part in methods that use other learning principles. For example, in social skills training, modeling is combined with reinforcement of desired behaviors by the trainer as well as by others in the client's environment.

A HISTORICAL PERSPECTIVE

During the 1960s, the clinical application of operant theory began to spread from its base in psychology to other disciplines. Its debut in social work occurred in the latter part of that decade with the introduction of behavioral practice models based on, to a large extent, operant principles. (Again, the term *behavioral* will be used to refer to approaches that incorporate such principles.) If there was a prime mover, it was perhaps Edwin J. Thomas at the University of Michigan School of Social Work. The "big bang" took place in a series of dramatic and controversial presentations at the 1967 Annual Program Meeting of the Council of Social Work Education, where Thomas and his associates unveiled their "socio-behavioral" approach to social work (Thomas, 1967b). Doctoral students trained in behavioral methods at Michigan found positions at other schools, where they introduced behavioral methods in their teaching and began to develop and test behavioral practice models (Reid, 1994). Among them (and where they went) were Sheldon Rose (Wisconsin), Eileen Gambrill (California at Berkeley), William Butterfield (Washington University), Clayton Shorkey (Texas), and Martin Sundel (Harvard). Supporting these developments were several doctoral students enrolled at the Columbia University School of Social Work during the late 1950s and 1960s. Although they had not been trained in behavioral practice in that program, they were attracted to behavioral models because of their scientific credentials and the importance that they attached to research. Members of this group included Richard Stuart, who later joined Thomas at the University of Michigan and became, like Thomas, a pioneer in the promotion of behavioral methods in social work; Scott Briar; Henry Miller; Harvey Gochros; William Reid; Arthur Schwartz; and Tony Tripodi. Briar, in particular, became a leading and influential exponent of behavioral approaches and the single-system designs used to test them. In the early 1970s, he became dean at the University of Washington School of Social Work, where he recruited faculty, including Steven Schinke, Rona Levy, Cheryl Richey, and Robert Schilling, who made significant contributions to behavioral practice and research. Schwartz and Reid went to the University of Chicago, where Schwartz introduced behavioral methods into the curriculum and produced an early text on behavioral social work (Schwartz & Goldiamond, 1975). Schwartz, in turn, recruited Elsie Pinkston, who joined the Chicago faculty in the early 1970s. Pinkston's appointment was of particular significance with respect to the dissemination of operant theory in social work. A student of Donald Baer (University of Kansas), a leading developer of applications of operant theory in clinical practice, Pinkston brought to social work both a strong operant orientation and skills in testing its applications through single-system designs. She quickly developed a research program in which operant methods were applied to problems of children and aged, among other groups, and attracted students who contributed to the behavioral literature. This program resulted in a text on effective practice methods with evidence-based case studies by her students (Pinkston et al., 1982). (A number of her former students, in fact, are contributors to the present volume). She also influenced (in an operant direction!) the efforts of William Reid and Laura Epstein to develop a short-term, task-centered model of social work practice (Reid & Epstein, 1972).

Previous practice movements in social work, such as the psychoanalytic, had quickly established roots in agency practice and evolved with considerable interaction between the agency and academic worlds. For the behavioral movement, the main points of entry and centers of influence were academic institutions. Main attractions of operant and other behavioral approaches to the faculty and their students who embraced them were their strong research tradition, the clarity of their language and procedures, and hard evidence that could, in fact, make a difference in the lives of clients. A generation previously, social work faculty might not have been as interested in such attractions, but the social work professoriat had changed considerably with the influx of faculty trained in the new doctoral programs. These faculty were more empirically oriented than their predecessors and had become disillusioned with the research-allergic psychoanalytic methods dominant at the time. Moreover, many perceived these methods as contributing to the belief being spread not only in academic journals but also in the national media that social work was "ineffective" (Reid, 1994). With their scientific warrants and a track record of effectiveness, the behavioral approaches were welcome indeed.

However, the enthusiasm was far from universal. "Behavior modification" was considered in many quarters, especially by practitioners and academics wedded to more traditional methods, a mechanistic, simplistic, and manipulative form of practice that seemed to deny the importance of the client's thoughts and feelings and of the client-practitioner relationship. Thus, the major dissemination path for behavioral ideas was from academic to practice settings, through such means as student training, faculty-initiated agency projects, books, journal articles, and workshops. At the same time, psychologists and psychiatrists in multidisciplinary settings were introducing behavioral methods to social workers. As these processes gathered momentum in the 1970s, antipathy toward behavioral approaches lessened. Since the antipathy was based largely on misconceptions, simple exposure to behavioral practice was a major corrective factor. The apparent effectiveness of behavioral methods was also persuasive. But increasing tolerance did not necessarily lead to conversion, a point that will be explored further herein. In social work, the academic establishment has retained its role as the major disseminator of behavioral methods to the world of practice.

INFLUENCE ON SOCIAL WORK PRACTICE

Operant theory has made extensive contributions to social work practice. I will consider its contributions both at a general level and in relation to specific problems and populations.

General Contributions

Operant theory has enriched social work with an empirically based and testable approach to understanding and changing social problems at all levels of practice. Thus far, its major contribution has been in the area of analysis and remediation of problems in the context of work with individuals and small groups.

The theory and its applications have demonstrated that an effective approach to human problems is to help people identify those problems in terms of specific behaviors and to help them change those behaviors in a direct and efficient manner. Thus, if parents have difficulty with their children, one pinpoints the behaviors that define the difficulty and works on those. One need not assume that such problems are the "symptoms" of underlying pathologies or remote historical events that must be addressed before it becomes possible to change anything in the present. Nor need one assume that direct changes in presenting difficulties will necessarily be undone by replacements of those difficulties ("symptom substitution"). By presenting problems and problem change in this way, operant theory helped instigate and support a general reorientation in social work thinking toward a view of human functioning as under control of present determinants and responsive to change in those determinants (Reid, 2002). If it is possible to help clients identify and change particular overt behaviors in meaningful and lasting ways through operant procedures, then it should be possible to help them identify and change particular cognitions (through cognitive therapy) or to help them act more wisely by adding to their knowledge in specific areas (through psychoeducational approaches) or to be more effective in particular interpersonal situations by helping them learn new ways of interacting (through social skills training). As a result of this shift, a more optimistic view of the potential of human change has emerged and, with it, a range of new interventions to develop that potential. Operant theory thus has become part of a point of view and burgeoning technology that is remaking direct practice in social work.

At a more specific level, operant theory and derivative methods have contributed several important concepts and principles to the core knowledge of the profession. The notion that positive reinforcement can be a powerful means of change is perhaps the most obvious addition. Social workers have become aware that reinforcers can take various forms and that they not only can foster desirable behavior but also can inadvertently maintain unwanted behavior. Such ideas are now commonplace in standard texts on social work micropractice (Hepworth, Rooney, & Larsen, 2002). Social workers have also learned about the limitations of punishment as a means of change and the usefulness of time out as a mild and effective consequence with children. More generally, most social workers have become familiar with basic contingency management methods in parent training: to reinforce positive behavior; to ignore negative behavior or, if necessary, to use time out to control it; and to suggest appropriate behavior. Most know about the use of point systems and token economies in home and institutional settings. Of all behavioral methods in the social work literature, one of the most frequently discussed today is social skills training. As noted previously, operant methods are important components of such training.

In addition to contributing specific methods to core practice knowledge, operant theory has also affected the development of other social work perspectives. For example, in their provocative and influential critique of social work's long-term love affair with psychotherapy, Specht and Courtney (1994) devise an alternative, "nonpsychotherapeutic" role for social work. They envision a "community based system of care," in which social services would be provided through the modern equivalent of settlement houses. Individualized help for personal problems would be among the offerings, but the help would take the form of behavioral intervention in which operant methods would have a major role. The task-centered model of social work practice (Reid, 2000; Reid & Epstein, 1972; Tolson, Reid, & Garvin, 2003) had its origins in the traditions of more action-oriented approaches used in social work, such as problem solving, crisis theory, and short-term psychosocial treatment. As the model evolved, it incorporated operant methods because they fit well into its action framework and enabled its users to take advantage of the new, research-supported technologies it offered. Finally, operant perspectives and methods have influenced a number of family intervention models of interest to social workers, including different family preservation approaches (Fraser & Nelson, 1997) and functional family therapy (Barton & Alexander, 1981). Contingency contracting, contingency management, and skill building have been among the procedures incorporated.

Problems and populations

The contribution of operant theory to work with selected problems and populations is summarized in table 3.1. The problems and populations were selected to show the breadth and variety of the contribution. As the table suggests, these methods have been used across virtually all major populations and problem areas of concern to social workers, not only as a source for intervention methods but also as a means of understanding behavior. The table could, of course, have been expanded considerably.

Evidence of Use in Practice

Thus far, I have considered the influence of operant theory from the standpoint of the social work literature and some general impressions about practice. However, evidence about the actual use of operant approaches in practice is another matter. Here one must make use of data on the practice activities of social workers.

Unfortunately, such data are in short supply. Only a few surveys have investigated to any degree of scale the orientations and methods that practitioners use in their work. Although the surveys report only use of behavioral methods in general, it is reasonable to assume that such methods, to a considerable extent, are based on operant theory. In one survey Jayaratne (1982) found that 30 percent of 489 National Association of Social Workers members responding reported some use of a behavioral approach in their practice; use was higher among more recent graduates. In a study by Strom (1994) of social workers in private practice, the comparable percentage was 37. A similar percentage (36) was found for social workers in Jensen, Bergin, and Greaves's (1990) survey of the practice

TABLE 3.1 Social Work Applications of Operant Theory to Selected Problems/Populations

Problem	Illustrative uses of operant theory/methods	Illustrative social work literature
Adolescent conduct disorder and emotional problems, residential settings.	Point reinforcement system (token economy)	Wong (1999)
	Level system (clients proceed through levels with gradually increasing privileges and responsibilities)	
	Continuum of response-reduction procedures (e.g., prompts, point fines, time outs)	
Adolescent sexual behavior	Use of operant theory to explain adolescent sexual behavior investigated in survey	DiBlasio & Benda (1990)
Alcoholism/ addiction	Contingency contracting between client and others with reinforcement of nonusing behavior	Fischer (2001)
	Use of environmental contingencies by spouse to control partner's drinking	Barber & Gilbertson (1998); Thomas, Santa, Bronson, & Oyserman (1987)
	Community reinforcement of nonuse through structuring contingencies pertaining to family, social life, and work	Fischer (2001); Smyth (1998)
Anxiety: phobias	Contingency analysis of factors reinforcing phobic reactions; use of positive reinforcement following successful completion of exposure trials	Thyer (1987, 2001)
Child behavior problems, child maltreatment, family settings	Understanding unwitting parental reinforcement of behavior and the unwanted creation of coercion cycles between parents and children through negative reinforcement	Corcoran (2000a, 2000b); Dangel & Polster (1982); Gammon & Rose (1991)
	Parent training: teaching parents methods of specifying goals for change, tracking change, managing contingencies to effect change, and generalizing from class to home setting; use of group to provide positive reinforcement	Pinkston & Jackson (1975); Pinkston & Smith (1998)

continued

TABLE 3.1 (*continued*)

Problem	Illustrative uses of operant theory/methods	Illustrative social work literature
Frail elderly	Guided trial, interruption, and reinforcement to improve eating habits in residential setting	Blackman & Pinkston (1982)
	Procedures for caregivers, including contracting, cueing (verbal and physical), modeling, differential reinforcement, and environmental reprogramming	Pinkston (1997); Pinkston, Green, Linsk, & Young (2001)
Health	Use of differential reinforcement to reduce incidence of asthma attacks and other health related problems with a psychogenic component	Butterfield & Werking (1981)
Mental illness, severe, chronic, residential settings	Training in social, coping, and independent living skills through modeling, prompting, shaping, differential reinforcement, behavioral assignments, token economies	Bradshaw (1996, 2000)
Mental Retardation	Interruption, differential reinforcement of incompatible behavior	Underwood, Figueroa, Thyer, & Nzeocha (1989)
School under-achievement and behavior problems	Identification of antecedents, self-monitoring of performance, self-reinforcement, parental reinforcement of performance through point systems, social skills training, teacher use of contingency management	Hubek & Reid (1982); Larkin & Thyer (1999); LeCroy & Goodwin (1979); Polster, Lynch & Pinkston (1981);Whitfield (1999)

orientations of different mental health professionals. The most recent study I was able to locate (Timberlake, Sabatino, & Martin, 1997) obtained questionnaire data from 2640 experienced clinical social workers (22 median years of experience) randomly sampled from Board Certified Diplomates of the American Board of Examiners in Clinical Social Work, most of whom were in private practice. Somewhat less than half of the respondents (43 percent) reported frequent use of a behavioral approach.

From the foregoing studies of social work practice, one can surmise that behavioral methods have become part of the social worker's repertory. Exactly how much is hard to tell given the nature of the practitioner surveys, which asked respondents to indicate from checklists whether they used an approach, and if so, perhaps also how often. In the samples studied, respondents typically report less use of behavioral approaches than psychodynamic, humanistic, and family systems. For example, in the study reporting its highest use (Timberlake et al. 1997), behavioral theory still finished behind psychosocial (84 percent), family systems (70 percent), cognitive (65 percent), ego psychology (61 percent), life-span development (59 percent), and self-psychology (51 percent) among others. However, there is reason to suppose that the data in these studies may underestimate the use of behavioral approaches. The two most recent studies (Strom, 1994; Timberlake et al. 1997) used samples of private practitioners who might be more likely to use psychodynamic and humanistic methods than might be typically found in samples of agency-based practitioners. The study using the best cross-sectional sample of social workers was conducted when the behavioral movement in social work was in its early stages and gave an indication that it was gaining strength. An up-to-date cross-sectional survey is needed.

Elsewhere I have argued that the dominant mode of practice in social work is some form of eclecticism, an argument supported by the studies cited above (Reid, 2002). Within this context, operant theory and its related intervention methods appears to function as one approach that clinical social workers draw on. It has become an important part of the social worker's kit of conceptual and practice tools.

Another way of assessing the influence of behavioral approaches in social work is to examine the extent to which they are taught in social work educational programs. Thyer and Maddox (1988) found from their review of catalogs of a sample of 67 schools of social work that 28 percent offered a course in behavior therapy and 39 percent included behavioral content as a part of other courses. In their review of 170 outlines of direct practice courses from 65 percent of schools with MSW programs, LeCroy and Goodwin (1988) note that "action-oriented and task-centered methods are increasingly being used to teach social work practice" (p. 47). Although there was no indication that courses used texts that could be described as primarily behavioral, LeCroy and Goodwin did notice a shift toward texts, such as that of Hepworth and Larsen (1982), that present content on behavioral methods. In their view, the trend was toward greater specificity in the formulation of practice methods. If so, behavioral methods, with their specificity and clarity, could contribute to this trend as well as benefit from it. These findings suggest that behavioral methods have become very much a part of the preparation for social work practice.

INFLUENCE ON SOCIAL WORK RESEARCH

Although operant approaches to understanding and changing human behavior need to be distinguished from the research methodology used to test them, these approaches have influenced social work research by introducing new forms of experimentation and by an ethos that demanded experimental testing. The best known contribution has been the single-subject (or systems) design (SSD), which social work researchers quickly seized on as a vehicle for testing not only behavioral methods but virtually all kinds of clinical social work interventions.

Indeed, Briar (1977) proposed that the profession develop a cadre of "clinical scientists" who could use such designs in their practice to test and develop effective interventions.

The first single-case studies (now referred to as single-system designs) began to appear in the late 1960s (e.g. Stuart, 1967; Thomas, 1967a). By1990 roughly sixty such studies completed by social work researchers had appeared in the literature—an estimate based on an analysis of Thyer and Boynton-Thyer's (1992) review of published literature relating to single-system designs. This level of output—on the order of approximately two to three published studies a year—was also found in Gorey's (1996) comprehensive meta-analytic review of social work effectiveness studies (nine published single-system designs during 1990–94).

The contribution of these single-system studies to the development of social work intervention knowledge is difficult to appraise. Most of the studies have tended to be one-shot affairs. There has been little evidence of the use of replication series (Barlow, Hayes, & Nelson, 1984) as a means of establishing the generality of the results. However, they certainly have provided evidence in support of the efficacy of a number of behavioral and other interventions for such problems as phobias, marital discord, child adjustment, and difficulties of the frail elderly. In a field in which any rigorous experimental test of an intervention is an uncommon event, the publication of even a few single-system designs a year has been salutary. Moreover, the single-system design has been widely used as a means of training social workers in the use of empirical and evaluation tools in practice (Bloom & Fischer, 1982; Bloom, Fischer, & Orme, 2003; Blythe, Tripodi, & Briar, 1994; Fraser, Lewis, & Norman, 1991). Although this initiative has had its detractors (Rubin & Knox 1996; Wakefield & Kirk, 1996), it has doubtlessly heightened student and practitioner involvement in the use of research tools in practice and has provided them with some skills in their application (Reid, 2002).

The development and testing of behavioral methods began to gather momentum in the 1970s through the use of more conventional group-experimental designs. In fact, behavioral interventions have dominated group experiments during the past quarter century. Reviews of social work research show that the most frequently tested approach has been behavioral, or more recently cognitive-behavioral, accounting from about a third to more than half of the experiments reviewed and the majority of those showing positive results (MacDonald, Sheldon, & Gillespie, 1991; Reid & Fortune, 2003; Reid & Hanrahan, 1982; Rubin, 1985; Thyer & Myers, 2000). The Reid and Fortune (2003) review, which covered experiments with positive outcomes reported during the past decade, provides details about more recent developments. Of the 107 experiments reviewed, almost half (49 percent) referred to the use of behavioral or cognitive-behavioral approaches (sometimes along with others). More than a third (36 percent) cited the use of reinforcement and feedback, a method that specifically reflects operant theory.

These data suggest that the single largest group of interventions of demonstrable effectiveness emerging from social work experiments contains behavioral or cognitive-behavioral components and further that these interventions may have more support from related research than other social work–tested interventions. If one considers interventions tested by social workers with support from related research as constituting the foundation of evidence-based practice in social work, then it is probably true that this foundation is largely behavioral or cognitive-behavioral.

OUTLOOK

A major contribution that operant theory has made thus far to social work has been to help lay the foundation for evidence-based practice. The validation of behavioral and cognitive-behavioral methods in social work and related disciplines has finally produced a critical mass of interventions that can make evidence-based practice a reality for a wide range of problems, especially in the mental health area. At least two trends should spur this development. One is the continuing generation of effective behavioral and cognitive-behavioral models in areas in which evidence-based practice is in a relatively inchoate stage, such as domestic violence. (For examples of such models, see Fals-Stewart, Kashdan, O'Farrell, & Birchler, 2002; Golden, Fals-Stewart, Reid, McGillicuddy, & Loneck, 2003.) The second is the growing attention to efforts to promote the dissemination and implementation of evidence-based practice in agency programs. Benchmarking studies have suggested that such efforts can successfully transport interventions tested in controlled studies (largely behavioral and cognitive-behavioral) to ordinary service contexts (Addis, 2002). The increasing emphasis on dissemination and implementation has given a new role to the main methodological contribution of the operant approach—the single-subject design. Such designs can be used to benchmark the extent to which interventions of established efficacy retain their effectiveness under typical practice conditions (Reid & Burton, in press).

Will operant theory continue to be a source of new developments in social work knowledge and practice? The answer to this question depends to a considerable extent on the amount and quality of research that might inform the theory. Without a sustained theory-driven research effort, the most likely scenario would be a continued refinement of existing techniques with extensions to new problems and populations, as noted previously. Innovations would result not from the development of the theory but from pragmatic inventions of program designers, drawing from such sources as their own experience, outcome research, and other approaches.

There is reason to believe that this scenario has actually taken place in behavior therapy in general. As Eifert and Plaud (1998a) have put it, "Much of mainstream behavior therapy has lost its link with basic research and behavior theory" (p. 1). Forsyth (1997) makes the point more dramatically: "The passion, mystery, and the majesty of theory-driven behavior therapy—as it was initially conceived by the inner circle of the founding members—has given way to technological proliferations and applications empiricism, and a proliferation of mini-theories that are only remotely connected (if at all) to the basic science and learning theory" (p. 61).

The result may be a stall in the progress of the behavioral therapy movement. Although it still may be producing effective methods, it might not be achieving the kind of dramatic increases in the level of effectiveness or the creation of breakthrough methods that might result from gains in theoretical understanding. As Foa and Kozak (1997) have noted, behavior therapy may have reached an "efficacy ceiling." Prevailing integrationist efforts "have yielded mixed results and improvements that have been more incremental than revolutionary (p. 6). As Hayes (1997) has commented, "there seems to be little evidence that effect sizes are noticeably increasing over time" (p. 518).

In general, the scene in behavior therapy has been reflected in developments in social work during the past two decades. Most new program designs that have made use of an operant approach have combined that approach with cognitive, psychoeducational, and other methods, usually under a cognitive-behavioral rubric. There has been little development of research programs that might inform operant theory. Applications of operant theory in social work may be in danger of using up their theoretical supplies. Although social work practice has been enriched by operant approaches as they have evolved, more is possible and more is certainly needed in a profession whose interventions are often no match for the problems they aim to resolve.

However, there are some encouraging signs. Some recent advances have been made in foundational operant constructs and principles through basic and applied research. For example, Baer and Pinkston (1997) have synthesized research and applications relating to antecedent control of behavior. Moreover, there is recognition of the need for operant theory and research to address more rigorously and imaginatively the processes of human cognition, language, and emotions as well as interactions in complex social systems (Eifert & Plaud, 1998b; Hawkins & Forsyth, 1997). Although cognitive events, as one type of behavior, have always fallen within the purview of operant theory (Thyer & Myers, 2000), they have not been studied systematically within that frame of reference. Needed bridging concepts have begun to emerge. For example, Eifert and Plaud (1998a) develop the notion of a "functional analysis of cognitive behavior" (p. 4). To illustrate this idea, they use the familiar observation that individuals experiencing a panic reaction become hypervigilant to changes in heart rate and other bodily functions. In a functional analysis, one might inquire into the adaptive value of the hypervigilance and attempt to determine its controlling contingencies. Increasing interest in operant behavior as rule-governed (Mattaini, 1996; Thyer, 1996) is another example of efforts to link behavioral and cognitive phenomena in ways that can be systematically studied.

Examples of recent research-based developments in operant theory that have effected such bridges include functional analytic psychotherapy (Kohlenberg, Kanter, Bolling, Parker, & Tsai 2002) and acceptance and commitment therapy (Hayes, Pankey, & Gregg, 2002). Both developments have been stimulated by experimental analysis of behavior under the control of verbal rules (Nelson-Gray, Gaynor, & Korotitsch, 1997). For instance, in treating anxiety through acceptance and commitment therapy, the practitioner attempts to extinguish or weaken functional relationships between bodily and emotional sensations (e.g. a feeling of tightness in the stomach, a sense of dread) and verbal rules associated with the sensations (e.g. something terrible will happen if the client speaks out). The goal is for the client to learn to accept the anxiety as an unpleasant sensation without his or her behavior being controlled by the verbal labeling and then to commit to change, that is, to act constructively despite the unpleasant sensation (Forsyth & Eifert, 1998).

Mattaini's (1996) formulations about changing larger systems through cultural design, Briggs and Paulson's (1996) multiple contingency framework for study of program implementation, and Pinkston, Green, Linsk, and Young's (2001) family ecobehavioral approach for elders are examples of extensions of operant theory to communities and formal organizations. Although these ideas need further development and testing, they reflect new thinking about operant concepts in areas that are especially relevant to social work.

These developments in basic and applied research and in theory building may be laying the groundwork for new developments in operant approaches. If operant theory moves in the directions indicated, it should increasingly form links with other fields of activity, including experimental cognitive psychology and brain research. Eventually one hopes for the development of a unified theory of behavior that would join together operant and respondent conditioning, cognitive-emotional phenomena, and biological processes.

If the signs of progress are to become progress that makes a real difference, more theory related research is needed at both basic and applied levels. As an applied profession, social work is largely dependent on experimental psychology and other sciences for basic research. However, applied research can be done in a way that informs theory. Theoretical models based on operant theory can be used both to understand phenomena and to test the theory (e.g. DiBlasio & Benda, 1990). In at least some treatment experiments, interventions could be derived from operant theory and tested in pure form, instead of being mixed together with other approaches in treatment packages. Other intervention components, if needed, could be introduced subsequently. Such experiments would be designed both to yield clinical benefits and to test theory-based hypotheses about how change might be brought about.

CONCLUSIONS

By any standard, operant theory has made a substantial contribution to social work practice and research. It has been a key force in a general shift in social work practice toward more emphasis on present determinants in human functioning and on straightforward methods of altering those determinants to effect positive change. It has provided a range of specific and effective intervention methods that social workers have incorporated into their practice repertories and has generated programs addressed to most of the problems and populations of concern to social workers. The single-subject research methodology tied to the theory has given social work researchers and practitioners important new tools for the evaluation and improvement of practice and has provided social work educators with ways to make research relevant and useful for their students. The recent growth in evidence-based interventions is due in large part to the experimental testing of behavioral and cognitive-behavioral interventions, which rest in large part on operant theory. Although developments in operant theory have been slowed by lack of theory-building research, there are signs of renewed interest in reforging connections to basic research and in expanding the theory in new and creative directions.

REFERENCES

Addis, M. E. (2002). Methods for disseminating research products and increasing evidence-based practice: Promises, obstacles, and future directions. *Clinical Psychology: Science and Practice, 9,* 367–378.

Baer, D. M., Wolf, M. M., & Risley, T. R. (1968). Some current dimensions of applied behavior analysis. *Journal of Applied Behavior Analysis, 1,* 1–97.

Baer, D. M., & Pinkston, E. M. (Eds.). (1997). *Environment and behavior.* Boulder, CO: Westview Press.

Barber, J. G., & Gilbertson, R. (1998). Evaluation of a self-help manual for partners of heavy drinkers. *Research on Social Work Practice, 8,* 141–151.

Barlow, D. H., Hayes, S. C., & Nelson, R. O. (1984). *The scientist practitioner: Research and accountability in clinical and educational settings.* New York: Pergamon Press.

Barton, C., & Alexander, J. F. (1981). Functional family therapy. In A. S. Gurman & D. P. Kniskern (Eds.), *Handbook of family therapy* (pp. 403–443). New York: Brunner/Mazel.

Blackman, D. K., & Pinkston, E. M. (1982). A training-maintenance program for reestablishing appropriate utensil use among the impaired elderly. In E. M. Pinkston, J. L. Levitt, G. R. Green, N. L. Linsk, & T. L. Rzepnicki (Eds.), *Effective social work practice* (pp. 413–426). San Francisco: Jossey-Bass.

Bloom, M., & Fischer, J. (1982). *Evaluating practice: Guidelines for the accountable professional.* Englewood Cliffs, NJ: Prentice Hall.

Bloom, M., Fischer, J., & Orme, J. G. (2003). *Evaluating practice: Guidelines for the accountable professional* (4th ed.). Boston: Allyn & Bacon.

Blythe, B., Tripodi, T., & Briar, S. (1994). *Direct practice research in human services agencies.* New York: Columbia University Press.

Bradshaw, W. (1996). Structured group work for individuals with schizophrenia: A coping skills approach. *Research on Social Work Practice, 6*(2), 139–154.

Bradshaw, W. (2000). Integrating cognitive-behavioral psychotherapy for persons with schizophrenia into a psychiatric rehabilitation program: Results of a three year trial. *Community Mental Health Journal, 36*(5), 491–500.

Briar, S. (1977). Incorporating research into education for clinical practice in social work: Toward a clinical science in social work. In *Sourcebook on research utilization* (pp. 132–140). Washington, DC: Council on Social Work Education.

Briggs, H. E., & Paulson, R. I. (1996). Racism. In M. A. Mattaini & B. A. Thyer (Eds.), *Finding solutions to social problems* (pp. 147–177). Washington, DC: American Psychological Association.

Butterfield, W. H., & Werking, J. (1981). Behavioral methods in primary health care. In S. P. Schinke (Ed.), *Behavioral methods in social welfare,* (pp. 287–302). New York: Aldine .

Corcoran, J. (2000a). *Evidence-based social work practice with families.* New York: Springer .

Corcoran, J. (2000b). Family treatment of preschool behavior problems. *Research on Social Work Practice, 10*(5), 547–588.

Dangel, R. F., & Polster, R. A. (Eds.). (1984). *Parent training: Foundations of research and practice.* New York: Guilford Press.

DiBlasio, F. A., & Benda, B. B. (1990). Adolescent sexual behavior: Multivariate analysis of a social learning model. *Journal of Adolescent Research, 5*(4), 449–466.

Eifert, G. H., & Plaud, J. J. (1998a). *From behavior theory to behavior therapy.* Needham Heights, MA: Allyn & Bacon.

Eifert, G. H., & Plaud, J. J. (1998b). From behavior theory to behavior therapy: An overview. In J. J. Plaud & G. H. Eifert (Eds.), *From behavior theory to behavior therapy,* (pp. 1–14). Needham Heights, MA: Allyn & Bacon.

Fals-Stewart, W., Kashdan, T. B., O'Farrell, T. J., & Birchler, G. R. (2002). Behavioral couples therapy for drug-abusing patients: Effects on partner violence. *Journal of Substance Abuse Treatment, 22,* 1–10.

Fischer, J. (2001). An eclectic approach to persons with substance-related disorders. In H. E. Briggs & K. Corcoran (Eds.), *Social work practice: Treating common client problems* (pp. 213–241). Chicago: Lyceum Books.

Foa, E. B., & Kozak, M. (1997). Beyond the efficacy ceiling? Cognitive behavior therapy in search of theory. *Behavior Therapy, 28*(4), 601–612.

Forsyth, J. P. (1997). In the name of the "advancement" of behavior therapy: Is it all in a name? *Behavior Therapy, 28,* 615–627.

Forsyth, J. P., & Eifert, G. H. (1998). Phobic anxiety and panic: An integrative behavioral account of their origin and treatment. In J. J. Plaud & G. H. Eifert (Eds.), *From behavior theory to behavior therapy* (pp. 38–67). Needham Heights, MA: Allyn & Bacon.

Fraser, M., Lewis, R., & Norman, J. L. (1991). Research education in M.S.W. programs: An exploratory analysis. *Journal of Teaching in Social Work, 4*(2), 83–103.

Fraser, M. W., & Nelson, K. E. (1997). Effectiveness of family preservation services. *Social Work Research, 21,* 138–154.

Golden, J., Fals-Stewart, W., Reid, W., McGillicuddy, N., & Loneck, B. (2003, January 18–21). *Behavioral Couples Therapy (BCT) with alcohol abusing violent couples.* Paper presented at the Seventh Annual Conference of the Society for Social Work and Research, Washington, DC.

Gorey, K. M. (1996). Effectiveness of social work intervention research: Internal versus external evaluations. *Social Work Research, 20*(2), 119–128.

Hawkins, R. P., & Forsyth, J. P. (1997). Bridging barriers between paradigms: Making cognitive concepts relevant for behavior analysts. *Journal of Behavior Therapy and Experimental Psychiatry, 28,* 3–6.

Hayes, S., Pankey, J., & Gregg, J. (2002). Acceptance and commitment therapy. In R. DiTomasso & E. Gosch, (Eds.), *Comparative treatments for anxiety disorders* (pp. 110–136). New York: Springer .

Hayes, S. C. (Ed.). (1989). *Rule-governed behavior: Cognition, contingencies, and instructional control.* New York: Plenum Press.

Hayes, S. C. (1997). Technology, theory and the alleviation of human suffering: We still have such a long way to go. *Behavior Therapy, 28,* 517–525.

Hepworth, D. H., & Larsen, J. (1982). *Direct social work practice: Theory and skills.* Homewood, IL: Dorsey Press.

Hepworth, D., Rooney, R., & Larson, N. (2002). *Direct social work practice: Theory and skills* (6th ed.). New York: Brooks/Cole.

Hubek, M. & Reid, W. J. (1982). Components of self management in special education classes. In R. T. Constable & J. P. Flynn (Eds.), *School social work: Practice and research perspectives* (pp. 220–230). Homewood, IL: Dorsey Press.

Jayaratne, S. (1982). Characteristics and theoretical orientations of clinical social workers: A national survey. *Journal of Social Service Research, 4,* 17–29.

Jensen, J. P., Bergin, A. E., & Greaves, D. W. (1990). The meaning of eclecticism: New survey and analysis of components. *Professional Psychology: Research and Practice, 21*(2), 124–30.

Kirby, K. C., Lamb, R. J., & Iguchi, M. Y. (1997). Stimulus control of drug abuse. In D. M. Baer & E. M. Pinkston (Eds.), *Environment and behavior* (pp. 173–184). Boulder, CO: Westview Press.

Kohlenberg, R., Kanter, J., Bolling, M., Parker, C., & Tsai, M. (2002). Enhancing cognitive therapy for depression with functional analytic psychotherapy: Treatment guidelines and empirical findings. *Cognitive and Behavioral Practice, 9,* 213–229.

Larkin, R., & Thyer, B. A. (1999). Evaluating cognitive-behavioral group counseling to improve elementary school students' self-esteem, self-control, and classroom behavior. *Behavioral Interventions, 14*(3), 147–161.

LeCroy, C. W., & Goodwin, C. C. (1988). New directions in teaching social work methods: A content analysis of course outlines. *Journal of Social Work Education, 24,* 43–49.

LeCroy, C. W., & Goodwin, D. L. (1979). Behavioral consultation and applied behavior analysis in the classroom. *School Social Work Quarterly, 1*(3), 219–228.

MacDonald, G., Sheldon, B., & Gillespie, J. (1992). Contemporary studies of the effectiveness of social work. *British Journal of Social Work, 22,* 615–643.

Mattaini, M. A. (1996). Public issues, human behavior, and cultural design. In M. A. Mattaini & B. A. Thyer (Eds.), *Finding solutions to social problems* (pp. 13–40). Washington, DC: American Psychological Association.

Mattaini, M. A., Twyman, J. S., Chin, W., & Lee, K. N. (1996). Youth violence. In M. A. Mattaini & B. A. Thyer (Eds.), *Finding solutions to social problems* (pp. 75–111). Washington, DC: American Psychological Association.

Milan, M. A. (1990). Applied behavior analysis. In A. S. Bellack, M. Hersen, & A. E. Kazdin (Eds.), *International handbook of behavior modification and therapy* (2nd ed., pp. 67–84). Washington, DC: American Psychological Association.

Nelson-Gray, R., Gaynor, S. T., & Korotitsch, W. J. (1997). Behavior therapy: Distinct but acculturated. *Behavior Therapy, 28,* 563–572.

Pinkston, E. M. (1997). A supportive environment for old age. In D. M. Baer & E. M.

Pinkston (Eds.), *Environment and behavior* (pp. 258–268). Boulder, CO: Westview Press.

Pinkston, E. M., Green, G. R., Linsk, N., & Young, R. N. (2001). A family eco-behavioral approach for elders with mental illness. In H. E. Briggs & E. Corcoran (Eds.), *Social work practice: Treating common client problems* (pp. 339–370). Chicago: Lyceum Books.

Pinkston E. M., & Jackson E. W. (1975). Modification of irrelevant and bizarre verbal behavior using parents as therapists. *Social Service Review, 49,* 46–63.

Pinkston, E. M., & Smyth, M. D. (1988). Contributions of parent training to child welfare: Early history and current thoughts. In R. J. Lutzker (Ed.), *Handbook of child abuse research and treatment. Issues in clinical child psychology.* (pp. 377–399). New York: Plenum Press.

Pinkston, E., M., Levitt, J. R., Green, G., Linsk, N. L., & Rzepnicki, T. L. (1982). *Effective social work practice.* San Francisco: Jossey-Bass.

Reid, W. J. (1994). The empirical practice movement. *Social Service Review, 68,* 165–184.

Reid, W. J. (2000). *The task planner.* New York: Columbia University Press.

Reid, W. J. (2002). Knowledge for direct social work practice: An analysis of trends. *Social Service Review, 76,* 6–33.

Reid, W. J., & Burton, J. (in press) Evidence-based practice: Breakthrough or buzzword? In S. A. Kirk (Ed.), *Mental disorders in the social environment: Critical perspectives.* New York: Columbia University Press.

Reid, W. J., & Epstein, L. (1972). *Task-centered casework.* New York: Columbia University Press.

Reid, W. J., & Fortune, A. E. (2003). Empirical foundations for practice guidelines in current social work knowledge. In A. Rosen & E. Proctor (Eds.), *Developing practice guidelines for social work intervention: Issues, methods, and research agenda.* New York: Columbia University Press.

Reid, W. J., & Hanrahan, P. (1982). Recent evaluations of social work: Grounds for optimism. *Social Work, 27,* 328–340.

Rubin, A. (1985). Practice effectiveness: More grounds for optimism. *Journal of the National Association of Social Workers, 30,* 469–476.

Rubin, A., & Knox, K. S. (1996). Data analysis problems in single-case evaluation: Issues for research on social work practice. *Research on Social Work Practice, 6*(1), 40–65.

Schwartz, A., & Goldiamond, I. (1975). *Social casework: A behavioral approach.* New York: Columbia University Press.

Skinner, B. F. (1974). *About behaviorism.* New York: Knopf.

Smyth, N. J. (1998). Substance abuse. In B. A. Thyer & J. S. Wodarski (Eds.), *Handbook of empirical social work practice* (pp. 123–152). New York: John Wiley & Sons.

Specht, H., & Courtney, M. E. (1994). *Unfaithful angels: How social work has abandoned its mission.* New York: Free Press.

Strom, K. (1994). Social workers in private practice: An update. *Clinical Social Work Journal, 22,* 73–89.

Stuart, R. B. (1967). Behavioral control of overeating. *Behavior Research and Therapy, 5,* 357–365.

Thomas, E. J. (1967a). Selecting knowledge from behavioral science. In E. J. Thomas (Ed.), *Behavioral science for social workers* (417–424). New York: Free Press.

Thomas, E. J. (Ed.). (1967b). *The socio-behavioral approach and applications to social work*. New York: Council on Social Work Education.

Thomas, E. J., Santa, C., Bronson, D., & Oyserman, D. (1987). Unilateral family therapy with the spouses of alcoholics. *Journal of Social Service Research, 10,* 145–162.

Thyer, B. (1987). Contingency analysis: Toward a unified theory for social work practice. *Social Work, 32*(2), 150–157.

Thyer, B. (1996). Behavior analysis and social welfare policy. In M. A. Mattaini & B. A. Thyer (Eds.), *Finding solutions to social problems* (pp. 41–60). Washington, DC: American Psychological Association.

Thyer, B. A. (1987). *Treating anxiety disorders*. Newbury Park, CA: Sage.

Thyer, B. A. (2001). Evidence-based approaches to community practice. In H.E. Briggs & K. Corcoran (Eds.), *Social work practice* (pp. 54–65). Chicago: Lyceum Books.

Thyer, B. A., & Boynton-Thyer, K. (1992). Single-system research designs in social work practice: A bibliography from 1965 to 1990. *Research on Social Work Practice, 2*(1), 99–116.

Thyer, B. A., & Maddox, K. (1988). Behavioral social work: Results of a national survey on graduate curricula. *Psychological Reports, 63,* 239–242.

Thyer, B. A., & Myers, L. L. (2000). Approaches to behavior change. In P. Allen-Meares & C. Garvin (Eds.), *The handbook of social work direct practice* (pp. 197–216). Thousand Oaks, CA: Sage .

Timberlake, E. M., Sabatino, C. A., & Martin, J. A. (1997). Advanced practitioners in clinical social work: A profile. *Social Work, 42,* 374–386.

Tolson, E., Reid, W. J., & Garvin, C. (2003). *Generalist practice: A task-centered approach* (2nd ed.). New York: Columbia University Press.

Underwood, L. A., Figueroa, R. G., Thyer, B. A., & Nzeocha, A. (1989). Interruption and DRI in the treatment of self-injurious behavior among mentally retarded and autistic self-restrainers. *Behavior Modification, 13*(40), 471–481.

Wakefield, J. C., & Kirk, S. A. (1996). Unscientific thinking about scientific practice: Evaluating the scientist-practitioner model. *Social Work Research, 20*(2), 83–95.

Whitfield, G. W. (1999). Validating school social work: An evaluation of a cognitive-behavioral approach to reduce school violence. *Research on Social Work Practice, 9*(4), 399–426.

Wong, S. E. (1999). Treatment of antisocial behavior in adolescent inpatients: Behavioral changes and client satisfaction. *Research on Social Work Practice, 9*(1), 25–44.

CHAPTER 4

ECOBEHAVIORAL SOCIAL WORK

Mark A. Mattaini
Sarah K. Moore

Although behavioral approaches to social work practice have been present at least since the 1920s (Orme & Stuart, 1981), they have expanded dramatically since the late 1960s. The real breadth of such approaches has only become apparent recently, in part because of emerging recognition of the ethical mandate to relying on evidence-based approaches to practice whenever possible (Gambrill, 1999). The natural science of behavior has an enormous amount to contribute to understanding and influencing the quality of transactional exchanges among people and their environments—and therefore, to social work. The science of behavior has been pursued by behavior analysts and those interested in a science of cultural practices, some of whom are social workers, for some decades, but much of what has been learned remains quite unfamiliar to most social workers. As a result, despite overwhelming evidence of their utility, many of the potential contributions of this science have yet to be realized.

The purpose of social work is to enhance adaptations among clients and the systems in which they are embedded, in ways that are consistent with social justice. Social work practice, therefore, is always contextual; this is why frameworks for practice developed during the later part of the twentieth century were often framed as *ecological* or *ecosystemic* (e.g., Germain & Gitterman, 1996; Meyer & Mattaini, 1995). Although behavioral social workers have often struggled with some of those frameworks, they have increasingly recognized the transactional and embedded nature of most social work practice. Ecobehavioral social work integrates that awareness with the science of behavior.

SOCIAL WORK AND SCIENCE

Behavioral social workers have often been their own worst enemies. In some cases, they have engaged in dichotomizing debates about, for example, whether social work is a "science" or an "art." The science of behavior cannot tell social workers everything they need to know in order to practice. It can, however, make important contributions that can have a profound impact on client and community well-being. Science can help.

Similarly, in recent years the social work profession has increasingly recognized the importance of the spiritual in practice, and some have viewed the spiritual and the scientific as antagonistic. The greatest scientists, however, often find the spiritual and the scientific ultimately indistinguishable. Einstein (n.d.) indicated:

> You will hardly find one among the profounder sort of scientific minds without a peculiar religious feeling of his own. . . . His religious feeling takes the form of a rapturous amazement at the harmony of natural law, which reveals an intelligence of such superiority that, compared with it, all the systematic thinking and acting of human beings is an utterly insignificant reflection. This feeling is the guiding principle of his life and work, in so far as he succeeds in keeping himself from the shackles of selfish desire (pp. 28–29).

The world-renowned biologist Ursula Goodenough has movingly argued that the best of science elicits reverence, gratitude, and a "covenant with Mystery" (1998, p. 167). Among social work behavior scientists, a similar recognition is increasingly common.

The Transactional Nature of the Science of Behavior

Practically all the behavior described as "scientific" relies on searching for, predicting, and testing connections among phenomena, particularly association and causation. Recent advances in scientific thinking increasingly recognize the omnipresent transactional complexities of such connections, which are often reciprocal and sometimes predictable only within limits (Capra, 1996). The social and systemic issues with which social workers and their clients struggle on a daily basis are similarly complex, and only a complex science of behavior and culture can begin to capture such issues adequately (Biglan, 1995). Contemporary behavioral theory recognizes that human behavior in the real world is embedded in a matrix of concurrent (supporting and opposing) contingencies (Malott, Malott, & Trojan, 2000), and that simultaneous examination of many of these may be required to understand how and why people and collectives act as they do.

It is here that ecological science can be helpful. For decades, ecological science has recognized that events are multidetermined; that is, they have multiple, often transactional, causes and cannot be adequately understood if amputated from context. Very early on, therefore, ecological scientists recognized that ecological science needed to rely on three iterative, transactional "tactics" (Bates, 1990): observations in the natural environment, experimentation (particularly in the natural environment but occasionally in the laboratory), and the development and refinement of conceptual frameworks (theory). These tactics constitute a single, coherent, interactive strategy for study, since conceptual frameworks guide decisions about what to observe. Observations suggest hypotheses that can be tested by experimentation; both observations and the results of experiments help refine conceptual frameworks, and those refined frameworks guide subsequent observations and experiments. The best of behavior and cultural-analytic science—and practice—is grounded in just this investigative paradigm.

Basic behavior analytic theory provides key guidance for this work. Particularly important is an understanding of *selection by consequences* (Skinner, 1981; see also responses to that seminal article published in Catania & Harnad, 1988). Skinner suggested that a common process, selection by consequences, explains directed change at the genetic, behavioral, and cultural levels. (Recent theory and research indicate that considerable change at each of those levels may be the result of random processes.) For our purposes here, this principle suggests that, all else being equal, individual behavior producing positive consequences tends to persist, whereas behavior followed by aversive consequences tends to fade. A similar process works at the cultural level; practices that produce positive outcomes tend to persist, and those that produce collectively harmful outcomes tend to be eliminated.

Of course, natural human and social phenomena are highly complex, so all else is seldom equal. Human behavior is highly sensitive to verbal mediation and verbal antecedents (rules, values). Most behavior participates in multiple contingencies (relations between behavior and consequences), some of which may reinforce it, and some of which may simultaneously punish it or reward incompatible alternatives. Behavioral and cultural outcomes may be uncertain, long-deferred, and sometimes intentionally concealed or manipulated. What is exciting is that the contemporary science of behavior can now begin to account for such complexities (e.g., Biglan, 1995; Mattaini, 1997, 1999) and can provide meaningful guidance for social work practice embedded in such transactional and multi-layered realities, thus addressing such critical social issues as the following:

- Parenting and raising successful children (Biglan, Metzler, & Ary, 1994; Henggeler, Schoenwald, Borduin, Rowland, & Cunningham 1998; Latham, 1994; Pinkston, 1997)
- The education crisis (Greer, 1996)
- Substance abuse (Meyers & Smith, 1995)
- Racism and sexism (Biglan, 1995; Briggs & Paulson, 1996; Daly, 1996)
- Environment degradation (see Greene, Winett, Van Houten, Geller, & Iwata, 1987, section 3)
- Sexual coercion (Biglan, 1996) and sexual abuse (Wolf & Pinkston, 1997)
- Child maltreatment (Dumas & Wahler, 1983; Lutzker, Bigelow, Doctor, Gershater, & Greene, 1998)
- Crime and violence (Cohen & Filipczak, 1971; Mattaini, 2001)
- Care for the elderly (Pinkston 1997; Pinkston & Linsk, 1984)
- Mental illness (Pinkston, Green, Linsk, & Nelson, 2000)
- And many others (Mattaini & Thyer, 1996; Sidman, 2001; Wodarski & Thyer, 1998).

A Science of Social Justice

Despite many distractions, the social work profession continues to see its mission as deeply grounded in social justice and human rights (Lowery, 2002). The science of behavior has much to contribute to efforts to extend social justice, at both theoretical and applied levels. Most oppression and most violations of human rights involve, at their core, the use of coercive or adversarial power (Lowery & Mattaini, 1999). Behaviorists have extensively studied the use of punishment and threats, and some of the most respected scholars in the field have integrated much of that research in recent years in ways that provide specific guidance for practice. Murray Sidman, in his essential work *Coercion and Its Fallout* (2001), documents the extensive, in fact almost exclusive, reliance on coercive processes in contemporary U.S. society, and the profoundly negative effects of that reliance, both individually and collectively. A major contribution of the science of behavior, according to Sidman, is a fine-grained understanding of the processes of coercion, threat, competition for individual gain, and induction of fear. Sidman describes the damaging effects of those processes on individual and collective well-being, as well as, critically, the nature of alternative, constructive sociocultural practices that are consistent with personal and collective well-being.

The state of the art in ecobehavioral social work practice goes far beyond mere behavior therapy (which emphasizes diagnosis of what is wrong with the individual client and how the professional should treat that deficit or disorder). Behavior therapy research certainly can contribute to effective, evidence-based practice. The term *therapy,* however, despite its seductive appeal (to professionals' egos and finances), is in most situations an overly limiting and often ethically questionable way to conceptualize social work practice. Ecobehavioral social work has the potential to move the field far beyond therapy into the realm of sharing power (Lowery & Mattaini, 1999) to construct improved transactional realities—thus contributing to the expansion of social justice.

How did social work (and allied fields) get to this exciting point in the development of ecobehavioral practice, and where is it going next? The next section selectively sketches the history of behavioral, and ultimately ecobehavioral, social work.

THE DEVELOPMENT OF ECOBEHAVIORAL SOCIAL WORK

There are only a few examples of pre-1960s social science practitioners who harnessed the power of a behavioral approach to address client needs. One example is the clinical teams of psychiatrists, psychologists, and social workers who formed "habit clinics" in the 1920s and used behavioral psychology as the basis for practice to help address the behavioral problems of preschool children (Orme & Stuart, 1981). Strong disciplinary interest in behavioral social work can be viewed as beginning with a full-day colloquium on sociobehavioral theory and its application to social work education and practice, which took place during the Council on Social Work Education's (CSWE) Annual Program Meeting in 1967 (Thomas, 1967). Several factors converged to bring behavioral theory and methods to the attention of the profession at that historical moment (Thomas, 1970). For four years prior to the CSWE colloquium, agency field instructors in the Detroit area had participated with University of Michigan faculty in special institutes focused on sociobehavioral knowledge and its practice applications. Those faculty members (especially Edwin G. Thomas) played a seminal role in promoting behavioral theory and methods in social work education and practice. Doctoral graduates of the program would go on to become leaders of the national behavioral social work movement. At the same time, growing numbers of studies of the efficacy of behavioral methods were being published and the results looked promising, but evaluations of more traditional approaches (Fischer, 1973; Geismar, 1972; Mullen, Dumpson, & Associates, 1972; Stuart, 1970; Wood, 1978) proved almost universally disappointing. Third, decreased funding for social programs in the early 1970s and the resultant increased competition among the helping professions further contributed to the need for social work "to legitimate its claim as a profession worthy of public support" (Witkin, 1996, p.70). Finally, the introduction and transfer of single-subject research designs to specific content areas in the field of social work (Bloom, 1975; Hersen & Barlow, 1976; Jayaratne & Levy, 1979; Kratochwill, 1978) favored support of behavioral theory and methods because of the conceptual congruence between structured behavioral interventions and single-subject research methods.

Many social workers, of course, were not open to changing their ways of thinking about practice, and the marketplace indeed became quite competitive and combative. An early debate on the pages of *Social Work* raised some oft-repeated concerns voiced by those wary of "abandon[ing] what we have practiced in favor of other approaches or points of view" (Bruck, 1968, p.45). Max Bruck argued that "behavior modification" makes unsubstantiated claims of effectiveness as a result of its reliance on single-subject designs; views people in terms of their symptoms and never truly addresses core disease; completely ignores "inner meditative forces" (p. 47) and the impact of physiology; artificially restricts analyses of behavior in ways that limit full contextual understanding; and, through the superficial treatment of symptomatology, ignores psychological phenomena that give rise to or provide motivation for observable behavior.

Carter and Stuart (1970) replied that Bruck "adopts a more stringent criteria for the demonstration of effectiveness in behavioral therapy than he does for psychodynamic theory" (p. 39); that people are more than their symptoms, but the "more" is not relevant to the scientific problem set by the symptoms; behaviorists do take "inner meditative forces," or "private events" (Skinner, 1953) into account; that physiology is not overlooked but "influences both the selection of environmental events that function as stimuli for the organism and the nature of its response to the stimuli" (Carter & Stuart, 1970, p. 44); that a stimulus can be defined as broadly as is necessary for intervention; and that determining the role environments play in behavior is the primary focus of behavioral analysis. Other debates raged in *Social Service Review* (Morrow & Gochros, 1970) and *Journal of Consulting and Clinical Psychology* (Eysenck, 1971; Portes, 1971), and many texts and articles appeared that reiterated the "misconceptions and popular myths about behavior modification" (Schwartz & Goldiamond, 1975, p.271; see also Fischer, 1978; Schinke, 1981; Thyer, 1983; Wodarski & Bagarozzi, 1979). Indeed, "cross-fertilization" (Perretz, 1967) had begun between the disciplines of social work and behavioral science, and the edge of discovery had been crossed.

Several "pioneer demonstrations" (Schinke, 1981) of community behavioral interventions with delinquent youth took place in the 1960s (Phillips, 1968; Schwitzgebel and Kolb, 1964), as did the preliminary investigations of home-based child management, or in situ family training (Hawkins, Peterson, Schweid, & Bijou, 1966; Wahler, Winkel, Peterson, & Morrison, 1965) and marital discord (Stuart, 1969). However, transfer of behavioral technology from psychological laboratory settings to the natural environments in which clients experienced the need for change occurred with increasing regularity in the 1970s. Behavioral assessments and interventions were enlisted to address almost every imaginable social problem (phobias, child abuse, spouse battering, anger management, medical disorders, smoking, obesity, depression, marital problems, antisocial behavior, social skill deficits, childhood mental disorders, substance abuse, and many others) across levels of individual, family, group, community, and organizational practices. Excellent literature reviews tracing this movement have been published over the years (e.g., Gambrill, 1995; Schinke, 1981; Thyer, 1983; Thyer & Hudson, 1987; Wodarski & Bagarozzi, 1979).

A parallel movement was occurring in social work education. By 1985, more than fifty textbooks of a behavioral nature had been written by social workers (Thyer, 1985). In 1988, Thyer and Maddox published a review of the course content on behavior therapy and single-subject research designs offered by sixty-seven of the ninety-nine accredited or preaccredited graduate schools of social work. They found that the sixty-seven schools offered thirty courses on the practice of behavior therapy or the principles of learning theory. In addition, they found evidence of a behavioral perspective in forty-four survey-type courses as well. Together, thirty-six different schools offered the seventy-four courses. The findings for single-subject designs were less promising, despite the CSWE's then recently updated Curriculum Policy Statement requiring that students of social work be taught designs suitable for the evaluation of one's own practice (Council on Social Work Education, 1982). Thyer and Maddox found only six full courses, but thirteen survey courses included content on this research methodology.

In the late 1970s, a great deal of interest emerged in so-called cognitive-behavior therapy. By the 1990s, however, behaviorists had come to recognize that cognitions are, in fact, covert behaviors that can be understood according to the same theoretical principles as overt behaviors, and that this perspective is both more parsimonious and clinically more useful than epistemic understandings rooted in unobservable and untestable hypothetical constructs. Emotional phenomena also had come to be understood as involving covert visceral and verbal behaviors. As discussed subsequently, this integrated perspective has led to strategically powerful interventional and preventive work.

In recent years, radical conceptual transformations have contributed to a vision of practice grounded in the science of behavior as *ecobehavioral*. The term *ecobehavioral* was coined in the 1970s on the pages of the *Journal of Applied Behavior Analysis*. The earliest article (Lutzker, Frame, & Rice, 1982) that reconceptualized child welfare practice from an ecobehavioral perspective provided guidance for similar transformations for other fields of practice. Predicated on emerging data indicating that variables such as poverty, joblessness, social isolation, and skills deficits of the children were risk factors for child abuse and neglect (Lutzker, Bigelow, Doctor, Gershater, & Greene, 1998), Lutzker and his colleagues's intervention project, Project 12-Ways, incorporated those variables within a multidimensional matrix for work with families in which child maltreatment was an issue. This approach was intended to act as a rudder for the practitioner adrift on Malott's "sea of concurrent contingencies" and to expand "context" to include many more channels for intervention (Malott et al., 2000). From these beginnings, a wide range of ecobehavioral applications has emerged over the past two decades.

THE BREADTH OF CONTEMPORARY AND EMERGING ECOBEHAVIORAL PRACTICE

Predictions about where science may lead are always risky. Nevertheless, current and emerging work suggests that the science of behavior has much more to contribute to social work practice with systems of all sizes. The material that follows highlights only a few areas in which ecobehavioral practice has particular promise. It is not a complete survey of current and emerging areas of ecobehavioral practice, which would require examination of the entire social work domain.

Work with Individual Clients

Every social worker providing consultation to individuals becomes involved at some point in cases in which the client, or someone in the client's transactional world, is seriously affected by substance abuse. Behavioral work over the past three decades has elaborated an approach for such work, the community reinforcement approach, which has consistently produced results that are substantially better, often by an order of magnitude, than those of traditional treatment for severe alcohol and drug abuse (Hunt & Azrin, 1973; Meyers & Smith, 1995). The model is also beginning to be adapted to particular cultural contexts, which social workers recognize as often essential in a diverse practice world (e.g., the University of New Mexico is developing a version of the community reinforcement approach that is specific to American Indian populations). Since the community reinforcement approach is no more (and often less) expensive than traditional treatment, there appears to be an ethical responsibility to at least consider it in work with those struggling to overcome substance abuse.

In the mental health arena, emerging behavioral approaches also have a great deal to offer. For example, adherence to medication schedules is a major issue in work with persons struggling with severe mental illness. Azrin and Teichner (1998), however, developed and tested a simple, single-session behavioral package that increased adherence in their sample from 73 percent (below the level generally shown to achieve adequate symptom control) to 94 percent (well within the adequate range). Another critical mental health issue is the treatment of depression; one approach that is demonstrably useful for serious depression is cognitive therapy. Unfortunately, the full cognitive-therapy package as developed by Beck, Rush, Shaw, and Emery (1978) is quite complex and usually is not implemented with fidelity to the model in everyday settings. Jacobson and his colleagues (Jacobson, Dobson, Truax, & Addis, 1996) discovered, however, that behavioral activation, one relatively straightforward component of the full Beck package, appears to produce results that are comparable to those produced by the full package. Lejuez and colleagues (2001) recently analyzed why this may be true in theoretical terms and developed a straightforward package that can be taught and implemented in standard agency settings more easily than can Beck's approach. Such a simple package may be much more realistic for application in everyday practice.

Other areas of practice with individuals in which behavioral theory and research are making contributions include HIV/AIDS, management of medical conditions and pain, violence prevention, weight control and eating disorders, poor academic performance and social skills deficits among children, and coping with trauma. In fact, in nearly every area in which social workers practice with individuals, ecobehavioral theory and research are making a contribution (Mattaini, 1997). The same is true for work with larger systems, including families.

Work with Families

There is by now an enormous literature outlining behavioral strategies for enhancing parenting and family life, including preventive approaches for raising successful children (e.g., Biglan, Metzler, & Ary, 1994; Hart & Risley, 1995; Latham, 1994) and interventions for families in which child maltreatment or severe conflict are concerns (Dumas & Wahler, 1983; Mattaini, McGowan, & Williams, 1996; Wolfe, 1987). For example, the only currently empirically supported approach to child behavior problems is the use of behavioral techniques (Corcoran, 2000), and parenting programs that take into account the transactional realities of families have proven more effective than those that focus more narrowly on managing children (Webster-Stratton, 1997). Well-structured parenting groups also offer opportunities for participants to assist one another with problems in their larger life space (Brunk, Henggeler, & Whelan, 1987)—which is one more indication of the importance of taking a broad ecobehavioral perspective.

A common problem that affects contemporary families is substance abuse. When the substance abuser is willing to enter treatment, a number of behavioral approaches, including the community reinforcement approach discussed previously, can be useful. In many cases, though, the abuser is not initially willing to enter treatment. Ecobehavioral approaches for working with family members and "concerned others" have been developed and have proven more effective than traditional "interventions," which rely on confrontation. The first of these approaches, and still perhaps the most widely useful, emerged as a component of the community reinforcement approach (Meyers & Smith, 1996; Sisson & Azrin, 1986). Two related approaches with evidence of effectiveness are unilateral family therapy (Thomas & Yoshioka, 1989) and pressures to change (Barber and Gilbertson, 1996). These behavioral strategies constitute an important resource for social workers in any setting in which family members wish to act to encourage their loved ones to enter treatment.

Seriously antisocial behavior by children and youth is another often-intractable problem that many social workers in family service, mental health, corrections, and school settings deal with every day. Although there are several useful approaches for addressing less serious antisocial behavior, when such behavior has become serious and habitual, many of those approaches fail to have the hoped-for impact. An approach with substantial empirical support, however, is multisystemic family treatment (MFT) (Henggeler et al., 1998). It explicitly attends to the multiple transactions that shape and maintain both problem behavior and possible positive alternatives in assessment and intervention. Rather than emphasize diagnosis and pathology, MFT relies on the development of collaborative partnerships (which, at their best, are an example of shared power) with everyone involved and works to identify critical antecedents and consequences of behavior within the transactional networks in which youth and families are embedded.

Family relationships in contemporary U.S. society are often highly conflictual and frequently involve enormous pain, both emotional and physical. Behavioral social workers and other behaviorists have developed and refined many data-based approaches for constructing fulfilling relationships and reducing the reciprocal aversive exchanges into which many families become trapped (Ginsberg, 1997; Griffee, 1994; Jacobson & Christensen, 1996; Mattaini, 1999; Serna, Schumaker, Sherman, & Sheldon, 1991; Stuart, 1980). Many of these approaches have demonstrated the power to make substantial change in relatively brief periods of time, which is important both for the families involved and because of the limited reimbursement often available for family work.

Work with Groups

Group work has always been an important social work modality, although course work related to this modality in schools of social work has declined dramatically in recent decades. Managed care has encouraged increased emphasis on groups, because under some circumstances (but not all), groups can be more efficient than work with individuals, and the preponderance of the research suggests that groups can, for many purposes, be at least as effective (Magen, 2002). Over the past three decades, behavioral group work has expanded substantially and has received considerable empirical support. Sheldon Rose (1977, 1989, 1998) has been the most important pioneer in this work. A notable phenomenon has been the blending of multiple models in group work (and to some extent in individual and family modalities). It is now common to find groups that explicitly incorporate social support as well as techniques such as behavioral rehearsal. Rose's early work (1977) clearly presaged this movement and provides theoretical rationale for such integration by examining group process and affective transactions within the group from a behavioral perspective.

An area of particular interest in behavioral group work is social skills training, of which there are many variations for different populations. Among these are assertiveness training (Rakos, 1991), aggression replacement training (Goldstein, Glick, & Gibbs, 1998), life and leadership skills groups (Mattaini, 2001), prevention groups pertaining to substance abuse and sexually transmitted diseases (Schinke, Forgey, & Orlandi, 1996), and training in positive interactions (LeCroy, 1994). Many of these approaches have reasonable, and some have very strong, empirical support. Most social skills groups are relatively structured, involving explicit description, modeling, and rehearsal of carefully specified skills. Notably, there is some evidence (Hayes, Kohlenberg, & Melancon, 1989) that, in some cases, an even more effective format may involve having group members interactively develop responses to challenging situations by relying on global ratings of effectiveness by other group members rather than predetermined definitions of supposedly optimal behavior.

Brannen and Rubin (1996) found that groups addressing both cognitive and relational behaviors can be useful for reducing some kinds of violence in families. Psychoeducation in multifamily groups, which involves both explicit teaching and construction of networks of mutual support, is the current state of the art in work with families of persons with severe mental illness (Farmer, Walsh, & Bentley, 1998; McFarlane, 1994); many aspects of such groups can be conceptualized as ecobehavioral in nature. Perhaps surprisingly for some readers, behaviorists working with persons with severe mental illness now also explicitly emphasize strategies to build empowerment, including self-help groups (Dickerson, 1998). Such groups emerge from nonbehavioral roots but are highly consistent with an ecobehavioral perspective, which can contribute to such groups in a number of ways, such as by encouraging behavioral specificity and clarifying self-management strategies. Empowerment-based group work often blends relatively seamlessly into work with larger systems, including organizations and communities.

Work with Organizations and Communities

Many critical social problems are deeply embedded in the networks within which people live out their lives and are best viewed as reflections of transactional cultural processes within organized collectives (organizations, families, communities, cultural groups, and the many other interlocking and overlapping networks that constitute modern society). For example, viewing individual young people as vectors of youth violence has not proved very useful (Astor, Vargas, Pitner, & Meyer, 1999); individually-based interventions have produced, at best, modest collective changes in the incidence of violence. In a society that relies heavily on the exercise of coercive power in most realms (family, education, economic, legal) (Sidman, 2001), in which, for example, most youth participate at some point in bullying (Walker, Colvin, & Ramsey, 1995), it is not surprising that substantial numbers will ultimately become involved in actions at the extreme end of the coercive continuum. Similarly, given that aggression is likely among those who experience aggression, it is only to be expected that a society in which the level of experienced social toxicity (Garbarino, 1999) is high will also have high levels of violence and other severe coercion. These understandings emerge from basic ecobehavioral theory and are strongly supported by empirical data.

Effective solutions to such culturally grounded issues are likely to involve intervention at the level of the transactional cultural practices maintained by social networks. A science of cultural practices (Biglan, 1995), a subdiscipline of the science of behavior, can provide the tools to begin to understand and influence such collective processes. The PEACE POWER strategy for constructing cultures of nonviolent power (Mattaini, 2001) is an example of an interventional approach that focuses tightly on constructing cultural practices that are inconsistent with coercion, threat, and violence while offering young people and the adults among whom they live out their lives alternative, higher-quality, constructive means for influencing their worlds—positive power. Projects based on this strategy can be finely adapted to local situations, cultures, and values and still maintain their roots in basic, empirically validated processes.

Construction of positive and enduring patterns of collective transactions that shape and support desirable actions is a widely useful strategy in work with organizations of all kinds. Daniels (2000) and his associates, for example, have developed simple yet powerful approaches for "bringing out the best in people" in work settings, strategies that increase both productivity and job satisfaction. Classroom cultures can be designed to incorporate classwide, peer-assisted self-management strategies that increase on-task behavior, instruction following, use of appropriate ways of gaining teacher approval, and academic skills (Mitchem, Young, West, & Benyo, 2001).

Ecobehavioral theory can also guide the development of community-wide strategies. Both the peace power strategy and the PeaceBuilders program (Embry, Flannery, Vazsonyi, Powell, & Atha, 1996) incorporate components for including families and the larger community in preventive programming, emphasizing a small set of potentially very powerful cultural practices that can be widely implemented. Biglan and his colleagues have implemented a number of community-wide prevention strategies and have pioneered the use of time-series designs to evaluate such strategies in rigorous but highly sensitive ways (Biglan, 1995).

Policy-Level Practice

Only limited ecobehavioral work has been conducted at the level of social policy, although there is a growing literature elaborating on theoretical principles that may be critical to guide policy development (e.g., Lamal, 1991, 1997; Mattaini & Thyer, 1996). In large part, these analyses involve clarification of the interlocking networks of contingencies involved in shaping, maintaining, and changing transactional patterns of cultural practices at larger sociocultural levels. A number of analyses of alternatives to welfare reform, for example, were prepared when reforms were occurring, some of which may have been useful to policy makers (Mattaini & Magnabosco, 1997; Nackerud, Waller, Waller, & Thyer, 1997).

Rakos (1993) has examined the behavioral processes involved in propaganda aimed at opinion change (e.g., in preparing the American people for the Gulf War). Behaviorists have also taken initial steps toward developing means of opinion change that do not rely on the partial truths and manipulations of motivations on which propaganda usually is based. Sanford and Fawcett (1980) developed a procedure called *consequence analysis* that basically relies on asking members of the public to specifically evaluate the multiple consequences of policy decisions to ensure that complex, interlocking ecobehavioral contingencies are weighed in reaching decisions. Sanford and Fawcett's research and preliminary results of a small Internet-based study we conducted (Moore & Mattaini, 2001) at least suggest that these procedures may lead to more thoughtful opinions and decisions.

Social workers often function in the policy arena. Seekins and Fawcett (1986) discussed variations of consequence analysis and other procedures that are useful to the scientist-advocate. So long as advocacy is based on thoughtful, honest evaluations of consequences (rather than slanted manipulation of information to support an agenda), there need be no conflict between the role of scientifically informed social worker and that of advocate. It is difficult, however, in a society that encourages everyone to work toward relatively immediate and individualized reinforcers, to act in ways that support long-term collective good. Ecobehavioral theory at least can help in understanding the roots of this problem and in elaborating cultural practices that would be required to increase the level of honesty, shared power, and altruism present in a culture (e.g., Lowery & Mattaini, 1999).

CONCLUSION

Finely textured, nuanced applications of the science of behavior to personal and collective human problems clearly have the potential to enrich social work practice at all levels in exciting and important ways. The major obstacles to such applications lie primarily in misunderstandings; for example, a belief that ecobehavioral social work focuses on only individual dysfunction (although dysfunction is a concept seldom used in such practice) asserts that there is no place for the spiritual dimension of humanity or fails to recognize and address oppression and coercive forces in the modern world. As has been shown, the contrary of each of these assertions is true. In addition, in contemporary society individual and collective violence is common, whole groups of people are systematically oppressed for the short-term advantage of privileged others, and many lives are not genuinely valued (despite rhetoric to the contrary). This reality requires the substantive attention of social workers as individuals and as a profession. Ecobehavioral practice, firmly grounded in the science of behavior, has essential contributions to make to this critical effort.

REFERENCES

Astor, R. A., Vargas, L. A., Pitner, R. O., & Meyer, H. A. (1999). School violence: Research, theory, and practice. In J. M. Jenson & M. O. Howard (Eds.), *Youth violence: Current research and recent practice innovations* (pp. 139–171). Washington, DC: NASW Press.

Azrin, N. H., & Teichner, G. (1998). Evaluation of an instructional program for improving medication compliance for chronically mentally ill outpatients. *Behaviour Research and Therapy, 36,* 849–861.

Barber, J. G., & Gilbertson, R. (1996). An experimental investigation of a brief unilateral intervention for the partners of heavy drinkers. *Research on Social Work Practice, 6,* 325–336.

Bates, M. (1990). *The nature of natural history.* Princeton, NJ: Princeton University Press. Originally published 1950.

Beck, A. T., Rush, A. J., Shaw, B. F., & Emery, G. (1978). *Cognitive therapy of depression.* New York: Guilford Press.

Biglan, A. (1995). *Changing cultural practices: A contextualist framework for intervention research.* Reno, NV: Context Press.

Biglan, A. (1996). Sexual coercion. In M. A. Mattaini & B. A. Thyer (Eds.), *Finding solutions to social problems: Behavioral strategies for change* (pp. 289–316). Washington, DC: American Psychological Association.

Biglan, A., Metzler, C. W., & Ary, D. A. (1994). Increasing the prevalence of successful children: The case for community intervention research. *The Behavior Analyst, 17,* 331–335.

Bloom, M. (1975). *The paradox of helping: Introduction to the philosophy of scientific practice.* New York: Wiley.

Brannen, S. J., & Rubin, A. (1996). Comparing the effectiveness of gender-specific and couples groups in a court-mandated spouse abuse treatment program. *Research on Social Work Practice, 6,* 405–424.

Briggs, H. E., & Paulson, R. I. (1996). Racism. In M. A. Mattaini & B. A. Thyer (Eds.), *Finding solutions to social problems: Behavioral strategies for change* (pp. 147–177). Washington, DC: American Psychological Association.

Bruck, M. (1968). Behavior modification theory and practice: A critical review. *Social Work, 13*(2), 43–55.

Brunk, M., Henggeler, S. W., & Whelan, J. P. (1987). Comparison of multisystemic therapy and parent training in the brief treatment of child abuse and neglect. *Journal of Consulting and Clinical Psychology, 55,* 171–178.

Capra, F. (1996). *The web of life*. New York: Anchor.

Carter, R. D., & Stuart, R. B. (1970). Behavior modification theory and practice: A reply. *Social Work, 15*(1), 37–50.

Catania, A. C., & Harnad, S. (1988). *The selection of behavior: The operant behaviorism of B. F. Skinner: Comments and consequences.* Cambridge, MA: Cambridge University Press.

Cohen, H. L., & Filipczak, J. (1971). *A new learning environment.* Boston: Authors Cooperative.

Corcoran, J. (2000). Family treatment of preschool behavior problems. *Research on Social Work Practice, 10,* 547–588.

Council on Social Work Education (1982). Curriculum policy statement for the master's degree and baccalaureate degree programs in social work education. *Social Work Education Reporter, 30,* 5–12.

Daly, P. M. (1996). Sexism. In M. A. Mattaini & B. A. Thyer (Eds.), *Finding solutions to social problems: Behavioral strategies for change* (pp. 201–220). Washington, DC: American Psychological Association.

Daniels, A. (2000). *Bringing out the best in people* (2nd ed.). New York: McGraw-Hill.

Dickerson, F. B. (1998). Strategies that foster empowerment. *Cognitive and Behavioral Practice, 5,* 255–275.

Dumas, J. E., & Wahler, R. G. (1983). Predictors of treatment outcome in parent training: Mother insularity and socioeconomic disadvantage. *Behavioral assessment, 5,* 301–313.

Einstein, A. (n.d.). *The world as I see it.* New York: Wisdom Library.

Embry, D. D., Flannery, D. J., Vazsonyi, A. T., Powell, K. E., & Atha, H. (1996). Peace-Builders: A theoretically-driven, school-based model for early violence prevention. *American Journal of Preventive Medicine, 12*(5, Suppl.), 91–100.

Eysenck, H. J. (1971). Behavior therapy as a scientific discipline. *Journal of Consulting and Clinical Psychology, 36,* 314–319.

Farmer, R. L., Walsh, J., & Bentley, K. J. (1998). Schizophrenia. In B. A. Thyer & J. S. Wodarski (Eds.), *Handbook of empirical social work practice* (pp. 245–270). New York: John Wiley and Sons.

Fischer, J. (1973). Is casework effective?: A review. *Social Work, 18,* 5–21.

Fischer, J. (1978). *Effective casework practice: An eclectic approach.* New York: McGraw-Hill.

Gambrill, E. (1995). Behavioral social work: Past, present and future. *Research on Social Work Practice, 5*(4), 460–484.

Gambrill, E. (1999). Evidence-based practice: An alternative to authority-based practice. *Families in Society, 80,* 341–350.

Garbarino, J. (1999). *Lost boys: Why our sons turn violent and how we can save them.* New York: Free Press.

Geismar, L. I. (1972). Thirteen cumulative studies. In E. M. Mullen, J. R. Dumpson, & Associates (Eds.), *Evaluation of Social Intervention.* San Francisco: Jossey-Bass.

Germain, C. B., & Gitterman, A. (1996). *The life model of social work practice.* New York: Columbia University Press.

Ginsberg, B. G. (1997). *Relationship enhancement family therapy.* New York: John Wiley & Sons.

Goldstein, A. P., Glick, B., & Gibbs, J. C. (1998). *Aggression replacement training: A comprehensive intervention for aggressive youth* (Rev. ed.). Champaign, IL: Research Press.

Goodenough, U. (1998). *The sacred depths of nature.* New York: Oxford University Press.

Greene, B. F., Winett, R. A., Van Houten, R., Geller, E. S., & Iwata, B. A. (1987). *Behavior analysis in the community, 1968–1986.* Lawrence: University of Kansas, Department of Human Development, Society for the Experimental Analysis of Behavior.

Greer, R. D. (1996). The education crisis. In M. A. Mattaini & B. A. Thyer (Eds.), *Finding solutions to social problems: Behavioral strategies for change* (pp. 113–146). Washington, DC: American Psychological Association.

Griffee, K. (1994). Acceptance and the family context. In S. C. Hayes, N. S. Jacobson, V. M. Follettee, & M. J. Dougher (Eds.), *Acceptance and change: Content and context in psychotherapy* (pp. 223–233). Reno, NV: Context Press.

Hart, B., & Risley, T. R. (1995). *Meaningful differences in the everyday experience of young American children.* Baltimore: Paul H. Brooks.

Hawkins, R. P., Peterson, R. F., Schweid, E., & Bijou, S. W. (1966). Behavior therapy in the home: Amelioration of problem parent-child relations with the parent in a therapeutic role. *Journal of Experimental Child Psychology, 4,* 99–107.

Hayes, S. C., Kohlenberg, B. S., & Melancon, S. M. (1989). Avoiding and altering rule-control as a strategy of clinical intervention. In S. C. Hayes (Ed.), *Rule-governed behavior: Cognition, contingencies, and instructional control* (pp. 359–385). New York: Plenum Press.

Henggeler, S. W., Schoenwald, S. K., Borduin, C. M., Rowland, M. D., & Cunningham, P. B. (1998). *Multisystemic treatment of antisocial behavior in children and adolescents.* New York: Guilford Press.

Hersen, M., & Barlow, D.H. (1976). *Single case experimental designs: Strategies for studying behavior change.* New York: Pergamon Press.

Hunt, G. M., & Azrin, N. H. (1973). A community-reinforcement approach to alcoholism. *Behaviour Research and Therapy, 11,* 91–104.

Jacobson, N. S, & Christensen, A. (1996). *Integrative couple therapy.* New York: W. W. Norton.

Jacobson, N. S., Dobson, K. S., Truax, P. A., & Addis, M. E. (1996). A component analysis of cognitive-behavioral treatment for depression. *Journal of Consulting and Clinical Psychology, 64,* 295–304.

Jayaratne, S., & Levy, R. (1979). *Empirical clinical practice.* New York: Columbia University Press.

Kerlinger, F. N. (1986). *Foundations of behavioral research* (3rd ed.). New York: Holt, Rinehart and Winston.

Kratochwill, T. R. (1978). *Single subject research: Strategies for evaluating change.* New York: Academic Press.

Lamal, P. A. (Ed.). (1991). *Behavioral analysis of societies and cultural practices.* New York: Hemisphere.

Lamal, P. A. (Ed.). (1997). *Cultural contingencies: Behavior analytic perspectives on cultural practices.* Westport, CT: Praeger.

Latham, G. I. (1994). *The power of positive parenting.* North Logan, UT: P & T Ink.

LeCroy, C. W. (1994). Social skills training. In C. W. LeCroy (Ed.), *Handbook of child and adolescent treatment manuals* (pp. 126–169). New York: Lexington Books.

Lejuez, C. W., Hopko, D. R., LePage, J. P., Hopko, S. D., & McNeil, D. W. (2001). A brief behavioral activation treatment for depression. *Cognitive and Behavioral Practice, 8,* 164–175.

Lowery, C. T. (2002). Social justice and international human rights. In M. A. Mattaini & C. T. Lowery (Eds.), *The foundations of social work practice: A graduate text* (3rd ed., pp. 25–47). Washington, DC: NASW Press.

Lowery, C. T., & Mattaini, M. A. (1999). The science of sharing power: Native American thought and behavior analysis. *Behavior and Social Issues, 9,* 3–23.

Lutzker, J. R., Bigelow, K. M., Doctor, R. M., Gershater, R. M., & Greene, B. F. (1998). An ecobehavioral model for the prevention and treatment of child abuse and neglect. In J. R. Lutzker (Ed.), *Handbook of child abuse research and treatment* (pp. 239–266). New York: Plenum Press.

Lutzker, J. R., Frame, R. E., & Rice, J. M. (1982). Project 12–ways: An ecobehavioral approach to the treatment and prevention of child abuse and neglect. *Education and Treatment of Children, 5,* 141–155.

Magen, R. H. (2002). Practice with groups. In M. A. Mattaini & C. T. Lowery (Eds.), *The foundations of social work practice: A graduate text* (3rd ed., pp. 208–227). Washington, DC: NASW Press.

Malott, R. W., Malott, M. E., & Trojan, E. A. (2000). *Elementary principles of behavior* (4th ed.). Upper Saddle River, NJ: Prentice Hall.

Mattaini, M. A. (1997). *Clinical practice with individuals.* Washington, DC: NASW Press.

Mattaini, M. A. (1999). *Clinical intervention with families.* Washington, DC: NASW Press.

Mattaini, M. A. (with the PEACE POWER Working Group). (2001). *Peace Power for adolescents: Strategies for a culture of nonviolence.* Washington, DC: NASW Press.

Mattaini, M. A., & Magnabosco, J. L. (1997). Reworking welfare: Untangling the web. In P. A. Lamal (Ed.), *Cultural contingencies: Behavior analytic perspectives on cultural practices* (pp. 151–167). Westport, CT: Praeger.

Mattaini, M. A., McGowan, B. G., & Williams, G. (1996). Child maltreatment. In M. A. Mattaini & B. A. Thyer (Eds.), *Finding solutions to social problems: Behavioral strategies for change* (pp. 223–266). Washington, DC: American Psychological Association.

Mattaini, M. A., & Thyer, B. A. (Eds.). (1996). *Finding solutions to social problems: Behavioral strategies for change.* Washington, DC: American Psychological Association.

McFarlane, W. R. (1994). Multiple-family groups and psychoeducation in the treatment of schizophrenia. *New Directions in Mental Health Services, 62,* 13–22.

Meyer, C. H., & Mattaini, M. A. (1995). The ecosystems perspective: Implications for practice. In M. A. Mattaini, C. T. Lowery, & C. H. Meyer (Eds.), *The foundations of social work practice: A graduate text* (2nd ed.). Washington, DC: NASW Press.

Meyers, R. J., & Smith, J. E. (1995). *Clinical guide to alcohol treatment: The community reinforcement approach.* New York: Guilford Press.

Mitchem, K. J., Young, K. R., West, R. P., & Benyo, J. (2001). CWPASM: A classwide peer-assisted self-management program for general education classrooms. *Education and Treatment of Children, 24,* 111–140.

Moore, S. K., & Mattaini, M. A. (2001). Consequence analysis: An on-line replication. *Behavior and Social Issues, 11,* 71–79.

Morrow, W., & Gochros, H. (1970). Misconceptions regarding behavior modification. *Social Service Review, 44,* 293–307.

Mullen, E. J., Dumpson, J. R., & Associates (Eds.). (1972). *Evaluation of social intervention.* San Francisco: Jossey-Bass.

Nackerud, L., Waller, R. J., Waller, K., & Thyer, B. A. (1997). Behavior analysis and social welfare policy: The example of Aid to Families with Dependent Children (AFDC). In P. A. Lamal (Ed.), *Cultural contingencies: Behavior analytic perspectives on cultural practices* (pp. 169–184). Westport, CT: Praeger.

Orme, J. G., & Stuart, P. (1981). The habit clinics: Behavioral social work and prevention in the 1920's. *Social Service Review, 55,* 242–256.

Perretz, E. A. (1967). [Review of the book Behavioral science for social workers.] *Journal of Education for Social Work, 3*(3), 117–120.

Phillips, E. L. (1968). Achievement Place: Token reinforcement procedures in a home-style rehabilitation setting for "pre-delinquent" boys. *Journal of Applied Behavior Analysis, 1,* 213–223.

Pinkston, E. M. (1997). A supportive environment for old age. In D. M. Baer & E. M. Pinkston (Eds.), *Environment and behavior* (pp. 258–268). Boulder, CO: Westview Press.

Pinkston, E. M., Green, G. R., Linsk, N. L., & Nelson, R. N. (2000). A family ecobehavioral approach for assisting elders with mental illness. In H. E. Briggs & K. Corcoran (Eds.), *Social work practice: Treating common client problems* (pp. 339–370). Chicago: Lyceum Books.

Pinkston, E. M., & Linsk, N. D. (1984). Behavioral family intervention with the impaired elderly. *Gerontologist, 24,* 576–583.

Pinkston, E. M., & Smith, M. (1998). Contributions of parent training to child welfare: Early history and current thoughts. In J. R. Lutzker (Ed.), *Handbook of child abuse research and treatment* (pp. 377–399). New York: Plenum Press.

Portes, A. (1971). Behavior therapy and critical speculation. *Journal of Consulting and Clinical Psychology, 36,* 320–324.

Rakos, R. F. (1991). *Assertive behavior: Theory, research, and training.* New York: Routledge.

Rakos, R. F. (1993). Stimulus control through the media: Propaganda and the Gulf War. *Behavior and Social Issues, 2,* 35–62.

Rose, S. D. (1977). *Group therapy: A behavioral approach.* Englewood Cliffs, NJ: Prentice Hall.

Rose, S. D. (1989). *Working with adults in groups.* San Francisco: Jossey-Bass.

Rose, S. D. (1998). *Group therapy with troubled youth: A cognitive-behavioral integrative approach.* Thousand Oaks, CA: Sage.

Sanford, F. L., & Fawcett, S. B. (1980). Consequence analysis: Its effects on verbal statements about an environmental project. *Journal of Applied Behavior Analysis, 13,* 57–64.

Schinke, S. P. (Ed.). (1981). *Behavioral methods in social welfare: Helping children, adults and families in community settings.* Hawthorne, NY: Aldine.

Schinke, S. P., Forgey, M. A., & Orlandi, M. (1996). Teenage sexuality. In M. A. Mattaini & B. A. Thyer (Eds.), *Finding solutions to social problems: Behavioral strategies for change* (pp. 267–288). Washington, DC: American Psychological Association.

Schwartz, A., & Goldiamond, I. (1975). *Social casework: A behavioral approach.* New York: Columbia University Press.

Schwitzgebel, R., & Kolb, D. (1964). Inducing behavior change in adolescent delinquents. *Behaviour Research and Therapy, 1,* 297–304.

Seekins, T., & Fawcett, S. B. (1986). Public policy-making and research information. *The Behavior Analyst, 9,* 35–45.

Serna, L. A., Schumaker, J. B., Sherman, J. A., & Sheldon, J. B. (1991). In-home generalization of social interactions in families of adolescents with behavior problems. *Journal of Applied Behavior Analysis, 24,* 733–746.

Sidman, M. (2001). *Coercion and its fallout* (2nd ed.). Boston: Authors Cooperative.

Sisson, R. W., & Azrin, N. H. (1986). Family member involvement to initiate and promote treatment of problem drinkers. *Journal of Behavior Therapy and Experimental Psychiatry, 17,* 15–21.

Skinner, B. F. (1953). *Science and human behavior.* New York: Macmillan.

Skinner, B. F. (1981). Selection by consequences. *Science, 213,* 501–504.

Stuart, R. B. (1969). Operant-interpersonal treatment for marital discord. *Journal of Consulting and Clinical Psychology, 33,* 675–682.

Stuart, R. B. (1970). *Trick or treatment: How and when psychotherapy fails.* Champaign, IL: Research Press.

Stuart, R. B. (1980). *Helping couples change: A social learning approach to marital therapy.* New York: Guilford Press.

Thomas, E. J. (1967). *The socio-behavioral approach and applications to social work.* New York: Council on Social Work Education.

Thomas, E. J. (1970). Behavioral modification and casework. In R. W. Roberts & R. H. Nee (Eds.), *Theories of social casework* (pp. 181–218). Chicago: University of Chicago Press.

Thomas, E. J., & Yoshioka, M. R. (1989). Spouse interventive confrontations in unilateral family therapy for alcohol abuse. *Social Casework, 70,* 340–347.

Thyer, B. A. (1983). Behavior modification in social work practice. In M. Hersen, P. Miller, & R. Eisler (Eds.), *Progress in behavior modification* (Vol. 15, pp. 173–226). New York: Plenum Press.

Thyer, B. A. (1985). Textbooks in behavioral social work: A bibliography. *The Behavior Therapist, 8,* 161–162.

Thyer, B. A., & Hudson, W. W. (Eds.). (1987). Progress in behavioral social work. *Journal of Social Service Research, 10*(2/3/4).

Thyer, B. A., & Maddox, K. (1988). Behavioral social work: Results of a national survey on graduate curricula. *Psychological Reports, 63,* 239–242.

Thyer, B. A., & Wodarski, J. S. (1990). Social learning theory: Toward a comprehensive conceptual framework for social work education. *Social Service Review, 64,* 144–152.

Wahler, R. G., Winkel, G. H., Peterson, R. F., & Morrison, D. C. (1965). Mothers as behavior therapists for their own children. *Behaviour Research and Therapy, 3,* 113–124.

Walker, H. M., Colvin, G., & Ramsey, E. (1995). *Antisocial behavior in school: Strategies and best practices.* Pacific Grove, CA: Brooks/Cole.

Webster-Stratton, C. (1997). From parent training to community building. *Families in Society, 78,* 156–171.

Witkin, S. L. (1996). If empirical practice is the answer, then what is the question? *Social Work Research, 20*(2), 69–75.

Wodarski, J. S., & Bagarozzi, D. (1979). *Behavioral social work.* New York: Human Services Press.

Wodarski, J. S., & Thyer, B. A. (1998). *Handbook of empirical social work practice: Vol. 2. Social problems and practice issues.* New York: John Wiley & Sons.

Wolf, S. C., & Pinkston, E. M. (1997). Structure for victim engagement in sexual abuse.

In D. M. Baer & E. M. Pinkston (Eds.), *Environment and behavior* (pp. 163–172). Boulder, CO: Westview Press.

Wolfe, D. A. (1987). *Child abuse: Implications for child development and psychopathology*. Newbury Park, CA: Sage.

Wood, K. M. (1978). Casework effectiveness: A new look at the research evidence. *Social Work, 23,* 437–458.

CHAPTER 5

Science and Evidence-Based Social Work Practice

Bruce A. Thyer

The current movement within social work to align the field so that it adheres to the principles of evidence-based practice is a welcome transmogrification of an enduring theme in the profession, one that has been a persistent, if muted, voice from the very beginnings of the discipline. The American Social Science Association was established in 1865; it was a group that called for the objective study of human behavior by means of the same tools of scientific inquiry that were proving so successful in the biological and physical sciences, which is, of course, the fundamental assumption of the approach known as *positivism*.

> "Social science" was understood by [American Social Science Association] members to refer to the whole realm of problematical relationships in human affairs. One became a "social scientist" by contributing to the store of esoteric knowledge and practical expertise . . . a *"new way to care for the insane or to administer charity"*—all of these were equally valuable contributions to "social science" (Haskell, 1977, p. 87, italics added).

Nearly one hundred people attended the inaugural meeting of the American Social Science Association, in response to Frank Sanborn's letter of invitation, sent on behalf of the Massachusetts Board of Charities:

> Dear Sirs—Our attention has lately been called to the importance of some organization in the United States, both local and national, whose object shall be the discussion of those questions related to the Sanitary Condition of the People, The Relief, Employment, and Education of the Poor, the Prevention of Crime, the Amelioration of the Criminal Law, the Discipline of Prisons, the Remedial Treatment of the Insane, and those numerous matters of statistical and philanthropic interest which are included under the general head of 'Social Science' (cited in Haskell, 1977, pp. 97–98).

The association's early statements of purpose made the following claims:

> This Association proposes to afford, to all persons interested in human improvement, an opportunity to consider social economics as a whole. . . . They are to collect all facts, diffuse all knowledge, and stimulate all inquiry, which have a bearing on *social welfare* (p. 102, italics added).

[We] shall consider Pauperism *actual* rather than legal, the relation and the responsibilities of the gifted and educated classes towards the weak, the witless, and the ignorant. We shall endeavor to make useful inquiries into the causes of Human Failure, and the Duties devolving upon Human Success. We shall consider the Hours of Labor, the relations of Employers and the Employed; the Employment of Women, by itself considered; the relation of Idleness to Female Crime; Prostitution and Intemperance; Workhouses (Haskell, p. 105, italics in original).

Clearly, this was among the very first social work membership organizations in the United States. The parent American Social Science Association went on to sprout numerous, more specialized offshoots, including, in 1879, the Conference on Charities. This was transformed in 1884 into the National Conference of Charities and Correction, described as "a forum for the communication of the ideas and values connected with scientific charity (Germain, 1970, p. 9). In 1917, the National Conference of Charities and Correction in turn became the National Conference on Social Work and emerged in 1957 as the National Conference on Social Welfare, which dissolved in the 1980s. A paper presented at the 1889 meeting of the National Conference of Charities and Correction was titled "Scientific Charity," and a 1894 article appearing in the influential journal *The Charities Review* was titled "A Scientific Basis for Charity." The movement called scientific charity (or scientific philanthropy), which evolved in the latter part of the 1800s, culminated in the pioneering work and writings of the American social worker Mary Richmond, whose 1917 text *Social Diagnosis* wholeheartedly endorsed a scientific (e.g., positivistic) approach to social work. Richmond, in turn, received an honorary master's degree from Smith College for "establishing the scientific basis of a new profession" (Germain, 1970, p. 12).

Apart from its disastrous embrace of psychoanalysis and its metastasized offspring, social work continued its advocacy of science throughout the early part of the twentieth century. In 1949 the independent Social Work Research Group was established and became the profession's major scientific interest-group (see Graham, Al-Krenawi, & Bradshaw, 2000). The Social Work Research Group was one of the seven original constituent groups that combined in 1955 to form the National Association of Social Workers, a group that had as one of its central missions the promotion of scientific research, which was to be nurtured by the creation of a research section within the new National Association of Social Workers. An editorial by Louis Towley, then a professor at the George Warren Brown School of Social Work at Washington University, asserted in the first issue of the new National Association of Social Work journal, *Social Work:* "Among the many things that are now within the reach of social work, one must surely mention first a broader, more intensive research effort" (Towley, 1956, p. 110). Alas, this was not to be. In the mid-1960s, the National Association of Social Work's Research Section was renamed the Council on Social Work Research, and it soon died of inanition. The forces of research were not to be denied, however, and widespread dissatisfaction with the limited support given to the promotion and use of scientific research by the existing professional organizations (e.g., the National Association of Social Work and the Council on Social Work Education) led the nationally known social work researcher Janet B. W. Williams to assemble a small group of supporters and, in 1994, form the independent membership organization the Society for Social Work and Research. The society struck a responsive chord within the profession and had grown by the end of the millennium to more than eight hundred members. Its well-organized, high-quality annual convention rapidly became the field's leading outlet for quality research presentations, and, in 1999, the society began providing a subscription to the independent journal *Research on Social Work Practice* to all members. The Society for Social Work and Research is now the field's major voice for increasing the role of science within social work, and in a very meaningful manner, it is carrying the banner of scientific charity into its third century of existence.

THE EMPIRICAL CLINICAL PRACTICE AND EMPIRICALLY SUPPORTED TREATMENT MOVEMENTS

The turn of the past century experienced the rise of two related movements, and though they did not exactly thrive, they came to exert a significant influence. The first is *empirical clinical practice,* a term derived from a book by the same title authored by the social workers Siri Jayaratne and Rona Levy (1979), and the second is *empirically supported treatments,* which is more largely the work of clinical psychologists.

The basic principles of empirical clinical practice involve advocating that social workers select interventions on the basis of their degree of scientific support, and that they empirically evaluate the outcomes of their practice using single-system research designs. In Jayaratne and Levy's (1979) own words:

> Empirical practice is conducted by clinicians who strive to measure and demonstrate the effect of their clinical practice by adapting traditional experimental research techniques to clinical practice. . . . The clinician would first be interested in using an intervention strategy that has been successful in the past. . . . When established techniques are available, they should be used, but they should be based on objective evaluation rather than subjective feeling (pp. xiv, 7).

The text is largely devoted to an explication of the methods of single-system research designs and selection and development of reliable and valid methods of assessment for the purposes of integrating credible outcome measures into evaluation efforts. A related book by a social worker, *The Role of Research in Clinical Practice* (Wodarski, 1981) expressed isomorphic views. Empirical clinical practice generated a flurry of articles and chapters (e.g., Corcoran, 1985; Ivanoff, Blythe, & Briar, 1987; Ivanoff, Robinson, & Blythe, 1987; Macdonald, 1994; Thyer, 1995, 1996a, 1996b; Thyer & Wodarski, 1998; Wodarski & Thyer, 1998) and did not escape controversy. Perhaps the most tangible result was the incorporation (largely due to the efforts of John Wodarski) of the mandate that social work research courses teach "designs for the systematic evaluation of the student's own practice . . . (and should) prepare them systematically to evaluate their own practice and contribute to the generation of knowledge for practice" into the Council on Social Work Education's (1982, pp. 10–11) influential *Curriculum Policy Statement,* where said standard today remains virtually unchanged.

Independent from empirical clinical practice but philosophically and conceptually related to it was the initiative of *empirically supported treatments* undertaken within the American Psychological Association. Spearheaded by David Barlow, then president of Division 12 (clinical psychology) of the association, the presidential *Task Force on Promotion and Dissemination of Psychological Procedures* was established in the early 1990s and charged with a twofold task:

1. To come up with a scientifically defensible set of criteria by which judgments can be made as to whether of not a given psychosocial treatment can be considered to be empirically supported, and

2. Once these criteria have been arrived at, undertake systematic reviews of the published research, and to develop lists of interventions that can be said to be empirically supported in the treatment of particular disorders.

These developments did not escape criticism and controversy either, but the bottom line is that the very capable individuals who served on this task force indeed accomplished both tasks, which remain ongoing initiatives within the American Psychological Association.

These evidentiary standards (see Chambless et al., 1996) included the following central elements: (1) at least two good between-group design experiments demonstrating efficacy in that they are (a) superior to pill or psychological place or to another treatment or (b) equivalent to an already-established treatment in experiments with adequate statistical power, or (2) a large series of single-case design experiments ($N > 9$) demonstrating efficacy that must have (a) used good experimental designs and (b) compared the intervention with another treatment (as in the first standard). Further criteria for both standards are that experiments must be conducted with treatment manuals, characteristics of the client samples much be clearly specified, and effects must have been demonstrated by at least two different investigators or investigative teams. Other nonscientific criteria are also important: what does the intervention cost (financial, time, resources, training)? Can the approach be used with diverse clientele? Is the intervention compatible with the values and ethics of the field?. These criteria are not explicit, but they are assumed, given the context of practice by members of ethical and professional health care disciplines.

Frankly, these are very modest standards indeed, but once in place, the task force began the process of examining the published journal literature to determine which interventions met these standards for various conditions or disorders.

Reports then began to appear that delineated these well-established treatments (Sanderson & Woody, 1995; Task Force, 1995); entire issues of professional journals (e.g., a 1996 issue of *Clinical Psychology: Science and Practice,* a 1998 issue of *Journal of Consulting and Clinical Psychology,* a 1998 issue of *Psychotherapy Research,* a 1998 issue of *Journal of Clinical Child Psychology*) and some books (e.g., Christophersen & Mortweet, 2001; Nathan & Gorman, 1998) began to appear that elaborated on these issues. The task force's work was favorably commented on in the influential *Mental Health: A Report of the Surgeon General* (Hatcher, 2000), and the empirically supported treatments movement continues within contemporary psychology. For example, contemporary accreditation standards for professional psychology training programs require "that all interns demonstrate an intermediate to advanced level of professional psychological skills, abilities, proficiencies, competencies and knowledge in the areas of: (a) Theories and methods of assessment and diagnosis and effective intervention (*including empirically supported treatments*) (Committee on Accreditation, 2000, p. 16, italics added). More strongly, accreditation site visitors need to assess whether practicum placements "provide a wide range of training and education through applications of empirically supported intervention procedures; [and] . . . which empirically supported procedures do the students practice in their practicum settings" (Committee on Accreditation, n.d., p. 37).

THE PRACTICE-GUIDELINES MOVEMENT

As it became evident that certain psychosocial and biological treatments were indeed efficacious for selected mental, physical, and psychosocial problems, various professional groups began a parallel movement to develop *practice guidelines,* defined as "systematically developed statements to assist practitioner and patient decisions about appropriate care for specific clinical circumstances" (Institute of Medicine, 1990, p. 2). Ideally, practice guidelines are based on scientific evidence, although some emerged based on the consensus judgments of so-called expert panels of health care providers and researchers. Matthew Howard and Jeff Jensen guest-edited a special section (May 1999) of *Research on Social Work Practice* devoted to articles discussing the emergence of practice guidelines in fields related to social work and of their pros and cons for social work practice (Howard & Jensen, 1999). Many thousands of practice guidelines have been developed, primarily in the medical fields, but an increasing number address so-called mental disorders. Organizations involved in the development and dissemination of practice guidelines include the American Psychiatric Association, the American Academy of Child and Adolescent Psychiatry, the Agency for Health Care Policy and Research, the interdisciplinary Practice Guidelines Coalition, the American Psychological Association, the American Association of Applied and Preventive Psychology, the National Association of Social Workers, and the Society for Social Work and Research.

The National Association of Social Workers has collaborated to a minor extent in the development of a few of the practice guidelines developed by the American Psychiatric Association (e.g., American Psychiatric Association, 1993), and the Society for Social Work and Research has sent representatives to a few national meetings of the Practice Guidelines Coalition. Efforts are underway to affiliate the society more formally as a full partner with the Practice Guidelines Coalition. In general, however, it is shameful how little social work organizations have been proactive in seeking involvement, input, and partnership with other groups actively developing practice guidelines. There is some consideration being given to the development of "disciplinary" practice guidelines, by and for social workers (e.g., Rosen & Proctor, 2003), but this has the potential to be a big blunder. Social work lacks a sufficiently strong disciplinary knowledge base to generate its own practice guidelines. By definition, practice guidelines make use of scientific research findings from multidisciplinary sources. To omit the fine work by psychologists, psychiatrists, and other health care professionals in developing science-based guidelines would result in grossly incomplete literature reviews. It makes no sense to use behavioral science knowledge developed from multidisciplinary sources to create guidelines supposedly limited for use by professional social workers. Human service problems require interventional knowledge from multidisciplinary sources and often require interdisciplinary, interventional programs. The development of social work practice guidelines would be an insular, retrograde step in the development of a genuine science of social work practice. Social work should collaborate with other disciplinary groups to develop practice guidelines that all human service professionals, regardless of discipline, can use and that are charged with helping clients who are experiencing particular problems.

THE EVIDENCE-BASED PRACTICE MOVEMENT

On December 13, 1999, the Surgeon General of the United States, David Satcher, M.D., stated on the National Public Radio news program *All Things Considered* that "Evidence-based treatment is treatment based upon the best available science." This is a more concise statement than the formal definition of evidence-based practice that Sackett, Richardson, Rosenberg, and Haynes (1997, p. 2) provide: "the conscientious, explicit, and judicious use of the current best evidence in making decisions about the care of individual patients." Gambrill is one the earliest voices to bring the evidence-based practice paradigm (and the word is deliberately chosen) to the attention of the social work community, stating that, "In EBP social workers seek out practice-related research findings regarding important practice decisions and share the results of their search with clients. If they find that there is no evidence that a method they recommend will help a client, they so inform the client and describe their theoretical rationale for their recommendations. Clients are involved as informed participants" (1999a, p. 346).

Persons (1999) presents the following simplified model for the evidence-based clinician to follow:

The evidence-based practitioner:

- Provides informed consent for treatment.
- Relies on the efficacy data (especially from [randomized controlled trials]) when recommending and selecting and carrying out treatments.
- Uses the empirical literature to guide decision-making.
- Uses a systematic, hypothesis-testing approach to the treatment of each case:
- Begins with careful assessment
- Sets clear and measurable treatment goals
- Develops an individualized formulation and a treatment plan based on that formulation
- Monitors progress towards the goals frequently and modifies or ends treatment as needed,

It is certainly recognized that the scientific foundations for social work practice vary considerably. For some problems, such as selected so-called mental disorders like major depression, panic disorder, or schizophrenia, several psychosocial interventions meet the standards of evidence-based practice and can be employed by social workers and their clients. Others enjoy less robust evidentiary foundations (e.g., child abuse and neglect, domestic violence), and some fields of practice (e.g., political action) are characterized by the virtual absence of any scientific outcome studies that can be used to guide practice. Evidence-based practice does not suggest that social work abandon these practice arenas—one must rely on more traditional sources of knowledge to guide one's work, such as practice wisdom, theory, authority, values, and history. However, it is incumbent on practitioners to keep abreast of scientific developments in these areas so as not to overlook important new practice-research findings.

The "face validity" of the merits of the evidence-based practice paradigm ensure its rapid dissemination throughout the health care fields, including the practice of social work. The recent *Mental Health: A Report of the Surgeon General* (see Hatcher, 2000) notes that, "A challenge for the nation in the near-term future is to speed the transfer of new evidence-based treatments and prevention programs into diverse service delivery settings and systems. . . . A range of treatments of well-documented efficacy exists for most mental disorders. . . . Gaps also exist between optimally effective treatment and what many individuals receive in actual practice. . . . A range of efficacious psychosocial and pharmacological treatments exist for many mental disorders in children." In Great Britain, the national government has funded the Centre for Evidence-Based Social Services, directed by the social worker Brian Sheldon, and the Australian federal government recently established a similar center, under the administrative leadership of the social worker Jim Barber. There is an emerging social work literature focused on the topic of evidence-based practice (e.g., Corcoran, 2000; Lloyd, 1998; Macdonald, 1998, 2001; Thyer, 2001, 2003a, 2003b; Thyer & Kazi, 2004; Thyer, Wodarski, Harrison, & Myers, in press). Academic advertisements have begun to explicitly recruit for faculty in the United States who have the background to teach from the evidence-based practice perspective, and at least one major school of social work, Washington University in St. Louis, has adopted evidence-based practice as the organizational framework for its master's of social work curriculum.

Although one might expect that a profession such as social work that prides itself on being a research-based discipline would have autonomously adopted the central ethos of evidence-based practice some time ago, several factors have mitigated against its earlier promulgation, including a generalized distrust of scientific research among a powerful minority in the profession; entrenched non-evidence-based practices in the service and educational communities; a failure to reinforce evidence-based practice when practitioners attempt to introduce it into social service agencies; insufficient dissemination of existing knowledge that pertains to psychosocial treatments of demonstrated efficacy and effectiveness; the failure of third-party payers to limit reimbursement for social workers who provide non-evidence-based interventions; the nonexistence of a legal precedent establishing a right to effective treatments, where these are known to have been developed; and a shortage of social work journals that emphasize the publication of practice-research findings related to evidence-based practice. Despite these impediments, the profession is slowly moving in the direction of evidence-based practice, and this trend is likely to accelerate in the next few years.

THE COCHRANE AND CAMPBELL COLLABORATIONS

Several large international interdisciplinary groups are similarly engaged in evaluating the evidence related to helping solve psychosocial problems, most notably the Cochrane Collaboration, which has its headquarters in Great Britain (see Gambrill, 1999b), and the Campbell Collaboration, which has its headquarters in the United States. Social workers are involved in both endeavors. Geraldine Macdonald, a professor of social work at the University of Bristol, is a social work member of the Cochrane Collaboration, which focuses on the design and conduct of systematic reviews of the literature, relating to intervention in various medical and other health care problems. These systematic reviews are not as potentially prescriptive as are practice guidelines (and deliberately so). They summarize what is known about the causes of given problem and of the most scientifically supported methods of intervention (Clark & Oxman, 2000). It should be noted that the systematic reviews simply summarize the empirical research findings—they do not tell clinicians what to do! Practice guidelines tell clinicians what to do, but they have no enforcement contingencies to mandate their application. They are purely aspirational and hortatory in application. Practice standards tell clinicians what to do and are backed up by some enforcement mechanism. At present, there are few practice standards in social work, in the sense of the previous sentence. The sources of knowledge used in the construction of these systematic reviews are hierarchically ordered; randomized controlled clinical trials are given the greatest weight, and expert opinion, unverified practice wisdom, and anecdote are given the least. As members of the Cochrane Collaboration give their attention to effective treatments for mental disorders, then the relevance of this work becomes more apparent for the discipline of social work.

The Campbell Collaboration is closely related conceptually, in spirit, and in methodology to the Cochrane Collaboration, but it differs in that its orientation "will consist of a number of review groups, initially focused on broad areas in education, crime and justice, social work, and social welfare interventions. Review groups will solicit and approve the production of systematic reviews . . . to present high-quality evidence about 'what works'—and what does not work. Targets for this information include members of the public, service providers, policy makers, educators and their students, and researchers" (Bullock, 2000, p. 13; see also www.campbell.se.upenn.edu).

Representatives from the Society for Social Work and Research attended the first national organizational meeting of the Campbell Collaboration, held in early 2001 on the campus of the University of Pennsylvania, and moves are currently afoot to have the society become a formal affiliate of this promising new group. There is an awareness that the majority of efforts in evidence-based practice have heretofore focused on the areas of health and mental health, but considerable work has been undertaken to review and evaluate the evidentiary foundations of interventions applicable to nonclinical psychosocial problems and to more-macro issues. Some preliminary research along these lines is found in the works of Macdonald (2001), Mattaini and Thyer (1996), Thyer (2001), and Wodarski and Thyer (1998).

EVIDENTIARY STANDARDS USED IN EVIDENCE-BASED PRACTICE

Considering the emphasis given to randomized controlled trials as a major source of evidence in judging the effectiveness of psychosocial interventions, the question may be asked as to what are the characteristics of adequately designed randomized controlled trials? The recently established journal *Evidence-Based Mental Health,* published by the BMJ Publishing Group, has provided a set of standards for acceptable randomized controlled trials, which include (among others) the following features:

- Random allocation of participants to comparison groups
- Follow-up (end-point assessment) of at least 80 percent of those entering the investigation
- Outcome measure of known or probable clinical importance
- Analysis consistent with study design
- Assessment or diagnosis of clients conducted with demonstrated reliability, using a reasonably reliable system (e.g., the *Diagnostic and Statistical Manual*) and/or reports of interrater agreement.

- Assessments conducted blindly, without assessors knowing the clients' group assignment (see "Purpose and Procedure," 2000, pp. 66–67).

Generally speaking, a randomized control trial possessing the previous features will be considered capable of producing more reliable and valid knowledge than studies lacking these methodological controls. There is a hierarchy of group-research designs, which includes, among others, randomized controlled trials possessing the previously mentioned features (the highest or strongest form of inquiry), quasi-randomized controlled trials, nonrandomized controlled trials, and cohort studies with case-by-case matching or statistical adjustment to create comparable groups, at the lower end. Prospectively designed studies are usually perceived as producing more valid information than retrospectively conducted ones. At the lowest end of the evidentiary scale (but still potentially valuable) are anecdotal reports, case histories, and small nonblind pre-experimental group studies. Note that these types of studies are capable of yielding conclusions that are accurate, but they do not do an adequate job of ruling out rival, more parsimonious explanations for any observed apparently positive effects.

Additional standards must be applied in the evaluation of social work interventions. For example, conclusions derived from outcome studies conducted with real-life clients seen by everyday practitioners in agency-based settings are likely to be more generalizable to social work practice than clients who were actively recruited on the basis of highly selected or circumscribed features, for example. Some areas of practice may not lend themselves to genuinely experimental evaluations (e.g., policy practice, community organization), and we must, perforce, rely on less stringent research methods, such as quasi-experimental or time-series studies. Evidence-based practice does not insist that practice be based on perfect evidence, only on the best scientific evidence that is currently available. A treatment supported by two well-designed randomized controlled trials has better evidence than one supported by only a single randomized controlled trial. A treatment supported by one quasi-experimental study with a positive outcome is better justified in practice than is an intervention lacking even this minimal level of evidentiary support. A newly developed intervention with positive outcomes obtained through several well-designed single-system research designs is more "evidence-based" than a treatment with no credible evaluation studies.

THE UNFORTUNATE ALTERNATIVE TO EVIDENCE-BASED PRACTICE

The movement toward evidence-based practice in social work is, in part, a reaction to the proliferation of bogus and ineffectual treatments provided by members of our discipline and practitioners in related fields (Lilienfeld, Lynn, & Lohr, 2003). Although the following story is not typical of mainstream social work practice, it illustrates the life-and-death nature of some interventional decisions.

Approximately four months after the surgeon general's interview on National Public Radio, cited previously in this chapter, on April 18, 2000, a ten-year-old girl named Candace Newmaker found herself in a fetal position and very tightly wrapped in a blue flannel blanket by her social worker. Four adults, including the social worker who possessed a master's of social work from a Council on Social Work Education–accredited program, placed pillows around and on top of the little girl and proceeded to push and pummel the child while screaming at her to work her way free. Candace was crying, saying that she could not breathe, could not find a way out, and was going to throw up. One therapist yelled, "Go ahead, die right now." Candace became quiet and unresponsive for fifteen minutes before she was finally unwrapped, unconscious, after the hourlong ordeal. She died the following day as a result of being suffocated during this "rebirthing training" session (Crowder & Lowe, 2000). The social worker and her colleagues were indicted, tried, and found guilty of child abuse that led to death. They face a sentence of up to forty years in prison. Needless to say, rebirthing therapy is not an evidence-based practice. The widespread adoption of evidence-based practice would curb the use of rebirthing therapy and the hundreds of similarly bogus and sometimes harmful treatments provided to child and adult social work clients. Adoption of evidence-based practice would jump-start the nascent efforts in social work to systematically evaluate the outcomes of established and newly developed psychosocial services, programs, and policies and to move the field more in the direction of being a genuinely progressive profession.

STEPS TO PROMOTE EVIDENCE-BASED SOCIAL WORK PRACTICE

There are several possible points of leverage that the social work profession might use to influence the development of evidence-based social work practice. Some are steps that can be taken by individuals, others by professional groups, and still others by outside entities.

The Council on Social Work Education's *Educational and Policy Statement and Accreditation Standards* should embrace the language of evidence-based practice and mandate that social work students be provided training in evidence-based practices (e.g., intervention and assessment methods), where these are known to have been developed. Content on human behavior in the social environment should be required to emphasize empirically supported theories and models, in lieu of historical or traditionally taught frameworks that either are now known to be false or lack credible evidence of validity. Research training should explicitly focus on applied research methodology and on evaluation research techniques, including at least one required graduate-level course in inferential statistics involving the use of a data-analysis package such as SPSS. A further ambitious standard would be the mandate that all direct-practice students, as a graduation requirement, empirically demonstrate that they have helped at least one client. The Council on Social Work Education's annual conference and its periodical, *Journal of Social Work Education,* should promote the dissemination of evidence-based practice as the issues pertain to social work training.

The National Association of Social Workers' journals should emphasize intervention research on the outcomes of social work practice (to enhance their usefulness to practitioners), and, perhaps most important, the next revision to the association's code of ethics should include the following practice standards:

> Clients should be offered as a first choice treatment, interventions with some significant degree of empirical support, where such knowledge exists, and only provided other treatments after such first choice treatments have been given a legitimate trial and been shown not to be efficacious.
>
> Clinicians should routinely gather empirical data on client's relevant behavior, affect, and reports of thoughts, using reliable and valid measures, where such measures have been developed. These measures should be repeated throughout the course of treatment, and used in clinical decision-making to supplement professional judgments pertaining to the alteration or termination of treatment. (Thyer, 1995, p. 95)

It is only when social workers have an ethical obligation to conduct evidence-based practice can we, as a profession, realistically expect it to take hold. As does the Council on Social Work Education's annual program meeting, the National Association of Social Workers' periodic regional and national conferences (if and when they are resumed) should promote and disseminate evidence-based practice content. The association should also take a much more proactive role in being involved in the numerous interdisciplinary, professional, and governmental initiatives aimed at developing practice guidelines and evidence-based practice.

Third-party payers and managed-care firms should only provide reimbursement when social workers provide evidence-based practice, where these have been established for given psychosocial problems, and some public, spirited person or organization should underwrite the legal expenses of a series of different clients who received non-evidence-based social work services, in circumstances where evidence-based practices are well established (e.g., major depression, panic disorder, obsessive-compulsive disorder, substance abuse) and consequently were harmed or simply failed to benefit from care. Claims should be very modest, perhaps seeking only reimbursement of the fees paid by the client who received bogus services (e.g., rebirthing therapy, primal-scream therapy, past-life regression therapy, facilitated communication, neurolinguistic programming, therapeutic touch—all services provided by contemporary social workers) and a small penalty. The aim is not to seek the award of substantial damages but to establish the legal precedent that social work clients have a *right* to receive evidence-based practices as first choice treatments (see Myers & Thyer, 1997). Larger settlements involving substantial punitive damage awards may be forthcoming once the clients' right to effective treatments were well established in different areas of practice. Such lawsuits would radically change the practice landscape, promoting evidence-based practice far more effectively than complainant journal articles and book chapters urging its adoption.

CONCLUDING REMARKS

Evidence-based practice has the potential to help the field of social work accomplish some of the noble goals of its predecessor organizations, organizations going back as far as the American Social Science Association founded in 1865. Evidence-based practice is, frankly, old wine in new bottles. Jayaratne and Levy's empirical clinical practice of the late 1970s is an earlier vintage that is still quite pleasing to the palate. Agreeably sweet, with a subtle tinge of astringency, it has aged well. Unfortunately, few social work agencies keep a supply on hand. There seems to be a concatenation of positive influences at work in these contemporary times that are tending to promote the general idea that clients have a right to effective treatments, where these have been established, and in many important areas of social work practice, effective treatments *are* known and well supported by credible scientific research studies. The Society for Social Work and Research is a major positive development; the Institute for the Advancement of Social Work and Research, proposed federal legislation to create a Center for Social Work Research under the auspices of the National Institutes of Health, the Cochrane and Campbell collaborations, the emergence of science-based practice guidelines, the impetus of managed care for health care providers to offer demonstrable effective interventions, the publication of a large and growing body of literature that supports the evidence-based practice movement—these are all constructive forces absent a mere two decades ago.

REFERENCES

American Psychiatric Association. (1993). *Practice guideline for eating disorders.* Washington, DC: Author.

Bullock, M. (2000, May/June). What is the Campbell Collaboration? *Psychological Science Agenda,* p. 13.

Chambless, D., Sanderson, W., Shoham, V., Johnson, S., Pope, K., Crits-Christoph, P., et al. (1996). An update on empirically validated therapies. *The Clinical Psychologist, 49*(2), 5–8.

Christophersen, E. R., & Mortweet, S. L. (2001). *Treatments that work with children: Empirically supported strategies for managing childhood problems.* Washington, DC: American Psychological Association.

Clark, M., & Oxman, A. D. (Eds.). (2000). *Cochrane reviewer's handbook: Version 4.1.* Oxford, England: The Cochrane Collaboration. Retrieved from http://www.cochrane.org/cochrane/hbook.htm

Committee on Accreditation. (2000). *Guidelines and principles for accreditation of programs in professional psychology.* Washington, DC: American Psychological Association.

Committee on Accreditation. (n.d.). *Site visitor workbook: Guidelines for the review of doctoral, internship, and post-doctoral residency programs* (6th ed.). Washington, DC: American Psychological Association.

Corcoran, J. (2000). *Evidence-based social work practice with families.* New York: Springer.

Corcoran, K. (1985). Clinical practice with nonbehavioral methods: Strategies for evaluation. *Clinical Social Work Journal, 13,* 78–86.

Crowder, C., & Lowe, P. (2000, May 19). 4 accused in 'rebirthing' death affidavit states girl, 10, smothered while adults pushed and therapist yelled 'Die right now.' *Denver Rocky Mountain News,* p. 5A.

Council on Social Work Education. (1982). Curriculum policy statement for the master's degree and baccalaureate degree program in social work education. *Social Work Education Reporter, 30*(3), 5–12.

Gambrill, E. (1999a). Evidence-based clinical practice: An alternative to authority-based practice. *Families in Society, 80,* 341–350.

Gambrill, E. (1999b). Evidence-based clinical practice, evidence-based medicine and the Cochrane Collaboration. *Journal of Behavior Therapy and Experimental Psychiatry, 30,* 1–14, 153–154.

Germain, C. (1970). Casework and science: A historical encounter. In R. Roberts & R. Nee (Eds.), *Theories of social casework* (pp. 3–32). Chicago: University of Chicago Press.

Graham, J. R., Al-Krenawi, A., & Bradshaw, C. (2000). The Social Work Research Group/NASW Research Section/Council on Social Work Research: 1949–1965: An emerging research identity in the American profession. *Research on Social Work Practice, 10,* 622–643.

Haskell, T. L. (1977). *The emergence of professional social science: The American Social Science Association.* Urbana: University of Illinois Press.

Hatcher, D. (2000). *Mental health: A report of the Surgeon General.* Public Health Service, Office of the Surgeon General, Center for Mental Health Services, and National Institute of Mental Health. Washington, DC: U.S. Government Printing Office. Available at http://purl.access.gpo.gov/GPO/LPS26276

Howard, M. O. & Jensen, J. (1999). Clinical practice guidelines: Should social work develop them? *Research on Social Work Practice, 9,* 283–301.

Institute of Medicine. (1990). *Clinical practice guidelines.* Washington, DC: National Academy Press.

Ivanoff, A., Blythe, B. J., & Briar, S. (1987). The empirical clinical practice debate. *Social Casework, 68,* 290–298.

Ivanoff, A., Robinson, E. A., & Blythe, B. J. (1987). Empirical clinical practice from a feminist perspective. *Social Work, 32,* 417–423.

Jayaratne, S. & Levy, R. L. (1979). *Empirical clinical practice.* New York: Columbia University Press.

Lilienfeld, S. O., Lynn, S. J., & Lohr, J. M. (2003). *Science and pseudoscience in clinical psychology.* New York: Guilford Press.

Lloyd, E. (1998). Introducing evidence-based social welfare practice in a national child care agency. In A. Buchanan & B. Hudson (Eds.), *Parenting, schooling and children's behaviour* (pp. 161–177). Aldershot, England: Ashgate.

Macdonald, G. (1994). Developing empirically based practice in probation. *British Journal of Social Work, 24,* 405–427.

Macdonald, G. (1998). Promoting evidence-based practice in child protection. *Clinical Child Psychology and Psychiatry, 31,* 71–85.

Macdonald, G. (2001). *Effectiveness interventions for child abuse and neglect: An evidence-based approach to planning and evaluating interventions.* New York: Wiley.

Mattaini, M. A., & Thyer, B. A. (Eds.). (1996). *Finding solutions to social problems: Behavioral strategies for change.* Washington, DC: American Psychological Association Press.

Myers, L. L., & Thyer, B. A. (1997). Should social work clients have the right to effective treatment? *Social Work, 42,* 288–298.

Nathan, P., & Gorman, J. (Eds.). (1998). *A guide to treatments that work.* New York: Oxford University Press.

Persons, J. B. (1999). Evidence-based psychotherapy: A graduate course proposal. *Clinical Science, 2,* 12.

Rosen, A., & Proctor, E. (Eds.). (2003). *Developing practice guidelines for social work interventions: Issues, methods, and research.* New York: Columbia University Press.

Sackett, D. L., Robinson, W. S., Rosenberg, W., & Haynes, R. B. (1997). *Evidence-based medicine: How to practice and teach EBM.* New York: Churchill Livingston.

Sanderson, W., & Woody, S. (1995). Manuals for empirically-validated treatments: A project of the Task Force on Psychological Interventions. *The Clinical Psychologist, 48*(4), 7–11.

Purpose and procedure. (2000). *Evidence-based Mental Health, 3,* 66–67.

Task Force on Promotion and Dissemination of Psychological Procedures. (1995). Training in and dissemination of empirically-validated psychological treatments: Report and recommendation. *The Clinical Psychologist, 48*(1), 3–23.

Thyer, B. A. (1995). Promoting an empiricist agenda within the human services: An ethical and humanistic imperative. *Journal of Behavior Therapy and Experimental Psychiatry, 26,* 93–98.

Thyer, B. A. (1996a). Forty years of progress towards empirical clinical practice? *Social Work Research, 20,* 77–81.

Thyer, B. A. (1996b). Guidelines for applying the empirical clinical practice model to social work. *Journal of Applied Social Sciences, 20,* 121–127.

Thyer, B. A. (2001). Evidence-based approaches to community practice. In K. Corcoran & H. E. Briggs (Eds.), *Social work practice: Treating common client problems* (pp. 54–65). Chicago: Lyceum Books.

Thyer, B. A. (2003a). Empirically-based interventions. In R. A. English (Ed.), *Supplement to the 19th edition of the encyclopedia of social work* (pp. 21–29). Washington, DC: NASW Press.

Thyer, B. A. (2003b). Principles of evidence-based practice and treatment development. In G. Greene & A. Roberts (Eds.), *Social worker's desk reference* (pp. 739–742). New York: Oxford University Press.

Thyer, B. A., & Kazi, M. A. F. (Eds.). (2004). *International perspectives on evidence-based practice in social work.* Birmingham, England: Venture Press.

Thyer, B. A., & Wodarski, J. S. (Eds.). (1998). *Handbook of empirical social work practice: Volume 1. Mental disorders.* New York: Wiley.

Thyer, B. A., Wodarski, J. S., Harrison, D. F., & Myers, L. L. (in press). *Cultural diver-*

sity and social work practice: An evidence-based approach. Springfield, IL: Charles C. Thomas.

Towley, L. (1956). NASW: A professional step. *Social Work, 1*(1), 109–112.

Wodarski, J. S. (1981). *The role of research in clinical practice.* Baltimore: University Park Press.

Wodarski, J. S., & Thyer, B. A. (Eds.). (1998). *Handbook of empirical social work practice: Vol. 2. Psychosocial problems and practice issues.* New York: Wiley.

PART TWO

APPLICATIONS

Part 2 presents examples of evidence-based behavioral social work practice. These eight chapters serve as models for developing practice aimed at addressing particular problems and client populations. Lynn McClannahan and Patricia Krantz (chapter 6) suggest factors for social workers to consider in choosing behavioral programs for families of children with autism. They also describe the roles of family and practitioner, which are crucial to successful program implementation and evaluation. In chapter 7, Susan Stern discusses the contributions of behavioral and family-systems theories as a basis for multisystemic therapy approaches with adolescents and their families. She presents evidence that furthers understanding of youth problem behavior in an ecological context that extends beyond family influences, practice principles, and challenges to successful implementation. In chapter 8, Steven Wolf addresses the sensitive topic of assessment and treatment of juvenile male perpetrators of sexual abuse. He articulates a set of organizing principles to guide interventions and a model for matching practice with research and clinical evidence.

Moving to adult populations, Matsujiro Shibano (chapter 9) draws on his experience in Japan to describe the role of operant theory and developmental research methods in designing effective parent-training programs. He presents an exemplar and discusses some of the issues he faced in disseminating a model parent-training program he adapted from his work in the United States. In chapter 10, Nathan Linsk and Christopher Mitchell address medication management as an example of how empirically based best practices can help support HIV-affected individuals and maximize outcomes. Using a case example, they describe an adherence program based on applied behavior analysis. Similarly, Glenn Green and Earlie Washington (chapter 11) discuss the use of behavioral theory and evidence in providing care for the elderly in adult day care centers. Their discussion is extended by Hanrahan, Luchins, Murphy, Patrick, Sachs, and Hougham (chapter 12), who focus on the issue of advanced dementia in the elderly. They use a case study to illustrate their evidence-based perspective and offer an extensive examination of model programs that are being used nationwide to provide appropriate care. In chapter 13, Wong, Wilder, Schock, and Clay lay a foundation for the practitioner seeking knowledge of advances in behaviorally based mental health treatment. They describe the contributions of behavioral research in the treatment, stabilization, and adjustment of persons with severe and persistent mental disorders.

CHAPTER 6

Some Guidelines for Selecting Behavioral Intervention Programs for Children with Autism

Lynn E. McClannahan and
Patricia J. Krantz

This chapter describes some evaluation dimensions that social work professionals can use to assist families in selecting effective intervention programs for children with autism. Although behavioral treatment technology emerged in the mid-1960s and continues to be extended and elaborated, nonscientific approaches to autism treatment also continue to proliferate. Not all agencies that lay claim to a behavioral approach are science based, and there are major, substantive differences among programs that use applied behavior analysis methodology. These circumstances are confusing to people unfamiliar with the field and often complicate placement decisions. However, there are empirically validated practices that appear to be indicators of effective, science-based intervention programs. We discuss the importance of sustained engagement with activities and other people, many opportunities to respond and practice new skills, staff members' frequent but discriminated use of behavior-descriptive praise, good relationship-building repertoires displayed by intervention personnel, careful attention to children's hygiene and appearance, a programmatic approach to the development of youngsters' social competence, an environment that supports the display of new skills and minimizes the occurrence of inappropriate behavior, and policies and practices that foster parents' participation in intervention and promote generalization of children's skills across persons and settings. These are not the only indexes of effective intervention programs for children with autism, but problems in these areas may seriously compromise children's progress in treatment.

SOME GUIDELINES FOR EVALUATING BEHAVIORAL INTERVENTION PROGRAMS FOR CHILDREN WITH AUTISM

Autism is a developmental disability that appears before the age of three and is characterized by impairments in social interaction, such as gaze aversion or the absence of communicative gestures; impairments in communication, such as mutism, language delays, stereotypic uses of language, and lack of pretend play;

and repetitive and stereotypic patterns of behavior such as preserving "sameness" of routines and engaging in repetitive motor mannerisms such as flapping hands or spinning objects (American Psychiatric Association, 1994).

Historically, a portion of the literature of autism treatment—perhaps a significant portion—has comprised ineffective approaches and treatment fads. Sensory integration, auditory integration training, facilitated communication, music therapy, hormone therapies such as secretin, immunological therapies such as intravenous immune globulin, and special diets were (or are) said to be helpful, but not one is adequately supported by scientific evidence, and research has shown that some are actually harmful (New York State Department of Health Early Intervention Program, 1999; Smith, 1996).

Since the publication of *Application of Operant Conditioning Procedures to the Behavior Problems of an Autistic Child* (Wolf, Risley, & Mees, 1965), hundreds of scientific studies have demonstrated the effectiveness of applied behavior analysis in building important skills and in diminishing the severe behavior problems of people with autism (Jacobson, Mulick, & Green, 1998). The contemporary intervention of choice is behavioral (Green, 1996); no other treatment approach has received comparable scientific support. However, agencies that use (or claim to use) a behavioral approach may differ greatly. For example, services may be delivered in hospitals, in outpatient clinics, in children's own homes, in specialized treatment centers, in special education classrooms in public schools, or in various combinations of these locations. Parents and siblings may be included in or excluded from participation. Those who provide intervention may be trained by others who are only slightly more experienced than they are or by senior professionals who have a great deal of education and experience in operant methodology and autism treatment. Staff supervision and mentoring may occur daily, weekly, monthly, or infrequently, or may be absent. Furthermore, behavioral intervention is not a single approach—applied behavior analysis includes many measurement procedures and many behavior-increase and behavior-decrease procedures that can be used singly or in combination to remediate various skill deficits and behavior problems. Given the diversity of services that purport to be behavioral, how can social work professionals and family members determine which agencies are most likely to deliver effective intervention to children who need help?

SOME EVALUATION DIMENSIONS

The following paragraphs present some empirically validated practices that appear to be indicators of program effectiveness. We also review some of the research that supports these practices and discuss their importance. To say that these practices represent "best practice" would be premature; there is so far little or no evidence to recommend one set of well-researched behavioral procedures over another. On ethical and humanitarian grounds, however, omissions of certain practices may be negative indicators of program effectiveness.

Engagement with Activities and Other Persons

A large body of research demonstrates relationships between engagement and the acquisition of new academic, social, language, and self-care skills (Greenwood, 1999). Conversely, people who do not interact with the physical or social environment have few opportunities to learn, and chronic inactivity increases the likelihood of behavior problems and health problems (Reid & Green, 1998).

In our setting, an evaluation protocol (McClannahan, Krantz, MacDuff, & Fenske, 1988) defines engagement as "scrutinizing, manipulating, or otherwise appropriately using instructional or leisure materials; visually attending to staff members or to materials they present; visually attending to another learner who is interacting with an instructor; or following directions" (p.7). Children are not scored as engaged if they are exhibiting stereotypic, disruptive, or other inappropriate behavior. When obtaining data on engagement, observers use a time-sampling procedure—every minute, on the minute mark, they count (from left to right) the number of students in a classroom or activity area and then immediately count the number of students who are engaged. These observations are averaged to obtain percentage engagement. Data-based feedback on students' engagement is provided to staff members as a part of their training program, and assessments of engagement are included in staff performance evaluations. More than a quarter of a century of repeated measures of the engagement of young people with autism show that, given an ongoing program of staff training and evaluation and an effective intervention system (McClannahan & Krantz, 1993), it is reasonable to expect group and individual engagement measures to be 80 percent or greater across time, staff members, settings, and activities.

Because high levels of engagement are characteristic of well-organized and effective human service agencies (Reid & Green, 1998), measures of engagement are one way to evaluate a program. During a visit to a single classroom or area, a parent or social work professional may collect successive one-minute time samples; on a tour of the program, it may be possible to collect one time sample in each classroom or activity area. In programs of poor quality, there may be no planned activities during some portions of the day, or learners may spend extended periods of time waiting (e.g., waiting for an activity to begin; standing in line to gain access to the cafeteria, bathroom, or gym). In programs of good quality, time samples should reveal mean engagement of 80 percent to 100 percent.

Opportunities to Respond

An opportunity to respond occurs when someone asks a question or gives an instruction that requests that a person perform a specific behavior (e.g., "What time is it?" or "Please get your coat"). Repeated instructions ("nags") and nonspecific directions ("Do it again") are not good examples of opportunities to respond; the former may teach children that they need not follow directions the first time they are given, and the latter may produce errors.

Unfortunately, in many public school classrooms, youngsters have few or no opportunities to respond during the school day (Stanley & Greenwood, 1983); but for children with and without developmental disabilities, increased opportunities to respond result in improved performance on measures of academic achievement (Delquadri, Greenwood, Stretton, & Hall, 1983). In programs that serve children with autism, opportunities to respond have been increased by means of enriched staff-child ratios; peer tutoring; small-group instruction, including choral responding (Kamps, Dugan, & Leonard, 1994); and integration of parents into the treatment process (Harris, 1983).

Discrete-trial teaching, often discussed in the literature of autism intervention (e.g., Anderson, Taras, & Cannon, 1996; Harris, 1983; Koegel, Russo, & Rincover, 1977; Sundberg & Partington, 1998), represents a specific type of presentation of opportunities to respond. In a discrete-trial paradigm, the teacher asks a question or gives an instruction, the student responds correctly or incorrectly or does not respond, the teacher delivers or does not deliver a reward, and there is a brief time interval before the next trial begins (McClannahan & Krantz, 1997). In some of the early applications of behavior analysis to autism intervention, discrete-trial teaching was virtually the only instructional procedure used (see Lovaas, 1977), and it is still widely used. Some of its important contemporary uses are teaching "readiness" skills (e.g., sitting quietly and looking at the instructor), motor- and verbal-imitation repertoires, and receptive-language tasks (e.g., pointing to objects or pictures). Many children who are exposed to lengthy discrete-trial teaching sessions respond with aggression or self-injury (Horner, Day, Sprague, O'Brien, & Heathfield, 1991), noncompliance (Mace et al., 1988), tantrums (Lovaas, 1977), or stereotypy. Often, these problems can be minimized by interspersing brief periods of discrete-trial instruction with other types of learning experiences, such as using computer software, independently practicing emerging skills (e.g., handwriting, spelling, bike riding), or following photographic or written activity schedules in the absence of verbal prompts from instructors (McClannahan & Krantz, 1999).

Although opportunities to respond are a relevant feature of good intervention programs, they are only one of many key features, and discrete-trial instruction is only one of several ways to provide opportunities to respond. In our setting, we count the number of opportunities to respond that staff members deliver during five-minute observation periods, and we invite staff members to predict the level of opportunities to respond that they will use during specific activities (this promotes correspondence between "saying" and "doing," which is important to the development of good intervention skills). Predictions are indexed to three levels: Low (zero to seven opportunities in five minutes), moderate (eight to fourteen opportunities), or high (fifteen or more opportunities). These categories are useful only with reference to children's activities. Some activities, such as receptive language development ("Touch your nose/hair/shoulders/knees") and verbal imitation ("Say 'ma,'" "Say 'mama'") call for many opportunities to respond; others, such as certain receptive language programs, call for moderate levels because the target responses require some time to execute ("Find the re-frigerator" and "Touch the dishwasher"); and still other activities, such as key-boarding, writing, dressing, and brushing teeth, call for few or no opportunities to respond (Do we want others to talk to us while we complete such tasks?).

When visiting agencies that serve children with autism, parents and profes-sionals may want to count or, at minimum, informally observe opportunities to respond, not only because they help learners remain engaged, but also because they create occasions for them to practice certain key responses. But it is also im-portant to recall that not all learning activities should be guided by verbal in-structions.

Behavior-Descriptive Praise

Nine of the first ten volumes of *Journal of Applied Behavior Analysis* (1968–1977) include one or more articles that describe praise as a reinforcer. In general- and special-education classrooms, praise has been shown to increase appropri-ate behavior (e.g., Hall, Lund, & Jackson, 1968) and task engagement (e.g., Broden, Bruce, Mitchell, Carter, & Hall, 1970). Unfortunately, for most children with autism, praise is not a functional reinforcer at the outset of intervention; when it is systematically paired with other reinforcers (initially, perhaps, pre-ferred foods and later, tokens), it acquires reward value.

Behavior-descriptive praise statements include both an indication of ap-proval and a specification of the response that is being approved (e.g., "Good, you pointed to the dime," "I like it when you use your napkin"). Such statements also provide good language models that can support next performances. For ex-ample, if the teacher instructs "Say 'I want'" and the child responds "I wan" (the child's best-yet approximation), the behavior-descriptive praise "Good, you said 'I want!'" not only indicates approval but also provides a model for the next ver-bal production.

In addition to confirming that students' responses are correct, behavior-specific praise helps make both staff members' and learners' day-to-day experi-ences more pleasant. Most people prefer to occupy work environments that feature praise ("Great, you covered your mouth when you coughed!") rather than correction ("Don't sneeze on me! Turn your head!"). Furthermore, because behavior-descriptive praise indicates which responses receive a staff member's attention, it is useful to staff trainers.

Good intervention environments feature behavior-specific praise that sup-ports behavioral receptivity and the shaping of new skills. In such settings, staff members *contingently* deliver praise—that is, they praise correct, socially ap-propriate responses and do not praise incorrect or inappropriate performances. In addition, they identify certain teaching activities in which praise is likely to be helpful and other activities in which it may not be useful. If verbal prompts are appropriate (e.g., "Five plus two equals seven; say 'seven'" or "Say, 'it's October'") or if the activity features social interaction, behavior-descriptive praise is often a helpful tool. If verbal prompts are not called for and may produce prompt dependence (e.g., during bathing, shoe tying, or face washing), praise may interrupt or postpone independent performances.

Relationship Building

In autism intervention, just as in social work practice, it is important to build relationships that result in positive social consequences for the people who are receiving help (Pinkston, Levitt, Green, Linsk, & Rzepnicki, 1982). Often, building relationships with children with autism begins when the therapist pairs herself or himself with items or activities that have already acquired reward value, such as preferred snacks or favorite toys. If this is successfully accomplished, the therapist's physical proximity, positive attention, and praise become reinforcers that can be delivered in many different contexts.

It is not difficult to observe staff members' relationship-building repertoires during even a brief visit to an autism treatment program. Individuals with good skills in this area have pleasant facial expressions, smile frequently, and speak enthusiastically to children who are responding correctly, but maintain neutral facial expressions and voice tone when students are displaying inappropriate behavior. When children earn rewards, staff members do not passively observe them playing with preferred toys or engaging in preferred activities; instead, they play *with* them, make friendly comments about the activities, and provide positive physical contact such as light touches, pats, or tickles (if these are rewarding to a child). During transitions from one activity to another (e.g., a walk to another classroom, the drinking fountain, the playground, or the lockers), staff members do not disengage; instead, they use transitions as additional opportunities to provide attention, praise, tokens, and other rewards for appropriate performances. Furthermore, their relationship-building skills are individualized on the basis of each child's observed likes and dislikes. Some children like hugs, and others enjoy tosses in the air; some like to sing and others do not enjoy singing; some like to run or to be chased, and others do not; some are very interested in noise-making toys, and others are fearful of them. Skillful therapists not only deliver highly preferred snacks, toys, or activities but also provide a wide array of rewards, teach children to make choices among the available rewards, and invent new activities that are based on the children's preferences.

In intervention programs of good quality, relationship-building repertoires extend to colleagues and consumers of services. Staff members publicly recognize one another's professional accomplishments, effectively communicate with one another about topics that may have an impact on treatment integrity, and take pride in children's progress. Although a small proportion of people begin their intervention careers with good relationship-building skills, most people develop and enhance these skills as a result of ongoing training and mentoring. Not all organizations foster these behavior patterns; some agency subcultures promote competition rather than cooperation (McClannahan & Krantz, 1993), place greater emphasis on punishment than reinforcement, or adhere to policies about instructional procedures or curricula that prevent good relationship building and individualization of rewards. When rewards are less frequent or less potent, both children and staff members are less likely to try new responses, and there are fewer opportunities to shape new skills.

Children's Hygiene and Personal Appearance

Prior to intervention, most children with autism have few, if any, personal-care skills. After treatment begins, it may take a considerable amount of instructional time before children achieve criterion performances of skills such as buttoning, zipping, washing hands, blowing one's nose, and taking a shower. In fact, initial instruction often focuses on basic issues, such as learning to use the toilet or cooperating with bathing, hair drying, and dressing.

A child who routinely arrives at a treatment setting with dirty hair, dirty hands and nails, mucous on his or her face, and urine-stained clothing is in a very vulnerable position because professional helpers (like most other members of the community) avoid close physical proximity, physical contact, and associated social attention, although these may be primary components of reinforcers. Therefore, while children are learning self-care repertoires, staff trainers and their trainees must ensure children's good hygiene and personal appearance; failure to do so may erode the effectiveness of their intervention programs and contribute to social disapproval and discrimination. In summary, personal appearance variables, such as clean face and hair, clean nose, unstained hands, absence of sores on hands and face, matching socks, and clean and unstained clothing, may be taken as indicators of program quality (McClannahan, McGee, MacDuff, & Krantz, 1990). The presence of programs to teach zipping, dressing, shoe tying, or nail clipping is important but not sufficient. If children appear dirty and unkempt, the treatment agency is failing to fulfill its mandate.

Social Competence

Social competence, like good personal appearance, helps people with developmental disabilities avoid disapprobation and enjoy a measure of social acceptance. The term *social competence* subsumes a broad array of responses and repertoires, such as sharing, being of assistance, complimenting others, and requesting assistance when appropriate (Walker & Calkins, 1986). Specifically, instructional goals for children who are learning to talk should include "please," "thank you," "excuse me," and "help me" as well as greetings and good-byes. Preschoolers and young children should learn to put away toys and instructional materials, pick up things that they drop, and use wastebaskets and recycling containers. They should also be taught to flush toilets, wash hands at relevant times, use tissues and napkins, tuck in their shirts, zip their pants, and tie their shoes. Teaching children with autism to walk with their hands in their pockets or to carry their own belongings provides alternatives to stereotypic motor movements such as hand flapping or repetitive finger play and thus enhances others' perceptions of their social competence.

Beyond early childhood, intervention personnel should help children acquire more-advanced social competencies, such as opening doors for others, picking up things that others drop, turning lights on if first to enter a room and turning them off if last to leave, expressing appreciation, and offering to help (McConaughy, Stowitschek, Salzberg, & Peatross, 1989; Salzberg, Agran, & Lignugaris/Kraft, 1986). Learning to request specific types of information and assistance (e.g., "What is this?" "Where should I put it?" "I can't reach it" "Can you show me how to do it?") are skills that are of lasting importance. In addition, a critical area of social competence is learning to complete tasks *at criterion*. If a student cleans his or her desk, is it really clean when the task concludes? After an adolescent shaves, does he appear clean shaven? Is the sink clean? Are the razor and shaving supplies put away?

A social competence curriculum is likely to have far-reaching implications for young people with autism; the evidence suggests that job loss and movement to more restrictive residential settings are often associated with social-skill deficits (Salzberg, Likins, McConaughy, & Lignugaris/Kraft, 1986; Walker & Calkins, 1986). Although not all of the examples of social competence described previously may be noted on a single visit to an intervention agency, one should expect to see some of these skills displayed and others being taught. Claims that these goals are too advanced for enrolled children may represent deficiencies in the curriculum or deficiencies in instructional technology.

Inappropriate Behavior

Effective programs are prosthetic environments that support the development of new skills and help people learn not to display dysfunctional behavior. Therefore, when visiting an autism intervention agency, one may observe a few children who are engaging in disruptive or self-injurious behavior, or perhaps several young people who occasionally display motor stereotypy or vocal noise; one should not expect to see frequent or widespread behavior problems. If dysfunctional behavior is ongoing, the agency is not meeting its responsibilities.

When inappropriate behavior occurs, closely observe the responses of intervention personnel. Under the best of circumstances, they will respond quickly in a manner that appears to be practiced; for example, a teacher or therapist might remove a token from a token board, turn a child's chair away from an activity area, or temporarily remove toys or snacks. In less desirable circumstances, staff members may appear to be embarrassed or uncertain as to how to respond. If the opportunity arises, ask a staff member what he or she is expected to do when problem behavior occurs. Optimal responses will be respectful of children's right to confidentiality but may describe some parameters of agency policy and refer visitors to someone who can answer the question in more detail.

Prevention is at least as important as treatment of severe behavior problems. Research shows that intervention environments that promote high levels of engagement with activities and other people not only decrease stereotypy, aggression, self-injury, and other inappropriate behavior (Konarski, Favell, & Favell, 1992; Krantz, MacDuff, & McClannahan, 1993) but also prevent their development (Reid & Green, 1998). This is an important reason for the examination of individual and group engagement, as discussed previously in this chapter.

Other indicators of prevention that can be observed during introductory visits to an agency are (a) the fact that there is far more attention to appropriate behavior than to inappropriate behavior, (b) children are frequently rewarded for displaying new skills, and (c) children have many opportunities to make choices. Of course, meaningful choices are individualized; very young children, children who recently entered treatment, and children with the most severe disabilities may select one of two snacks or toys. Others may choose from a broad array of activities or respond to nonspecific questions such as, "What would you like to do?" An important body of research indicates that when people with developmental disabilities have regular opportunities to make choices of preferred items and activities, they are less likely to engage in problem behavior (Lancioni, O'Reilly, & Emerson, 1996).

Family Participation in Intervention

It is well established that the therapeutic gains of children with autism often fail to generalize from the treatment setting to home and community settings or from intervention agents to parents, siblings, and relatives. It is also true that new skills acquired in home-based programs often do not transfer from home to the special education classroom or park or from the home therapist or parent to a grandparent or classroom aide. Baer (1999) notes that, "no one learns a generalized lesson unless a generalized lesson is taught" (p. 1); this axiom is especially relevant to people with autism.

Responsible treatment agencies include parents as partners in intervention, because it is unlikely that desirable outcomes can be achieved without their participation. Learning to set a table in the treatment center is not relevant in the absence of programming to promote skill generalization to home (and to successfully accomplish this, it may be necessary to know how many family members are present for breakfast or dinner, what condiments the family uses, or whether they use placemats). Initiating conversation with a therapist is of little value unless the social interaction program includes provisions for achieving skill transfer from therapist to parents. Learning to use the toilets at school and to buy snacks at the school store are splinter skills unless intervention agents take specific steps to ensure that the child can use the toilets at home, at church, and at the shopping center and can make purchases at the places his or her parents regularly shop. In summary, any curriculum for a child with autism is likely to be nonfunctional unless it is individualized to reflect his or her family members' interests, preferences, and usual activities and unless skill generalization is actively programmed to parents, siblings, and relatives and to home and community settings.

When selecting a treatment resource, a key evaluation dimension is an agency's expectations, policies, and procedures about family members' roles in intervention. Ideally, agency personnel encourage parents to advocate for their children, to give them key roles in selecting intervention goals, to provide instruction and hands-on training that enable them to be effective partners in intervention, and to support and reinforce their participation (Pinkston, et al., 1982). Agencies that discourage parent involvement are unlikely to represent good choices; treatment personnel come and go, but parents' responsibilities continue.

DISCUSSION AND IMPLICATIONS FOR PRACTICE

Although the well-documented practices described in the preceding paragraphs may be helpful indicators of program quality, there are some more general characteristics of intervention that are also predictive of positive outcomes for children. Two of these are age at intervention and program intensity: Treatment that begins earlier in a child's life and delivers many hours of intervention per day, week, or year is likely to produce greater benefits than intervention that begins later in life and delivers fewer hours (Jacobson et. al., 1998; Ramey & Ramey, 1998). These data set agendas for educating parents as well as pediatricians and other professionals in order to achieve increasingly early diagnoses and placements and for advocating for increased federal, state, and health insurance funding of early and intensive intervention. There is a growing body of data to support these initiatives. For example, Jacobson et al. (1998) report that, of children with autism who receive competently delivered, early, intensive behavioral intervention, 20 percent to 50 percent achieve normal functioning; 40 percent achieve meaningful, moderate gains; and only 10 percent continue to need intensive services in adulthood. These figures represent positive outcomes for children and families and substantial cost savings for government funding agencies.

A third indicator of program quality is the use of many versus few behavioral intervention procedures. In the best of circumstances, children with autism have opportunities to learn in many different ways that are defined by many different but well-documented procedures, such as discrete-trial training, incidental teaching, peer tutoring, video modeling and imitation, and use of photographic or written activity schedules (Krantz, 2000). Programs that confine their intervention efforts to single procedures and ignore the richness and depth of contemporary, empirically based practice may prevent children with autism from taking advantage of the wealth of learning opportunities available to their siblings and typical peers.

REFERENCES

American Psychiatric Association. (1994). *Diagnostic and statistical manual of mental disorders* (4th ed.). Washington, DC: Author.
Anderson, S. R., Taras, M., & Cannon, B. O. (1996). Teaching new skills to young

children with autism. In C. Maurice, G. Green, & S. C. Luce (Eds.), *Behavioral intervention for young children with autism: A manual for parents and professionals* (pp. 181–194). Austin, TX: Pro-Ed.

Baer, D. M. (1999). *How to plan for generalization.* Austin, TX: Pro-Ed.

Broden, M., Bruce, C., Mitchell, M. A., Carter, V., & Hall, R. V. (1970). Effects of teacher attention on attending behavior of two boys at adjacent desks. *Journal of Applied Behavior Analysis, 3,* 199–203.

Delquadri, J. C., Greenwood, C. R., Stretton, K., & Hall, R. V. (1983). The peer tutoring spelling game: A classroom procedure for increasing opportunity to respond and spelling performance. *Education and Treatment of Children, 6,* 225–239.

Green, G. (1996). Early behavioral intervention for autism. In C. Maurice, G. Green, & S. C. Luce (Eds.), *Behavioral intervention for young children with autism: A manual for parents and professionals* (pp. 29–44). Austin, TX: Pro-Ed.

Greenwood, C. R. (1999). Reflections on a research career: Perspective on 35 years of research at the Juniper Gardens Children's Project. *Exceptional Children, 66,* 7–21.

Hall, R. V., Lund, D., & Jackson, D. (1968). Effects of teacher attention on study behavior. *Journal of Applied Behavior Analysis, 1,* 1–12.

Harris, S. L. (1983). *Families of the developmentally disabled: A guide to behavioral intervention.* New York: Pergamon Press.

Horner, R. H., Day, H. M., Sprague, J. R., O'Brien, M., & Heathfield, L. T. (1991). Interspersed requests: A nonaversive procedure for reducing aggression and self-injury during instruction. *Journal of Applied Behavior Analysis, 24,* 265–278.

Jacobson, J. W., Mulick, J. A., & Green, G. (1998). Cost-benefit estimates for early intensive behavioral intervention for young children with autism: general model and single state case. *Behavioral Interventions, 13,* 201–226.

Kamps, D. M., Dugan, E. P., & Leonard, B. R. (1994). Enhanced small group instruction using choral responding and student interaction for children with autism and developmental disabilities. *American Journal on Mental Retardation, 99,* 60–73.

Koegel, R. L., Russo, D. C., & Rincover, A. (1977). Assessing and training teachers in the generalized use of behavior modification with autistic children. *Journal of Applied Behavior Analysis, 10,* 197–205.

Konarski, E. A., Jr., Favell, J. E., & Favell, J. E. (1992). *Manual for the assessment and treatment of the behavior disorders of people with mental retardation.* Morganton, NC: Western Carolina Center Foundation.

Krantz, P. J. (2000). Commentary: Interventions to facilitate socialization. *Journal of Autism and Developmental Disorders, 30,* 411–413.

Krantz, P. J., MacDuff, M. T., & McClannahan, L. E. (1993). Programming participation in family activities for children with autism: Parents' use of photographic activity schedules. *Journal of Applied Behavior Analysis, 26,* 137–138.

Lancioni, G. E., O'Reilly, M. F., & Emerson, E. (1996). A review of choice research with people with severe and profound developmental disabilities. *Research in Developmental Disabilities, 17,* 391–411.

Lovaas, O. I. (1977). *The autistic child: Language development through behavior modification.* New York: Wiley.

Mace, F. C., Hock, M. L., Lalli, J. S., West, B. J., Belfiore, P., Pinter, E., et al. (1988). Behavioral momentum in the treatment of noncompliance. *Journal of Applied Behavior Analysis, 21,* 123–141.

McClannahan, L. E., & Krantz, P. J. (1993). On systems analysis in autism intervention programs. *Journal of Applied Behavior Analysis, 26,* 589–596.

McClannahan, L. E., & Krantz, P. J. (1997). In search of solutions to prompt depend-ence: Teaching children with autism to use photographic activity schedules. In D. M. Baer & E. M. Pinkston (Eds.), *Environment and behavior* (pp. 271–278). Boulder, CO: Westview Press.

McClannahan, L. E., & Krantz, P. J. (1999). *Activity schedules for children with autism: Teaching independent behavior.* Bethesda, MD: Woodbine House.

McClannahan, L. E., Krantz, P. J., MacDuff, G. S., & Fenske, E. C. (1988). *Staff training and evaluation protocol.* Unpublished manuscript, Princeton Child Development Institute.

McClannahan, L. E., McGee, G. G., MacDuff, G. S., & Krantz, P. J. (1990). Assessing and improving child care: A personal appearance index for children with autism. *Journal of Applied Behavior Analysis, 23,* 469–482.

McConaughy, E. K., Stowitschek, J. J., Salzberg, C. L., & Peatross, D. K. (1989). Work supervisors' ratings of social behaviors related to employment success. *Rehabilita-tion Psychology, 34,* 3–15.

New York State Department of Health Early Intervention Program (1999). *Clinical practice guideline: The guideline technical report. Autism/pervasive developmental disorders, assessment and intervention for young children (age 0–3 years)* (Publi-cation No. 4217). Albany, NY: Author.

Pinkston, E. M., Levitt, J. L., Green, G. R., Linsk, N. L., & Rzepnicki, T. L. (1982). *Effec-tive social work practice.* San Francisco: Jossey-Bass.

Ramey, C. T., & Ramey, S. L. (1998). Early intervention and early experience. *Ameri-can Psychologist, 53,* 109–120.

Reid, D. H., & Green, C. W. (1998). *Determining quality outcome indicators in pro-grams for people who have the most significant disabilities.* Morganton, NC: Habil-itative Management Consultants.

Salzberg, C. L., Agran, M., & Lignugaris/Kraft, B. (1986). Behaviors that contribute to entry-level employment: A profile of five jobs. *Applied Research in Mental Retar-dation, 7,* 299–314.

Salzberg, C. L., Likins, M., McConaughy, E. K., & Lignugaris/Kraft, B. (1986). Social competence and employment of retarded persons. In N. Ellis & N. Bray (Eds.), *In-ternational Review of Research in Mental Retardation* (pp. 225–257). New York: Academic Press.

Smith, T. (1996). Are other treatments effective? In C. Maurice, G. Green, & S. C. Luce (Eds.), *Behavioral intervention for young children with autism* (pp. 45–59). Austin, TX: Pro-Ed.

Stanley, S. O., & Greenwood, C. R. (1983). How much "opportunity to respond" does the minority disadvantaged student receive in school? *Exceptional Children, 49,* 370–373.

Sundberg, M. L., & Partington, J. W. (1998). *Teaching language to children with autism or other developmental disabilities.* Danville, CA: Behavior Analysts.

Walker, H. M., & Calkins, C. F. (1986). The role of social competence in the commu-nity adjustment of persons with developmental disabilities: Processes and out-comes. *Remedial and Special Education, 7,* 46–53.

Wolf, M. M., Risley, T., & Mees, H. (1965). Application of operant conditioning proce-dures to the behavior problems of an autistic child. *Behavior Research and Ther-apy, 3,* 113–124.

CHAPTER 7

EVIDENCE-BASED PRACTICE WITH ANTISOCIAL AND DELINQUENT YOUTH: THE KEY ROLE OF FAMILY AND MULTISYSTEMIC INTERVENTION

Susan B. Stern

Current developments in intervention with aggressive, antisocial and delinquent youth parallel the theme of this book: family- and community-centered evidence-based treatment. Treatment-outcome research demonstrates that families are key change agents for antisocial and delinquent youth (Kumpfer, 1999; Stern, 2001). In like manner, best prevention practices draw attention to the family's importance in both the development and the early control of childhood aggression and conduct problems, which, in turn, strongly predict antisocial behavior and several related social problems among adolescents, including delinquency, violence, drug use, school failure and depression (Webster-Stratton & Taylor, 2001). These problems have profound negative consequences for the individual adolescent and, inevitably, for others in their environment and for society at large in terms of both human and economic costs.

This chapter focuses on understanding youth problem behavior in a systemic context that emphasizes, but goes beyond, family influences. Advances in research across adolescent problem areas converge to suggest additional important underpinnings for the design of effective intervention. First, sophisticated conceptual and statistical models have established that adolescent behavior is multiply determined by the reciprocal interaction of individual youth characteristics and characteristics of key social systems in which youth are embedded, which underscores the need for prevention and intervention programs that target not just the family but also multiple systems (Henggeler, 1991; Smith & Stern, 1997).

Second, problem behaviors do not occur in isolation. Adolescent antisocial behavior, delinquency, substance use, school dropout, risky sexual behavior, and teen pregnancy frequently co-occur (Allen, Leadbeater, & Aber, 1994; Ary, Duncan, Duncan, & Hops, 1999; Donovan, Jessor, & Costa, 1988). Furthermore, while some risk factors are unique to a specific problem area, on the whole, the risks for these interrelated behaviors across systems overlap substantially. Although not all adolescents experience multiple disorders, the evidence for a syndrome of problem behaviors for many youth implies the need for comprehensive services. Treatment needs to carefully address behaviors that may co-occur with delinquency, and prevention programs require an integrated approach that targets the similar and most powerful risk factors and strengthens common protective factors (Ary et al., 1999; Thornberry, Huizinga, & Loeber, 1995). Therefore, although this chapter specifically focuses on antisocial and delinquent behavior, it is more widely applicable to intervention with high-risk youth and families.

In the following sections, the empirical literature on risk and protective factors across system domains is reviewed with attention to highlighting strong and modifiable determinants of antisocial behavior and delinquency.[1] In line with the central thrust of this chapter, emphasis is on the prominent role of family processes alone and in interaction with other systems. Family treatment approaches that address these factors share several principles and strategies to guide effective practice; these are underscored following a review of empirically supported models. The remainder of the chapter spotlights multisystemic therapy (Henggeler, Schoenwald, Borduin, Rowland, & Cunningham, 1998), one of the leading empirically supported ecological and family-based intervention models for adolescent antisocial and delinquent behavior. Last, I will touch on the need to bridge the gap between research and practice and consider implications for the social work profession of research on multisystemic therapy and other evidence-based treatments for families with adolescents who have behavioral and emotional difficulties.

RISK AND PROTECTIVE FACTORS ACROSS SYSTEMS

Multiple risk factors across systems shape the development and maintenance of antisocial behavior and delinquency with family processes and peer relations playing key roles (Thornberry et al., 1995; U.S. Department of Health and Human Services, 1999). Risk factors increase the likelihood of a particular outcome but do not necessarily cause the outcome to occur. In addition, there is no single risk factor for antisocial behavior and delinquency; it is the accumulation and interaction of risk across family and other domains that increases the likelihood of adverse youth outcomes (Mrazek & Haggerty, 1994). Risk factors also vary in their salience across developmental periods (U.S. Department of Health and Human Services, 2001). Patterson and Yoerger (1993) have identified two developmental pathways for delinquency: an early onset path beginning before puberty, when family factors have the greatest impact, and a trajectory of adolescent late starters for whom peers and school may be more predominant (Simons, Wu, Conger, & Lorenz, 1994). Protective factors decrease the likelihood of youth engaging in problem behavior and may moderate or lessen the impact of risk factors in a youth's ecology (Jessor, Van Den Bos, Vanderryn, Costa, & Turbin, 1995).

---

1. Research on the development of antisocial behavior and delinquency are considered together because much of the behavior in question is similar and the distinction between the legal and psychopathological definitions is not clear cut (Tolan, Guerra, & Kendall, 1995).

As do the additive and interactive effects of risks, multiple protective processes have the greatest effect on reducing delinquency (Thornberry et al., 1995).

Direct Family Influences

Within the family, weak relationships between parent and child, conflict, and ineffective family management practices all significantly increase risk for anti-social behavior and delinquency (Loeber & Stouthamer-Loeber, 1986; Smith & Stern, 1997). Low attachment or bonding, rejection, and hostility, as well as lack of parents' support and involvement in their child's life characterize poor affective relationships and consistently have been linked with delinquency (Krohn, Stern, Thornberry, & Jang, 1992; Loeber & Stouthamer-Loeber, 1986). In contrast, family closeness is protective. Ties of affection and warmth encourage parent-child involvement and positive family interaction that, in turn, decrease the likelihood of deviant behavior (Kumpfer & DeMarsh, 1986; Patterson, Reid, & Dishion, 1992). According to social control theory (Hirschi, 1969), bonds to family and social institutions also promote conventional values, which inhibit antisocial and delinquent behavior, and attachment to parents can restrain youth even in situations of temptation. Studies of resilience (e.g., Werner & Smith, 1992) showing that a strong ongoing bond with one parent or another caregiver or adult in a child's life can be protective increase the relevance of the research findings on affective relationships and delinquency for the diversity of family constellations in a multicultural society.

Family management encompasses both socialization practices that shape and reinforce socially desirable and competent behavior and the critical parenting skills needed to control undesirable behavior. Of these, ineffective discipline practices (e.g., inconsistent, lax, or harsh coercive discipline) and inadequate monitoring and supervision particularly place youth at risk for problem behavior (Loeber & Stouthamer-Loeber, 1986). Effective monitoring requires adult caregivers to know where their children are, whom they are with, and what they are doing when they are not in sight, and it protects against both deviant behavior and association with deviant peers—a powerful proximal predictor of delinquency.

High levels of family conflict, including multiple forms of family violence, also increase risk for delinquency and youth violence as well as other behavioral and emotional problems (Thornberry, 1994; Thornberry et al., 1995). Family conflict, not surprisingly, lessens parent-adolescent involvement, which, in turn, contributes to inadequate monitoring and association with deviant peers (Ary et al., 1999). Negative communication and problem-solving skill deficits exacerbate family conflict and are associated with delinquency and other adolescent negative outcomes in a number of studies (e.g., Alexander, 1973; Hops, Tildesley, Lichtenstein, Ary, & Sherman, 1990) but not as strongly as are other family processes (Forehand, Miller, Dutra, & Chance, 1997; Smith & Stern, 1997). Notwithstanding, family intervention that targets communication and problem solving diminishes antisocial behavior, thus supporting their inclusion in intervention (Bry, Conboy, & Bisgay, 1986; Gordon, Arbuthnot, Gustafsond, & McGreen, 1988; Klein, Alexander, & Parsons, 1977). It also should be noted that antisocial youths' poor communication and problem-solving skills may interact with individual risk factors, including a cognitive bias to attribute hostile intent to others and beliefs supporting the use of aggression as a legitimate means to deal with conflict (Dodge & Frame, 1982; Slaby & Guerra, 1988).

Findings from contemporary studies suggest that the relationship between family processes and delinquency or other adverse youth outcomes holds up across ethnic groups (Boyd-Franklin & Bry, 2000; Forehand et al., 1997; Kumpfer, 1999), although important culturally specific differences emerge in a few studies that, if replicated, have implications for theory and intervention (see, e.g., Catalano et al., 1992). There are also contradictory findings across studies that examine the same family process. Illustrative of this, Smith and Krohn (1995) have found that parent control, which includes both monitoring and discipline, is not associated with decreased delinquency for Hispanic adolescents, in contrast with African American and Caucasian adolescents.[2] Other studies have found that parental monitoring similarly decreases deviant behavior for Hispanic and African American youths (Gorman-Smith, Tolan, Zelli, & Huesmann, 1996; Lamborn, Dornbusch & Steinberg, 1996). A notable study for the strength of its design and sample found a strong consistent role for the effects of high monitoring predicting lower rates of adolescent deviance across two ethnic groups—African American and Hispanic—and four urban settings (Forehand et al., 1997). Not intended as a full review, these examples underscore the need for more research that is representative of the diversity of families social workers serve, in order to better inform our understanding of cultural similarities and differences in family processes and youth outcomes. Equally imperative is the need for clinicians to know the research on family processes, given their significance in multiple studies for adolescent behavior, but to individualize assessment and monitor outcomes for each family.

The family risk factors thus far described encompass dynamic interactional family *processes*. Several additional family factors may increase risk for antisocial and delinquent behavior, including parental criminality, antisocial personality disorder, substance abuse, and mental health status as well as family poverty, stress, and social isolation (Kumpfer, 1999; Patterson et al., 1992; Smith & Stern, 1997). Although there are undoubtedly multiple pathways by which these factors affect youth outcomes, including genetic and cognitive ones, there is strong evidence that many influence behavior at least partially by disrupting parenting and family relationships (Conger & Elder, 1994; Conger, Patterson & Ge, 1995; Stern & Smith, 1995; Stern, Smith, & Jang, 1999). As one would expect, families coping

---

2. It is possible that Smith and Krohn's inclusion of discipline along with monitoring in their measurement of control contributes to their differing findings. There may be more cross-cultural variation in discipline than in other parenting processes.

with the effects of poverty, mental illness, and other forms of adversity face greater challenges in parenting. Moreover, because it is known that the risks associated with family adversity and parent mental health status negatively affect treatment engagement and outcome, interventions to improve parenting and parent-adolescent relationships must also address parental pressures and the wider ecology of family life.

Interacting Risk Factors with Family Processes

Family processes influence adolescent antisocial behavior and delinquency not only directly but also in interaction with other system influences. Most notably, family processes play a strong, indirect role through their interaction with peer association. Likewise, family processes are linked with risk factors at the school system level, indirectly affecting delinquency through lack of school success (Thornberry, Lizotte, Krohn, Farnworth, & Jang, 1991), and at the community level where neighborhoods with high crime, disorganization, and mobility and low support present barriers to effective parenting (Peebles & Loeber, 1994; Sampson, 1993; Stern & Smith, 1995).

With respect to peer association, family processes either can increase risk or be protective. To begin with, poor monitoring increases drift into a deviant peer group, especially during adolescence, when youth spend more unsupervised time with their peers (Dishion, Patterson, Stoolmiller, & Skinner, 1991; Snyder, Dishion, & Patterson, 1986). Developmental transitions require shifts in monitoring, and as antisocial children reach early adolescence, monitoring is particularly significant for preventing arrest risk (Ary et al., 1999; Patterson et al., 1992). In addition, troubled relationships and low parent-adolescent involvement contribute to inadequate monitoring, which increases problem behavior both directly and indirectly by promoting association with deviant peers, which is the final pathway to delinquency (Ary et al., 1999). On the other hand, attachment to parents and a supportive relationship protects against negative peer influences, either by preventing contact with deviant peers or by lessening the effects (Poole & Regoli, 1980; Warr, 1993). Importantly, even in the presence of delinquent peers, parents' involvement can counter peer influence and mitigate delinquency (Warr, 1993).

Coercion Theory

Patterson and colleagues (1982, 1992) have developed and tested a social learning model of the development and progression of antisocial behavior that incorporates the primary risk factors across systems. According to social learning theory, the beginnings of antisocial behavior are learned in the family, where daily interactions shape both prosocial and problem behavior in young children. When children whine, throw tantrums, or in other ways do not comply with adult requests, Patterson's coercion model assumes that less skilled or stressed parents unintentionally reinforce these behaviors by giving in and failing to provide appropriate consequences. When parents attempt to discipline but then back off, children learn that aversive behavior "works," and aggressive behavior is strengthened through positive reinforcement. In a reciprocal manner, parent behavior is negatively reinforced by cessation of aversive child behavior, thereby perpetuating cycles of inconsistent parenting, which, in turn, contribute to further antisocial behavior. Children who demonstrate impulsive, unresponsive, or overactive behavior are especially likely to resist efforts to control them (Maccoby, Snow, & Jacklin, 1984), which precipitates the "coercive cycle."

At the same time that the young aggressive child is developing coercive behaviors, he or she fails to learn the behaviors necessary for successful relationships with peers and in school. Upon entering school, a child who behaves aggressively is rejected by prosocial peers and is more likely to turn to other rejected and disruptive children, who reinforce one another's negative behaviors. Lacking behavioral and social competencies, the aggressive child also is at risk for academic difficulties. Peer rejection and school failures predict association with a deviant peer group, leading eventually to delinquency (Patterson et al., 1992). Meanwhile, at home, the additional problems outside the family intensify caregiver stress and further erode family control and climate (Ambert, 1992, 1997; Stern & Smith, 1999). As coercive interactions continue to escalate in multiple settings, protective parent behaviors that can moderate risk, such as youth advocacy, seeking information and support, and parent-school involvement, may become less likely as caregivers are confronted by the demands of parenting a difficult youth (Boyd-Franklin & Bry, 2000; Stern & Smith, 1999).

Tests of coercion theory based on observational data in families of aggressive children support the reciprocal effects described at the micro level of family interaction (Dishion, Patterson, & Kavanagh, 1992; Patterson & Dishion, 1988). Research also supports the developmental model of antisocial behavior with adolescents, taking into account peer and school influences as well as family management practices, especially coercive interactions and poor monitoring (Dishion, Patterson, & Reid, 1988; Dishion et al., 1991; Patterson, DeBaryshe, & Ramsey, 1989). A study involving older adolescents than had been observed previously found that the model generalized from antisocial behavior to an array of problem behaviors (Ary et al., 1999).

EVIDENCE-BASED INTERVENTION

Consistent with the empirical evidence, among those concerned with improving the delivery of juvenile justice and mental health services, there has been a shift toward recognizing the family's role in the attenuation as well as development of delinquency and other disorders through interventions targeted toward enhancing parenting and strengthening families. By viewing the family as part of the solution, practitioners can draw on and promote the protective factors available in many families, such as the positive aspects of parental or extended family love and concern, while empowering caregivers with knowledge and skills to reduce risk factors. From a prevention perspective, there is accumulating evidence that family interventions are stronger and more durable than those focused solely on youth (Kumpfer, 1999). With respect to treatment outcomes, I will review the most promising research-based family interventions, but it is also critical to articulate what does *not* work. A host of traditional interventions with antisocial and delinquent youth either have little evidence of effectiveness or have demonstrated iatrogenic effects, which is not surprising because association with deviant peers is a potent predictor of delinquency. The many programs that cluster youth together, whether in residential or therapy groups, fly in the face of compelling evidence. An influential study that documented negative peer influences illustrates the value of incorporating an understanding of risk factors across systems to inform prevention and intervention. Dishion and Andrews (1995) compare parent training alone (targeting family management) with adolescent groups alone (targeting youths' self-regulation deficits) and with a combined condition. Only parent training alone produced positive long-term outcomes. Counter to expectations of enhanced effects, the combined treatment showed no change for youth problem behavior, because, most likely, positive parenting changes and negative peer influence cancelled each other out. "Best practices," then, are clearly family focused and attentive to multiple systemic levels, from the individual to the cultural, and to the reciprocal interactions among them.

There is no one evidence-based treatment model for adolescent antisocial behavior and delinquency. There are, however, several empirically supported approaches that need to be continuously evaluated as they are adapted to various communities and diverse cultural groups. Each incorporates knowledge of risk and protective factors, builds on family interaction therapy and research, and is part of a program of ongoing research that informs evolving model development. Among these, multisystemic therapy (Henggeler & Borduin, 1990; Henggeler et al., 1998) and functional family therapy (Alexander, J., Pugh, C., Parsons, B., Sexton, T., 2000) were developed specifically to treat delinquency, although both now target a range of problems of at-risk youth and their families, while multidimensional treatment foster care (Chamberlain & Mihalic, 1998) addresses a similar group of youth requiring out-of-home placement. Multidimensional family therapy (Liddle, 1992; Liddle & Hogue, 2000) and brief strategic family therapy (Szapocznik & Kurtines, 1989; Szapocznik & Williams, 2000) concentrate on youth substance abuse and related problems. All but multisystemic therapy are described briefly below; multisystemic therapy will be discussed in detail in the following section.

Functional family therapy (FFT) is a family systems model with a strong behavioral orientation that gives attention to the *function* of behavior in the family relational system. It is a phase-oriented model in which FFT therapists initially concentrate on engagement and motivation by interrupting the family blaming process and developing a collaborative set. Once this has been accomplished, a behavior-change phase targets parenting deficits and the establishment of positive communication and problem-solving interactions. A more multisystemic generalization phase focuses on the family's relational needs and interactions with their environment. FFT began as a clinic model but has since been extended to include home-based services. Treatment outcome studies show that FFT decreases recidivism and out-of-home placement, improves family supportive relationships and climate, has favorable sibling effects, and is cost-effective (Alexander et al., 2000; Alexander & Parsons, 1973; Barton, Alexander, Waldron, Turner, & Warburton, 1985; Gordon et al., 1988; Gordon, Graves, & Arbuthnot, 1995; Klein et al., 1977). Besides outcome evaluations, research on FFT has examined in-session therapy process questions, most notably the change of negative, blaming family communication and the effects of therapist characteristics and behavior on process and outcome (Alexander, Barton, Schiavo, & Parsons, 1976; Newberry, Alexander, & Turner, 1991; Robbins, Alexander, & Turner, 2000). The model currently is being evaluated in increasingly multicultural contexts, although data are not yet published (Alexander et al., 2000).

Multidimensional treatment foster care (MTFC) is an extension of Patterson's social learning treatment to youth at risk of out-of-home placement for chronic and severe antisocial behavior, emotional disturbances, and delinquency. Development of the model speaks to both the difficulties of behavioral family intervention for delinquency in community settings (Dishion & Patterson, 1992) and the irony and ineffectiveness of placing antisocial youth together in groups and living arrangements. MTFC trains and supervises community families or experienced foster parents in family management to bring the adolescent's behavior under control. Concurrently, the youth's family receives parenting skills and family therapy and is supported toward reintegration and management of the adolescent. The youth is given skills training to get along with peers and in school and is closely supervised and cut off from delinquent peers. A case manager coordinates community contacts with parole or probation officers, the school, and others. MTFC is reported to be a cost-effective alternative to residential treatment, hospitalization, or incarceration (Chamberlain & Mihalic, 1998). It significantly reduced incarceration, compared with alternative residential care, in two studies (Chamberlain, 1990; Chamberlain & Reid, 1998) and facilitated quicker, less restrictive placement for youth discharged from a state mental hospital (Chamberlain & Reid, 1991). Current extensions of the model include research on MTFC for girls with involvement in both the juvenile justice and the mental health systems and replications at new sites (Chamberlain & Mihalic, 1998; Chamberlain & Moore, 2002). The former is exciting because much of the delinquency research on both family processes and intervention has been with boys, and less is known that is specific to female delinquency development and treatment implications.

Multidimensional family therapy (MDFT) and brief strategic family therapy (BSFT) show promising evidence of treatment effectiveness and relevance for family delinquency intervention, given the co-occurrence of drug use. Each approach has been developed with ethnically diverse urban youth and families. Both have roots in structural or structural strategic family therapy, but in response to changing family needs, clinical experience, and research findings, they have been broadened into more ecological approaches over the years. Both target risk and protective factors for youth substance abuse and both may be either clinic or home/community-based or a combination. Unlike the behavioral systems approaches, MDFT and BSFT do not explicitly "teach" skills; they focus more on modifying parenting behavior and parent-adolescent interactions through in-session enactment and restructuring (Minuchin, 1974).

MDFT and BSFT have each demonstrated favorable youth and family functioning outcomes in research studies (e.g., Liddle et al., 2001; Santisteban et al., 2003). Investigators of each approach have conducted significant research on engagement, the therapeutic alliance, and therapy change process (Liddle, 1995; Schmidt, Liddle, & Dakof, 1996; Santisteban et al., 1996). BSFT researchers have concentrated on understanding immigration and acculturation issues in diverse Hispanic families and on developing culturally responsive engagement and intervention strategies (Kurtines & Szapocznik, 1996). MDFT researchers explore strategies to address parent-adolescent reconnection and break impasses and are especially attentive to adolescent alliance building and understanding and using culturally relevant themes for African American youth (Diamond & Liddle, 1999; Jackson-Gilfort & Liddle, 1999; Liddle, Rowe, Dakof, & Lyke, 1998).

As is evident in this overview of treatment outcome studies, the findings from family processes and family intervention research converge to underscore that families play a key role in and pose a frontline defense against adolescent disorders. Although these brief overviews do not do justice, familiarity with each of the approaches offers the social work practitioner an introduction to research-based models and methods to enhance practice. The approaches share several themes with one another and with multisystemic treatment. Each approach has evolved over years of (continuing) clinical research and has been modified in response to family needs, changing contexts, and research findings. Each has a heavy emphasis on engagement and on being nonblaming, respectful, and empowering of families. Each approach is family based and targets parenting and family interactions. Each approach further acknowledges the multiple influences on youth development and the ecology of family life. All the models reviewed offer systematic and planful yet individualized and flexible methods for working with families.

I selected multisystemic therapy to expand on in this chapter for several reasons. First, of the models previously mentioned, it is the only one that was designed as an ecological model from its inception. Based on Bronfenbrenner's (1979) theory of social ecology, multisystemic therapy has a consistency and coherence in integrating knowledge of risk and protective factors in a youth's and a family's ecology throughout its assessment and treatment procedures. Second, it is the most extensively studied model and is considered to have the strongest evidence of treatment efficacy and effectiveness, as I will review subsequently. Third, though created to address antisocial and delinquent behavior, multisystemic therapy has been expanded to treat a range of serious youth problems, thus enhancing its potential relevance to social workers across multiple service systems (e.g., juvenile justice, mental health, child welfare). Fourth, there is a broad-based call for systems-level reform in child and adolescent services, with the intent of creating culturally competent, child-centered, and family-focused community-based comprehensive systems of care. The principles and procedures of multisystemic therapy are compatible with the values and principles supported by the National Institute of Mental Health's 1984 initiative establishing the Child and Adolescent Service System Program and with consumer advocacy groups (Henggeler et al., 1998). Among the core principles, intervention efforts not only need to include parents and other caregivers but also need to empower family members in a collaborative partnership in service planning and delivery (Henggeler, 1994: Stroul & Friedman, 1994). Finally, I view multisystemic therapy as essentially a social work model of a person in her or his reciprocally interacting environments.

MULTISYSTEMIC THERAPY

Multisystemic therapy (MST) is an ecological family- and community-based treatment model that draws on contemporary theoretical models with strong research evidence of the multisystemic influences (e.g., intrapersonal, family, peer, school, community) on youth behavior (Henggeler et al., 1998). Although similar to other family therapy models in targeting changes in both youth behavior and the family system as a whole, MST explicitly and systematically targets the multiple domains in which youth behavior is embedded. This does not necessarily mean that the worker intervenes in each system; rather, MST emphasizes empowering parents and other caregivers with the skills and support to develop and carry out change strategies across the key systems linked with adolescent problem behavior (Henggeler et al., 1998; Smith & Stern, 1997).

A set of nine guiding principles provides a structured framework within which MST case conceptualization and intervention occurs. At the same time, treatment is individualized and highly flexible, enabling practitioners to build on each family's specific strengths and to be responsive to their cultural context. An ecological assessment of strengths and needs occurs across each of the systems that have been linked with antisocial behavior. Following assessment, treatment is tailored for and with each family, drawing heavily on behavioral and cognitive-behavioral interventions with strong evidence of effectiveness as well as strategies from other empirically based or pragmatic problem-focused approaches such as structural and strategic family therapies. The flexibility of the MST framework allows for the integration of other interventions as new research becomes available, although flexibility should not be confused with eclecticism. MST is a prescriptive approach in that it tries to match research-informed treatment to specific youth and family situations. Monitoring throughout treatment provides feedback on the success or failure of selected strategies and accountability for outcomes. When treatment is not working, the MST therapist, supervisor, and treatment team develop hypotheses about barriers to intervention and generate ideas for overcoming them.

Services are provided using a family-preservation model in the youth's home and community, thus increasing access and engagement in treatment as well as ecological validity. As in the other approaches, extensive attention is given to engagement. Even though home-based treatment can facilitate engagement, it does not guarantee it, especially when engagement is viewed as an ongoing process signifying emotional investment and active participation and follow-through in intervention plans (Cunningham & Henggeler, 1999; Stern, 1999). MST's reported rate of engagement and treatment completion is high (Cunningham & Henggeler, 1999). When barriers to engagement occur, therapists identify what systemic obstacles exist and develop strategies to overcome them.

MST Treatment Principles

According to the first principle of MST (Henggeler et al., 1998), the overarching purpose of assessment is to determine the fit between problems that are occurring and the ecological context. To this end, the therapist helps the family identify any problems and strengths at the individual, family, peer, school, and community levels or interactions among them that might be linked with the problems. With their consent, additional information may be sought outside the family to gain the broader picture that multiple perspectives will often provide. Research on risk and protective factors across systems informs the process, helping a practitioner conduct a systematic yet individualized assessment. Not all families show the same risks, and each family has unique strengths and resources, often as a result of their cultural context. Moreover, the same processes can manifest differently across families. For example, close family bonds are protective in studies across racial and ethnic groups, yet may appear to be dissimilar, depending on the cultural context—teasing and sharing confidences or more formal interactions based on cultural concepts of "respect" might equally characterize warm, supportive relationships for different families (Boyd-Franklin & Bry, 2000). Understanding how a family's culture contributes to problems and potential solutions is an important component of assessing the fit between identified problems and the broader systemic context (Brondino et al., 1997).

Once information is gathered, the therapist sets goals in collaboration with the family and develops hypotheses that are testable based on observable and measurable events so that interventions can be continuously evaluated, consistent with one of the nine MST principles (Henggeler et al., 1998). Because MST is a present-focused and future-oriented model, proximal causes are considered before distal ones when generating hypotheses, although the latter are considered when they are linked with and impact current functioning (Henggeler et al., 1998). As for assessment, treatment effectiveness is monitored using multiple perspectives (e.g., father, grandmother, teacher, probation officer), and MST holds providers (therapist, supervisor, and support team) accountable for identifying and overcoming barriers to reaching treatment goals.

In addition to using empirically validated techniques, several principles guide the selection of treatment strategies. As presented in the treatment manual (Henggeler et al., 1998), interventions targeting specific, well-defined problems are present focused and action oriented, developmentally appropriate for both youth and caregivers, require daily and weekly effort by everyone involved in carrying out tasks and working on achieving goals, and are designed to promote responsible behavior and decrease irresponsible behavior. In accordance with another MST principle and the social work profession's values, treatment is strengths based. More specifically, the identified strengths within each system are used as levers for change.

Finally, as a logical extension of the social ecology model and a strengths perspective, two principles address the need for intervention to target sequences of behavior within and between the multiple systems (e.g., school and home) that maintain the identified problems and to promote the durability of treatment changes by empowering caregivers to similarly address family members' needs across ecological contexts.

Intervention Strategies

Intervention strategies in MST fall into five main categories (Henggeler et al., 1998). At its core, MST intervention emphasizes the modification of parenting practices and the strengthening of family functioning, which might include helping families cope with marital or family transition issues. Second, a group of intervention strategies target changing relationships with peers, specifically disengaging youth from deviant peers, fostering connection to prosocial peers and activities, and developing social competence and problem-solving skills. In line with the research on parent-peer linkages, empowering caregivers to monitor peer relationships and implement change strategies is central to success. Knowing other parents of peers and forming a network facilitate monitoring and supervision. A third set of interventions promotes academic and social competence in school and attends to the family-school linkage. Parents' involvement in their children's school life and monitoring of academic performance lessen the likelihood of the school failure and dropout outcomes associated with delinquency (Farrington, 1992).

Fourth, the MST manual (Henggeler at al., 1998) describes interventions to strengthen family linkages with community supports. Given the traditional strength of social workers in this area, I will highlight only two points. Assisting families to obtain resources both in the community and from formal agencies is an important component of family preservation programs and social work practice. But when seeking informal support, priority should be given to helping families find social support in their own environment. Therapy ends, parenting and support groups end, and it is hoped that multiple agency involvement ends, whereas grandparents, aunts, uncles, cousins, neighbors, coworkers, churches, temples, synagogues, boys and girls clubs, and so forth are embedded in a family's natural ecology. Second, when a reciprocal exchange of support can be negotiated instead of always having to depend on others for support, caregivers are empowered and mutually beneficial relationships are more likely to endure.

And fifth, the MST manual provides guidelines for deciding when individually oriented intervention might be required and outlines empirical interventions for a range of difficulties such as caregiver substance abuse or psychiatric problems, youth cognitive and problem-solving deficits, and victimization sequelae.

During MST engagement and intervention, therapists use an iterative process to identify obstacles to implementation, to test hypotheses about their role, and to generate solutions (Henggeler et al., 1998). Strategies for overcoming common barriers are described for each of the intervention areas. Of course, these do not cover all situations, and therapists need to actively and creatively problem solve with families when difficulties arise. Although such a process is not unique to MST, its structured, systematic use is exceptionally integrated throughout the model.

MST Research Outcomes

Reviewers and federal agencies alike have recognized MST either as a highly promising or an exemplary intervention model for antisocial and delinquent behavior (Elliot, 1998; Kazdin & Weisz, 1998; Kumpfer, 1999; McBride, VanderWaal, VanBuren, & Terry, 1997; U.S. Department of Health and Human Services, 1999). Reviewers largely note that MST has shown significant and sustained positive results across settings in modifying family processes and in attenuating adolescents' serious antisocial behavior, including long-term reductions in delinquency recidivism, incarceration, and costs (Washington State Institute for Public Policy, 1998). MST has reduced long-term rates of rearrest or out-of-home placement in three randomized trials with violent and chronic juvenile offenders (Borduin et al., 1995; Henggeler, Melton, & Smith, 1992; Henggeler, Melton, Brondino, Scherer, & Hanley, 1997; Henggeler, Melton, Smith, Schoenwald, & Hanley, 1993). In contrast, compared with usual community treatment, MST had limited effects in a study of substance abusing or dependent juvenile offenders with high rates of psychiatric comorbidity (Brown, Henggeler, Schoenwald, Brondino, & Pickrel, 1999; Henggeler, Clingempeel, Brondino, & Pickrel, 2002; Henggeler, Pickrel, & Brondino, 1999; Schoenwald, Ward, Henggeler, Pickrel, & Patel, 1996). As suggested by the researchers, poor treatment fidelity and the need for enhancements to multisystemic therapy specific to a challenging population of drug-using offenders may have contributed to the disappointing outcomes. In addition, two small randomized trials respectively suggest that MST may be effective with juvenile sex offenders (Borduin, Henggeler, Blaske, & Stein, 1990) and with child abuse and neglect (Brunk, Henggeler, & Whelan, 1987), although findings should be viewed cautiously, given the small sample sizes, the lack of follow-up in the maltreatment study, and no completed replications; encouragingly, a large clinical trial of MST for adolescent maltreatment is in progress. And finally, a randomized trial testing the effectiveness of MST as an alternative to psychiatric hospitalization for youth with serious emotional disorders initially showed favorable results on measures of symptoms, family functioning, out-of-home placement, and cost dimensions (Henggeler, Rowland, et al., 1999; Schoenwald, Ward, Henggeler, & Rowland, 2000), but unlike the long-term data for antisocial behavior, outcomes were not maintained at one year (Henggeler et al., 2003). Findings regarding changes in family functioning vary across studies, and two recent meta-analyses found no effects when individual study outcomes are pooled (Littell, 2004; Woolfenden, Williams, & Peat, 2003). Extensions of MST to new settings are under way, including research on MST implementation in school and neighborhood settings (Cunningham & Henggeler, 2001; Randall, Swenson, & Henggeler, 1999). Of note, families in MST studies tend to be economically disadvantaged, and a high percentage are African American. Treatment outcomes are reported to be equally effective for African American and white youth and families in studies that have examined this issue (Brondino et al., 1997).

Most of the research on multisystemic treatment has been conducted by Scott Henggeler, the model developer, and his colleagues, so a large, well-designed independent clinical trial of MST for serious young offenders currently under way in Ontario, Canada, is notable. The Ontario study involves 409 youths and their families in eight agencies across four communities. Interim results of the study show no overall differences between MST and services as usual on conviction rates and other key offending outcomes, with neither having desired effects on criminal behavior; changes in family functioning and youth and caregiver mental health, however, favor multisystemic treatment (Leschied & Cunningham, 2002). The study results regarding the long-term effectiveness of MST in reducing youth offending should be interpreted cautiously because follow-up is ongoing, some patterns that emerged in the data require further analysis, and several possible factors may have contributed to the outcomes. Quite aside from its substantive findings, the Ontario study underscores the importance of rigorous research evaluations as treatments deemed to be evidence-based are extended to new populations and contexts and become widely adopted, as I discuss in the next section. This point is further reinforced in a forthcoming systematic review of outcomes of multisystemic therapy (Littell, 2004). Its meta-analysis findings are considerably less favorable than those reported in individual studies, and the author's conclusion of no significant multisystemic impact on out-of-home placements, recidivism, or family functioning is at odds with previous reviewers' positive assessment of multisystemic treatment's evidence base.[3]

BRIDGING THE RESEARCH-PRACTICE GAP

As a result of the many favorable reviews of its evidence base, MST has been widely disseminated and targeted in federal efforts to move empirically sup-

---

3. Meta-analysis of outcomes from multiple studies may support a different conclusion than those drawn from the results of single studies or an unsystematic review. It is possible that a meta-analysis of any of the other models described in this chapter could raise issues similar to those identified in Littell's (2004) multisystemic review.

ported treatments into real-world, community-based practice settings to bridge the gap between efficacy and effectiveness (Brown et al., 1997; Hoagwood, Hibbs, Brent, & Jensen, 1995). A strength of multisystemic therapy is that from the beginning it has addressed serious adolescent problems reflective of actual practice in the natural environments of youths and families. It has been suggested that MST is *effective* when implemented with integrity in community settings. Nonetheless, caution is warranted when drawing conclusions about effectiveness, considering the mixed findings presented in the previous section. Moreover, there are several challenges to its dissemination. Foremost is the challenge to implement MST with fidelity and to identify the critical supports necessary to achieve this (Schoenwald, Brown, & Henggeler, 2000). A number of studies have shown that clinicians' adherence to the nine underlying MST principles is linked to favorable youth outcomes (Henggeler, et al., 1997; Henggeler, Pickrel, et al., 1999; Huey, Henggeler, Brondino, & Pickrel, 2000; Schoenwald, Henggeler, Brondino, & Rowland, 2000). Low levels of adherence and more modest outcomes than in previous studies occurred when the original developers of MST did not directly supervise treatment implementation and adherence as typical of agency conditions. Even so, analysis of adherence data indicated that outcomes were substantially better in cases in which treatment adherence ratings were high, underscoring the importance of implementing treatment as intended. These findings also speak to the critical role of supervision required for skilled implementation of MST. Efforts to boost adherence have included development of a supervisory manual (Henggeler & Schoenwald, 1998) and refinement of procedures (Schoenwald, Henggeler, et al., 2000), along with research on the links between supervision fidelity and therapist adherence to the treatment protocol (Henggeler, Schoenwald, Liao, Letourneau, & Edwards, 2002). In addition, MST has extensive training and consultation and organizational protocols, as well as a quality assurance system that is itself multisystemic and extends from the clinical to the organizational level (Henggeler & Schoenwald, 1999; Schoenwald, 1998; Schoenwald, Brown, et al., 2000). With respect to these efforts and implications for program and policy decisions, a current large multisite study funded by the National Institute of Mental Health (Sonja Schoenwald, principal investigator) is further investigating factors that can affect treatment adherence and transportability in the broader context of community-based practice, ranging from practitioner-level to organizational and extra-organizational characteristics and practices.[4] This study has the potential to shed significant light on multisystemic therapy's effectiveness.

Social workers historically have been attentive to the ecological context of individuals and families, so it would not be surprising if some dismissed MST as nothing new. Indeed, the ideas behind MST are not that different from and reflect

---

4. Along the same lines as MST, all the models reviewed in this chapter either have or are in the process of developing treatment manuals, training protocols, and procedures for monitoring therapist adherence and treatment progress and outcome, as well as tackling important issues of dissemination and effectiveness.

what is usually considered good social work practice. However, despite the caveats noted, MST clearly warrants our attention in light of its empirical underpinnings and extensive research program, which should be considered in conjunction with the mixed evidence of effectiveness for other family preservation programs (Blythe, Salley, & Jayaratne, 1994) and little evidence of effectiveness for practice as usual with children and adolescents in community agencies (Hoagwood et al., 1995; Taylor, Eddy, & Biglan, 1999; Weisz, Donenberg, Han, & Weiss, 1995). Littell (2004) suggests that social work practitioners might try to improve multisystemic outcomes, keeping the need for rigorous evaluation in mind, a point with which I strongly concur. MST provides a valuable framework for evidence-based social work practice. What MST does beyond embracing an ecological approach that targets the known determinants of antisocial and delinquent behavior across multiple systems is twofold. First, it operationalizes a set of empirically grounded principles associated with successful outcomes and monitors adherence to them to explicitly guide case conceptualization and therapist activity. Second, MST therapists incorporate empirical intervention strategies throughout treatment.

Bridging the gap between research on empirically based practice and real-world implementation calls for a professional commitment to accountability for outcomes and requires partnerships among researchers, providers, families, policy makers, and funders (Stern, 2001). Several initiatives are already under way. The Office of Juvenile Justice and Delinquency Prevention has launched a "strengthening families" technology transfer program and is compiling and disseminating family-based model programs, including the ones previously discussed, for delinquency prevention (Kumpfer, 1999). The office also has funded the development of "Blueprints for Violence Prevention" for the dissemination of programs they judge exemplary (MST, FFT, and MTFC are among these) and for technical assistance to communities to support implementation efforts (Elliot, 1998). In tandem with these valuable initiatives, we need careful evaluation of their outcomes and further research on the numerous issues above and beyond treatment integrity critical to the dissemination of evidence-based models (see, e.g., Schoenwald & Hoagwood, 2001). Transporting evidence-based programs from research to community settings is neither a simple nor a one-way process and requires attention to the mutual "fit" with the complexities of contemporary practice and the unique strengths and characteristics of an agency, its practitioners, and the youth and families served. As social workers, we can bring our wealth of expertise in community-based practice and understanding of diverse families to this task and the exciting opportunities currently available for further development, dissemination, and evaluation of evidence-based family models—all in the service of improving outcomes for youth and families.

REFERENCES

Alexander, J. F. (1973). Defensive and supportive communication in normal and deviant families. *Journal of Consulting and Clinical Psychology, 40,* 223–231.

Alexander, J. F., Barton, C., Schiavo, R. S., & Parsons, B. V. (1976). Behavioral interventions with families of delinquents: Therapist characteristics and outcome. *Journal of Consulting and Clinical Psychology, 44*(4), 656–664.

Alexander, J. F., & Parsons, B. V. (1973). Short-term behavioral intervention with delinquent families: Impact on family processes and recidivism. *Journal of Abnormal Psychology, 81,* 219–225.

Alexander, J. F., Pugh, C., Parsons, B., & Sexton, T. (2000). Functional family therapy. In D. S. Elliott (Series ed.), *Blueprints for violence prevention.* Golden, CO: Venture Publishing.

Allen, J. P., Leadbeater, B. J., & Aber, J. L. (1994). The development of problem behavior syndromes in at-risk adolescents. *Development and Psychopathology, 6,* 323–342.

Ambert, A. M. (1992). *The effect of children on parents.* New York: Haworth Press.

Ambert, A. M. (1997). *Parents, children, and adolescents: Interactive relationships and development in context.* New York: Haworth Press.

Ary, D. V., Duncan, T. E., Duncan, S. C., & Hops, H. (1999). Adolescent problem behavior: The influence of parents and peers. *Behaviour Research and Therapy, 37,* 217–230.

Barton, C., Alexander, J. F., Waldron, H., Turner, C. W., & Warburton, J. (1985). Generalizing treatment effects of Functional Family Therapy: Three replications. *American Journal of Family Therapy, 13,* 16–26.

Blythe, B. J., Salley, M. P., & Jayaratne, S. (1994). A review of intensive family preservation services research. *Social Work Research, 18,* 213–224.

Borduin, C. M., Henggeler, S. W., Blaske, D. M., & Stein, R. (1990). Multisystemic treatment of adolescent sexual offenders. *International Journal of Offender Therapy and Comparative Criminology, 35,* 105–114.

Borduin, C. M., Mann, B. J., Cone, L. T., Henggeler, S. W., Fucci, B. R., Blaske, D. M., et al. (1995). Multisystemic treatment of serious juvenile offenders: Long term prevention of criminality and violence. *Journal of Consulting and Clinical Psychology, 63,* 569–578.

Boyd-Franklin, N., & Bry, B. H. (2000). *Reaching out in family therapy: Home-based, school, and community interventions.* New York: Guilford Press.

Brondino, M. J., Henggeler, S. W., Rowland, M. D., Pickrel, S. G., Cunningham, P. B., & Schoenwald, S. K. (1997). Multisystemic therapy and the ethnic minority client: Culturally responsive and clinically effective. In D. K. Wilson, J. R. Rodrigue, & W. C. Taylor (Eds.), *Health-promoting and health-compromising behaviors among minority adolescents* (pp. 229–250). Washington, DC: American Psychological Association.

Brown, T. L., Henggeler, S. W., Schoenwald, S. K., Brondino, M. J., & Pickrel, S. G. (1999). Multisystemic treatment of substance abusing and dependent juvenile delinquents: Effects on school attendance at posttreatment and 6-month follow-up. *Children's Services: Social Policy, Research, and Practice, 2,* 81–93.

Brown, T. L., Swenson, C. C., Cunningham, P. B., Henggeler, S. W., Schoenwald, S. K., & Rowland, M. D. (1997). Multisystemic treatment of violent and chronic juvenile offenders: Bridging the gap between research and practice. *Administration and Policy in Mental Health, 25,* 221–238.

Bronfenbrenner, U. (1979). *The ecology of human development: Experiments by design and nature.* Cambridge, MA: Harvard University Press.

Brunk, M., Henggeler, S. W., & Whelan, J. P. (1987). A comparison of multisystemic therapy and parent training in the brief treatment of child abuse and neglect. *Journal of Consulting and Clinical Psychology, 55,* 311–318.

Bry, B. H., Conboy, C., & Bisgay, K. (1986). Decreasing adolescent drug use and school failure: Long-term effects of targeted family problem-solving training. *Child & Family Behavior Therapy, 8,* 43–59.

Catalano, R. F., Morrison, D. M., Wells, E. A., Gillmore, M. R., Iritani, B., & Hawkins, J. D. (1992). Ethnic differences in family factors related to early drug initiation. *Journal of Studies on Alcohol, 53*(3), 208–217.

Chamberlain, P. (1990). Comparative evaluation of specialized foster care for seriously delinquent youths: A first step. *Community Alternatives: International Journal of Family Care, 2,* 21–36.

Chamberlain, P., & Mihalic, S. F. (1998). *Blueprints for violence prevention: Multisystemic therapy.* D. S. Elliott (Series ed.), University of Colorado, Center for the Study of and Prevention of Violence. Boulder, CO: Blueprints Publications.

Chamberlain, P., & Moore, K. J. (2002). Chaos and trauma in the lives of adolescent females with antisocial behavior and delinquency. *Journal of Aggression, Maltreatment & Trauma, 1,* 79–108.

Chamberlain, P., & Reid, J. B. (1991). Using a specialized foster care community treatment model for children and adolescents leaving the state mental hospital. *Journal of Community Psychology, 19,* 266–276.

Chamberlain, P., & Reid, J. B. (1998). Comparison of two community alternatives to incarceration for chronic juvenile offenders. *Journal of Consulting and Clinical Psychology, 66,* 624–633.

Conger, R. D., & Elder, G. H. (1994). *Families in troubled times: Adapting to change in rural America.* New York: Aldine de Gruyter.

Conger, R. D., Patterson, G. R., & Ge, X. (1995). It takes two to replicate: A mediational model for the impact of parents' stress on adolescent adjustment. *Child Development, 65,* 541–561.

Cunningham, P. B., & Henggeler, S. W. (1999). Engaging multiproblem families in treatment: Lessons learned throughout the development of multisystemic therapy. *Family Process, 38*(3), 265–286.

Cunningham, P. B., & Henggeler, S. W. (2001). Implementation of an empirically based drug and violence prevention and intervention program in public school settings. *Journal of Clinical Child Psychology, 30,* 221–232.

Diamond, G. S., & Liddle, H. A. (1999). Transforming negative parent-adolescent interactions. *Family Process, 38,* 5–26

Dishion, T. J., & Andrews, D. W. (1995). Preventing escalation in problem behaviors with high-risk young adolescents: Immediate and one-year outcomes. *Journal of Consulting and Clinical Psychology, 63,* 538–548.

Dishion, T. J., & Patterson, G. R. (1992). Age effects in parent training. *Behavior Therapy, 23,* 719–729.

Dishion, T. J., Patterson, G. R., & Kavanagh, K. A. (1992). An experimental test of the coercion model. In J. McCord & R. E. Tremblay (Eds.), *Preventing antisocial behavior: Interventions from birth through adolescence* (pp. 53–282). New York: Guilford Press.

Dishion, T. J., Patterson, G. R., & Reid, J. (1988). Parent and peer factors associated with early adolescent drug use: Implications for treatment. In E. Radhert & J. Grabowski (Eds.), *Adolescent drug abuse: Analysis of treatment research, NIDA Research Monograph* (Vol. 77, pp. 69–93). Washington DC: U.S. Government Printing Office.

Dishion, T. J., Patterson, G. R., Stoolmiller, M., & Skinner, M. L. (1991). Family, school, and behavioral antecedents to early adolescent involvement with antisocial peers. *Developmental Psychology, 27*(1), 172–180.

Dodge, K. A., & Frame, C. M. (1982). Social cognitive biases and deficits in aggressive boys. *Child Development, 53*, 620–635.

Donovan, J. E., Jessor, R., & Costa, F. M. (1988). Syndrome of problem behavior in adolescence: A replication. *Journal of Consulting and Clinical Psychology, 56*(5), 762–765.

Elliott, D. S. (Series ed.). (1998). *Blueprints for violence prevention.* University of Colorado, Center for the Study and Prevention of Violence. Boulder, CO: Blueprints Publications. Available at http://www.colorado.edu/cspv/blueprints

Farrington, D. (1992). Juvenile delinquency. In J. C. Coleman (Ed.), *The school years* (pp. 122–163). London: Routledge.

Forehand, R., Miller, K. S., Dutra, R., & Chance, M. W. (1997). Role of parenting in adolescent deviant behavior: Replication across and within two ethnic groups. *Journal of Consulting and Clinical Psychology, 65*(6), 1036–1041.

Gordon, D. A., Arbuthnot, J., Gustafsond, K. E., & McGreen, P. (1988). Home-based behavioral systems family therapy with disadvantaged juvenile delinquents. *American Journal of Family Therapy, 16,* 243–255.

Gordon, D. A., Graves, K., & Arbuthnot, J. (1995). The effect of functional family therapy for delinquents on adult criminal behavior. *Criminal Justice and Behavior, 22,* 60–73.

Gorman-Smith, D., Tolan, P. H., Zelli, A., & Huessmann, L. R. (1996). The relation of family functioning to violence among inner-city youths. *Journal of Family Psychology, 10,* 115–129.

Henggeler, S. W. (1991). Multidimensional causal models of delinquent behavior. In R. Cohen & A. Siegel (Eds.), *Context and development* (pp. 211–231). Hillsdale, NJ: Erlbaum.

Henggeler, S. W. (1994). A consensus: Conclusions of the APA task force report on innovative models of mental health service for children, adolescents, and their families. *Journal of Clinical Child Psychology, 23*(Suppl.), 3–6.

Henggeler, S. W., & Borduin, C. M. (1990). *Family therapy and beyond: A multisystemic approach to treating the behavior problems of children and adolescents.* Pacific Grove, CA: Brooks/Cole.

Henggeler, S. W., Clingempeel, W. G., Brondino, M. J., & Pickrel, S. G. (2002). Four-year follow-up of multisystemic therapy with substance-abusing and substance-dependent juvenile offenders. *Journal of the American Academy of Child and Adolescent Psychiatry, 41,* 868–874.

Henggeler, S. W., Melton, G. B., Brondino, M. J., Scherer, D. G., & Hanley, J. H. (1997). Multisystemic therapy with violent and chronic juvenile offenders and their families: The role of treatment fidelity in successful dissemination. *Journal of Consulting and Clinical Psychology, 65,* 821–833.

Henggeler, S. W., Melton, G. B., & Smith, L. A. (1992). Family preservation using multisystemic family therapy: An effective alternative to incarcerating serious juvenile offenders. *Journal of Consulting and Clinical Psychology, 60,* 953–961.

Henggeler, S. W., Melton, G. B., Smith, L. A., Schoenwald, S. K., & Hanley, J. H. (1993). Family preservation using multisystemic treatment: Long-term follow-up to a clinical trial with serious juvenile offenders. *Journal of Child and Family Studies, 2,* 283–293.

Henggeler, S. W., Pickrel, S. G., & Brondino, M. J. (1999). Multisystemic treatment of substance abusing and dependent delinquents: Outcomes, treatment fidelity, and transportability. *Mental Health Services Research, 1,* 171–184.

Henggeler, S. W., Rowland, M. D., Halliday-Boykins, C., Sheidow, A. J., Ward, D. M., Randall, J., et al. (2003). One-year follow-up of multisystemic therapy as an alternative to the hospitalization of youths in psychiatric crisis. *Journal of the American Academy of Child and Adolescent Psychiatry, 42,* 543–551.

Henggeler, S. W., Rowland, M. D., Randall, J., Ward, D. M., Pickrel, S. G, Cunningham, P. B., et al. (1999). Home-based multisystemic therapy as an alternative to the hospitalization of youth in psychiatric crisis: Clinical outcomes. *Journal of the American Academy of Child and Adolescent Psychiatry, 38,* 1331–1339.

Henggeler, S. W., & Schoenwald, S. K. (1998). *The MST supervisory manual: Promoting quality assurance at the clinical level.* Charleston, SC: MST Institute.

Henggeler, S. W., & Schoenwald, S. K. (1999). The role of quality assurance in achieving outcomes in MST programs. *Journal of Juvenile Justice and Detention Services, 14,* 1–17.

Henggeler, S. W., Schoenwald, S. K., Borduin, C. M., Rowland, M. D., & Cunningham, P. B. (1998). *Multisystemic treatment of antisocial behavior in children and adolescents.* New York: Guilford.

Henggeler, S. W., Schoenwald, S. K., Liao, J. G., Letourneau, E. J., & Edwards, D. L. (2002). Transporting efficacious treatments to field settings: The link between supervisory practices and therapist fidelity in MST programs. *Journal of Clinical Child & Adolescent Psychology, 31,* 155–167.

Hirschi, T. W. (1969). *Causes of delinquency.* Berkeley, CA: University of California Press.

Hoagwood, K., Hibbs, E., Brent, D., & Jensen, P. (1995). Introduction to the special section: Efficacy and effectiveness in studies of child and adolescent psychotherapy. *Journal of Consulting and Clinical Psychology, 63,* 683–687.

Hops, H., Tildesley, E., Lichtenstein, E., Ary, D., & Sherman, L. (1990). Parent-adolescent problem-solving interactions and drug use. *American Journal of Drug and Alcohol Abuse, 16,* 239–258.

Huey, S. J., Henggeler, S. W., Brondino, M. J., & Pickrel, S. G. (2000). Mechanisms of change in multisystemic therapy: Reducing delinquent behavior through therapist adherence and improved family and peer functioning. *Journal of Consulting and Clinical Psychology, 68,* 451–467.

Jackson-Gilfort, A., & Liddle, H. A. (1999). Culturally specific interventions for African American adolescents. *Family Psychologist 15,* 6, 12.

Jessor, R., Van Den Bos, J., Vanderryn, J., Costa, F. M., & Turbin, M. S. (1995). Protective factors in adolescent problem behavior: Moderator effects and developmental change. *Developmental Psychology, 31*(6), 923–933.

Kazdin, A. E., & Weisz, J. R. (1998). Identifying and developing empirically supported child and adolescent treatments. *Journal of Consulting and Clinical Psychology, 66,* 19–36.

Klein, N. C., Alexander, J. F., & Parsons, B. V. (1977). Impact of family systems intervention on recidivism and sibling delinquency: A model of primary prevention and program evaluation. *Journal of Consulting and Clinical Psychology, 45,* 469–474.

Krohn, M. D., Stern, S. B., Thornberry, T. P., & Jang, S. J. (1992). The measurement of family process variables: The effect of adolescent and parent perceptions of family life on delinquent behavior. *Journal of Quantitative Criminology, 8,* 287–315.

Kumpfer, K. L. (1999). *Strengthening America's families: Exemplary parenting and family strategies for delinquency prevention.* U.S. Department of Justice. Retrieved June 5, 2001, from http://www/strengtheningfamilies.org

Kumpfer, K. L., & DeMarsh, J. P. (1986). Family environmental and genetic influences on children's future chemical dependency. In S. Griswold-Ezekoye, K. L. Kumpfer, & W. Bukoski (Eds.), *Childhood and chemical abuse: Prevention and intervention* (pp. 49–91). New York: Haworth.

Kurtines, W. M., & Szapocznik, J. (1996). Structural family therapy in contexts of cultural diversity. In E. Hibbs & R. Jensen (Eds.), *Psychosocial treatment and research with children and adolescents.* Washington, DC: American Psychological Association.

Lamborn, S. D., Dornbusch, S. M., & Steinberg, L. (1996). Ethnicity and community context as moderators of the relations between family decision making and adolescent adjustment. *Child Development, 67,* 283–301.

Leschied, A. W., & Cunningham, A. (2002). *Seeking effective interventions for serious young offenders: Interim results of a four-year randomized study of multisystemic therapy in Ontario, Canada.* London, Ontario: Centre for Children and Families in the Justice System.

Liddle, H. A. (1992). A multidimensional model for treating the adolescent who is abusing alcohol and other drugs. In W. Snyder & T. Ooms (Eds.), *Empowering families: Family centered treatment of adolescents with alcohol, drug abuse, and mental health problems* (pp. 91–100). Rockville, MD: U.S. Department of Health and Human Services, Office of Treatment Improvement.

Liddle, H. A. (1995). Conceptual and clinical dimensions of a multi-dimensional, multi-systems engagement strategy in family based adolescent treatment. *Psychotherapy, 32,* 39–54.

Liddle, H. A., Dakof, G. A., Parker, K., Diamond, G. S., Barrett, K., & Tejeda, M. (2001). Multidimensional family therapy for adolescent drug abuse: Results of a randomized clinical trial. *American Journal of Drug and Alcohol Abuse, 27,* 651–688.

Liddle, H. A., & Hogue, A. (2000). A family based developmental-ecological preventive intervention for high-risk adolescents. *Journal of Marital and Family Therapy, 26(3),* 265–279.

Liddle, H. A., Rowe, C. L., Dakof, G. A., & Lyke, J. (1998). Translating parenting research into clinical interventions for families of adolescents. *Clinical Child Psychology and Psychiatry, 3,* 419–443.

Littell, J. H. (2004, January). Systematic and nonsystematic reviews of effects of multisystemic therapy. Paper presented at the 8th Annual Conference of the Society for Social Work and Research, New Orleans, LA.

Loeber, R., & Stouthamer-Loeber, M. (1986). Family factors as correlates and predictors of juvenile conduct problems and delinquency. In M. Tonry & N. Morris (Eds.), *Crime and Justice: An Annual Review of Research, 7,* 29–149.

Maccoby, E. E., Snow, M. E., & Jacklin, C. N. (1984). Children's dispositions and mother-child interaction at 12 and 18 months: A short-term longitudinal study. *Developmental Psychology, 20*(3), 459–472.

McBride, D., VanderWaal, C., VanBuren, H., & Terry, Y. (1997). *Breaking the cycle of drug use among juvenile offenders.* Washington, DC: National Institute of Justice.

Minuchin, S. (1974). *Families and family therapy.* MA: Harvard University Press.

Mrazek, P. J., & Haggerty, R. J. (Eds.). (1994). *Reducing risks for mental disorders: Frontiers for preventive intervention research.* Washington, DC: National Academy Press.

Newberry, A. M., Alexander, J. F., & Turner, C. W. (1991). Gender as a process variable in family therapy. *Journal of Family Psychology, 5,* 158–175.

Patterson, G. R. (1982). *Coercive family process.* Eugene, OR: Castalia Publishing.

Patterson, G. R., DeBaryshe, B. D., & Ramsey, E. (1989). A developmental perspective on antisocial behavior. *American Psychologist, 44*(2), 329–335.

Patterson, G. R., & Dishion, T. (1988). Multilevel family process models: Traits, interactions, and relationships. In R. A. Hinde & J. Stevenson-Hinde (Eds.), *Relationships within families: Mutual influences.* Oxford: Clarendon.

Patterson, G. R., Reid, J. B., & Dishion, T. J. (1992). *Antisocial boys.* Eugene, OR: Castalia Publishing.

Patterson, G. R., & Yoerger, K. (1993). Developmental models for delinquent behavior. In S. Hodgins (Ed.), *Crime and mental disorders* (pp. 140–172). Newbury Park, CA: Sage.

Peebles, F., & Loeber, R. (1994). Do individual factors and neighborhood context explain ethnic differences in juvenile delinquency. *Journal of Quantitative Criminology, 10,* 141–157.

Poole, E. D., & Regoli, R. M. (1980). Parental support, delinquent friends, and delinquency: A test of interaction effects. *Journal of Criminal Law and Criminology, 70*(2), 188–193.

Randall, J., Swenson, C. C., & Henggeler, S. W. (1999). Neighborhood solutions for neighborhood problems: An empirically based violence prevention collaboration. *Health Education and Behavior, 26*(6), 806–820.

Robbins, M. S., Alexander, J. F., Newall, R. M., & Turner, C. W. (1996). The immediate effect of reframing on client attitude in family therapy. *Journal of Family Psychology, 10,* 28–34.

Sampson, R. (1993). Family and community level influences on adolescent delinquency in the inner city of Chicago. Paper presented at the 60th anniversary meeting of the Society for Research in Child Development, New Orleans, March, 1993.

Santisteban, D. A., Copatsworth, J. D., Perez-Vidal, A., Kurtines, W. M., Schwartz, S. J., Murray, E. J., et al. (2003). Efficacy of brief strategic family therapy in modifying Hispanic adolescent behavior problems and substance use. *Journal of Family Psychology, 17,* 121–133.

Santisteban, D. A., Szapocznik, J., Perez-Vidal, A., Kurtines, W. M., Murray, E. J., & Laperriere, A. (1996). Efficacy of intervention for engaging youth and families into treatment and some variables that may contribute to differential effectiveness. *Journal of Family Psychology, 10*(1), 35–44.

Schmidt, S. E., Liddle, H. A., & Dakoff, G. A. (1996). Changes in parenting practices and adolescent drug abuse during multidimensional family therapy. *Journal of Family Psychology, 10*(1), 12–27.

Schoenwald, S. K. (1998). *Multisystemic therapy consultation guidelines.* Family Services Research Center, Medical University of South Carolina, Charleston.

Schoenwald, S. K., Brown, T. L., & Henggeler, S. W. (2000). Inside multisystemic therapy: Therapist, supervisory, and program practices. *Journal of Emotional and Behavioral Disorders, 8,* 113–127.

Schoenwald, S. K., Henggeler, S. W., Brondino, M. J., & Rowland, M. D. (2000). Multisystemic therapy: Monitoring treatment fidelity. *Family Process 39,* 83–103.

Schoenwald, S. K., & Hoagwood, K. (2001). Effectiveness, transportability, and dissemination of interventions: What matters when? *Psychiatric Services, 52,* 1190–1197.

Schoenwald, S. K., Ward, D. M., Henggeler, S. W., Pickrel, S. G., & Patel, H. (1996). MST treatment of substance abusing or dependent adolescent offenders: Costs of reducing incarceration, inpatient, and residential placement. *Journal of Child and Family Studies, 5,* 431–444.

Schoenwald, S. K., Ward, D. M., Henggeler, S. W., & Rowland, M. D. (2000). Multisystemic therapy versus hospitalization for crisis stabilization of youth: Placement outcomes 4 months postreferral. *Mental Health Services Research, 2(1),* 3–12.

Simons, R. L., Wu, C., Conger, R. D., & Lorenz, F. O. (1994). Two routes to delinquency: differences between early and late starters in the impact of parenting and deviant peers. *Criminology, 32,* 247–275.

Slaby, R. G., & Guerra, N. G. (1988). Cognitive mediators of aggression in adolescent offenders: 1. Assessment. *Developmental Psychology, 24,* 580–588.

Smith, C. A., and Krohn, M. D. (1995). Delinquency and family life among male adolescents: the role of ethnicity. *Journal of Youth and Adolescence, 24,* 69–93.

Smith, C. A., & Stern, S. B. (1997). Delinquency and antisocial behavior: A review of family processes and intervention research. *Social Service Review, 71,* 382–420.

Snyder, J., Dishion, T. J., & Patterson, G. R. (1986). Determinants and consequences of associating with deviant peers during preadolescence and adolescence. *Journal of Early Adolescence, 6,* 29–43.

Stern, S. B. (1999). Challenges to family engagement: What can multisystemic therapy teach family therapists? *Family Process, 38(3),* 281–285.

Stern, S. B. (2001). Outcomes research for children and adolescents: Implications for children's mental health and managed care. In N. W. Veeder & W. Peebles-Wilkins (Eds.), *Managed care services: Policy, programs and research* (pp. 187–212). New York: Oxford University Press.

Stern, S. B., & Smith, C. A. (1995). Family processes and delinquency in an ecological context. *Social Service Review, 69,* 703–731.

Stern, S. B., & Smith, C. A. (1999). Reciprocal relationships between antisocial behavior and parenting: Implications for delinquency intervention. *Families in Society, 80,* 169–181.

Stern, S. B., Smith, C. A., & Jang, S. J. (1999). Urban families and adolescent mental health. *Social Work Research, 23,* 15–27.

Stroul, B. A., & Friedman, R. M. (1994). *A system of care for children and youth with severe emotional disturbance* (Rev. ed.). Washington, DC: Georgetown University Child Development Center.

Szapocznik, J., & Kurtines, W. M. (1989). *Breakthroughs in family therapy with drug-abusing and problem youth.* New York: Springer.

Szapocznik, J., & Williams, R. A. (2000). Brief strategic family therapy: Twenty-five years of interplay among theory, research and practice in adolescent behavior problems and drug abuse. *Clinical Child and Family Psychology Review, 3,* 117–135.

Taylor, T. K., Eddy, J. M., & Biglan, A. (1999). Interpersonal skills training to reduce aggressive and delinquent behavior: Limited evidence and the need for an evidence-based system of care. *Clinical Child and Family Psychology Review, 2*(3), 169–182.

Thornberry, T. (1994). *Violent families and youth violence: Fact sheet #21.* Washington, DC: Office of Juvenile Justice and Delinquency Prevention.

Thornberry, T. P., Huizinga, D., & Loeber, R. (1995). The prevention of serious delinquency and violence: Implications from the program of research on the causes and correlates of delinquency. In J. C. Howell, B. Krisberg, J. D. Hawkins, & J. J. Wilson (Eds.), *A sourcebook: Serious, violent, and chronic juvenile offenders* (pp. 213–237). Newbury Park, CA: Sage.

Thornberry, T. P., Lizotte, A. J., Krohn, M. D., Farnworth, M., & Jang, S. (1991). Testing interactional theory: An examination of reciprocal causal relationships among family, school and delinquency. *Journal of Criminal Law and Criminology, 82,* 3–35.

Tolan, P. H., Guerra, N. & Kendall, P. C. (1995). Introduction to special section: Prevention and prediction of antisocial behavior in children and adolescents. *Journal of Consulting and Clinical Psychology, 63,* 515–517.

U.S. Department of Health and Human Services (1999). *Mental health: A report of the Surgeon General.* Rockville, MD: U.S. Department of Health and Human Services, National Institutes of Health, National Institute of Mental Health.

U.S. Department of Health and Human Services (2001). *Youth violence: A report of the Surgeon General.* Rockville, MD: U.S. Department of Health and Human Services, Centers for Disease Control and Prevention, National Center for Injury Prevention and Control; Substance Abuse and Mental Health Services Administration, Center for Mental Health Services; and National Institutes of Health, National Institute of Mental Health.

Warr, M. (1993). Parents, peers, & delinquency. *Social Forces, 72*(1), 247–264.

Washington State Institute for Public Policy (1998). *Watching the bottom line: Cost-effective interventions for reducing crime in Washington.* Olympia, VA: The Evergreen State College.

Webster-Stratton, C., & Taylor, T. (2001). Nipping early risk factors in the bud: Preventing substance abuse, delinquency, and violence in adolescence through interventions targeted at young children (0 to 8 years). *Prevention Science, 2,* 165–192.

Weisz, J. R., Donenberg, G. R., Han, S. S., & Weiss, B. (1995). Bridging the gap between laboratory and clinic in child and adolescent psychotherapy. *Journal of Consulting and Clinical Psychology, 63,* 688–701.

Werner, E. E., & Smith, R. S. (1992). *Overcoming the odds: High risk children from birth to adulthood.* New York: Cornell University Press.

Woolfenden, S. R., Williams, K., & Peat, J. K. (2003). Family and parenting interventions in children and adolescents with conduct disorder and delinquency aged 10–17 [Corchrane Review]. *The Corchrane Library, 3.*

CHAPTER 8

PATTERNS OF JUVENILE MALE SEXUAL AGGRESSION: AN OPERANT APPROACH TO UNDERSTANDING AND INTERVENING EFFECTIVELY

Steven C. Wolf

Sexual abuse is a complex and serious social problem. It strongly and negatively affects its victims and their families, and it degrades a community's quality of life. Successful intervention into sexual abuse demands an equally complex response that integrates the efforts of family members, community contacts—often the juvenile or criminal justice systems, churches, schools, and perhaps others—as well as the identified perpetrator of sexual abuse (Wolf, 1985; Wolf, Conte, & Meinig, 1988). Social workers, by philosophy and training, are uniquely qualified to engage these multiple clinical and direct practice systems. What social work lacks is an organizing principle to guide their interventions and a model for matching practice with research and clinical evidence (evidence-based practice). This chapter describes an evidenced-based, behavioral practice model of intervention with the perpetrators of sexual abuse.

LITERATURE REVIEW

That some persons sexually use, exploit, and abuse others is now well established. Twenty years ago, the National Institute of Mental Health estimated that between 200,000 and 450,000 juvenile males sexually abused others each year (Ageton, 1983).[1] An unknown number of adult males similarly perpetrate sexually each year. In a now-classic study, Abel, Becker, Mittelman, Rouleau, and Murphy (1987) document the highly repetitive and chronic nature of sexual abuse. Able and colleague's findings are bolstered by the anecdotal self-reports of men with histories of sexually abusing others (Becker & Stein, 1988; Conte, Wolf, & Smith, 1989; Wolf, 1997). These studies document the early onset of sexual abusing and suggest that this behavior is often generational. In one study (Conte et

---

1. Because the vast majority of sexual abusers in clinical practice will be male, and because the research reported here deals with males exclusively, I will throughout the chapter refer to abusers as males and use masculine pronouns.

al., 1989), 50 percent of adult sexual abusers interviewed reported having first sexually abused before age twenty; 40 percent at or before age fourteen; and 20 percent before age ten. These same men report having acted out multiple paraphilias and having abused multiple victims. In a later study of juvenile male sexual abusers, Wolf (1997) found similar patterns. In both studies, the individuals averaged more than five victims each.

Hudson, Ward, and McCormack (1999) conducted a path analysis of the offending behavior of a sample of sex offenders. Their findings are similar to those of Conte et al. and Wolf, showing planning, sexual arousal, and distorted and self-excusing thinking as the main components of sexual abuse.

This similarity of approach has been repeatedly observed by clinicians and appears to be a common thread in treatment models as diverse as psychodynamic, family systems, and behavioral. Each perspective has used a kind of cycle-of-offending construct to describe the highly patterned nature of these individuals' abuse. But *cycle* is a limited, imprecise choice of terms, for it implies a continuous process wherein the end causes the beginning (Carich, 1999; Lane, 1994, 1997).

Challenging the idea of cycles of offending, Barry Maletzky, writing as editor of the journal *Sexual Abuse* (1998), stated:

> A cycle is a repeating series of occurrences, each event of which triggers the next and brings the whole back to the initial starting point. . . . A cycle is self-perpetuating, as once entered, it repeats endlessly because each step promotes the next. It is common for clinicians to refer to deviant cycles when describing a series of behaviors eventuating in sexual abuse, but it appears that they are describing instead a *chain* of behavior triggered by an internal or external stimulus with a sexual goal that, once realized, terminates the sequence.

So-called cycles of sexual abusing also imply that there is a regular relationship between the behavior and its consequence; that operant contingencies exist between the act of sexually abusing and its outcome. Belief in such contingencies points to examination of the flow of sexually abusive behavior from onset to conclusion for evidence of these operant contingencies. Their existence would have strong implications for how abuse might be stopped and prevented in the future. Discovery of such evidence would confirm Maletzky's (1998) assertion that the cycle is, in reality, a chain.

Several behavioral studies of adult (Conte et al., 1989; Hudson, Ward, & McCormack, 1999) and juvenile (Wolf, 1997; Zolondek, Abel, Northey, & Jordan, 2001) male sexual abusers have used behavioral approaches to examine the self-reports of sexual abusers. These authors found that sexual abuse, at least in their samples, is highly stable, and they found reliable similar patterns in both adult and juvenile male sexual abusers.

An operant model (Skinner, 1938) of sexual aggression (Laws & Marshall, 1990; McGuire, Carlisle, & Young, 1965; Rosen & Beck, 1988), assumes that a behavior chain is under the control of two principle factors: (1) how strongly and how closely each behavioral response is rewarded (Barbaree, 1990) and (2) the strength of the actor's expectation that the chain will end in gratification (Wolf & Pinkston, 1997). Thus, the outcome of each node in the abuse chain acts as a consequent reinforcer (S^R) for those behaviors (R) that they immediately follow and sets the occasion (S^D) for the occurrence of those behaviors that they immediately precede (Baer, 1992; Walker, 1969).

In this case, the consequent produced at each node is assumed to be sexual arousal and the expectation of achieving additional sexual gratification. These consequents act as conditioned reinforcers (S^R) of the previous sexually aggressive behavior (R) and as the discriminative stimulus (S^D) for the next response. Simply put, when some element of sexually aggressive behavior occurs and pleasant thoughts and feelings follow, it is rewarded. When this happens, this behavior is more likely to occur again in similar conditions. Thus rewarded—and sexually interested—the actor is also more likely to pursue further sexual gratification. When the sexually aggressive behavior is closely followed by punishment, its likelihood of recurrence is diminished (Baer, 1992).

APPROACH: APPLIED BEHAVIOR ANALYTIC MODEL

Informed by operant models and the behavioral research that Conte, Wolf, and Smith (1989) report, Wolf and Pinkston (1997) constructed an operant model of sexual aggression. This model predicted that the powerful reinforcers of sexual arousal and anticipation of gratification would strongly and reliably shape sexually abusive behavior. It further predicted that the actual pattern of offending, if it existed, would proceed from some triggering event—through selecting a person to victimize—would include a strategy for approaching, engaging, and controlling the victims, would achieve sexual abuse of the targeted victim, and would finish in a process of self-excusing and emotional distancing from feelings of culpability for the abuse.

In this study, twenty sexually abusive youth were interviewed. Data supporting the existence of an operant model was obtained. These data are summarized in figure 8.1 and described in the following section. This study used a closeness-of-fit model to measure the fit between the predicted model and that described by subjects. In this model, perfect agreement between self-report and the model would result in a score of 1.0. A less-than-perfect fit would produce a score of less than 1.0. The authors assumed that closeness-of-fit lower than about 0.5 would indicate a weak or poorly described relationship between that predicted and that observed. In this study, the lowest closeness-of-fit score was 0.63.

Node 1: Releasing Conditions
(Aggregate Closeness-of-Fit = 0.82)

S^D1. Most of these youth report that unpleasant feelings often were a precondition, or trigger, for the onset of sexual thinking (95 percent). Of this group, 80 percent report that they would often have sexual thoughts—including a desire to masturbate or offend—while experiencing "bad" feelings. Thirty-nine

FIGURE 8.1   Operant Chain of Sexual Abuse

Node 1: Releasing Conditions
$SD^1 \rightarrow R^1 \rightarrow SR^1$
$\downarrow$

Node 2: Target Selection
$SD^2 \rightarrow R^2 \rightarrow SR^2$
$\downarrow$

Node 3: Movement to Contact
$SD^3 \rightarrow R^3 \rightarrow SR^3$
$\downarrow$

Node 4: Sexual Abuse
$SD^4 \rightarrow R^4 \rightarrow SR^4$
$\downarrow$

Node 5: Risk Management
$SD^5 \rightarrow R^5 \rightarrow SR^5$
$\downarrow$

Node 6: Reconstitution
$SD^6 \rightarrow R^6 \rightarrow SR^6$

percent said that anger was, for them, a clear trigger for seeking sexual arousal. Seven percent claim that frustration or boredom would trigger sexual thoughts.

R1.   All participants reported that they responded to the presence of "bad" feelings or other unpleasant feelings by becoming sexual, including escaping to sexual fantasy, masturbating, or thinking about being sexual. Once sexually interested, 85 percent reported that they actively sought some sort of physical, sexual outlet.

S^R1.   Of participants, 95 percent reported that, as a consequence of thinking about sex, they experienced (and enjoyed) an increase in their sense of physical well-being. Seventy-five percent reported an improvement in emotional feelings and thoughts.

Clearly, these youth share a common experience in which thinking about sex—abusive or otherwise—is reinforced by improvements in their physical and emotional condition. However, none of the subjects was able or willing to identify when, why, or under what conditions they made the decision to be sexually abusive rather than sexually appropriate.

These youth further report that feeling sexually excited increased their interest in and attention to locating and selecting a target person with whom to be sexual (S^D2).

Node 2: Target Selection (Aggregate Closeness-of-Fit = 0.63)

R2.   These subjects report infinite variety in the characteristics of the potential victims to whom they are attracted. In 55 percent of the cases, they reported that some combination of the characteristics of the person and the setting was what most attracted them to a potential sexual target. Gender alone was what caused 30 percent of them to select a target, and 20 percent reported that the person's behavior was sufficient to cause them to be selected as a sexual target, irrespective of the victim's looks, age, or gender. Fifteen percent reported that being alone with a person, regardless of their gender or attractiveness, was sufficient for their being selected as a sexual partner or victim.

S^{R}2.   Continuing the response pattern of Node 1, all subjects reported that being close to a selected sexual target improved how they felt physically and emotionally. Eighty-five percent stated that being close to a sexual target made them feel sexually aroused or generally excited. Only 20 percent said that they were physically excited without being sexually aroused. One youth reported that being close to his selected target turned him off sexually.[2]

In general, for this sample, the characteristics of the target and the setting act as primary elements in eliciting sexual excitement. With individual variation, nearly all of these juveniles' report that proximity to the sexual target provides an important consequent improvement in both mood and physical feeling. As with the previous node, these responses, and the attendant increase in sexual arousal and expectation of sexual success, become the stimulus discriminator (S^{D}3) for the next node: movement to contact.

Node 3. Movement to Contact (Aggregate Closeness-of-Fit = 0.71)

R3^a (Premeditation, Closeness-of-Fit = 0.89).   In this node, 95 percent of these juveniles consciously plan where and how they will make contact with their intended victim. All but one of the twenty subjects had a location selected for sexual abusing before approaching their target sexually for the first time. This single subject reported that he was more inclined to sexually approach a potential victim when they happened to arrive in a suitable location for abuse. This subject further reported that he would stay close to a selected victim until they entered a location suitable for abuse.

R3^b (Analyzing Risk, Closeness-of-Fit = 0.63).   Eighty-five percent of subjects reported that, before approaching a target victim, they would try to figure out a strategy that would work best in gaining sexual access to a particular individual. Sixty-five percent stated that, before trying to sexually abuse, they would "test" a selected target in some manner to get a sense of their likelihood of reporting or resisting being abused. Sixty-five percent also recalled that, when a victim resisted, they would withdraw, try to distract the victim from thinking about the abuse, or leave the target alone. Sixty-five percent reported that they

---

2. Although this youth described feeling reduced sexual arousal with physical approach to his target, he reported having a full erection concurrent to target proximity.

would try again with this same victim on another occasion. In response to probe questions, one youth described believing the targets he selected were all abusable and that he simply had to be in the right place when the victim was most vulnerable to his approach.

R3^c (Approach, Closeness-of-Fit = 0.63).   Ninety percent reported that, before offending, they would bribe their target victims by doing things for them they knew the target would really appreciate. Eighty-five percent stated that they would touch their intended victims in nonsexual ways to "get them used" to being touched. These same subjects reported that they would then progress to touching more sensitive (sexual) parts of the victim's bodies until—having desensitized the victim—they had full sexual access to the victim.

Seventy percent of the subjects also reported a willingness to use threats, coercion, and overt force to gain sexual access to their victims. Sixty-percent stated that they had threatened a victim with physical violence to gain sexual access.

Of interest is that, while discussing their sexual offending, almost all of the subjects suggested that the use of force, by itself, was gratifying, sexually and otherwise. Although none of the subjects admits to having raped, their description of having used physical force, threats, and weapons when abusing suggests that they have done so.

S^{R}3.   Seventy-five percent of subjects reported that this planning, testing, and approaching of their victims increased their sexual arousal and overall enjoyment of the abuse. Twenty percent reported no increase in arousal at this stage but reported that they were already highly aroused. One youth suggested that he could not become more aroused without achieving orgasm. Only one youth reported a decrease in his sexual arousal at this stage. However, he also reported that he had at least a partial erection, sexually penetrated his victim, and reached orgasm.

At each step of Node 3, the subjects reported that the presence, in one youth's words, of an "abusable" target, may be the most common final trigger of the sexual abuse. Their reports suggest that proximity to an abusable target is sufficient for their selection as a possible victim.

Node 4: Sexual Abuse (Aggregate Closeness-of-Fit = 1.00)

R4.   All of these subjects report that they have sexually abused at least one victim by touching. All report that they have abused their victim or victims more than once. In the course of their sexual abuse, 90 percent reported having at least touched the chest and genitals of their victims to gain sexual gratification. Sixty percent attempted to get their victims to touch them sexually; to perform oral sex on them, to masturbate them, or to penetrate them anally. Half report that, in addition to touching their victims sexually, they made their victim look at their genitals (an act of sex-offender exhibitionism).

S^R4. All of these youth report being sexually aroused while they were sexually abusing. Eighty percent reported that the experience exceeded or was close to meeting their expectations. Fifty-three percent reported that they ejaculated while abusing. Seventy-five percent said that they also ejaculated after the abuse while fantasizing about what they had done. Twenty percent reported that the experience of abusing was nowhere close to being as gratifying as they expected. These same subjects report that this failure to achieve the level of gratification they expected caused them to think of and, in many cases, overtly plan how they could improve their experience of abusing in the future.

Node 5: Risk Management (Aggregate Closeness-of-Fit = 0.85)

S^D5^a Internal. After abuse, these subjects described undergoing a significant change in the valence of their thinking and behavior, experiencing a loss of sexual arousal and their attraction to sexual abuse, and developing a fear of the consequences associated with having abused. Specifically, at some point after the abuse incident, all of the participants reported a loss of sexual arousal or interest in sex. This loss of sexual arousal seems to function as a stimulus discriminator, focusing the abusers' actions on trying to minimize the possible consequences of their abusive behavior. Eighty-five percent of these subjects reported that when their sexual arousal declined, they felt generally all right but were afraid of being caught and punished. Ten percent recalled not worrying about any negative consequences for having abused. Only one person reported feeling "really terrible about the abuse and worrying about having hurt [the] victim." This subject reported abusing again despite this fear and guilt.

R5^a. Although not all subjects reported being concerned about being caught and punished for having abused, all said that they engaged in protective and excusing self-talk about their abusive actions. Fifty percent told themselves that the abuse was all right because the victims liked it. Twenty percent told themselves that the victim was too young to remember being abused. Ten percent told themselves that the abuse was not really their fault for some reason. Five percent told themselves that the abuse was the victim's fault, and 5 percent "forgave" themselves because they "would never" abuse again.

S^D5^b External. Note that this condition is same as for Internal S^D5^a.

R5^b. Ninety-five percent of these youth reported that they did something to prevent their victims from reporting the sexual abuse. Of these, 45 percent threatened their victims to keep them from telling. Forty-five percent offered their victims gifts or favors to keep them from telling. Forty percent of these subjects used multiple strategies. Thirty-five percent asked the victims forgiveness as a strategy to keep them from telling.

S^{R}5.   As a consequence of this self-protective talk, 50 percent of subjects reported that their excuses made them feel better—less guilty—immediately. Forty-five percent said they felt better in a few days. Ninety-five percent of these youth reported that their strategies were either very effective or rather effective in reducing their guilt about committing sexual abuse and their anxiety about being caught and punished. It is possible that, in these cases, the passage of time without discovery and punishment was more salient to these subjects than any self-protective excuses they made. Only one individual reported that his excuses did not reduce his feelings of anxiety for having abused. This is the same individual who reported being turned off by being close to his chosen victim and losing sexual arousal as it became clear that he could successfully sexually abuse his victim. These bad feelings, however, did not interfere with this individual's willingness to continue sexually abusing.

Node 6: Reconstitution (Aggregate Closeness-of-Fit = 0.91)

S^{D}6.   Subjects experience relief from guilt and fear of discovery.

R6^a Rationalization.   As the initial fear of discovery and punishment began to decline, these subjects described initiating a process of self-talk, reminding themselves of their good qualities. Some of the self-validating responses included telling themselves that they were "really good guys" (35 percent), "it [the abuse] just happened" (20 percent), and that it was not their fault (20 percent).

S^{D}6.   Note that this condition is the same as S^{D}6 external.

R6^b Distancing.   Eighty-five percent of these subjects sought validation from others. Sixty-five percent acted more friendly and interested in family members and friends. Fifteen percent reported that attending church or reading the Bible made them feel all right again.

S^{R}6.   Ninety-five percent stated that these strategies of self-approval and other-approval were effective in reducing their feelings of guilt or anxiety. Twenty-six percent recalled that this strategy also actually improved their feelings of self-worth. The effectiveness of these rationalizing and distancing strategies may explain why, even in the face of likely discovery and punishment, sexual offenders often repeat their patterns of sexual aggression.

IMPLICATIONS FOR ASSESSMENT AND TREATMENT: PRACTICE PRINCIPLES

The main element in understanding and treating sexually abusive persons is that their sexual use, exploitation, and abuse of vulnerable persons are the visible center of a complex chain of conditions and events. This chain is nested within multiple individual and social systems, many of them overtly antisocial and covertly antagonistic of smaller, weaker persons. The behaviors that make up the abuse chain are reinforced at multiple points by immediate sexual gratification, gaining access to nonsexual social rewards such as feelings of self-efficacy, and an expectation that greater sexual pleasures are close at hand. The strength of sexual arousal and anticipation, along with an impaired ability to empathize, act to disinhibit—or, from a learning theory perspective, reciprocally inhibit—the fear of being caught and punished.

Each of these principles is reported in research literature and forms the evidence on which practice is based. Acknowledging these principles, the social worker is obliged to engage the appropriate clinical behaviors in his or her evaluation, treatment planning, and practice. This is evidence-based practice. Evidence-based practice is the application of systematically gained and empirically tested knowledge to clinical care. In this case, it is the application of the principles of behavioral chaining to the evaluation, description, and treatment of patterns of sexually abusive behavior.

Evidence

As described previously, the individuals in this study, like their older counterparts, evidenced highly developed patterns of sexual preference for abuse (Miranda & Corcoran, 2000). They are strongly attracted to, and sexually reinforced by, abusive sexuality, such that they are willing to risk freedom and punishment to achieve it. When not sexually abusing, they engage in sexual daydreams and often masturbate repeatedly to thoughts and memories of their abusing (Sagel & Stermac, 1990; Swaffer, Hollin, Beech, Beckett & Fisher, 2000).

In general, they are antisocial in their attitudes, beliefs, and actions, even though often they mask this with a pro-social, highly moral stance. They lack genuine empathy for their victims, as differentiated from the situational empathy displayed by abusers once caught and fearing punishment. Such empathy is self-serving and short-lived (Beckett, Beech, Fisher, & Fordham, 1994).

They plan their abuse before acting out both overtly and covertly in sexual masturbation fantasies. They know the timing and location of all possible risk elements. They calculate the likelihood that their victim of choice will report being abused. They are willing to use threats, actual force, and physical violence to gain sexual access to their victims.

They do not voluntarily relinquish this preference for abusive sexuality, nor do they readily discuss and disclose their abusive behavior. They are only dissuaded from abusing by the strict enforcement of external controls and the sure and immediate certainty of punishment.

Intervention

Three things must be accomplished in treating this problem. First, the social factors of the abuser's environment, including social support for the abusive behavior, that facilitate abuse must be identified and contained. Second, the sexual abuse chain's reinforcers must be weakened. Third, a constellation of nonabusive sexual and social patterns must be taught and reinforced to alter the abuser's pattern of sexual interest and arousal.

The first step is the behavioral assessment. A behavioral assessment is a systematic, guided examination of the client's sexual abuse chain, the fantasies that shape it, and the social factors that may support its development and maintenance. In evidence-based practice, the clinician systematically observes and records his or her findings, guided by principles arising from research. The findings of this examination are compared with those reported in literature. Concurrence between observations and findings assures the clinician that he or she is supported by the careful work of her peers. Nonconcurrence suggests the need for further observation, consideration of observational errors, or dissimulation by the client.

Before the behavioral assessment can begin, some kind of therapeutic alliance must be established. This is difficult in the extreme since, among individuals who sexually abuse, dissimulation is the rule rather than the exception and is at the core of their abusing. Dissimulation exemplifies the antisocial and robust self-protective strategies inherent in their personalities. In the abuser's mind, the social worker or clinician is the enemy. To overcome this reluctance, the social worker must engineer an environment in which the abuser can feel relatively safe. The social worker must orchestrate an approach that will engage the client to the degree that he can discuss his abusive behavior in some detail. One approach is the use of an orientation protocol such as the one described subsequently.

Orientation Protocol

The orientation protocol intends to acquaint the abuser, his or her family, significant others, and other social support members with the nature, structure, and risks inherent in the assessment and treatment process for sexual abusers and persuade them that it is in their best interest to cooperate. In this regard, it must be remembered that the risks of disclosing being a sexual abuser are very real. To admit to being sexually abusive is to risk public humiliation, the possible loss of family and friends, and incarceration.

This protocol aims to (1) empower the social support network in a process in which their role, input, and support is valued and, in fact, expected, in the treatment of the client (even when the social system is as abusive as the client); (2) engage the social support network as active participants in a process of helping the sexual abuser receive appropriate treatment designed to prevent expression of the sexually abusive behavior; (3) educate the social support network and the client as to the social worker's or clinician's legal, philosophical, theoretical, and practical beliefs about the problem of sexual abuse and the role of behavioral assessment and treatment in controlling this problem; and (4) provide the social support network and the client with accurate information as well as an appropriate and accurate language for discussing the problem of sexual abuse, thus desensitizing the abuser and those attending the session to discussing the behavior and desensitizing the individuals to the nature of treatment. The orientation makes the empirical knowledge of the field available and accessible to the client and his social support network. The steps of this protocol are described in exhibit 8.1.

Behavioral Assessment

The sexual abuser behavioral assessment has three goals: (1) to identify and describe the structure, content, targets of, and reinforcer strength inherent in the individual's sexual abuse chain; (2) to analyze the abuser's current access to victims and thereby his risk to reabuse in the short run; and (3) to analyze the psychological, developmental, and environmental factors unique to this particular abusive individual that facilitate or inhibit the abusive behavior and might inhibit or facilitate a return to abuse.

A sexual abuser assessment begins with collecting and reviewing all the victim and witness statements available subsequent to gaining consent from the abuser/client. The sexual abuse chain described in research is used as a focusing lens for reviewing these statements and in subsequent interviews with the abuser and his social system. The victim and witness statements are, in this manner, disaggregated into the step-by-step process of abuse charted by the chain. Inconsistencies, information gaps, and/or vagueness in the victim's or client's descriptions of chain events are noted and addressed during client and collateral interviews.

Two clinical strategies are effective in gaining cooperation and generating important information. The first strategy is to begin the assessment by examining the abuser/client's life story. This is a strategic choice, because it engages a core characteristic common to sexual abusers: narcissism. Ask the client to list and describe in order every location at which he has lived. Ask about his quality of life at each address; where he went to school; what activities he engaged in; who his friends were; the evolution of his genogram; his relationships with parents, siblings, and other adults; his victories and tragedies. In this way, one can learn a great deal about his developmental history and the social values and forces that surrounded his development; values and forces that may come into play in the development and furthering of his abusing. Start with very broad, open-ended questions and proceed to questions of increasing specificity. This information is key to discovering the factors that facilitate or inhibit his sexual abuse behavior.

A technique for facilitating this strategy is to place a long—at least six feet—sheet of paper between the clinician or social worker and the client to sketch the client's life-story time line between the client and the evaluator. This is a good way to engage clients, to show your interest in them as a person, to document the richness of their lives, and to identify key elements in the client's life. What you learn about the abuser/client can be compared with the findings of psychological testing.

Once these basics of the client's life story are documented on the sheet, the

EXHIBIT 8.1:   Orientation Protocol (Therese Wolf)

Before conducting a sex offender-specific assessment, the therapist conducts a one- to two-hour orientation session with all available social support network members and the client. This orientation session provides the social support network and the client an opportunity to learn about and to decide whether they wish to become engaged in the evaluation and treatment processes.

Because, in general, the client and his social support network are unfamiliar with the treatment of sexual aggression and typically experience some level of trauma as a result of the disclosure of sexual abuse, the orientation session enables the social support network and/or the client to achieve the following goals:

1. To empower the social support network in a process in which their role, input, and support is valued and, in fact, expected, in the treatment of the client;

2. To engage the social support network as active participants in a process of helping the client receive appropriate treatment designed to prevent expression of the sexually aggressive behavior;

3. To educate the social support network and the client as to Northwest Treatment Associates' philosophical, theoretical, and practical beliefs about the problem of sexual aggression and the role of evaluation and treatment in controlling this problem; and

4. To provide the social support network and the client an appropriate and accurate language for discussing the problem of sexual aggression, thus normalizing the behavior and desensitizing the individuals to the nature of treatment.

Engaging the client and the social support network in assessment and treatment is defined as a "complex, reciprocal process concerning the relationship between the therapist, the client and their family [social support network] as well as the specific adjustments the therapist makes over time to accommodate a particular family" (Jackson & Chable, 1985). This engagement is a relationship, often unequal in power and knowledge, between the client group and therapist that includes complex and often-conflicting agendas. It overtly confirms the need for the therapist to consider the particular idiosyncrasies of each client group with regard to the sensitive nature of sexual abuse.

The orientation process facilitates this engagement and enables the therapist to begin assessing the client and his social support network in a nonthreatening and nonintrusive way. Information gathered during this orientation session will enable the therapist to strategize how to best

EXHIBIT 8.1: *(continued)*

approach the client and his social support network and how to most effectively conduct the actual evaluation.

Assisting the social support network in achieving these goals begins when the orientation session is first scheduled. The therapist explains the purpose of the orientation session as an opportunity for all involved parties to address their concerns and to learn about the evaluation and treatment processes. In general, the orientation session is scheduled at a time that is convenient for the social support network, to ensure that as many significant individuals as possible can attend.

Because each client's social support network is different, the participants in the orientation session vary from case to case. In the case of an adolescent sexual offender, the client, his or her guardian(s), parents, foster parents, or whomever is responsible for his or her care are strongly encouraged to attend. In the case of an adult sexual offender, his or her spouse or significant other, older nonvictim children, siblings or other close family members, and friends may be asked to attend. Beyond these individuals, probation officers, child welfare workers, and others may also be invited. Although siblings may be encouraged to attend, if a sibling is also a known victim, the therapist should carefully assess his or her inclusion in the orientation session, including the sibling's willingness to attend and his or her vulnerability to further victimization by attending.

The orientation session consists of five steps:

1. Define the purpose of the session as one in which the client and his or her social support network have the opportunity to discuss the events that have resulted in the referral, gather accurate information about the evaluation and treatment processes as well as the therapist, and decide what they, as the youth's caretakers/friends/support system, wish to do next.

2. Reframe and address potential resistance or fear about discussing sexual aggression and its impact by acknowledging that, in general, the issue generates much anxiety, anger, or confusion for clients and their social support network.[1] Recognize the family as the "expert" about parenting and living with the youth and request their assistance in understanding their unique experience by eliciting their questions, concerns, and comments.[2]

---

1. The term *family* can be appropriately substituted with other descriptors, depending on who attends at the session.

2. The social support network's denial of the sexual offense is reframed in a similar manner. Its existence is therefore made overt and normalized while providing an opportunity to "get beyond" denial as the process progresses.

EXHIBIT 8.1: (*continued*)

3. The therapist communicates expertise in and comfort with discussing sexual aggression while normalizing the behavior for the client and social support network. The therapist uses clear and accurate language to describe the sexual behaviors alleged, educates the family as to the occurrence of such behavior in the general population, describes the assumptions held about sexually aggressive behavior and its course, communicates acceptance of the youth despite clear statements of the inappropriateness of the behavior, places clear responsibility on the youth for the behavior, and discusses the role family and friends can serve in assisting the youth in developing control.

4. The therapist explains the sex-offender evaluation process and its relation to treatment. The written "Informed Consent to Evaluate" is reviewed carefully as the therapist outlines issues of the legal rights of the client, fees, limited confidentiality, mandated reporter status, personal nature of the material discussed, dissemination of the sex-offender report, and use of client data for research.

5. The therapist suggests that the client and his or her social support network take ample time to review the document again, discuss it with their attorney if desired, and review their impressions from this meeting before deciding whether they wish to proceed with the evaluation process. The client group is "reminded" that it is a consumer of a service and, as such, has some options as to how and with whom they obtain treatment. Information about alternative treatment agencies is provided to all clients. If the group decides to continue with the evaluation process, all necessary forms are signed and sessions are scheduled. If the social support network decides to wait, a day for a final decision is selected.

---

social worker can begin sketching in the abuser/client reports of his own sexual history: where, when, and how did he learn about sex? What was his first sexual experience; with whom it occurred; how it felt; what his impressions of this experience are now; what his experiences are with pornography, with masturbation, and with other paraphiliac behaviors; whether he was sexually abused or felt abused at the time?

The second strategy is to organize questions about the sexual abuse. One technique is to start with the abuse itself (Node 4), not moving between nodes until there is a thorough and complete picture of the actual abuse—almost a slow-motion image, a clear picture of the location and the time of day, the weather, the surrounding occurrences, the location of key persons, how the victim and the abuser came to be in that location at that time, how each was dressed (clothing that can be easily removed and put on is often key to the abuser's strategy), and all the steps leading up to the abuse itself. From there, work backward node by node to discover first why the abuser thought this person could be abused, why they were attracted to this person, and what they did to gain access to the victim (see Node 3).

After a clear timeline of the abuse is developed, move forward and examine how the abuser felt afterward: what they said to themselves and what they did to make themselves feel better; what they said or did to prevent discovery (see Node 5); and finally what they did to "get past" the abuse episode (see Node 6). A sexual abuse behavioral assessment is complete when every term in each node of the individual abuser's chain is known.

Treatment

It is impossible to adequately describe the treatment of sexually abusive persons in the space allotted for this chapter. Quite literally, the good texts and journals describing elements of this process would fill a large room to overflowing (Gill & Cavanagh Johnson, 1993; Marshall, Laws, & Barbaree, 1990; Salter, 1988; Schlank & Cohen, 1999). What follows, then, is a general discussion of the larger bits of work with this population. Absent are discussions of the implications of working with court-mandated persons; issues of being a social workers and acting as an agent of the state; concerns about confidentiality specific to work with sexual abuse; and the simple question of who the client is, the abuser or the community. The reader is directed to the journals listed in the bibliography of this chapter and is encouraged to seek out consultation and training with a therapist experienced in work with sexual abusers.

That being said, treatment proceeds from the behavioral assessment. Knowing the chain, the social worker knows the types of behavior and victims that are attractive to the abuser. The social worker knows specifically which thoughts, expectations, and outcomes reinforce their abusive actions. The social worker knows how the abuser excuses his behavior and the locations and victim types the abuser will most likely select to abuse. Finally, the social worker knows the types of circumstances under which the abuser will most likely reenter his abuse chain. The social worker now has a body of information—knowledge—about the abuser/client's life and actions that can be compared with that reported in literature that will ground work in theory and empirical knowledge and guide intervention.

When the social worker has gained this knowledge of the abuser client, what remains is weakening of the social supports for sexual abuse and the sexual attraction to abuse and reinforcement of attraction to appropriate sexuality. To accomplish this, most sexual abuser programs use a combination of individual behavioral and cognitive-behavioral treatment, group treatment, and family treatment modalities (Knopp, Freeman-Longo, & Stevenson, 1992).

Group therapy is a powerful means of overcoming the abuser's reluctance to self-disclose. It provides a safe, peer-type atmosphere that offers informed challenges to the individual abuser's distortions and rationalizations and supports making nonabusive choices.

Individual behavioral therapy provides a one-on-one venue to address the minutiae of the client's pattern of abusive sexuality, to use powerful counterconditioning methods to weaken abusive patterns and sexual preferences, to create and reinforce appropriate sexual patterns and preferences, and to practice various nonabusive social skills in a safe, therapeutic environment.

Family therapy is the venue in which the abuser/client can practice and reinforce behaving in nonabusive ways toward family members. Even in those situations in which the sexual abuse took place outside the family, abusive patterns related to the sexual chain are often present. Family therapy can be a powerful means of "abuse-proofing" members—eliminating sexual and gender myths, teaching a means and language for identifying and bringing attention to abuse patternlike behaviors—and reconstructing the role of the abuser as an appropriate parent and/or child caregiver.

In summary, the task of treating sexual abusers is about identifying and describing their sexually abusive chain, locating it in its social and family context, understanding how these social factors facilitate or inhibit the chain's expression, using behavioral and other techniques to systematically weaken and restructure the abusive habits inherent in the individual's abuse chain, and restructuring the abuser's social context so as to inhibit reinitiation of the abusive chain.

REFERENCES

Abel, G., Becker, J., Mittelman, M., Rouleau, J., & Murphy, W. (1987). Self-reported sex crimes of non-incarcerated paraphiliacs. *Journal of Interpersonal Violence, 2*(1), 3–25.

Ageton, S. S. (1983). *Sexual assaults among adolescents: A national study.* Final report of the National Center for the Prevention and Control of Rape. Washington, DC: National Institute of Mental Health.

Baer, D. M. (1992). Personal communication.

Barbaree, H. (1990). Stimulus control of sexual arousal: Its role in sexual assault. In W. L. Marsall, D. R. Laws, & H. E. Barbaree (Eds.), *Handbook of sexual assault: Issues, theories and treatment of the offender* (p. 116). New York: Plenum Press.

Becker, J., & Stein, R. (1988). The assessment of adolescent sexual offenders. In R. J. Prinz (Ed.), *Advances in behavioral assessment of children and families* (Vol. 4, pp. 97–118). JAI Press.

Beckett, R. C., Beech, A. R., Fisher, D., & Fordham, A. S. (1994). *Community-based treatment for sex offenders: An evaluation of seven programmes.* London: Home Office.

Carich, M. S. (1999). In defense of the assault cycle: A commentary. *Sexual Abuse: A Journal of Research and Treatment, 11*(3), 249–251.

Conte, J., Wolf, S. C., & Smith, T. A. (1989). What sexual offenders tell us about prevention strategies. *Child Abuse and Neglect, 13,* 293–301.

Gill, E., & Cavanagh, J. T. (1993). *Sexualized children: Assessment and treatment of sexualized children and children who molest.* Rockville, MD: Lauch Press.

Hudson, S. M., Ward, T., & McCormack, J. C. (1999). Offense pathways in sexual offenders. *Journal of Interpersonal Violence, 4*(8), 779–798.

Knopp, F. H., Freeman-Longo, R., & Stevenson, W. F. (1992). *Nationwide survey of juvenile and adult sex offender treatment program and models.* Orwell, VT: Safer Society Press.

Lane, S. (1994). The cycle. In G. Ryan (Ed.), *Interchange: Cooperative newsletter of the Adolescent Perpetrator Network.* Denver, CO: C. Henry Kempe Center.

Lane, S. (1997). The sexual abuse cycle. In G. Ryan & S. Lane (Eds.), *Juvenile sexual offending: Causes, consequences and correction* (pp. 77–121). San Francisco: Jossey-Bass.

Laws, D., & Marshall, W. (1990). A conditioning theory of the etiology and maintenance of deviant sexual preference and behavior. In W. L. Marshall, D. R. Laws, & H. E. Barbaree (Eds.), *Handbook of sexual assault: Issues, theories and treatment of the offender* (pp. 226). New York: Plenum Press.

Maletzky, B. M. (1998). Defining our field II: Cycles, chains, and assorted misnomers [Editorial]. *Sexual Abuse: A Journal of Research and Treatment, 10*(1), 1–4.

McGuire, R. J., Carlisle, J. M., & Young, B. A. (1965). Sexual deviation as conditioned behavior. *Behavior Research and Therapy, 2,* 185–190.

Miranda, A. O., & Corcoran, C. L. (2000). Comparison of perpetration characteristics between male juvenile and adult sexual offenders: Preliminary results. *Sexual Abuse: A Journal of Research and Treatment, 12*(3), 179–188.

Rosen, R. C., & Beck, J. G. (1988). *Patterns of sexual arousal: Psychophysiological processes in clinical applications.* New York: Guilford Press.

Sagel, Z., & Stermac, L. (1990). The role of cognition in sexual assault. In W. L. Marshall, D. R. Laws, & H. E. Barbaree (Eds.), *Handbook of sexual assault: Issues, theories and treatment of the offender* (pp. 161–174). New York: Plenum Press.

Salter, A. (1988). *Treating child sex offenders and victims: A practical guide.* New York: Sage.

Skinner, B. F. (1938). *The behavior of organisms: An experimental analysis.* New York: Appleton-Century-Crofts.

Swaffer, T., Hollin, C., Beech, A., Beckett, R., & Fisher, D. (2000). An exploration of child abusers' sexual fantasies before and after treatment. *Sexual Abuse: A Journal of Research and Treatment, 12*(1), 61–68.

Walker, E. L. (1969). Reinforcement—"the one ring." In J. T. Tapp (Ed.), *Reinforcement and behavior* (pp. 47–62). New York: Academic Press.

Wolf, S. C. (1985). A multi-factor model of deviant sexuality. *Victimology: An International Journal, 10*(1-4), 359–374.

Wolf, S. C. (1997). *Victim engagement patterns among male juvenile sexual offenders.* Unpublished doctoral dissertation, University of Chicago.

Wolf, S. C., & Pinkston, E. M. (1997). Structure of victim engagement in sexual abuse. In D. M. Baer & E. M. Pinkston (Eds.), *Environment and behavior* (pp. 163–172). Boulder, CO: Westview Press.

Zolondek, S. C., Abel, G. G., Northey, W. F., & Jordan, A. D. (2001). The self-reported behaviors of juvenile sexual offenders. *Journal of Interpersonal Violence, 16*(1), 73–85.

CHAPTER 9

Behavioral Family Treatment in Japan: Design and Development of a Parent Training Program

Matsujiro Shibano

In Japan, a child's right to live in a safe environment has been severely threatened by the fact that the number of the children suffering from abuse and neglect by their own parents or caretakers has been increasing quadratically for the past ten years (figure 9.1). Although it is imperative to establish an effective reporting system and protective intervention procedures based on accurate risk assessment, the development of resources that contribute to the prevention of child abuse and neglect is now widely recognized as extremely important. Among needed resources in the community is parent training, heretofore not considered seriously because the Japanese historically have believed that society should not intervene in the parenting function of the family. Increasingly, however, Japanese families have suffered from the lack of effective parenting models as a result of the steady increase of nuclear families and the decline of multiple-generation households. Behavioral parent training in groups is expected to be one of the most cost-effective primary preventive measures for nuclear families not to become candidates for child maltreatment.

Fourteen years ago, a behavioral group parent-training program, or *Fureai-Koza* (positive parent-child communication) program, was initiated at the main children's center in Kobe. This program was based on the behavioral parent education program developed by Pinkston and her colleagues at the University of Chicago (Pinkston et al., 1981, Shibano, et al., 1982). The *Fureai-Koza* project is a joint project of the Department of Children and Family of Kobe City and the Society for the Study of Mother-Child Communication at Kwansei Gakuin University. From the beginning, a major goal of the *Fureai-Koza* project was the dissemination of the group parent-training program to the 105 local children's centers scattered around the city. Since each center is located in the middle school district to which the families have easy access, it is important to disseminate the *Fureai-Koza* program to each center as a means of preventing child abuse and neglect.

FIGURE 9.1 Number of Child Abuse and Neglect Cases Treated by Children and Family Centers in Japan

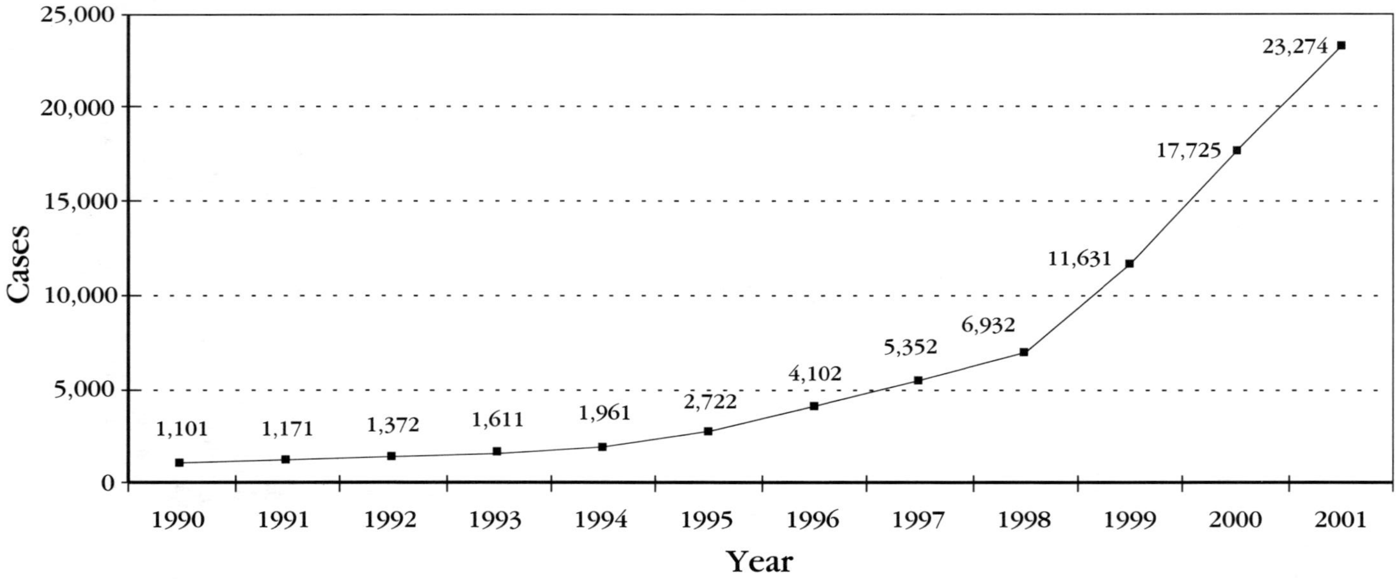

DESIGN AND DEVELOPMENT OF BEHAVIORAL PARENT TRAINING IN JAPAN: BRIEF LITERATURE REVIEW

Takeda and Tatsuki (1978) introduced the basic concepts of behavioral parent training and the basic operant procedures that professionals and parents can use to modify the child's negative behaviors in family settings. These concepts and procedures are mainly based on studies by Patterson, Reid, Jones, and Conger (1975), Gelfand and Hartman (1975), Miller (1975), and Patterson (1976). In the mid-1980s, Shibano began to evaluate the possibility of applying the behavioral parent training on a group basis to Japanese families (Shibano, 1989). Kuwata and Shibano (1990) have found that the behavioral group parent training was effective in reducing the anxiety of mothers with babies younger than one year old. In the series of studies by Yamagami and her colleagues (1998), the behavioral parent training was applied to families with physically or emotionally disturbed children (Takada, 1991). The studies reported that the various operant procedures to modify the ineffective basic social skills of children were successfully conveyed to the mothers. In 1988 the *Fureai-Koza* project was established to design and develop a group parent-training program that could be administered with ease by the local children's center's staff members, who usually have a limited amount of knowledge about behavioral training.

Shibano (1984) introduced the idea of research and development of the intervention programs and the procedures of developmental research and utilization, originally proposed by Thomas (1978). In the course of developing the *Fureai-Koza* program, Shibano consistently emphasized the significance of developing social work interventions in the research and development perspective (Nakagawa & Shibano, 1993). Later he adopted and tried to simplify the design and development procedures advocated by Thomas (1984) and Thomas and Rothman (1994) in order to make it easier for practitioners to implement the integrated procedures of research and development as well as dissemination (utilization). Shibano (2000) proposed modified design-and-development procedures as practice model-development procedures. He and his colleagues published a series of practice models that they had designed and developed as a result of implementation of the modified procedures. They included models of family reunification for institutionalized children (Endo & Shibano, 1998), behavioral staff training for care workers in nursing homes (Endo & Shibano 1999), and child-protective-service case management with a multimedia CD-ROM manual (Shibano, 2001).

It is believed that practice models or intervention programs thus designed and developed are, by nature, the ones with an evidence-based practice component embedded, since one of the most important features of the modified design-and-development is iteration or repetitive process to improve an initial and tentative model. In iteration, repetitive evaluation of the initial model is essential. Evaluation procedures based on evidence are integrated into the model.

MODIFIED DESIGN-AND-DEVELOPMENT PROCESS AND
BEHAVIORAL GROUP PARENT TRAINING PROGRAM

The original developmental research and utilization procedures that Thomas (1978) advocated comprised five distinctive steps: (1) analysis, (2) development, (3) evaluation, (4) diffusion, and (5) adoption. Thomas later added the "design" phase as the second step of the procedure to establish his intervention design and development model (Thomas 1984). More recently, Thomas and Rothman (1994) further elaborated the model. In their elaborated model, the developmental process is more clearly and rationally delineated as the innovative creation of intervention programs based on information integration and an iterative design-redesign process. The modified design and development procedures used to design and develop the *Fureai-Koza* program have only four phases, and the emphasis is on the fourth phase or dissemination. In figure 9.2, the first and second phases of Thomas and Rothman's design and development model are integrated into the first phase of the modified design and development model and the fourth and fifth phase are integrated into the third phase. The second phase and the third phase are looped, to suggest that the iteration (the repeated process of returning to the previous phase after evaluation) takes place when the initial intervention program is not satisfactory and its redesign is in order. The loop in the third phase represents the iterative process to modify and improve the initial and tentative program on the basis of ongoing evaluation. As mentioned previously, through this iterative process, an evaluation procedure with tools to gather evidential data are also to be developed and installed into the final program package for dissemination. The modified design and development puts more emphasis on the diffusion or dissemination of the program finalized after iteration. The specific procedures will be discussed in the following section.

A series of both quantitative and qualitative research studies was conducted to gather and analyze information on the needs that two-generation families burdened with child rearing have with respect to parenting. The relevant literature was also reviewed for possible intervention procedures to meet the identified needs. On the basis of these studies and literature reviews, an initial and tentative program for group parent training was prepared. The initial program has five distinct goals to meet the identified needs and three operational modes to attain the goals, as is shown in figure 9.3. The goals are to have necessary and sufficient knowledge of child development, to have necessary and sufficient parenting skills, to enjoy child rearing, to be (feel) socially related or not socially isolated, and to take a respite from parenting. The first and second goals are attained through the didactic mode (by conveying behavioral principles and procedures to the families by means of lectures) and the coaching mode (e.g., role-playing or behavioral rehearsal). The third, fourth, and fifth goals are attained through the curator mode, which involves various means to create a positive atmosphere, such as preparing a relaxing setting, providing babysitters, building group cohesiveness, and so forth. These elements were combined in the tentative *Fureai-*

FIGURE 9.2   Modified Design and Development Process Chart

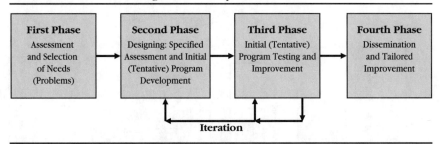

Iteration

Koza model, the immediate aim of which is to reduce parental burden and anxiety pertaining to child rearing and a long-term goal of which is the prevention of child abuse and neglect (see figure 9.4).

Figure 9.4 provides an outline of the initial program in which a session is held on a weekly basis for five consecutive weeks. A group of ten families is recruited through the monthly municipal newsletter.

The knowledge and skills of behavioral parenting are to be conveyed didactically to the families without use of unfamiliar behavioral terms. Instead, terms coined by White (1985) were adopted to explain the operant procedures useful to understand the child-mother interactions and to modify parenting behaviors. Notably, most of the basic operant procedures fall nicely into White's three basic categories of parenting skills: consultant, limit setter, and architect. The consultant role employs the various operant procedures to increase behaviors. The limit-setter role employs the various operant procedures to decrease behaviors. The architect role employs the various operant procedures to set up environments in which the positive behaviors are more likely to take place and the negative behaviors are less likely to occur. A series of lectures or statements were embedded into the program, as is depicted in figure 9.4. Role-playing that represented the coaching mode was also incorporated into the program to supplement the didactic mode. As for the curator mode, group work was done to develop group cohesiveness in order to help the families relate to one another and ultimately to cope with social isolation. Refreshments and free discussion time were provided after each session to make the families more comfortable. Babysitters were provided so that the parents could enjoy the lectures and exchange information without being preoccupied with their children. The seven-session program was finalized after the iterations in the third phase.

DESIGN, DEVELOPMENT, AND DISSEMINATION OF *FUREAI-KOZA* WITH AN EMBEDDED EVIDENCE-BASED PRACTICE COMPONENT

A distinct characteristic of the modified design and development is the fourth phase, in which the devices are adopted to make it possible to disseminate

FIGURE 9.3 *Fureai-Koza* Program Elements: Needs, Goals, and Operational Modes

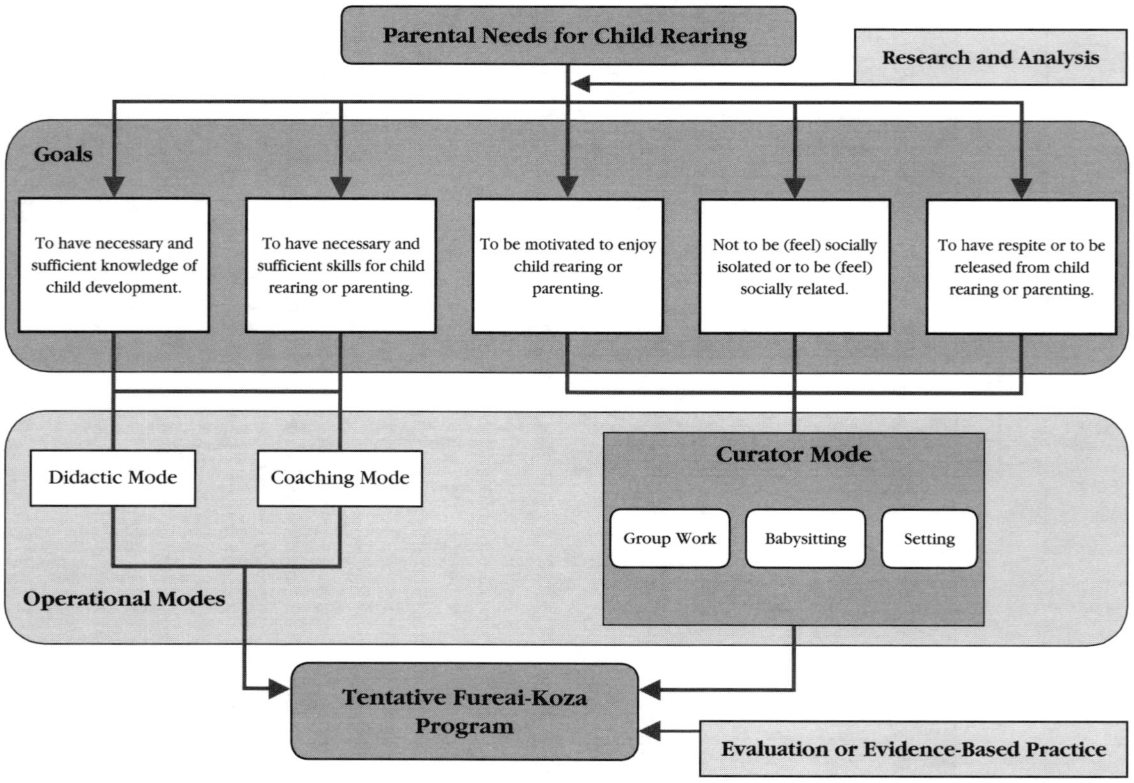

FIGURE 9.4 Tentative Five-Session *Fureai-Koza* Program (Three-Year Version)

Time	Session 1	Session 2	Session 3	Session 4	Session 5
9:30	Reception	Reception	Reception	Reception	Reception
10:00	Salutation	Salutation	Salutation	Salutation	Salutation
10:05	Self-introduction	Seal affixing for attendance	Seal affixing for attendance	Seal affixing for attendance	Seal affixing for attendance
10:10	Orientation: Explaining program overview	Amusement: Introducing games with children	Amusement: Games with children	Amusement: Games with children	Amusement: Games with children
10:20					
10:30		Lecture 1: Child development consultant role	Lecture 2: Limit-setter role	Lecture 3: Architect role	
10:50	Questionnaire: Child rearing anxiety scale (pre)	Group discussion	Role playing	Questions and answers	Questionnaire: Child rearing anxiety scale (post) evaluation
11:20	Explaining homework	Explaining homework	Group discussion	Group discussion	
11:30	Chatting time without staff	Chatting time without staff	Chatting time without staff	Chatting time without staff	Farewell party: Awarding certification
	Homework 1	Homework 2			

Fureai-Koza to the 105 local children's centers in Kobe. The devices are catering; module development; multimedia, interactive manual development; Web site development; and the evidence-based practice component.

Catering

The full-scale *Fureai-Koza* was catered to a local children's center at which the main children's center staff implemented the program in cooperation with local center staff. Local center staff who were interested in adopting *Fureai-Koza* watched experienced staff administer the program. More than a dozen of the local centers have had *Fureai-Koza* catered over the past decade, but few actually adopted it, despite their positive regard for the program. The reason why they decided not to adopt the program was that they believed that the full-scale program was a bit overwhelming to the understaffed local centers. The average local children's center is staffed with a manager and one or two workers in addition to college-student volunteers. Given this understaffed situation, the centers were quite reluctant to participate in the program's administration. They tended to consider the catered *Fureai-Koza* a single-shot event conducted by outsiders.

Module Development

An intervention program should be easy to implement in understaffed settings, and it should be easily modified to various settings, since each agency that adopts the program varies in size, staff, budget, and so on. Thomas (1984) emphasizes the importance of module development when dissemination is undertaken. In cases in which a program is too complex to implement as a total package, it can be broken down into meaningful components. A module is an independent unit of the program that contains a manual guiding implementation and necessary materials, such as teaching materials. Each module can be implemented alone or in combination with other modules, depending on family needs and the resources available at the agency. At the beginning of the *Fureai-Koza* project, the modules were planned and developed in accordance with the categories of the identified needs of the families. The three modes to meet parents' needs were also made into modules. The following modules were identified: program administration, lecture, homework (to supplement the coaching mode), evaluation (to evaluate the program by having the participating families evaluate the program at the last session), babysitter, and free discussion time. The lecture module comprised six submodules: (1) child development, (2) role-playing, (3) consultant role 1 (how to increase positive behaviors), (4) consultant role 2 (how to use a chore chart or behavioral contracting), (5) architect role (how to prepare prosthetic environments and shape behaviors), and (6) limit-setter role (how to decrease negative behaviors). These modules and submodules can be used in many different ways in accordance with the different settings' various needs, staff, and resources. In an understaffed agency with limited resources, for instance, the combination of the child-development, program administration, and babysitter modules could be used for families interested in general information on child development and social contacts as respite.

There is an additional module that has much to do with evidence-based practice. The evaluation module aims to evaluate the effectiveness of the program by monitoring the behavior of the participants so that necessary improvements can be made. Since the module is also one of the devices necessary for dissemination of *Fureai-Koza,* it will be discussed subsequently.

Multimedia, Interactive Manual Development

Successful program dissemination requires a good manual to guide program implementation. One of the practical criteria of the good manual is that the program can be replicated just by following the manual. Many print manuals fail to meet this criterion. In the *Fureai-Koza* project, an audiovisual, multimedia manual was developed. The interactive multimedia manual includes a CD-ROM and a set of print texts. The CD-ROM (authored with Macromedia Director Version 8.0J) contains all the aforementioned modules and includes both text and video clips. Some of the video clips delineate the easy-to-follow procedures required to prepare the modules. Others are video clips of the lectures or submodules, which can be shown to families as teaching materials in combination with the print texts. One of the advantages of the CD-ROM manual is that its contents can be manipulated easily to facilitate learning by referring to the modules and video clips with the click of a mouse. A videotape version of the manual was also developed for local children's centers at which a personal computer was not available. The sequence of the basic components of the videotape manual is presented in figure 9.5. A package of the CD-ROM, the VHS cassette, and the print text materials was delivered to each local children's center.

Web Site Development

A Web site is another powerful device for diffusion of the intervention program. In fact, such a site can be used as a manual when the entire contents of the manual are incorporated into the Web site. Those who are interested in the program have easy access to the Web site: they need only search for the site and click to open it to access the whole interactive manual. Another advantage of a Web page is that the user can easily contact staff who have developed the program to ask questions via e-mail.

The *Fureai-Koza* home page is available in Japanese at www.kobekko.or.jp/age3/index.html. At the time of this writing, only a portion of the program is available to the public, so it does not yet function fully as an interactive manual; however, the entire interactive manual will be available online soon. The *Fureai-Koza* Web site allows for the program to be disseminated beyond the local children's centers directly to self-help groups in the community and even to individual

FIGURE 9.5 Sequence of Elements of Videotape Manual

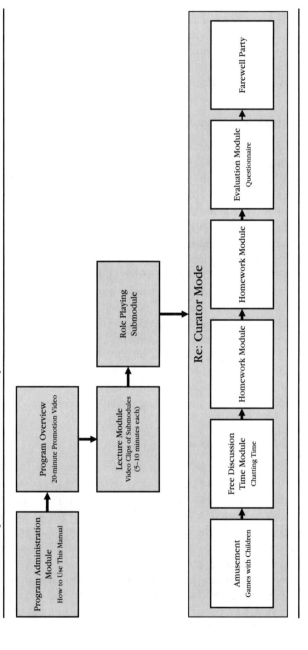

families who are difficult to reach. This means it is important that follow-up service by e-mail is available, in order to avoid the misuse of the program.

Evidence-Based Practice Devices

Fureai-Koza has been undertaken according to a simplified version of Thomas and Rothman's design and development model, but with more emphasis on dissemination. In the early phases of design and development and modification, a series of planned research and literature review is imperative to the design of an initial intervention program; thus, the concept of evidence-based practice is naturally incorporated into the process. As mentioned previously, the five goals of the group parent-training program and the program content to attain the goals were induced by deliberate analysis of the evidence gained from our systematic research and literature review. Furthermore, the program has a module in which some devices are packaged to make it possible to improve the program so that it may be better accepted by the community and disseminated on a larger scale.

The devices packaged in the evaluation module are a subjective evaluation form for program participants, which is administered on the last day of the program; an anxiety scale on child rearing developed by Makino (1982), which is administered in a pre-post manner; a scale on parental attitude toward child, which is the Japanese version of Hudson's (1982) "Index of Parental Attitude"; and a questionnaire filled out by program participants to provide information on the relationship between participants' attributes and evaluation results. These devices are delivered in the form of durable hard copies as a module package to each local children's center, at which the necessary number of photocopies are made.

With these devices, evaluation results are accumulated to form a clinical database. The data are analyzed on a regular basis for use as clinical feedback information for improvement of the disseminated program. This evaluation system is depicted in figure 9.6.

EVALUATION OF DISSEMINATION AND IMPLICATIONS

Three versions of *Fureai-Koza* have been developed so far: (1) for families with a six-month-old (zero-year version), (2) for families with a one-and-a-half-year-old (year-and-half version), and (3) for families with a three-year-old (three-year version). In 1999 the city of Kobe decided to fund a grant for the three-year version to be administered in 105 local children's centers. However, none of the local children's centers administered the full-scale program, because the city granted only three sessions' worth of budget to each center. Each center then combined the modules differently to implement its unique *Fureai-Koza* in accordance with the needs of the target families. In late 1999 the efforts of *Fureai-Koza* dissemination were evaluated. Because space is limited in this chapter, only some

FIGURE 9.6 Evidence-Based Practice Component Embedded in the *Fureai-Koza* Program

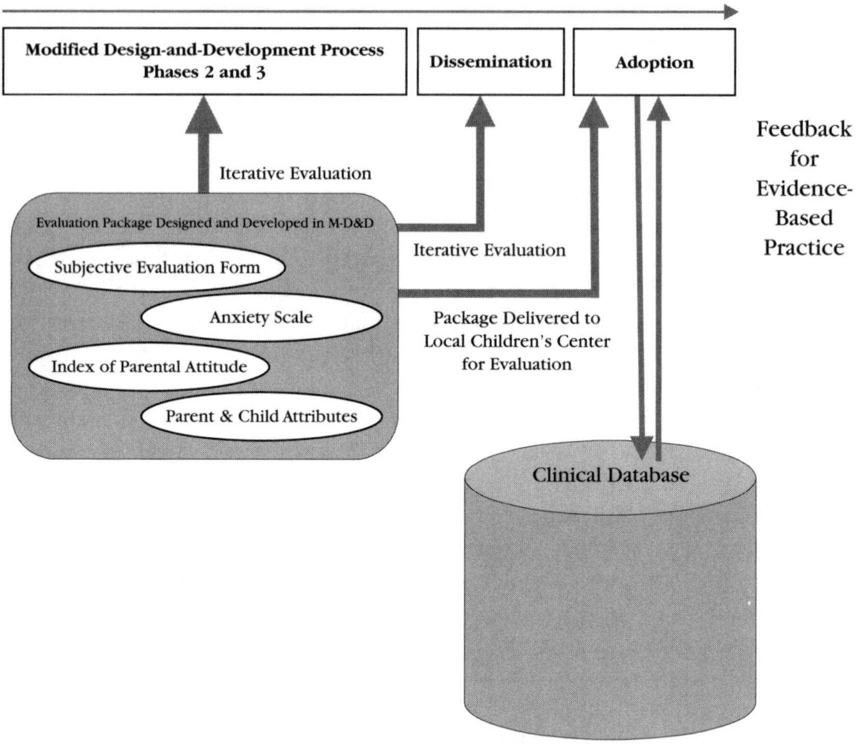

selected evaluation results are reported; their implications are discussed in the remainder of this chapter.

Method

A questionnaire sent to the 105 local children's centers in December 1999 comprised the following four areas of inquiry: (1) overall evaluation of the difficulty in administering *Fureai-Koza,* (2) selection of submodules or lectures and evaluation of the difficulty in administering them, (3) evaluation of the attitudes of the participants, and (4) identification of the areas that need to be improved.

Results

Data from questionnaires returned by 68 percent (71) of the local children's centers were analyzed using SPSS. The majority of the centers (82 percent) implemented a three-session program by combining three to four relevant submodules in accordance with the particular needs of the families participating in their programs. The average number of participating families per local children's center was 44 (98 at the maximum and 8 at the minimum), which means that more than four thousand families participated in the program.

The overall difficulty in introducing *Fureai-Koza* at the local children's centers was evaluated on a five-point Likert-type scale (1 = "very difficult," 2 = "difficult," 3 = "neutral," 4 = "easy," and 5 = "very easy"). Of the local centers, 38 percent (27) reported that preparation for the program was difficult (a rating of 1 or 2), and about 20 percent (14) considered it easy (a rating of 4 or 5). Similarly, about 37 percent (26) indicated that the program was difficult to administer (a rating of 1 or 2), and about 27 percent (19) reported that it was easy to administer (a rating of 4 or 5). The modes in both questions were "3" (about 42 percent and 37 percent, respectively). In addition, in response to the question "Did the introduction of the program hinder daily routines?" about 30 percent (21) of local centers answered either "much" or "somewhat," and 31 percent (22) answered either "not at all" or "hardly." Although the centers had some difficulty in introducing the program, it appears that the introduction was not particularly troublesome for the majority of centers.

With respect to the selection of appropriate submodules, the centers did appear to have some difficulty; however, their difficulties did not extend to leading discussions after presentation of audiovisual materials of the modules. The limit-setter module (how to decrease negative behaviors) was the leading choice; about 91 percent of all the local centers chose it. The second most popular module was the role-play module (74 percent) and the third most popular was the child-development module (59 percent). The consultant module (how to increase positive behaviors) was chosen as the most difficult module by only 28 percent of the local centers. The families interested in *Fureai-Koza* may have more difficulty in decreasing negative behaviors than in increasing positive behaviors. It may also be the case that they are preoccupied with, or pay more attention to, negative behaviors and are indifferent to the positive ones. The limit-setter module contains skills such as positive and negative punishment but also skills such as differential reinforcement of other behaviors, differential reinforcement of alternative behaviors, and differential reinforcement of incompatible behaviors. If parents use these nonpunishment skills to decrease negative behaviors, they may have a better chance to avoid situations in which they can be abusive.

The overall attitude of the families participating in *Fureai-Koza* was evaluated by center staff. Approximately 52 percent (37) of the respondents said that the families were either "very enthusiastic" or "enthusiastic" about participating in the program. They also said that they did not have much difficulty in helping families develop group cohesiveness.

Six program areas were identified as the ones to be improved. The top two areas were securing babysitters (approximately 84 percent of the centers reported that this could be improved) and the contents of submodules (almost 83 percent). Since most of the local centers are understaffed, they have to secure enough babysitters from outside the center. With tight budgets, they usually cannot afford to hire them and thus usually depend on volunteers who they have difficulty in securing. Since the contents of the submodules were developed on the basis of the needs of limited samples, it is not surprising to know that there is much room for improvement. This will be discussed in the following section.

IMPLICATIONS

The *Fureai-Koza* project is now in the final phase of the design and development process. Although the first trial of the program's dissemination to the local children's centers appeared to proceed smoothly, there is room for improvement in some areas. Among them are securing enough babysitters and improving of the submodule contents (lectures). It is important that the babysitter module function in order for the parents to have respite during the program period. Because it was aware of this, Kobe's Department of Children and Community began to play a tentative mediator role. The department recruits college-student volunteers for *Fureai-Koza* babysitting and assigns them to the local centers. This centralized system is yet to be evaluated. Since it is difficult to believe that the department will be able to continue in this role, a localized system must be developed such that each local center is able to recruit its own student volunteers.

In addition, the contents of the submodules must be tailored to meet the specific needs of the families at each center. However, there seems to be a catch-22 situation in which module content should be general enough for dissemination but specific enough for adoption. A module for such tailoring needs to be developed. It is only the beginning of the final phase of *Fureai-Koza's* design and development and the dissemination efforts continue to realize the evidence-based parent training program in the community.

REFERENCES

Endo, F., & Shibano, M. (1999). Environmental modification based on operant techniques to alleviate the agitated behavior of an elderly person in a residential care unit. *Japanese Journal of Behavior Therapy, 24*(1), 1–14.

Endo, W., & Shibano, M. (1998). R&D of a program for early reunification of institutionalized children. *Journal of Social Work Studies, 23*(4), 291–302.

Gelfand, D. M., & Hartman, D. P. (1975). *Child behavior: Analysis and therapy.* New York: Pergamon Press.

Hudson, W. W. (1982). *The clinical measurement package.* Illinois: Dorsey Press.

Kuwata, S., & Shibano, M. (1990). R&D in social work practice: An example of R&D of a program for parenting skills training for mothers with under a year old babies. *Kwansei Gakuin University Sociology Department Studies, 61,* 49–82.

Makino, K. (1982). Living of mothers with infants: Child rearing anxiety. *Family Education Studies, 3,* 34–56.

Miller, W. H. (1975). *Systematic parent training.* Champaign, IL: Research Press.

Nakagawa, C., & Shibano, M. (1993). A trial of DR&U and Dissemination of Fureai-koza by means of catering. *Kwansei Gakuin University Sociology Department Studies, 67,* 131–142.

Patterson, G. R. (1976). *Living with children.* Champaign, IL: Research Press.

Patterson, G. R., Reid, J. B., Jones, R. R., & Conger, R. (1975). *Social learning approach to family intervention: Families with aggressive children.* Eugene: Castilia.

Pinkston, E. M., Friedman, B. S., & Polster, R. A. (1981). Parents as agents for behavior change. In S. P. Schinke (Ed.), *Behavioral methods in social welfare* (pp. 29–40). New York: Aldine.

Shibano, M. (1984). R&D in social work. *Journal of Juvenile Problems, 33,* 65–79.

Shibano, M. (1989). Fureai-Koza: Behavioral parent training project. *Growing Children, 1,* 83–130.

Shibano, M. (2000). Innovation in child and family services: Research and development of practice models and manuals. *Kwansei Gakuin University Sociology Department Studies, 85,* 55–65.

Shibano, M. (2001). *Case management manual for child abuse and neglect.* Tokyo: Yuhikaku.

Shibano, M., Cox, W. H., Rzepnicki, T. L., & Pinkston, E. M. (1982). A single-parent intervention to increase parenting skills over time. In E. M. Pinkston et al. (Eds.), *Effective social work practice* (pp. 422–434). San Francisco: Jossey-Bass.

Takada, H. (Ed.). (1991). *Problematic behaviors of children with disabilities.* Osaka, Japan: Niheisha.

Thomas, E. J. (1978). Mousetraps, developmental research, and social work education. *Social Service Review, 52,* 468–483.

Thomas, E. J. (1984). *Designing interventions for the helping professions.* Beverly Hills, CA: Sage.

Thomas, E. J., & Rothman, J. (1994). An integrative perspective on intervention research. In J. Rothman & E. J. Thomas (Eds.), *Intervention research: Design and development for human service* (pp. 3–23). New York: Haworth Press.

Yamagami, T. (Ed.). (1998). *Parent training program for those who raise children with disabilities: Classroom for mothers.* Osaka, Japan: Niheisha.

CHAPTER 10

ADHERENCE TO HIV THERAPIES: CAN APPLIED BEHAVIOR ANALYSIS HELP?

Nathan L. Linsk and
Christopher G. Mitchell

In the past twenty years, HIV/AIDS has emerged as a major infectious disease that has significant social, emotional, community, and societal impacts. As knowledge about this epidemic and its treatment evolve, support and management continue to become more complex. Interventions were initially launched rapidly with minimal evaluation, in an effort to reach people quickly, because many people were severely ill or dying. Therefore, in addition to medication treatments, social treatments such as case management, psychosocial counseling, support groups, and alternative therapies were quickly launched without considerations of best practices. The need for both individualized and group evaluations of interventions continues to be critical, not only to ensure that the best interventions are selected for individuals but also to ensure that funds are allocated most effectively. This article addresses an emerging aspect of the HIV situation, medication management, as an example of how empirically based best practices can help support the affected individual and maximize outcomes.

BACKGROUND

As a result of antiretroviral combination therapy, being the primary means of treating HIV infection in developed countries, care management has become increasingly complicated from the perspective of the medical provider, social care providers, and people living with HIV and AIDS. The regimens are difficult for even the most educated and motivated patients. The notion of "adherence to treatment" has evolved to describe efforts to successfully achieve behaviors necessary to take complex medications. This offers an alternative to "compliance," which focuses on following the orders of the provider. Adherence interventions have been suggested that are centered on the person who must make decisions about taking the drugs rather than the provider (Noring, Duber, Birkhead, & Agins, 2001).

To prevent the rapid development of viral resistance to antiretroviral therapy, it is crucial that patients fully understand and are able to adhere to their medication schedule. However, the medication therapy requirements are complex; the regimen for an individual may have various storage (refrigeration), dietary, and specific scheduling requirements. Dosages may be needed three to four times daily, although less frequent dosages may be viable for some. Recently, new regimens have emerged that involve dosages one or two times per day, which are effective for only some patients. The treatments have multiple potential medication interactions and side effects. It is common for people living with HIV/AIDS to take three or more antiretroviral medications, antitubercular medication, and two or more medications to prevent opportunistic infectious. A medication regimen of ten to twelve, or as many as thirty or more, pills each day is not uncommon. To ensure adherence to such complicated regimens, HIV-positive people require a great deal of support.

The consequences of nonadherence may be so severe that it is best to delay treatment rather than risk treatment errors. As combination therapy proceeds, the virus may be rapidly mutating, and the mutations may lead to changes in the virus that are resistant to the drugs being used and to related drugs. In effect, drug resistance means that the drug in question, and its relatives in the available array of antiretroviral drugs, no longer have any clinical effect for the individual. The likelihood of developing drug resistance increases with medication errors. Furthermore, the development of resistant viral strains, if transmitted to others, may create a situation in which the drugs are ineffective for a whole community of people. This has been the case with tuberculosis in the past decade; not only has there been a surge of tuberculosis in a society that once believed the disease could be eliminated but also multidrug resistant strains have emerged. From a public health perspective, drug resistance is associated with both multidrug resistance issues and transmission of a resistant virus, which may, in fact, lead to a worsening of the epidemic in the community.

The consequences of developing drug resistance are significant (Bangsberg et al., 2000; Linsk & Bonk, 2000). For the individual, nonadherence-related resistance may make unavailable a whole class of promising drugs and lead to the loss of the opportunity to achieve the objective of antiretroviral therapy, which is an undetectable level of the virus. Although some immune restoration occurs, unfortunately viral eradication cannot be achieved in the foreseeable future. Clearly people who cannot complete the care regimens will be left out of the hopeful promises of new antiviral treatments. Nonadherence is associated with a long-term decline in health status or death, not to mention a personal sense of failure that may well occur if someone does not successfully take medications.

How can these mutations be prevented? The chief means to reduce the chance of viral resistance to drugs is in absolute consistency in use of the medications. This means taking the medication at the required time and amount continuously and on an ongoing basis. No longer can the person forget doses, take drug holidays, or decide not to take the drug because he or she does not feel like it or for other reasons. The virus is unforgiving. The medical provider cannot rely on a standard protocol to prescribe the optimal plan for each person with HIV. The provider and the patient work together to make decisions, which may be challenging when neither has a good history of working with the other.

In the case of HIV/AIDS, the estimated level of adherence needed for effective treatment and minimal development of resistance is estimated to exceed 95 percent, and there are significantly more favorable outcomes if adherence can take place at the 99 percent level (Paterson et al., 1999). For example, this would be missing one or fewer doses over a one month, three times a day regimen, which exceeds usual expectations for behavioral maintenance.

Given that close to 100 percent adherence to drug therapies is assumed to be necessary to promote effective therapy and to reduce the risk of drug resistance, practitioners are challenged in terms of how to assess whether any individual will be able to achieve this objective. As Barthwell (1997) points out, medical practitioners, drug companies, AIDS advocates, and drug treatment workers have all questioned the suitability of HIV treatment for clients who are "deemed less likely to adhere, a dangerous process that can lead to discrimination" (p. 2).

Studies of other diseases reveal that higher levels of nonadherence are normative in medical care. Estimates of noncompliance range from 20 percent to 40 percent for short-term responses to acute diseases, to 50 percent for longer-term symptomatic chronic diseases such as diabetes, and even higher for long-term chronic illnesses that require lifestyle changes, such as hypertension (Sherbourne, Hays, Ordway, DiMatteo, & Kravitz, 1992). Studies have found that patient adherence is largely unrelated to socioeconomic status and education, is not a matter of simply obeying instructions, and is related to various factors (Barthwell, 1997; Chesney, 1997; Friedland, 1997). Given that many people living with HIV experience problems with literacy, homelessness, substance abuse, and mental illness, adherence interventions must incorporate several components that respond to special needs.

LITERATURE REVIEW

Predating the use of current combination antiretroviral therapy, several studies have pointed out the association between availability and use of HIV treatment by race, sex, and injection drug-use status. Chaisson, Keruly, and Moore (1995) measured disease progression and survival in 1372 HIV-positive patients. They found no relation between disease progression and sex, race, injection drug use, income, level of education, or insurance status. However, given that almost half of HIV-infected individuals are infected in association with injection drug use (their own use or that of a partner), the challenge of determining the relationship between effective outcomes of adherence interventions for HIV antiretroviral therapy continues to be compelling. Bangsberg, Tulsky, Hecht, and Moss (1997) make a case for antiretroviral therapy for HIV-positive homeless people, but they caution that it may be ethically necessary to delay treatment until the patient's life is stabilized if there is a strong likelihood that immediate treatment will result in resistance. They note that all HIV-positive homeless people are not unstable, however. Of homeless and marginally housed HIV-positive people in San Francisco, 72 percent could name a primary care clinician they had visited on average of six times in the previous year. Those in methadone maintenance and in residence hotels may be more likely to adhere than those on the streets or not in recovery. The authors note that barriers to adherence are often as much system related as they are patient related. Adherence requires confidential and convenient clinic locations, flexible appointment scheduling, secure places to store medication, and perhaps transportation to clinic and pharmacists (Bamberger et al., 2000).

A few studies have examined adherence and coexisting situations, such as substance use and the impact on adherence to medications. In a retrospective study of 57 HIV-infected injection drug users, Ferrando, Wall, Batki, and Sorensen (1997) assessed adherence to Azido-Thymidine (AZT, the first antiretroviral therapy drug) in methadone maintenance treatment programs and found no correlation between adherence to AZT and recent illicit drug use. Similarly, adherence was not associated with psychiatric status. Wall et al. (1995) studied 25 HIV-infected drug users in methadone treatment in San Francisco and found that health care interactions—including nursing follow-up, monitoring pill counts, and feedback on CD4+ (or T cells, a measure of immune function) levels—showed significant improvements in adherence, but that this only occurred when the supervision was present. Freedman, Rodriguez, and French (1996) found that reasons for nonadherence among injection drug users included hoarding or selling of medication, stockpiling medications for future use if they were to become sick, forgetfulness, confusion about regimen, fear of overdosing or interaction with illicit drugs, and side effects. Broers, Morabia, and Hirshcel (1994) studied 150 injection drug users and 162 other HIV-positive people who began taking AZT between 1989 and 1992. The drug users needed more time than others to accept AZT therapy, but they were as compliant with treatment as others: 81.3 percent versus 83.2 had good compliance (but insufficient for antiretroviral therapy). Former drug users and injection drug users receiving methadone began taking AZT more often and complied better than did active drug users. On the basis of the extant literature, then, substance abuse, homelessness, and psychiatric illness were associated with less treatment and worse adherence.

The case for good research on this topic is even more compelling because those infected by injection drug use are more likely to be Hispanics and African Americans, the fastest-growing risk-behavior groups in terms of HIV prevalence. To help a person with HIV make decisions about whether to begin treatment and how to be successful, practice approaches need to be comprehensive, tied to research and theory, and carefully evaluated.

There are no universally recognized evidence-based best practices regarding treatment adherence and HIV, although there are several guidelines. The standard guidelines in the United States are "Guidelines for the Use of Antiretroviral Agents in HIV-1-Infected Adults and Adolescents," developed by a panel on clinical practices for treatment of HIV infection convened by the Department of Health and Human Services (2003). These guidelines state the following predictors of optimal adherence to HIV medications and optimal viral suppression includes: "(1) availability of emotional and practical life supports; (2) a patient's ability to fit medications into his or her daily routine; (3) understanding that suboptimal adherence leads to resistance; (4) recognizing that taking all medication doses is critical; (5) feeling comfortable taking medications in front of others; and (6) keeping clinic appointments" (p. 10). Several specific strategies are suggested, including negotiating a treatment plan with the patient; assessing the patient's readiness to take medication; educating the patient; developing a plan for the specific regimen, which may include practice sessions; using daily or weekly pill-boxes, timers, and other devices; informing the patient about side effects; engaging and educating family and friends; using community-based case managers and peer educators; and "trusting relationships between the patient, clinician and the health care team" (Department of Health and Human Services, 2003, pp. 10–11).

THEORETICAL APPLICATIONS

In conceptualizing adherence, practitioners need to have a broad understanding that places medication-related behavior in the complex social and emotional context of the patient. This broader definition of adherence not only includes the prescribed use of medication and the prompts and intervention techniques suggested to support their medication adherence but also denotes keeping appointments with health service providers; pursuing and securing the recommended ancillary services (e.g. mental health services, substance abuse treatment, housing, public aid); and following through with other treatment plan recommendations, which are ideally made collaboratively between the patient and the treatment team.

Much HIV research and practice, particularly in the prevention area, has used a "health belief model" (Hochbaum, 1958; Rosenstock, 1974; Strecher & Rosenstock, 1999) to conceptualize intervention. This model posits likelihood of action as a combination of the individual's perception of a specific situation in terms of the degree of harm that will occur as a consequence of not taking a particular action as well as their perception that a positive action will reduce that harm. Modifying factors are included in this approach, including individual characteristics such as age, sex, ethnicity, personality, socioeconomic status, and knowledge. Cues to action include education, symptoms, and information, including media information. Likelihood of action is then considered the difference between perceived benefits minus perceived barriers to behavior. In terms of applied behavioral analysis, this approach might be considered an aversive stimulus—the perceived health problem—and the individual's behavior to avoid that negative outcome. Application of this to adherence would include patient-education materials that explain or depict the dangers of nonadherence, the benefits of adherence, and the individual's need to make an informed decision. Much HIV/AIDS education, as well as antismoking and other health education, has taken this type of approach, often with the assumption that if people understand the risk, they will accordingly modify their behavior.

A more recent application of theory to HIV/AIDS, including adherence and compliance issues, uses the conceptual framework of the "transtheoretical model of change," which is elaborated on by Prochaska and DiClemente (1982). This theoretically eclectic model emphasizes *intentional* behavior change (Grimley, Prochaska, Velicer, Blais, & DiClemente, 1994). According to this model, individuals progress through specific stages as they struggle to adopt and/or eliminate certain behaviors. The stages are precontemplation, contemplation, preparation, action, and maintenance (DiClemente et al., 1991). Recognition of where a patient is on this continuum is essential to identification of the medical and/or psychosocial interventions and assistance necessary to effect behavior change. Applied to persons with HIV/AIDS under medical care, the stages-of-change framework can be useful in recognizing and understanding how patients may approach adherence differently and require different types of intervention supports depending on where they find themselves in the stages of change. For instance, the issues related to adherence will differ quite significantly between a patient who has just made the decision to commence antiretroviral medication and a patient who has been successfully maintaining antiretroviral medication for many months.

Midwest AIDS Training and Education Partners has used this transtheoretical model of change to develop the RIMES/EARS (Readiness, Initiation of Treatment, and Maintenance and Evaluation / Engage, Assess, Recommend, and Support) adherence initiative. This initiative allows progress to be monitored and readjusted as needed (Linsk, Lubin, Sherer, & Schechtman, 1998). The model is useful for training and patient education, but it has not been specifically evaluated or monitored.

TOWARD A BEHAVIOR ANALYSIS APPROACH

It may be surprising that adherence to HIV drugs has not been the focus of applied behavior analysis practice or research. Only one unpublished article investigates monitory reinforcement combined with structured training to find improved adherence (Rigsby et al., 1999). The requirements of medication adherence, however, are extremely relevant to an empirically and theoretically based practical approach. Application of behavior analysis may have utility in terms of assessment of readiness to use these complex drugs; how best to construct an adherence program; and, perhaps most particularly, how to monitor adherence and goal achievement.

Toward these ends, an adherence program will be described that uses both the technology and principles of applied behavior analysis to help people with HIV make decisions about initiating and maintaining antiretroviral therapy.

ASSESSMENT

Various methods to establish recording and data-collection methods for people with HIV/AIDS–related medications have been put forward, including logs, pillboxes, computerized medication dispensing systems that record the number of times a bottle is opened, and self-report by the person taking the drugs or report by significant others. Clinicians may ask their patients and clients to bring in these records; some clinicians have even included telephone call systems, both in which the provider or another staff member calls the client on a regular interval or unexpectedly and in which the provider or staff member uses a page and call-back system. Although these approaches have various results, a behavior analysis approach may have the advantage of offering a useful analytic system to establish whether the person is ready to use the drugs, whether they achieve their behavioral objectives, and whether the regimen needs to be adjusted.

Toward that end, a standard data-recording system might be developed and implemented prior to the initiation of therapies. Several practitioners and researchers have suggested simulated adherence trials in which the individual uses placebos, often such everyday substances as jellybeans or mints, to simulate the regimen. A recording method that incorporated which stimuli patients use to remind themselves to take the drugs, an incident-by-incident record of whether they responded to the stimulus, whether the response would be to take the drug or some other response, and the consequence of their taking or not taking the drug would be useful data for patients and for their helpers. This record could then be brought to the subsequent session and reviewed with the provider. An example of a simple log is provided in table 10.1.

In this hypothetical example, John takes his medication four times a day. The data-collection form enables him to record the details of each dosage time on a daily basis. John has selected cues to use for each dosage time, brushing teeth, lunch time, washing dishes, and so on. On this day, he was successful in taking his medications only for two of the four doses. However, the data form enables him to indicate what worked and what did not (mediators); these mediators can then be used to redesign the program if needed. John also indicates the consequences of taking or not taking the drugs. In this case, it is apparent that there are not very strong reinforcers, only filling out this log. His expressed guilt and anger as negative consequences are items for discussion and further analysis.

The functional analysis reveals that the person adhered only 50 percent of the time that day, and over the course of the week, the person's adherence rate was about 65 percent. This is too low of an adherence level to achieve viral load reduction. When the patient brings the log to the practitioner, they can jointly review the log, reinforce positive progress, and address problems. In addition, the patient and practitioner can discuss consequences. In fact, the consequences are not easily recorded, because there seldom is a direct consequence of taking the drug appropriately or not and what comes later. The practitioner may decide to work on developing positive reinforcers for adherence before recommending initiation of ongoing treatment.

Given this baseline analysis, which might be recorded graphically, John might choose to work on drug adherence before initiating the actual drug regimen. Once the regimen is initiated, continued use of the recording method will allow

TABLE 10.1 Adherence Behavior Analysis Log Example

Time of required dosage	Antecedents: Did you use a cue to remember the dosage?	Behavior: Were you able to take the drug as required? Note any modification of the plan.	If so, what helped you to do so?	If not, why not?	Consequence: Was there a consequence to taking or not taking the drug?
Morning dose: 8:00 a.m.	Brushing teeth	Yes, able to take log	Putting "pill" by tooth-brush night before	OK	Rewarded self by filling out log
Afternoon dose: 1:00 p.m.	After lunch	No, lunch delayed and then I was in a hurry		Too busy	Felt guilty and worried about it
Evening dose: 7:30 p.m.	Washing dishes after dinner	Yes, remembered to do it	Having the log in the kitchen		Not really
Night dose: 11:00 p.m.	Setting alarm clock	No		Too tired to remember	Angry at self next morning

for monitoring use of the drugs, which might be available to a person doing his or her own self-analysis, to the adherence helper (who might be a nurse, social worker, psychologist, or case manager), or to the physician who is primarily responsible for medical management.

It is important to have an ongoing plan for how long the person will maintain this kind of analysis. If the person is successful, it may be important to reduce data-collection demands while taking care to maintain positive supports for taking the drugs. If there are side effects of the drugs that are unpleasant, it will be especially important to offer the individual positive consequences, which might be available through a recording, self-reward, and feedback system. Another option for feedback and support may be the use of a group modality.

Finding sufficiently powerful reinforcers is a challenge for this type of approach. However, the use of a behavioral database and attention to how to reduce the negative and increase the positive consequences of taking these drugs is a starting point.

There is no ongoing program for adherence that will endure over time. Instead, the person needs to be aware of what is changing about his or her health situation, what will change in terms of treatment, and what is changing in his or her environment. The comprehensive program needs to be adjusted any time that there is a change in any dimension of adherence. Use of an applied behavior analysis framework, at least episodically, may enable the person to maintain accurate adherence over time or, at a minimum, help him or her become clear about when adherence is not working.

CONCLUSION

Cross-case data clearly are needed to develop and evaluate a behavioral medication-adherence approach. To date, most evaluations have been programmatic rather than systematic and have used a single case design applied across a suitable number of people who use the approach. In addition, the particular needs of subpopulations must be considered and addressed. Although the labor intensity of this approach may appear to be an additional responsibility for HIV-positive people and their caregivers, the critical nature of adherence is an excellent justification for taking on that responsibility.

Adherence to HIV medication does not have a strong base of evidence-based treatment guidelines. However, the approach uses the major features of applied behavior analysis, although it is not always operationalized in the manner noted in this article. Nonetheless, providers often take a baseline, sometimes retrospectively; analyze the findings with the client; formulate an intervention; and evaluate the results. Given that the behavior is so specific and can be counted in terms of pills taken, data is readily available. Often the client is asked to self-report behavior, but this entails reliability issues, particularly after more than two days. Use of a more explicit evidence-based behavior analysis approach may be helpful to clients and providers alike.

REFERENCES

Bamberger, J. D., Unick, J., Klein, P., Fraser, M., Chesney, M., & Katz, M. H. (2000). Helping urban poor stay with antiretroviral HIV drug therapy. *American Journal of Public Health, 90*(5), 699–701.

Bangsberg, D., Tulsky, J., Hecht, F., & Moss, A. (1997). Protease inhibitors in the homeless. *Journal of the American Medical Association, 278*(1), 63–65.

Bangsberg, D. R., Hecht, F. M., Charlebois, E. D., Zolopa, A. L., Holodniy, M., Sheiner, L., et al. (2000). Adherence to protease inhibitors, HIV-01 viral load and development of drug resistance in an indigent population. *AIDS, 14,* 357–366.

Barthwell, A. G. (1997). Substance use and the puzzle of adherence. *Focus: A Guide to AIDS Research and Counseling, 12*(9), 1–3.

Broers, B., Morabia, A., & Hirshcel, B. (1994). A cohort study of drug users' compliance with zidovudine treatment. *Archives of Internal Medicine, 154*(10), 1121–1127.

Chaisson, R. E., Keruly, J. C., & Moore, R. D. (1995). Race, sex, drug use and progression of HIV. *New England Journal of Medicine, 333*(12), 751–756.

Chesney, M. (1997, November). *Overview of adherence to medical treatment.* Keynote address presented at Adherence to New HIV Therapies, A Research Conference. Forum for Collaborative HIV Research, National Minority AIDS Council, National Institutes of Health Office of AIDS Research, Washington, DC.

Department of Health and Human Services. (2003). Guidelines for the use of anti-retroviral agents in HIV-1–Infected adults and adolescents. Available at http://AIDSinfo.nih.gov

DiClemente, C., Prochaska, J., Velicer, W., Fairhurst, S., Rossi, J., & Velasquez, M. (1991). The process of smoking cessation: An analysis of precontemplation, contemplation and preparation stages of change. *Journal of Consulting and Clinical Psychology, 59,* 295–304.

Ferrando, S., Wall, T., Batki, S., & Sorensen, J. L. (1997). Psychiatric morbidity, illicit drug use and adherence to zidovudine (AZT) among injection drug users with HIV disease. *American Journal of Drug and Alcohol Abuse, 22*(4), 475–487.

Freedman, R. C., Rodrigues, G. M., & French, J. R. (1996). Compliance with AZT treatment regimens of HIV-seropositive injection drug users. *AIDS Education and Prevention, 8*(1), 57–81.

Friedland, G. (1997, November). *State of the science: Why adherence is an issue in HIV therapy.* Keynote address presented at Adherence to New HIV Therapies, A Research Conference, Forum for Collaborative HIV Research, National Minority AIDS Council, National Institutes of Health Office of AIDS Research, Washington, DC.

Grimley, D., Prochaska, J., Velicer, W., Blais, L., & DiClemente, C. (1994). The transtheoretical model of change. In T. Brinhaupt & R. Lipka (Eds.), *Changing the self: Philosophies, techniques and experiences* (pp. 201–227). Albany, NY: SUNY Press.

Hochbaum, G. M. (1958). *Public participation in medical screening programs: A sociopsychological study* (PHS Publication No. 572). Washington, DC: U.S. Government Printing Office.

Linsk, N. L., & Bonk, N. (2000). Adherence to treatment as social work challenges. In V. J. Lynch (Ed.), *HIV/AIDS at the year 2000: A sourcebook for social workers* (pp. 211–227). Boston: Allyn & Bacon.

Linsk, N. L., Lubin, B., Sherer, R., & Schechtman, B. A. (1998). *The MATEC adherence initiative* [Online]. Available from the Midwest AIDS Training and Education Partners, www.matec.info.

Noring, S., Dubler, N. N., Birkhead, G., & Agins, B. (2001). A new paradigm for HIV care: Ethical and clinical considerations. *American Journal of Public Health, 91*(5), 690–694.

Paterson, D., Swindells, S., Mohr, J., Brester, M., Vergis, E., Squier, C., et al. (1999, February). How much adherence is enough? A prospective study of adherence to protease inhibitor therapy using MEMS caps [Abstract No. 92]. *6th Conference on Retroviruses and Opportunistic Infections,* Chicago.

Prochaska, J. O., & DiClemente, C. C. (1982). Transtheoretical therapy: Toward a more integrated model of change. *Psychotherapy Theory, Research and Practice, 19*(3), 276–288.

Rigsby, M. O., Rosen, M., Beauvais, J., Cramer, J. A., Rainey, P. M., O'Mally, S. S., et al. (1999). *Monetary reimbursement combined with structured training increases adherence to antiretroviral therapy.* Unpublished manuscript.

Rosenstock, L. M. (1974). Historical origins of the health belief model. *Health Education Monographs, 2,* 328–335.

Sherbourne, C. D., Hays, R. D., Ordway, L., DiMatteo, M. R., and Kravitz, R. L. (1992). Antecedents of adherence to medical recommendations: Results from the medical outcomes study. *Journal of Behavioral Medicine, 15*(5), 447–468.

Strecher, V. J., & Rosenstock, I. M. (1999). The health belief model. In A. Baum, S. Newman, J. Weinman, R. West, & C. McManus (Eds.), *Cambridge handbook of psychology health and medicine* (pp. 113–117). Cambridge, England: Cambridge University Press.

Wall, T., Sorensen, J., Batki, S., Delucchi, K. L., London, J. A., Chesney, M. A., et al. (1995). Adherence to zidovudine (AZT) among HIV-infected methadone patients: A pilot study of supervised therapy and dispensing compared to usual care. *Drug and Alcohol Dependence, 37,* 261–269.

CHAPTER 11

BEHAVIORAL PROGRAMMING AND STAFF DEVELOPMENT IN ADULT DAY CARE

Glenn R. Green and
Earlie M. Washington

Adult day care programs have come of age. It is estimated that there are more than three thousand centers operating in the United States that provide assistance for the elderly and their families. As with child day care programs, adult day care programs are located in various community locations, including church basements, as adjuncts to senior centers, nursing homes and hospitals, freestanding settings, storefronts, assisted care centers, and community centers. Several surveys and studies have provided a rich review of the treatment or intervention models of providing adult day care services (Von Behren, 1986; Weisset et al., 1990). These different models share many common elements, including structured activities—such as exercise programs, recreational services, educational activities, community events, health and medication monitoring, and case management. Transportation to and from the center, daily lunches, and opportunities for socialization are also common. Many programs include religious activities, family support and education groups, coordination of in-home services, and assistance with daily activities such as bathing, grooming, and other needed personal assistance.

As are many social service programs, adult day care programs are struggling with a variety of clinical and nonclinical issues. Adequacy of referrals, admission criteria, accreditation, populations served, cognitive and other impairments of the clientele, funding and reimbursement, and marketing are the dominant issues that adult day care programs face.

Because people are living longer than ever before, the problems and needs of the elderly in community and residential settings continue to merit attention, research, and investigation of effective helping approaches. Being old is not a disease; it is the normal process of aging that is often accompanied by physical, social, and environmental changes. The skills and behaviors that may have served the elderly well when they were younger are no longer adaptive when they are older. In addition to changes that are the result of normal aging, newly developed behavioral, social, and medical problems may occur. Chronic illnesses; medication and medication management; sleep disorders; newly required health care changes, such as checking blood sugar for adult-onset diabetes—all must be newly managed. Most elderly adapt, modify, originate, and change as they have done throughout their lives.

The elderly participate in adult day care services for a variety of reasons. Although there are no typical participants in adult day care, many are older than eighty years of age and have functional limitations with respect to activities of daily living. Most elderly and their families choose to participate in an adult day care program in order to address specific concerns, such as loneliness, self-care issues, inability to be alone, safety considerations, or perhaps lack of activity. In addition, some participants in adult day care programs display problem behaviors exhibited by many participants in institutional settings such as nursing homes. Participants with excess behaviors such as screaming, repetitive questioning, aggression or wandering, and deficit behaviors (e.g., self-care deficits, lack of social initiation, attention problems) challenge staff, volunteers, and other participants in adult day care settings.

The purpose of this chapter is to review the major clinical considerations in adult day care programs with specific attention to behavioral interventions. The purpose is also to examine and illustrate how staff can be effectively educated and trained to develop and implement behavioral interventions in operating adult day care programs. Case examples exemplify the strength of behavioral programming with impaired and disabled elderly participants in this community setting.

CLINICAL PARAMETERS OF ADULT DAY CARE

Four different clinical factors are important to the successful and effective operation of an adult day care program drawing on different disciplines including education, social work, gerontology, and psychology: (1) minimum intervention, (2) normalization of the environment and activities, (3) targeting of treatable problems and support autonomy, and (4) individualized interventions.

Robert Kahn (1975) developed the concept of minimum intervention as a guiding clinical principle in work with geriatric populations. The concept asserts that the preferred intervention is the minimum intervention necessary to successfully affect the problem situation. Minimum intervention does not mean or translate into no intervention, ineffective intervention, or lack of intervention. When a treatment is proposed with an elderly population, Kahn asserts that specific attention must be given to the risks and to the possibility that the intervention can either create dependence of the older person or result in the possibility of unintended yet problematic outcomes. The dependence may occur despite reasonable objectives, laudable goals, and positive intentions.

The normalization of the environment and its corresponding activities are concepts historically used within the field of rehabilitation (Wolfensberger, 1979). Normalization is also important because of problems with generalization and extension of treatment effects. The physical, interpersonal, and functional aspects of environments for individuals with disabilities, including senior citizens, should be as normal as feasible so as to support adaptive behaviors (Pinkston, 1997). There is an obvious requirement to have supportive, adaptive, safe, and accessible environments for adult day care programs and to establish varied activities in those settings. The concept of normalization would, for example, suggest that it is appropriate to have impaired senior citizens attend religious services at their churches instead of religious services provided on site at an adult day care program.

Zarit and Zarit (1998) discuss the importance of concentrating on problems that are treatable and that support an individual's autonomy. An individual whose spouse has recently died may be lonely, depressed, lack money management skills, or have feelings of being out of control. The death of the spouse cannot be changed, but the skills, behaviors, and feelings corresponding to that significant event can be targeted and affected. The reality of intervention with elderly clients in adult day care programs is that many of the psychosocial problems presented are also very difficult to modify. Often the maintenance of a skill or support of continuing specific skills and behaviors is an appropriate goal. A lifelong history of learning coupled with chronic illnesses and diseases may seriously reduce the possibility of significant changes, and a successful outcome may be defined as no change or even as limiting skill or behavior deterioration. Green, Linsk, and Pinkston (1986) describe a home-based intervention with a cognitively impaired senior citizen and his wife. The husband would accuse his wife of leaving him alone for hours when she simply left the room or took the garbage out. A clear behavioral pattern emerged in which she would deny the accusation, he would accuse her again, and a lengthy argument would occur. The wife was taught a differential reinforcement intervention in which she ignored the accusation and reinforced natural and normal conversations. Notably, data show that the frequencies of the accusations were not affected, but the duration of each accusation was significantly reduced.

Individualized interventions are often necessary to successfully continue and maintain a senior citizen's adaptive skills and behaviors. In addition, individualized interventions may assist impaired senior citizens in successfully negotiating and operating in a variety of environments. Specific behavioral deficits and excesses occur that are so severe that individualized interventions, conducted within the parameters of the adult day care program, are warranted. Examples include behavioral excesses or deficits that interfere with the participant's and other participants' daily activities or abilities to gain reinforcement and support. These behavioral excess and deficits, therefore, are appropriate targets of clinical interventions.

Behavioral Programming

When specific problems arise, an individualized behavior management program may offer an effective problem-solving approach. Although details of behavior management programs with the elderly have been specified elsewhere (Pinkston, Green, Linsk, & Young, 2000), clinical interventions in adult day care programs present many challenges that are not unique to this population, although their specific content may be. Examples of intervention issues include the selection of change agents from staff members, the development of appropriate clinical goals, intervention specification, the design of education and programs, the monitoring of clinical programs, and the evaluation of their effectiveness. With consideration to environmental issues, modeling, increasing opportunities for reinforcement, reinforcement, and cueing, adaptive behaviors can be strengthened, problematic behaviors minimized, and new behaviors encouraged. The following behavioral techniques have been shown to be easy to implement and are self-sustaining (Burgio & Burgio, 1986; Carstenson, 1988; DeRoos & Pinkston, 1997).

Structuring the environment. The physical and functional environment can be developed to encourage and support adaptive and positive behaviors. The challenge for many adult day care programs is working within fundamental site limitations. If programs wish to encourage socialization, the site must allow and encourage participant interaction. It is equally important to structure environments to safely permit deviant and problem behaviors, such as wandering and repeated questioning. Participants with Alzheimer's disease, for example, frequently wander and pace. They also often engage in repetitive activities such as restacking papers, turning light switches on and off, or taking and replacing items numerous times. An environment can be structured to allow wandering but not reinforcing the behavior, thereby ensuring that the wandering occurs safely. Environmental restructuring is also advantageous in that it is easy to implement and is sustainable.

Modeling appropriate behaviors. Modeling appropriate behaviors is a designated staff and volunteer activity. In a natural manner, modeling demonstrates to the senior citizen an appropriate behavior that is reinforced and used both to strengthen existing positive behaviors and to elicit new behaviors. For individuals with cognitive impairments, modeling is especially powerful because it provides strong environmental cues of acceptable activities. Adult day care programs have abundant opportunities for modeling. Modeling appropriate eating behaviors, for example, for individuals who may have lost those skills may cue and encourage the behavior.

Increasing opportunities for reinforcement. The creation of rich and multiple opportunities for reinforcement in adult day care programs is another behavioral technique. Staff and volunteers are taught to create, manipulate, and structure the setting so as to create an atmosphere of success, enjoyment, and reinforcement for impaired senior citizens. Activities and events are adapted to the capability of the participants in the program, and there are multiple opportunities to engage in potentially reinforcing activities with minimum guidance and assistance. Many opportunities for reinforcement may be missed or unrecognized by impaired participants, so increasing cues leading to reinforcement may be beneficial to them. A group leader can be taught to ask questions that are easy to answer, to guide the answer of the participant who has dementia, or even to supply a partial answer for the participant. Praise and other reinforcing events can be used to approximate the correct response. The correct answer from the participant is not always the goal, but participation in the activity and group discussion may be.

At times, it is necessary to implement individualized intervention because the problem behaviors are of a significant magnitude or severity as to interfere with everyday functioning of the adult day care participant. The senior citizen who stands up at incorrect times on the bus, who overeats, or who disrupts group activities by screaming displays problematic behaviors. These behaviors may also create problems in the home for family members, and they often increase the risk of nursing home placement.

Contingent positive reinforcement.   The use of positive reinforcement, which is the presentation of a reinforcing stimulus contingent on a specific participant behavior, is a powerful technique in increasing the occurrence, intensity, or duration of that behavior the future. A critical element, as specified previously, is to select behaviors that are changeable and goals that are attainable.

In the development of individual behavioral goals, it is important to define problems appropriately for an older population. A problem may be pacing or low rates of group participation. If the problem is pacing, the goal is often to decrease pacing. As with most goals that target a decrease in problematic behaviors, the intervention technique may tend toward punishment, time out, or extinction-based procedures. Given the amount of deprivation commonly found in the elderly, a more effective and humane approach in adult day care settings is to increase behaviors that are incompatible with the targeted behavior and that represent desirable alternatives. Instead of targeting pacing, a more appropriate goal is to target sitting, a behavior that is a suitable alternative.

Cueing.   Cueing is the use of antecedent stimuli (e.g., a question asked by a staff member) to prompt desired behavior (e.g., a verbal response by the elderly participant). The staff member obtains the participant's attention, asks the question, waits for a response, repeats the question if necessary, and guides the response if appropriate. Operant theory encompasses behavioral consequences but also acknowledges the powerful role of antecedent events in the recurrence of behavior (Baer, 1997; Baer & Pinkston, 1997). The role of antecedent events and cues to behaviors are particularly important for the impaired elderly who are trying to recover previously existing behavior patterns after some form of trauma. Many times, cueing may be an effective behavioral intervention to encourage behaviors, and it provides opportunities for behaviors to be reinforced (Pinkston, 1997; Pinkston, Levitt, Green, Linsk, & Rzepnicki, 1982; Pinkston & Linsk, 1984b).

These behavioral interventions, when used by trained staff, can be implemented in adult day care program sites. In addition, well-developed and implemented behavioral interventions have been shown to have a profound impact on participants in the programs (DeRoos & Pinkston, 1997). Direct-care staff have the greatest contact with adult day care participants and make logical change agents. Additional investigation, however, is warranted to ascertain effective training protocols, including consultation, ongoing education, follow-up and booster sessions, and in-service training. The most effective and meaningful intervention is worthless unless the intervention technique is implemented in a manner as developed and programmed to allow for systematic evaluation.

Recent literature suggests that staff can increase their knowledge and skill, and thereby their effectiveness, through training. DeRoos and Pinkston (1997) demonstrated that short-term group instruction and on-the-job training with staff in adult day care programs were effective in increasing reinforcement by staff, cueing, and the use of contracts. A variety of educational programs for direct-service staff—including lectures, discussions, reading materials, films, and other media—can increase knowledge of behavioral principles and intervention procedures (Cuff, 1977; Delameter, Conners, & Wells, 1984; Gardner, 1972; Schinke & Wong, 1977). Knowledge of a skill, however, does not guarantee that a skill is used or used appropriately (Bernstein, 1984; Delameter et al., 1984). Training and educational programs to develop and use skills may require modeling the desired behavior for staff (Gladstone & Spencer, 1977); structuring practice opportunities; providing feedback and evaluative information about performance (Parsonson, Baer, & Baer, 1974); and providing reinforcement (Delameter et al., 1984), usually within an interrelated package (Pinkston, 1997).

STAFF TRAINING AND ELDERLY SUPPORT PROJECT

The Elderly Support Project staff at the University of Chicago designed a training program to teach paraprofessional staff of adult day care centers effective behavioral and caregiving techniques. The program was designed to minimize staff time and agency resources required for training, and it incorporated behavioral techniques into the ongoing activities of both the staff and the agencies.

Program Sites

On-site training and program implementation was chosen in order to avoid the problem of poor generalization from the training setting to an application setting. The Elderly Support Project staff of the University of Chicago's School of Social Service Administration conducted this research with twenty-one different staff members from five different adult day centers in metropolitan Chicago. All the centers were private, nonprofit organizations and were funded primarily by the State of Illinois. At all centers, participants and staff were representative of the socioeconomic and ethnic status of the communities usually served by the adult day centers. Adult day care services were designed to facilitate social interaction among the participants and to provide nutrition, education, daily physical exercise, counseling, family respite, transportation, continuous supervision, personal care, and referral services. The total enrollment of elderly participants was approximately fifty African American elderly per center, and average daily attendance was twenty-five senior citizens.

Adult Day Care and Staff Participants

Specific referral criteria were established for adult day care participants in the project. Participants must have (1) been older than sixty years of age; (2) diagnosed with severe psychological problems and/or brain dysfunction, including chronic and acute brain syndromes, reactive mental disorders, depressions that would otherwise prevent community functioning, schizophrenia, senile psychosis, arteriosclerotic brain disease, acutely confused states, or physical impairments such as cardiovascular accidents, arthritis, fractures, or spinal cord injuries; and (3) exhibited a functional disability greater than warranted by their health status.

Staff included individuals employed full-time at the centers that had significant direct contact with adult day care participants. Participation in the training program was encouraged but voluntary. A total of twenty-one staff participated: the mean age of the staff was forty-two, and ages ranged from twenty-three to seventy-one; the staff members were primarily female (90 percent); most staff were high school graduates; the staff, on average, had been working in adult day centers for three years; and staff members were primarily African American (86 percent).

Methodology

The research included single-subject designs to evaluate and compare changes in participants within adult centers. Pretests and posttests assessed changes in staff skills, focusing on the effectiveness of the selected behavioral procedures (Pinkston et al., 1982; Pinkston & Linsk, 1984a). Change in senior citizens' behaviors was assessed using direct observation and structured assignments.

Direct observations.   Researchers directly observed the elderly participants' adaptive and problematic behaviors and the interaction between staff and participants. Observations were made of staff intervention skills to establish baseline and postintervention effects of training. Staff-recorded instruments monitored the frequency of specific behaviors with targeted senior citizens. At the end of the ten training sessions, independent observers used structured observation to evaluate changes in the staff members' skills in implementing the new procedures during four structured activities, each oriented toward a specific set of the techniques taught. During this phase, the staff member was asked to create and manage a brief structured activity with an elderly participant. Staff responses were then noted. The structured evaluations enabled researchers to determine whether staff reasonably used each of the skills previously taught.

Staff Training

A short-term training model was selected and tested. The training model was developed to teach staff to design and implement behavioral interventions with targeted participants (DeRoos & Pinkston, 1997). Training, assessment, and evaluation of the training occurred in ten on-the-job training sessions and five subsequent consultation sessions.

The model included (1) group instruction sessions educating staff on the use of operant procedures, including reinforcement, task analysis, cueing, and contracting; (2) unstructured observation of staff in the adult day care setting and follow-up sessions providing corrective feedback and reinforcement; (3) structured observations to evaluate the staff members' skills in implementing operant procedures; and (4) the use of charted single-case evaluations of interventions for targeted adult day care participants. Elderly Support Project trainers used various methods, including instructions, feedback, modeling, and instructional materials to teach the behavioral techniques and to change behaviors of staff.

Fifteen- to thirty-minute formal, group instruction meetings were held once a week for ten weeks. Written exercises, oral explanations, and checklists pertaining to the treatment techniques were presented. Time was allowed for questions and answers. Each week, staff completed a written exercise and demonstration exercises. Prior to each session, the project trainer observed the staff members and identified examples of situations in which operant techniques might be useful. These situations were useful in illustrating the procedures being taught that week. At the instructional meeting, staff identified positive reinforcement and reinforcing activities for targeted adult day care participants to rehearse reinforcement with targeted participants. Staff members were also trained to complete a task analysis of participant behavior, to cue participants to perform specific behaviors, to use contingency contracts, and to implement differential reinforcement of incompatible behaviors. Discussions included how to develop activities programs that would promote more opportunities for participants' positive behavior and challenge participants who were reestablishing or relearning a skill, such as using eating utensils at lunch. Task assignments and worksheets with clear specification of the assignment goals were distributed once a week. Criteria defining success, emphasis of specific subtasks, and use of a task checklist were delineated.

Retraining occurred when staff had great difficulty demonstrating a skill or completing a written assignment or if a staff member did not respond to the trainer's cues. The trainer required the staff member to rehearse the tasks and provided ample positive feedback. Since many of the techniques were new, especially to these paraprofessional staff, feedback was essential.

Family Training

Subsequent to staff training, family training also began at two of the five centers. Family caregivers in the five centers were invited to participate. Fifteen family members began the training sessions. The family training taught caregivers to operationally define behavioral deficits and excesses; to monitor behavior through observation and data collection; to graph data; and to design, implement, and evaluate an intervention. A similar curriculum was used for families and staff.

Caregivers were taught to monitor, evaluate, and increase their own reinforcing activities. The structure of the training model consisted of ninety-minute group sessions. During the first meeting, project staff explained the primary aims of the project and the rationale, outlined responsibilities, explained the data-collection techniques, and distributed the pretests. Staff briefly outlined the skills to be taught, emphasized their usefulness, and explained how participants and their caregivers might benefit. Examples of previous successes by the project were discussed.

Homework tasks were assigned during each session. These assignments required caregivers to record observation data, to complete a reinforcement survey, and to answer a caregiver-efficacy survey. Training was always followed by a telephone call to each caregiver at home to provide reinforcement, answer questions, provide feedback, and give clarification to those having difficulties as well as to remind the caregivers to attend the subsequent training session.

The second training session assessed the baseline data collected during the previous week. The major session task was to teach caregivers to select and design an intervention, to practice the behavioral procedures, and to analyze their own involvement in reinforcing activities. The principles of reinforcement, reinforcement of incompatible behaviors, cueing, ignoring, and praise were all taught. Contracting was used as a tool to increase appropriate behavior and to decrease inappropriate behavior. Intervention decisions were outlined. The third and fourth training sessions reviewed, assessed, and refined the caregivers' progress as well as their own satisfaction with the intervention plans they had developed.

RESULTS

All twenty-one staff members at the five centers completed their training program, and the training procedures taught them skills necessary to conduct assessments and interventions.

Pretraining and posttraining tests were administered to the twenty-one staff members. Testing focused on the structured assignments about reinforcement, task analysis, cueing, and behavioral contracting. Staff completed four structured assignments before training, and four six months later, after training. Figures 11.1, 11.2, 11.3, and 11.4 compare the pretest and posttest scores.

Reinforcement

The staff members were asked to implement positive reinforcement techniques with targeted participants before training and after training. As is illustrated in figure 11.1, staff increased their use of positive reinforcement. The differences ranged from 20 percent to 60 percent, and the majority of the improvement scores clustered around 40 percent.

Task Analysis

Task analysis involved staff detailing a participants' specific desired behavior; noting the chain of events, including the antecedents and consequences to those specific behaviors; simplifying that chain of behaviors; and writing a clear specification of each step required for goal accomplishment. The task analysis also detailed staff skills necessary for the enhancement of participants' ongoing behaviors. Before training, the majority of the staff correctly completed fewer than 40 percent of their task analyses; after training, most staff correctly completed 80 percent to 100 percent of the analyses. Improvements in scores between the pretest and posttest ranged from 40 percent to 100 percent; the average was about 60 percent.

Cueing Task

Figure 11.3 presents correct cueing performed by staff. Cueing was the presentation of a stimulus, usually verbal directions or material prompts, to evoke desired behavior. At pretest, the majority of staff was unfamiliar with cueing and demonstrated difficulty in its use, completing fewer than 40 percent of the cueing tasks correctly. At posttest, most staff correctly completed 100 percent of the cueing task. In addition, staff members who were taught to cue targeted behaviors effectively maintained their scores when they were evaluated six months later.

Behavioral Contracting

Figure 11.4 shows staff improvement in the use of behavioral contracting. Contracting involves a joint agreement designed by two parties. The adult day care participants and staff agreed who would be involved, what and when the behavior or activity was expected, where the behavior was to occur, and what reinforcement would be used as the consequence. Staff members then designed a contract connecting the elements. In general, the staff performed substantially better at posttest than pretest. Several staff members correctly completed 60 percent to 70 percent of the behavioral contracting assignments at pretest, which indicates some familiarity with contracting knowledge. For these staff members, the training enhanced their previous knowledge, resulting in superior scores (100 percent) at posttest.

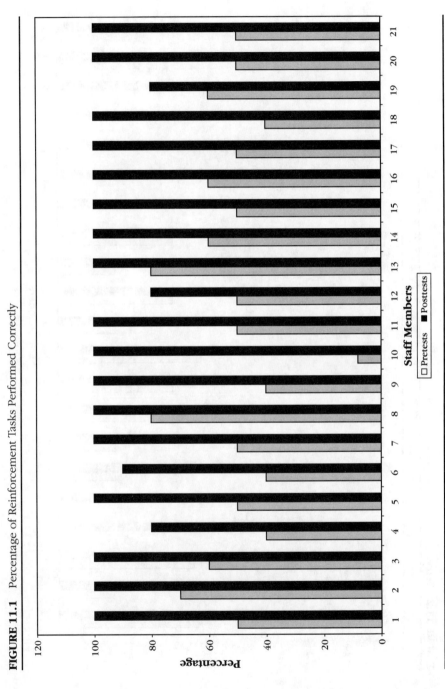

FIGURE 11.1 Percentage of Reinforcement Tasks Performed Correctly

FIGURE 11.2 Percentage of Task Analysis Perfomed Correctly

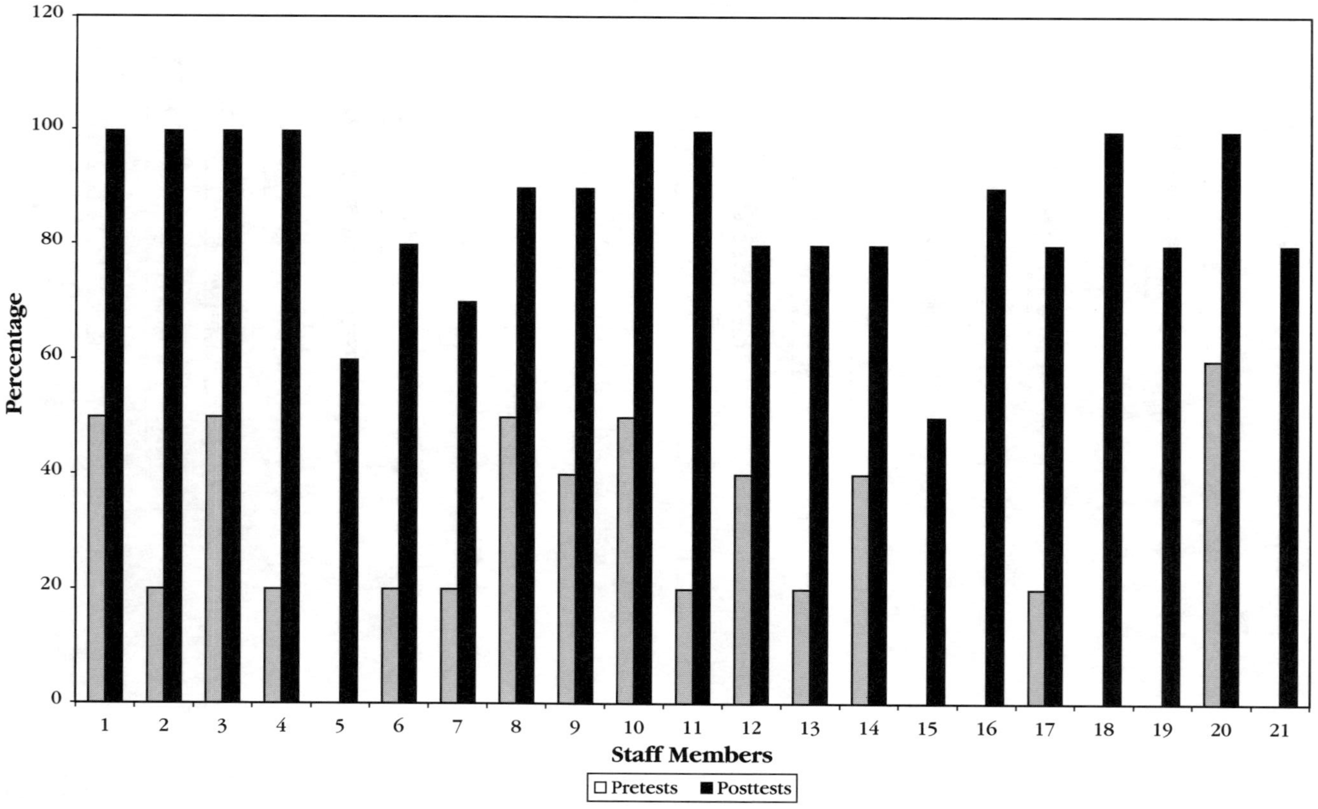

FIGURE 11.3 Percentage of Cueing Tasks Performed Correctly

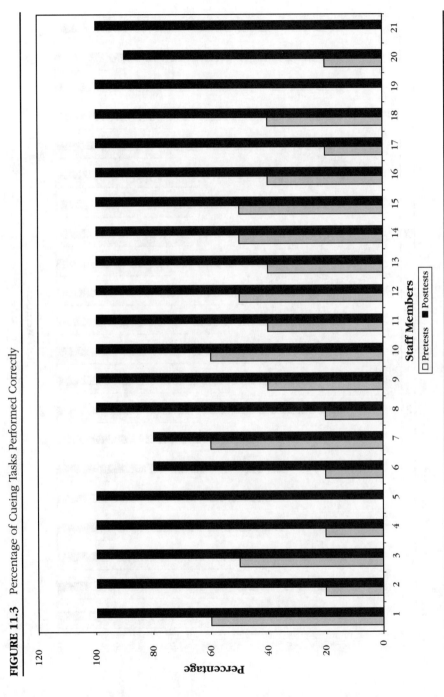

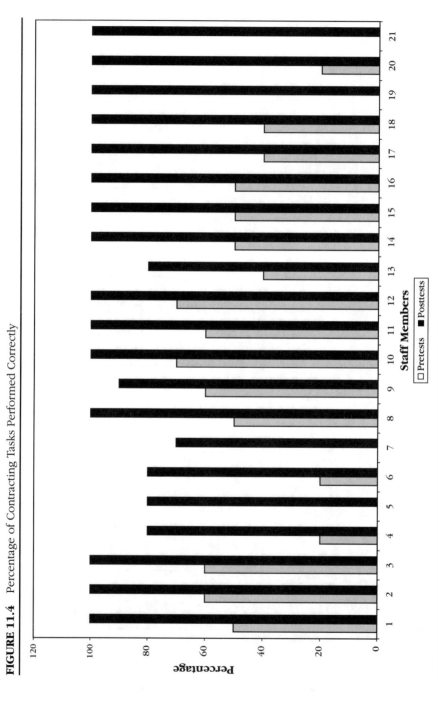

FIGURE 11.4 Percentage of Contracting Tasks Performed Correctly

RESULTS OF FAMILY EDUCATION SESSIONS

A four-week group-based education and training program was developed for family members who were providing caregiving to participants in the adult day care programs. It was hypothesized that behavioral techniques are useful for family members in caregiving situations. The program's educational structure and short-term time frame was intended to be sufficiently interesting and to allow for sufficient time to train and educate the caregivers. Only 15 families agreed to participate. Potentially, 150 families associated with the five centers could have participated, so the actual number recruited was quite small. Nevertheless, the participation level was higher than in any other family programs currently ongoing at any center. The staff at all centers reported that previous attempts to organize family-support or training groups had failed. The situation implies that efforts should focus on the identification and removal of barriers to family participation or the finding of different methods to help with family problems. Recurring issues that family members indicated were barriers preventing participation in center activities include: unavailable transportation, scheduling problems, insufficient time, a tired caregiver, interfering child care responsibilities, the elderly client not going out at night, and the caregiver wanting to be alone with the client at night.

This situation contrasts sharply with our experience using a home-based intervention model for a similar but slightly more impaired sample of elderly and their caregivers (Green, Linsk, & Pinkston, 1986; Pinkston & Linsk, 1984a; Pinkston, Green, Linsk, & Nelson, 2001; Pinkston, Linsk, & Young, 1988). In this home-based model, more than 50 percent of caregivers and their elderly relatives were successfully engaged in the program with very positive results.

THE JOHNSON CASE

Mr. Johnson was an eighty-six-year-old white male with neuromuscular damage from a stroke, exacerbated by arthritis and Parkinson's disease, who uses a wheelchair for mobility and has a hearing impairment moderated by a hearing aid. He needed assistance with twelve of thirteen activities of daily living. He also has some memory loss. The targeted problem was his lack of participation in group activities, during which he sat in his wheelchair with his head bowed and eyes closed.

Staff members' goal was to increase Mr. Johnson's participation in group activities, specifically, participation in one morning group activity and one afternoon group activity. A staff member monitored Mr. Johnson during the group activities. If he participated for at least five minutes, he received a score of "1," indicating achievement of the desired goal. Otherwise, he received a score of "0." Data collection took place each day that Mr. Johnson was at the center. In the baseline week, the staff monitored and recorded how often Mr. Johnson achieved the goal, how long he participated, and the activities in which he engaged. A reinforcement survey was completed and illustrated activities he enjoyed, such as playing various games, watching television, reading a newspaper and magazines, and playing with animals, especially puppies and cats. Staff used this information to develop additional reinforcement opportunities. A contingency contract was written in which he agreed to participate in a group activity for five minutes each morning and each afternoon. Before each activity, staff reminded him of the contract and requested that he participate in the upcoming activity.

During intervention, Mr. Johnson participated in all five of the designated morning group activities (current events discussions and exercise classes). He also participated in all five of the designated afternoon activities (baking cookies, three bingo games, and one exercise class).

THE LINCOLN CASE

Mrs. Lincoln, a seventy-seven-year-old African American woman with dementia, was in good enough physical condition to attend the center three days a week. The staff considered her hostile. Aggressive behavior toward a specific male participant, Mr. Haley, was seen as her most serious problem. She often made negative comments about him, which staff members described as "criticizing" and "putting him down." This behavior usually provoked laughter from other participants and retaliation from Mr. Haley. As a result, Mrs. Lincoln became isolated and had few opportunities for positive experience at the center. The goal was for her to increase the number of positive comments to Mr. Haley and others at the site and to increase her positive social experiences.

The staff recorded her behavior during thirty-minute intervals between 10:30 a.m. and 4:00 p.m. each of the three days she attended. Staff recorded both positive and negative comments made to Mr. Haley and the other participants. During baseline, the staff observed zero positive statements and thirteen negative statements to Mr. Haley, as well as zero negative statements and zero positive statements to other participants during the designated times.

A contingency contract was completed in which Mrs. Lincoln agreed to speak positively to Mr. Haley, once in the morning and once in the afternoon for one week. When she accomplished that goal, she was to be selected Senior of the Week. Once she was selected Senior of the Week, her picture would be taken and posted so that staff, family members, participants, and visitors would know of her accomplishment. When she made a positive statement about Mr. Haley or another participant, the staff also praised her by commenting on how nice it was of her to do so.

During the intervention week, improvement resulted. Mrs. Lincoln's negative comments to Mr. Haley and other participants decreased to zero and one, respectively. She increased her positive comments about Mr. Haley to twelve and comments about other participants to six comments. Reinforcement used in the contract was extremely effective. Mrs. Lincoln was excited about the possibility of being named Senior of the Week. Staff posted Mrs. Lincoln's picture at the center, creating the desired positive attention to her.

SUMMARY

This research demonstrates that adult day care staff can be taught to use behavioral techniques that result in important improvements in selected participants. The findings also suggest that the family caregiver's involvement is difficult to obtain. Although family training in previous home-based research was useful, cooperation for this project in a four-session group-training program in the day center was impossible to achieve on a large scale. This finding was supported by findings elsewhere (see DeRoos & Pinkston, 1997).

This research also showed the difficulties involved in consistent coordination of family and day center resources to enhance the social functioning of the elderly. Day center staff demonstrated, for example, commitment to use newly developed behavioral skills. Engagement of family members was more inconsistent. With fewer than 10 percent of eligible families participating, the vast majority of families did not learn the effective behavioral techniques and interventions that positively affect their loved ones. Even so, effective staff interaction benefits elderly participants by reducing confusion, increasing positive activities, and increasing opportunities for positive consequences.

PROGRAM IMPLICATIONS AND RECOMMENDATIONS

The collection of successes and difficulties in this research makes it difficult to determine a set of policy implications pertaining to the training and support of family caregivers. An important implication is the sustaining of family caregiving and prevention of early institutionalization of the elderly. This study reports the successful implementation of a training model for adult day center caregivers of impaired elderly persons.

Because of the small number of individuals studied; participation by the elderly, their family and staff; the limited geographic representation, and the exploratory nature of this investigation, it is difficult to make definitive conclusions and recommendations. Further investigation is clearly warranted, including exploration of issues such as long-term use of newly learned behavioral techniques, the role of supervision, or the use of booster sessions to maintain skills. The following recommendations may serve as useful guides, even as a beginning point, for additional investigation, specific policy questions and clinical initiatives with an elderly population, community-based adult day care programs, and caregivers of those elderly individuals:

1. The behavioral model is an effective approach in training staff working with the elderly, and staff can correctly reinforce and cue positive behaviors. Client improvement can occur;

2. Family caregivers frequently use the training sessions to learn behavior management techniques. The data imply the need for flexible training models that can incorporate ways to respond to individual family needs;

3. Policymakers and funding sources must be cognizant of the needs of caregivers and the elderly; and

4. The power of behavioral interventions to decrease institutionalization of the elderly is still unexamined; however, it is clear that caregivers, professionals, and family members can contribute to the well-being of the family during its clinical involvement.

REFERENCES

Baer, D. M. (1997). Some meanings of antecedent and environmental control. In D. M. Baer & E. M. Pinkston (Eds.), *Environment and behavior.* Boulder, CO: Westview Press.

Baer, D. M., & Pinkston, E. M. (1997). *Environment and behavior.* Boulder, CO: Westview Press.

Bernstein, G. S. (1982). Training behavior change agents: A conceptual review. *Behavior Therapy, 13,* 1–23.

Burgio, L. D., & Burgio, K. L. (1986). Behavioral gerontology: Applications of behavioral methods to the problems of older adults. *Journal of Applied Behavior Analysis, 19*(4), 321–328.

Carstensen, L. L. (1988). The emerging field of behavioral gerontology. *Behavior Therapy, 19,* 259–281.

Cuff, G. N. (1977). A strategy for evaluating a short course on behavior modification. *Mental Retardation, 2,* 48.

Delameter, A. M., Conners, C. K., & Wells, K. C. (1984). A comparison of staff training procedures: Behavioral application in the child psychiatric inpatient setting. *Behavior Modification, 8,* 39–58.

DeRoos, Y., & Pinkston, E. M. (1997). Training adult day care staff. In D. M. Baer & E. M. Pinkston (Eds.), *Environment and behavior* (249–257). Boulder, CO: Westview Press.

Gardner, J. M. (1972). Teaching behavior modification to nonprofessionals. *Journal of Applied Behavior Analysis, 5*(4), 517–521.

Gladstone, B. W., & Spencer, C. J. (1977). The effects of modeling on the contingent praise of mental retardation counselors. *Journal of Applied Behavior Analysis, 10*(1), 75–84.

Green, G. R., Linsk, N. L., & Pinkston, E. M. (1986). Modification of verbal behavior of the mentally impaired elderly by their spouses. *Journal of Applied Behavior Analysis, 19*(4), 329–336.

Kahn, R. L. (1975). The mental health system and the future aged. *Gerontologist, 15*(1), 24–31.

Parsonson, B. S., Baer, A. M., & Baer, D. M. (1974). The application of generalized correct social contingencies: An evaluation of a training program. *Journal of Applied Behavior Analysis, 7*(4), 427–437.

Pinkston, E. M. (1997). A supportive environment for old age. In D. M. Baer & E. M. Pinkston (Eds.), *Environment and behavior.* Boulder, CO: Westview Press.

Pinkston, E. M., Green, G. R., Linsk, N. L., & Young, R. N. (2000). A family ecobehavioral for elders with mental illness. In H. Briggs & K. Corcoran (Eds.), *Social work practice: Treating common client problems* (pp. 339–370). Chicago: Lyceum Books.

Pinkston, E. M., Levitt, J. L., Green, G. R., Linsk, N. L., & Rzepnicki, T. L. (1982). *Effective social work practice.* San Francisco: Jossey-Bass.

Pinkston, E. M., & Linsk, N. L. (1984a). Behavior family intervention with the impaired elderly. *The Gerontologist, 6*(24), 576–583.

Pinkston, E. M., & Linsk, N. L. (1984b). *Care of the elderly: A family approach.* New York: Pergamon Press.

Pinkston, E. M., Linsk, N. L., & Young, R. N. (1988). Home-based behavioral family treatment of the impaired elderly. *Behavior Therapy, 19,* 331–344.

Schinke, S. P., & Wong, S. E. (1977). Evaluation of staff training in group homes for retarded persons. *American Journal of Mental Deficiency, 82,* 130–136.

Von Behren, R. (1986). *Adult day care in America: Summary of a national survey.* Washington, DC: National Council on Aging, National Institute on Adult Day Care.

Weisset, W. G., Elston, J. M., Bolda, E. J., Zelman, W. N., Mutran, E., & Mangum, A. B. (1990). *Adult day care: Findings from a national survey.* Baltimore: Johns Hopkins University Press.

Wolfensberger, W. (1979). *Normalization: The principle of normalization in human services.* Toronto, Ontario, Canada: National Institute on Mental Retardation.

Zarit, S. H., & Zarit, J. M. (1998). *Mental disorders in older adults: Fundamentals of assessment and treatment.* New York: Guilford Press.

CHAPTER 12

PROVIDING APPROPRIATE CARE IN ADVANCED DEMENTIA

*Patricia Hanrahan, Daniel J. Luchins,
Kathleen Murphy, Gail Patrick,
Greg Sachs, and Gavin Hougham*

The personal and social costs of dementia are enormous. The chronic and impoverishing nature of the dementing disorders requires extensive resources to provide care from public health institutions such as nursing homes and hospitals. However, family members are usually the first line of support for persons with dementia. In this chapter, we describe the nature and extent of dementia, its epidemiology, and the related use of health and mental health services. We then describe the kinds of problems that emerge as dementia progresses, particularly in the advanced stages of the disease. Next we review our research on palliative care and hospice for persons with advanced dementia. We begin by describing the nature of palliative care and hospice, because these services provide an important context for many of the problems and issues that are discussed.

Palliative care focuses on the relief of symptoms and pain control for patients whose disease is not responsive to curative treatment. Rather than make aggressive efforts to prolong life, palliative care aims to improve the quality of life by easing physical decline and death. Palliative care can be provided at any time during the course of terminal illness.

Hospice programs provide palliative care, funding for medications, and support to dying patients and their families. An interdisciplinary team that includes doctors, nurses, and social workers provides services. Paraprofessionals provide respite care and assist with health care. Funding is available through the Medicare hospice benefit and other third-party payers. Historically, to access these benefits, the patient must have only six months to live; however, change of this limit has been under discussion.

Palliative care is the cornerstone of hospice services; however, access to hospice has rarely been available in end-stage dementia, mostly because the course of illness has been much longer than six months (Christakis & Escarce, 1996; Hanrahan & Luchins, 1995a). Yet the aging population in industrialized countries will demonstrate a growing need for palliative care and hospice for persons who are dying from dementia.

DEMENTIA: NATURE AND SCOPE OF THE PROBLEM

What is dementia? Dementia is a progressive cognitive impairment that often arises from Alzheimer's disease, although vascular dementia is another frequent cause (Hanrahan, Luchins, & Ovsiew, 1999). As the disease progresses, it is accompanied by increasing functional impairment in the activities of daily living, beginning with instrumental activities, such as shopping and balancing a checkbook. Ultimately, it renders its victims bed-bound and unable to communicate verbally (Reisberg, Ferris, DeLeon, & Crook, 1982). In advanced dementia, functional impairments occur in all or most activities of daily living; there is severe cognitive decline and a loss of the ability to engage in purposeful activities. A more extensive description of these problems can be found in the Global Deterioration Scale (Reisberg et al., 1982).

Although the duration of the illness varies from two to ten years, dementia is a terminal disease in which death is often caused by medical complications. For example, in end-stage dementia, patients frequently have problems swallowing food and aspiration pneumonia can develop. The shock of the initial diagnosis to individuals and their families can be so overwhelming that the medical team often finds it difficult to communicate the fact that the illness is terminal during initial visits to the clinic. This strongly supports the need for ongoing communication about care plans. Social workers can play an important role in exploring care needs and long-term plans as well as in helping family members cope with the attendant and often severe disruptions to their own lives.

PUBLIC HEALTH SIGNIFICANCE: EPIDEMIOLOGY AND HEALTH AND MENTAL HEALTH SERVICES

The prevalence of dementia increases with age; about one-third of individuals older than eighty-five years of age and one-half of those older than ninety-five have dementia (Bachman et al., 1993; Skoog, Nielson, Palmertz, Andreasson, & Svanborg, 1993; Wernick & Reisches, 1994). Because life spans have lengthened, the number of elders has increased as well and will continue to do so. The proportion of elders in the population is further increased by the aging of the baby boomer generation. There are currently about four million persons with dementia in the United States; this number is expected to increase to fourteen million by the year 2050 (Brookmeyer, Gray, and Kawas, 1998). These demographic trends, together with the debilitating nature of the disease, make it an epidemiological time bomb with major personal and social implications. As the population ages, dying with dementia will become one of the most common ways in which older people end their final years of life. Services for dying dementia patients and their families are an important and often neglected component of end-of-life care.

Service Utilization: Community Care

Most persons living with mild and moderate dementia are likely to remain in the community if they have family support. Even in cases of severe dementia, individuals with a family caregiver are most likely to die at home, although brief nursing home or hospital stays may precede death (Collins & Ogle, 1994). Family members provide a great deal of care for their demented loved ones in order to keep them at home, averaging ten hours a day of care (Rice, Fox, & Max, 1993). Even when patients are institutionalized, family caregivers provide care for an average of about an hour and a half a day. Other components of community care include physician services, prescriptions, transportation, other home health services, case management, respite, and adult day care. Facilitating access to these services through case management is a key role for social workers (Linsk, Hanrahan, & Pinkston, 1991).

Institutional care. Nursing homes and hospitals also provide a great deal of care for dementia patients. Half or more of nursing home patients have dementia, and their length of stay in nursing homes is about three years (German, Rovner, & Burton, 1992; Strahan & Burns, 1991; Welch, Walsh, & Larson 1992). State and county mental hospitals care for dementia patients as well, especially if the patients have severe behavioral or psychiatric problems. One-fifth of the patients in state hospitals are elderly and one-third have Alzheimer's disease or related disorders (Moak & Fisher, 1990). Most of these patients were admitted late in their lives, when behavioral and psychiatric problems complicated their dementia. There is also greater use of general hospitals by patients with dementia (Ernst & Hay, 1994). Social workers in these settings need to be aware of the prevalence and care needs of dementia patients and their families.

As we will discuss, in the end stages of the disease, these patients have had little access to a very important service for dying patients: hospice care (Christakis & Escarce, 1996; Hanrahan & Luchins, 1995a). Rather, at a time of great need, their care has been inappropriate, minimal, or absent.

PROBLEMS AMONG SEVERELY DEMENTED PATIENTS

Several types of problems emerge as dementia progresses, including deficits due to dementia, behavioral problems, medical complications arising from functional impairments, and caregiver issues. It is crucial for social workers to understand and assess these problems in order to develop appropriate care plans with families.

Behavioral problems are quite common in dementia and increase with the severity of the disease. Frequently reported behavioral problems include apathy, disinhibition, wandering, agitation, aggression, and binge eating (Burns, Jacoby, & Levy, 1990; Colenda & Hamer, 1991; Mega, Cummings, Fiorello, & Gornbein, 1996; Teri, Larson, & Reifler, 1988). Pinkston and her colleagues have developed an array of behavioral interventions that are particularly helpful for persons in the mild and moderate stages of dementia (Pinkston & Linsk, 1984). Other behavioral approaches have been developed, and psychoactive medications can be helpful as well (Engel, Burgio, & McCormick, 1990; Hanrahan, Luchins, & Ovsiew, 1999; Meco, Alessandria, Bonifati, & Giustini, 1994; Schneider, Pollack, & Lyness, 1990; Teri & Uomoto, 1991). Task-centered treatment provides a useful approach for integrating behavioral and service linkage issues within a problem-solving framework (Fortune & Reid, 1999; Naleppa & Reid, 2003).

Using these interventions to help family and other caregivers to deal with the behavior problems that are common in dementia is an important role for social workers. However, as dementia becomes more severe, it is increasingly important to assess the possibility that what are perceived as behavioral problems actually are masking untreated pain. Pain can sometimes be manifested and perceived as a behavioral problem, especially in those whose ability to verbalize is compromised.

Medical Complications

In advanced dementia, complications due to the disease frequently occur. The majority of forty-seven patients in our demonstration hospice program had more than one complication; more than half had swallowing problems, pressure ulcers, aspiration pneumonia, dehydration, or malnutrition; urinary tract infections were also common (Luchins, Hanrahan, & Murphy, 1997). Other painful conditions associated with old age are also likely to be present, such as osteoarthritis and cardiovascular problems. A history of stroke or head trauma is also often associated with dementia. Similar findings were reported in a British study (McCarthy, Addington-Hall, & Altmann, 1997).

Caring for the Caregivers

Clinicians need to remain alert to the needs of family caregivers as well as the needs of persons with dementia. Family caregivers often deal with considerable strain and are themselves at risk for psychiatric disorders, such as depression, sleep disorders, and anxiety (Gallagher, Rose, Rivera, Lovett, & Thompson, 1989; Goldman & Luchins, 1984; Hougham, Stocking, & Sachs, 2002; Pruchno & Resch, 1989). Among persons who report feeling strained by caring for disabled spouses, the risk of mortality is 63 percent higher than among comparable non-caregivers (Schulz & Beach, 1999). Self-medication to manage these problems frequently occurs. The level of family burden is likely to be high at the initial onset of dementia, when families first begin to deal with the demands of the disease (Hougham et al., 2002). This is often followed by a period of lower burden as the patient becomes moderately impaired. The burden rises again late in the course of dementia, when it is apt to be most difficult to manage.

There is relatively little research to guide interventions for family caregivers of dying patients. Depression may be improved by helping caregivers to maintain or develop social ties and to value their role in providing care (Haley, LaMonde, Han, Burton, & Schonwetter, 2003). When clinical depression develops among caregivers, psychoactive medications are very effective. Respite care, funded by hospice, can greatly ease the burden of caring for dying family members.

PALLIATIVE CARE AND HOSPICE SERVICES

Hospice and palliative care were initially provided primarily to cancer patients, but the needs of terminally ill dementia patients and their families have gained increased attention over the past decade. Families often exhaust the limited benefits provided by public and private insurance, because dementia can last from two to ten years. Helpful but costly services such as home care and respite care are beyond the means of many families in the later stages of the illness. In a case study of family caregivers of dementia patients, one husband described himself as in need of hospice services for himself as well as his severely demented wife because he was "desperate, financially and physically drained" (Luchins, Hanrahan, & Litzenberg, 1998). Hospice services that are funded by Medicare, such as respite, focus on the needs of the caregiver–patient dyad and are especially relevant to the families of end-stage dementia patients.

It is increasingly recognized that the benefits of palliative care, which concern easing physical decline and the dying process, apply to end-stage dementia patients. Their prognosis is limited; they have significant medical problems and are often in need of palliative care in the form of symptom relief and pain control. Although some end-stage dementia patients are in a vegetative state, others are at least intermittently aware of their environment and of pain and discomfort from complications of their dementia. The most severely deteriorated patients are at stage seven of the Global Deterioration Scale (Reisberg et al., 1982). They are dependent in all or most of their activities of daily living, unable to engage in purposeful activities, and their speech is limited to a few words a day. Typically, they are no longer able to recognize their loved ones. Family members and other proxy decision-makers may view their quality of life as quite poor.

Despite being incurably ill, severely demented patients often receive aggressive rather than palliative care at the end of life in acute-care hospital settings (Ahronheim, Morrison, Baskin, Morris, & Meier, 1996: Morrison & Su, 2000) and in chronic-care facilities (Evers, Dushyant Purohit, Perl, Khan, & Marin, 2002). Nursing home patients are often transported to emergency rooms, where they undergo painful but futile procedures (Kleinfield, 2003). Many dementia patients die in nursing homes after a protracted stay, but there is very little provision of grief and bereavement services for their survivors in these settings (Murphy, Hanrahan, & Luchins, 1997). These problems challenge the social work, health, and human services system to develop more appropriate responses.

WHAT IS APPROPRIATE HEALTH CARE FOR END-STAGE DEMENTIA PATIENTS?

Hospice developed in this country primarily as a service for cancer patients. Because palliative care and hospice had been so rarely used in advanced dementia, we explored attitudes toward these modes of care in a national survey of physicians, family members of dementia patients, and gerontologists (Luchins & Hanrahan, 1993). In all, more than fourteen hundred of those surveyed responded. This response rate, at 61 percent, is considered fairly good for survey research. A continuum of care from most aggressive, at level one, to palliative care only, at level five, was presented based on the work of Volicer and his colleagues (1986).

At level one, everything possible would be done to keep the patient alive, including aggressive care such as resuscitation, tube feeding, and medication for acute illness. Level five was described as focusing on comfort and control of pain while forgoing aggressive care. The majority clearly preferred level five, which was the least aggressive level of care. This preference was expressed by physicians who were gerontologists (61 percent), other gerontologists (55 percent), and family members (71 percent). A very small minority, ranging from 2 percent to 4 percent, favored highly aggressive care in which everything would be done to prolong life.

Family and professional caregivers were also quite positive about the role of hospice in end-stage dementia. Ninety percent of the family members and 91 percent of professionals viewed hospice care as appropriate for the end stages of dementia. These findings are consistent with related research (Danis et al., 1991; Diamond, Jernigan, Moseley, Messina, & McKeown, 1989; Michelson, Mulvihill, Hsu, & Olson, 1991; Payne, Taylor, Stocking, & Sachs, 1996).

Another major finding from the study was that relatively few respondents were aware of hospice programs that served dementia patients, which confirmed our clinical experience. The majority of professionals (91 percent) and family members (68 percent) were aware of hospice programs for cancer patients, but only about one-fifth knew of hospice programs that included dementia patients. This combination of positive attitudes toward hospice and lack of knowledge of available hospice programs suggested unmet need, which led to our next studies.

FEASIBILITY OF PROVIDING PALLIATIVE CARE AND HOSPICE SERVICES

A series of pilot studies, including our own, suggest that the provision of palliative care through hospice programs is a feasible alternative for severely demented patients (Brechling, Heyworth, Kuhn, & Peranteau, 1989; Hanrahan & Luchins, 1995b; Hanrahan, Raymond, McGowan, & Luchins, 1999; Luchins et al., 1997; Volicer et al., 1994; Volicer, Rheaume, Brown, Fabiszewski, & Brady, 1986). In collaboration with Meridian Hospice in Chicago, we established our first small pilot program for persons in the end stages of dementia and their families (Hanrahan & Luchins, 1995b). In this, as in all of our demonstration programs, enrollment in hospice was limited to those patients whose families believed that palliative care was an appropriate alternative for the terminal phase of their loved ones' illness.

Meridian Hospice provided home care to eleven individuals with advanced dementia and their families. As our later research indicated, survival time was a key issue in enabling access to hospice because the Medicare hospice benefit required physicians to certify that the patient was likely to die within about six months. The preferred outcome of aggressive care is to prolong survival time. However, in palliative care, extended survival time takes second place to improving the quality of life by easing physical decline and death. During the two years that we evaluated the program, eight of the eleven patients died. Their average survival time in hospice was seven months, which was fairly close to eligibility requirements for Medicare-funded hospice.

Our case studies at Meridian Hospice suggest a good fit between the kinds of services provided and the needs of both patients and family caregivers (Luchins et al., 1998). Family caregivers viewed respite, education, counseling, and bereavement services as very important and were quite satisfied with hospice care. Families also viewed the patients themselves as benefiting from skilled and individualized palliative care provided at home. These benefits included home visits by the hospice physician and nurses, palliative care, case-managed home health care, service provision in the home environment, and the high quality of staff care.

In related research, the provision of palliative care in dementia special care units was compared with traditional long-term care units at two Department of Veterans Affairs hospitals (Volicer et al., 1994). In most cases, advance proxy planning with family members limited aggressive medical interventions (Volicer et al., 1986). The patients themselves were too impaired to communicate their preferences. No such systematic planning program was in place in the traditional units. The dementia special care units decreased both patient discomfort and costs compared to the more traditional program.

ACCESS TO HOSPICE CARE: UNMET NEED

Although Meridian Hospice and other pilot programs supported the feasibility of hospice for end-stage dementia patients, the fact that very few of the professional and family caregivers in our earlier survey were aware of hospices that served dementia patients suggested unmet need (Luchins & Hanrahan, 1993). In order to explore this issue further, we conducted a national survey of all the hospices belonging to the National Hospice and Palliative Care Organization (Hanrahan & Luchins, 1995a). The proportion of hospice programs that responded was quite high at 70 percent, or 1,184 programs, so it is likely that our findings represented the typical pattern of hospice care at the time.

Our main question was, How many dementia patients received hospice services (excluding those with some other terminal illness, such as cancer)? In other words, we wanted to know how many had a primary diagnosis of dementia. Although the responding hospices served 138,503 patients in 1990, these programs reported serving less than 1 percent of patients with a primary diagnosis of dementia and no other terminal illness. A conservative estimate of the proportion of people who die from dementia is at least 7 percent (Ewbank, 1999; Hoyert, 1996). Thus, the vast majority of people who died of dementia did not receive hospice care, suggesting a major gap in the service delivery system. A later study had similar findings (Christakis & Escarce, 1996).

Barriers to Service Delivery

To understand problems in accessing hospice services, we asked hospice staff what problems occurred in their efforts to serve dementia patients relative to other patients. The main obstacle was the difficulty in predicting the survival time of dementia patients. As we have noted, patients needed to have a prognosis of death within six months to receive the Medicare hospice benefit. Because survival time in dementia ranges from two to ten years, it is very difficult to predict when patients will be within six months of death. From the perspective of access to hospice, then, the preferred outcome is a survival time of six months or less after hospice enrollment. This problem led us to our next study: identifying factors that predict death in end-stage dementia in the hope of increasing access to hospice. This study aimed to increase access to hospice by developing admission guidelines.

CRITERIA FOR ENROLLING DEMENTIA PATIENTS IN HOSPICE

Apart from the pioneering efforts of Volicer and his colleagues in studying institutional hospice (1993), very little was known about factors that influenced survival time in end-stage dementia when we began our studies. In order to develop guidelines for hospice programs, we established and tested enrollment criteria for the admission of end-stage dementia patients to hospice care. The criteria included the characteristics of advanced dementia and the presence of medical complications of the disease. After our initial test of the guidelines with Meridian Hospice, we recruited eight more Midwestern hospices that were willing to enroll dementia patients as part of our demonstration project (Hanrahan & Luchins, 1995b; Luchins et al., 1997). We again demonstrated that hospice care was feasible for dementia patients. Because replication is such an important component of establishing consistent findings, we conducted another replication in a large program provided by Great Lakes Hospice (Hanrahan, Raymond, McGowan, & Luchins, 1999).

While the study was in progress, the National Hospice and Palliative Care Organization had developed its own guidelines, so we retrospectively examined the application of these guidelines to our sample (Stuart et al., 1996). The guidelines paralleled our own but with the addition of a more detailed description of medical complications including the use of Stage Seven C of Functional Assessment Staging (FAST) as an appropriate cutoff point for enrollment (Reisberg, 1988; exhibit 12.1). Although these extremely impaired patients were more likely to die within six months, many very impaired patients in our study could not be scored on the FAST because their disease did not progress in the order required for its use.

IMPLICATIONS: DECREASED ACCESS?

Although the functional assessment staging can identify a subgroup of appropriate candidates for hospice, relying solely on this measure might actually decrease access to hospice care for many severely demented patients who do not meet such stringent criteria. Without hospice, sudden clinical events may occur for which the goals of care have not been discussed with the patients or their families (Ahronheim et al., 1996). Undesirable and aggressive interventions may then occur by default. At this point in the disease, dementia patients themselves are too impaired to indicate their preferences. For example, pneumonia frequently occurs in advanced dementia. Yet family members are often not consulted as proxy decision-makers about whether to focus primarily on palliative care to relieve discomfort or on more aggressive treatment, such as the use of antibiotics.

The number of hospice programs has grown substantially in the last three decades, and the number of patients served has quadrupled (Ogle, Mavis, & Wang, 2003). Data collected by the National Hospice and Palliative Care Organization suggests that access to hospice for dementia patients may be increasing as well. Unfortunately, the average length of stay for terminally ill patients has decreased by 25 percent (Wilson & Reisfield, 2003). However, patients and their families could benefit from earlier access to hospice services. Otherwise clinical care is often characterized by poor control of pain and symptoms and inadequate attention to family needs.

NEED FOR NEW CARE PARADIGMS

The apparent trend to limit hospice to persons so very late in the course of their terminal illnesses suggests the need for other models of care in institutional settings, such as nursing homes and hospitals, as well as in geriatrics and primary care practice in the community. Because so many nursing home residents have dementia, hospice and palliative care should be an important component of their health care plan. However, 70 percent of nursing homes have no hospice patients at all, despite the fact that 75 percent of persons admitted to nursing homes die within two years (Hazzard, Bierman, & Blass, 1994; Petrisek & Mor, 1999).

There are several barriers to offering hospice care within nursing homes as a treatment alternative (Zerzan, Sterns, & Hanson, 2000). In an effort to improve nursing homes, federal policy has designated the primary goals of care to be rehabilitation and restoration of function. This emphasis is an appropriate response

EXHIBIT 12.1: Functional Assessment Staging (FAST)

(Check highest consecutive level of disability)
1. No difficulty either subjectively or objectively.
2. Complains of forgetting location of objects. Subjective work difficulties.
3. Decreased job functioning evident to coworkers. Difficulty in traveling to new locations. Decreased organizational capacity.*
4. Decreased ability to perform complex tasks (e.g., planning dinner for guests, handling personal finances (such as forgetting to pay bills), difficulty marketing, etc.)
5. Requires assistance in choosing proper clothing to wear for the day, season, or occasion; for example, patients may wear the same clothing repeatedly, unless supervised.*
6. (a) Improperly putting on clothes without assistance or cueing (e.g., may put street clothes on over night clothes, or put shoes on wrong feet, or have difficulty buttoning clothing) occasionally or more frequently over the past weeks.*
   (b) Unable to bathe properly (e.g., difficulty adjusting bath-water temperature) occasionally or more frequently over the past weeks.*
   (c) Inability to handle mechanics of using the toilet (e.g., forgets to flush the toilet, does not wipe properly or properly dispose of toilet tissue) occasionally or more frequently over the past weeks.*
   (d) Urinary incontinence (occasionally or more frequently over the past weeks).*
   (e) Fecal incontinence (occasionally or more frequently over the past weeks).*
7. (a) Ability to speak limited to approximately a half a dozen intelligible different words or fewer, in the course of an average day or in the course of an intensive interview.
   (b) Speech ability is limited to the use of a single intelligible word in an average day or in the course of an intensive interview (the person may repeat the word over and over).
   (c) Ambulatory ability is lost (cannot walk without personal assistance).
   (d) Cannot sit up without assistance (e.g., the individual will fall over if there are not lateral armrests on the chair).
   (e) Loss of ability to smile.
   (f) Loss of ability to hold up head independently.

---

*Scored primarily on the basis of information obtained from a knowledgeable informant.

to reports of poor quality of care, abuse, and neglect in nursing homes. The assessment of potentially treatable conditions is required. Paradoxically, these goals make the provision of palliative care more difficult. Patients in the end stages of dementia and other terminal diseases may experience weight loss, dehydration, pressure sores, or functional decline. All these conditions have been identified as markers of potentially treatable conditions, yet palliative care has not been included as an acceptable treatment response in the regulations as they currently exist. This problem is not limited to dementia patients. Conditions such as pressure sores are more likely when patients' mobility is decreased as a result of terminal illnesses, and curative treatment is not always the best option as death approaches (Eisenberger & Zeleznik, 2003; Sachs, 2003).

Nursing homes and treating physicians may avoid being cited for violating regulations, for example, for not using a feeding tube for a dying malnourished patient if the patient's advance directives or family guardian requests the avoidance of such aggressive care. Anecdotal evidence, however, suggests that such advance planning and family consultation rarely occurs. For example, in a nursing home setting, staff contacted family members about the condition of their relatives with dementia an average of only one time in twenty-two months (Murphy, 2002). This was hardly conducive to the provision of palliative care in which frequent and ongoing communication with proxy decision-makers is essential. The need for better provision of palliative care in nursing homes, hospitals, and the community is further supported by studies suggesting that there is a great deal of undiagnosed pain among the elderly, particularly those with dementia.

UNDIAGNOSED PAIN, BEHAVIORAL PROBLEMS, AND PALLIATIVE CARE IMPLICATIONS

The assessment of pain is inadequate among the elderly, which leads both to underrecognition of pain and to inadequate pain control (Gagliese & Melzack, 1997; Herr & Mobily, 1996). Studies on the prevalence of pain among nursing home patients report results ranging from 45 percent to as high as 80 percent (American Geriatrics Society, 1998; Ferrell, 1995). Pain problems are common among community-dwelling elders as well (25 percent to 50 percent; American Geriatrics Society, 1998). Pain in this population is most often due to chronic conditions, such as arthritis and musculoskeletal problems. Complications due to dementia are another frequent source of pain, especially in the advanced stages of the disease (Luchins, Hanrahan, & Murphy, 1997).

The difficulty of assessing pain and symptoms among the elderly is an especially important problem in dementia. It is truly a nightmare scenario for those who are dying of dementia to be in frequent pain and unable to express it while their health care staff are not aware of this common problem. Unfortunately, this nightmare appears to be an all-too-frequent reality. Because social workers are often called on to develop plans for treating behavior problems, it is very important to consider the possibility that these problems are masking patients' untreated pain.

Behavioral Problems and Untreated Pain

As dementia progresses, the patient becomes less able to communicate verbally with family and health care staff, has poor judgment, and has difficulty in recalling painful episodes. Although complications of dementia often include painful illnesses, such as urinary infections, the severely demented patient is unable to tell the doctor or family member that pain and discomfort are present, let alone the nature of the pain. Instead, the demented patient's distress may be viewed as a behavior problem, such as agitation, or as a psychiatric symptom, such as depression (American Geriatrics Society, 1998; Cohen-Mansfield, 1986; Cohen-Mansfield & Werner, 1998, Eisdorfer, Cohen, & Paveza, 1992).

Agitation in the form of aggression is prevalent in institutional settings as well as in the community (Colenda & Hamer, 1991). In hospital and nursing home settings, the antecedent to aggressive behavior is most often some form of patient-staff exchange (Bridges-Parlet, Knopman, & Thompson, 1994). The link between aggression and untreated pain is fairly strong among persons with severe dementia, especially when their ability to report pain verbally is impaired (Cohen-Mansfield, Billig, Lipson, Rosenthal, & Pawlson, 1990; Cohen-Mansfield, Werner, & Marx, 1990). Aggression in nursing homes was especially high among persons who had two or more pain-related diagnoses and among people with arthritis (Feldt, Ryden, & Miles, 1998; Feldt, Warne, & Ryden, 1998). Pain appeared to be particularly likely when patients were moved, as one would expect in the case of joint pain caused by arthritis or disuse. Nursing assistants observed, for example, "She winces when we move her, . . . protects her arm and says 'ouch' when we get her up and dress her" (Feldt, Warne, & Ryden, 1998, p. 20). Nursing assistants reported pain in two-thirds of the sample, yet more than half of those believed to be in pain did not receive any pain medication. Unfortunately, this appears to be a common problem.

Although dementia patients' perception of pain is likely to remain intact, they often do not receive medication to control pain (Farrell, Katz, & Helme, 1996; Sengstaken & King, 1993). For example, Feldt and her colleagues (Feldt, Ryden, and Miles, 1998) found that cognitively impaired patients received significantly fewer opioid analgesics than did cognitively intact patients in the first and second forty-eight hours after surgery for hip fractures.

Similar findings were reported among patients who were hospitalized with pneumonia or hip fracture. More than half of the dementia patients died within six months, compared with 12 percent to 13 percent of the patients who were cognitively intact (Morrison & Su, 2000). Yet demented patients were subjected to as many aggressive, painful, or uncomfortable treatments and received less medication for pain. Among demented patients with hip fractures, only 24 percent received a standing order for pain medications. No documentation was found of any discussions with family members about whether the goal of care should focus more on prolonging life or easing death. Social workers are well suited to taking up the challenge of initiating this neglected but vital dialogue with families.

There is some evidence to suggest that the problem of inadequate use of pain medications is being recognized in chronic care facilities, which have increased their use of nonnarcotic pain medications among dementia patients over time (Evers et al., 2002). However, the use of narcotic pain medications was still less than half as likely among dementia patients compared to nondementia patients with similar medical complications (14 percent versus 38 percent).

These problems have led to recommendations to presume that agitation in advanced-dementia patients is the result of pain and to treat it with a physical assessment and pain medication as the first course of action. Guidelines have been developed for staff and family caregivers that call for providing pain medication before any activity that involves changing the patient's position. Anecdotally, Brenner (1998) reported that this procedure decreased agitation in the Jacob Perlow Hospice.

Palliative care modalities need to be developed and evaluated in addition to hospice, such as palliative care programs in nursing homes, hospitals, outpatient clinics, and home health care agencies. Palliative treatment is also an appropriate alternative for comorbid conditions in advanced dementia, such as diabetes, cardiovascular problems, and cancer as well as preventive care, such as mammograms and flu shots (Sachs, 1994).

PEACE: PALLIATIVE EXCELLENCE IN ALZHEIMER CARE EFFORTS

In response to the combination of highly restricted availability of hospice for dementia in the community and nursing homes, together with the likelihood of undiagnosed pain in advanced dementia, we initiated a demonstration project. The Palliative Excellence in Alzheimer Care Efforts, or PEACE, project, was designed to increase access to palliative care and hospice in two settings: in nursing homes through services contracted from the Hospice of Michigan and in the primary-care geriatrics practice of the University of Chicago (Hanrahan et al., 2002; Murphy et al., 2000; Shega et al., 2003).

The PEACE Project with the Hospice of Michigan

This project served patients with advanced dementia whose prognosis was too uncertain for hospice admission and provided these patients with palliative care and partial hospice services. Patients from three nursing homes received services from the Hospice of Michigan in the nursing home setting, with consent from their family caregivers. At intake, Hospice of Michigan staff met with family members to discuss the feasibility of palliative care. A family manual was provided for their review and subsequent reference while making these decisions. For those family caregivers who chose palliative care, the attending physician at the nursing home was notified of the patient's enrollment in PEACE. Project aims and goals were reviewed with the attending physician. Care was then provided as a team approach under the direction of a palliative care physician (Dr. Murphy) who was an on-site consultant to the nursing homes.

Conditions for which palliative care may be appropriate, or clinical choice points, were identified for each patient. This assessment also involved identifying possible causes for comorbid conditions and complications; whether any current conditions were likely to be causing the patient pain; and current medications. A palliative care plan was developed based on this assessment. Patients were then followed through biweekly rounds by the PEACE team, although care was available around the clock should an urgent condition arise. Patients whose survival was likely to be about six months were referred to full hospice services with Hospice of Michigan.

Family caregivers in the PEACE program welcomed the opportunity to discuss palliative care alternatives for their demented relatives, and many chose this option. Medical conditions that could be treated with palliative care, or clinical choice points, were identified for forty-one patients. Problems that have been commonly cited in nursing homes studies—notably, agitation and polypharmacy—proved to be important clinical choice points (Hanrahan et al., 1999; Nasman, Bucht, & Erikson, 1993). Agitation was often accompanied by painful comorbid conditions and/or complications. In response, pain medications were increased. Coughs and falls were also common choice points for providing palliative care.

Case study. An eighty-five-year-old woman was enrolled in the PEACE program; her dementia was believed to be combined in nature: Alzheimer's disease and vascular dementia. She had repeated loud vocalizations and agitation. Her extreme resistance to routine caregiving was disruptive and distressing to both family and nursing home staff. She had been given sedatives, hypnotics, antidepressants, and various antipsychotics as a trial to treat her behaviors. The PEACE team reviewed her medical chart and interviewed the family about her pain history. She had rheumatoid arthritis; osteoarthritis; diabetic neuropathy; previous pelvis, rib, and cervical fractures; and a history of trigeminal neuralgia. She was not receiving any pain medications. She was placed on low doses of opiates and her behavior improved remarkably. Her family and the nursing home staff were very surprised and pleased with her improvement.

Our preliminary findings suggest that the palliative care team proved beneficial for nursing home patients with advanced dementia and their families. Polypharmacy was regularly addressed with decreases in excessive or inappropriate medication use. One patient avoided being intubated for decreased appetite and was given finger foods instead. In some cases, the outcome of palliative care for these problems appeared to include preventing unnecessary and expensive hospital transfers. Although these outcomes are promising, they are best viewed as benchmarks in the absence of a comparison group that did not participate.

The University of Chicago PEACE Program

The University of Chicago PEACE program aimed to integrate palliative care with the primary care of patients with dementia throughout the course of the disease. This disease-management model is similar to proposals for MediCaring (Lynn, 1996). The model includes "advance planning, patient centered care, family support, and a palliative care focus from the diagnosis of dementia through its terminal stages" (Shega et al., 2003). The University of Chicago Geriatrics Section at the Windermere Senior Health Center conducted the demonstration project. Program goals for the advanced stages of dementia include offering hospice to all patients and their families; helping patients to die in their desired location, which was usually at home; and avoiding undesired invasive medical procedures or hospitalization.

Preliminary findings suggest that the 150 patients enrolled in the project have had adequate pain control and that both patients and their families were highly satisfied with their care. Hospice care was provided to half of the patients that have died to date. Death occurred at home for about two-thirds of the patients, which was usually in accord with their preferences. In response to this positive feedback, the research initiative is being transformed to become a part of regular care at the clinic.

Taken together, these findings from the two components of the PEACE demonstration project suggest the feasibility of new care paradigms for providing palliative care and hospice to dementia patients. Expansion of this model would create the ability to integrate a palliative approach into the mainstream of medicine.

IMPLICATIONS FOR SOCIAL WORK

Palliative care principles should be part of the education and practice of social work in order to address the needs and demographics of the increasing numbers of older adults who are suffering from dementia. Throughout the course of dementia, social workers can play a key role in treatment by providing behavioral interventions, service linkage, and advocacy. Program development, analysis, and evaluation are also important roles.

The initial diagnosis is a special opportunity to begin a dialogue about long-term treatment plans with family members and those patients who are still able to participate. Advance planning may then help to prevent unnecessary aggressive care when that is the patient's preference or the preference of family members as proxy decision-makers. Although advance directives are best initiated soon after the initial diagnosis, more often this does not occur, but it can still be initiated in nursing home and hospital settings. Social workers in these settings can engage family members in ongoing dialogue about whether the goal of care for their loved ones should focus more on prolonging life or easing death.

Social workers can also provide invaluable assistance to dementia patients and their families as case managers by linking them with community services such as adult day care and home health care as well as by advocating for their admission to hospice programs. As we have noted, behavioral problems are common in dementia and increase as the disease progresses. The pioneering efforts of Dr. Pinkston and her colleagues (1984) provide social workers with an invaluable resource for behavioral interventions that is especially useful in the mild and moderate stages of dementia.

In the more advanced stages of dementia, appropriate health services are often unavailable. Assessment should address the likelihood of untreated pain. Better programs are needed for patients who are dying of dementia and for their family caregivers. Social workers are well suited to introduce, adapt, and evaluate the PEACE demonstration project model as a new paradigm of care. Advocacy, program development, and evaluation are needed to improve the service environment and to inform policy debate.

REFERENCES

Ahronheim, J. C., Morrison, R. S., Baskin, S. A., Morris, J., & Meier, D. E. (1996). Treatment of the dying in the acute care hospital. *Archives of Internal Medicine, 156*(18), 2094–2100.

American Geriatrics Society (AGS) Panel on Chronic Pain in Older Persons. (1998). The management of chronic pain in older persons. *Journal of the American Geriatrics Society, 46*(5), 635–651.

Bachman, D. L., Wolf, P. A., Linn, R. T., Knoefel, J. E., Cobb, J. Z., Belanger, A. J., et al. (1993). Incidence of dementia and probable Alzheimer's disease in a general population. *Neurology, 43*(3, pt. 1), 515–519.

Brechling, B. G., Heyworth, J., Kuhn, D., & Peranteau, M. F. (1989). Extending hospice care to end-stage dementia patients and families. *American Journal of Alzheimer's Care and Related Disorders and Research, 4*(3), 21–29.

Brenner, P. R. (1998). The experience of Jacob Perlow Hospice: Hospice care of patients with Alzheimer's disease. In L. Volicer & A. Hurley (Eds.), *Hospice care for patients with advanced progressive dementia* (pp. 257–275). New York: Springer.

Bridges-Parlet, S., Knopman D., & Thompson, T. (1994). A descriptive study of physically aggressive behavior in dementia by direct observation. *Journal of the American Geriatrics Society, 42*(2), 192–197.

Brookmeyer R., Gray S., & Kawas C. (1998). Projections of Alzheimer's disease in the United States and the public health impact of delaying disease onset. *American Journal of Public Health, 88*(9), 1337–1342.

Burns, A., Jacoby, R., & Levy, R. (1990). Psychiatric phenomena in Alzheimer's disease. 4: Disorders of behaviors. *British Journal of Psychiatry, 157,* 86–94.

Christakis, N. A., & Escarce, J. J. (1996). Survival of Medicare patients after enrollment in hospice programs. *New England Journal of Medicine, 335*(3), 172–178.

Cohen-Mansfield, J. (1986). Agitated behaviors in the elderly: 2. Preliminary results in the cognitively deteriorated. *Journal of the American Geriatrics Society, 34*(10), 722–727.

Cohen-Mansfield, J., Billig, N., Lipson, S., Rosenthal, A. S., and Pawlson, L. G. (1990). Medical correlates of agitation in nursing home residents. *Gerontology, 36,* 96–97.

Cohen-Mansfield, J., & Werner, P. (1998). Predictors of aggressive behaviors: A longitudinal study in senior day care centers. *Journals of Gerontology. Series B, Psychological Sciences and Social Sciences, 53*(5), 300–310.

Cohen-Mansfield, J., Werner, P., & Marx, M. S. (1990). Screaming in nursing home residents. *Journal of the American Geriatrics Society, 38*(7), 785–792.

Colenda, C. C., & Hamer, R. M. (1991). Antecedents and interventions for aggressive behavior of patients at a geropsychiatric state hospital. *Hospital and Community Psychiatry, 42,* 287–292.

Collins, C., & Ogle, K. (1994). Patterns of pre-death service use by dementia patients with a family caregiver. *Journal of the American Geriatrics Society, 42,* 719–722.

Danis, M., Southerland, L. I., Garrett, J. M., Smith, J. L., Hielema, F., Pickard, C. G., et al. (1991). A prospective study of advance directives for life-sustaining care. *New England Journal of Medicine, 324*(13), 882–888.

Diamond, E. L., Jernigan, J. A., Moseley, R. A., Messina, V., & McKeown, R. A. (1989). Decision-making ability and advance directive preferences in nursing home patients and proxies. *Gerontologist, 29*(5), 622–626.

Eisdorfer, C., Cohen, D., & Paveza, G. (1992). An empirical evaluation of the Global Deterioration Scale for staging Alzheimer's disease. *American Journal of Psychiatry, 149,* 195–198.

Eisenberger, A., & Zeleznik, J. (2003). Pressure ulcer prevention and treatment in hospices: A qualitative analysis. *Journal of Palliative Care, 19*(1), 9–14.

Engel, B. T., Burgio, L. D., & McCormick, K. S. (1990). Behavioral treatment of incontinence in the long-term care setting. *Journal of the American Geriatrics Society, 38*(3), 361–363.

Ernst, R. L., & Hay, J. W. (1994). The U.S. economic and social costs of Alzheimer's disease revisited. *American Journal of Public Health, 84*(8), 1261–1264.

Evers, M. M., Dushyant Purohit, B. S., Perl, D., Khan, K., & Marin, D. B. (2002). Palliative and aggressive end-of-life care for patients with dementia. *Psychiatric Services, 53,* 609–613.

Ewbank, D. C. (1999). Deaths attributable to Alzheimer's disease in the United States. *American Journal of Public Health, 89*(1), 90–92.

Feldt, K. S., Ryden, M. B., & Miles, S. (1998). Treatment of pain in cognitively impaired compared with cognitively intact older patients with hip fracture. *Journal of the American Geriatrics Society, 46*(9), 1079–1085.

Feldt, K. S., Warne, M. A., & Ryden, M. B. (1998). Examining pain in aggressive cognitively impaired older adults. *Journal of Gerontological Nursing, 11,* 14–22.

Farrell, M. J., Katz, B., Helme, R. D. (1996). The impact of dementia on the pain experience. *Pain, 67*(1), 7–15.

Ferrell, B. A. (1995). Pain evaluation and management in the nursing home. *Annals of Internal Medicine, 123*(9), 681–687.

Fortune, A. E., & Reid, W. J. (1999). *Research in social work* (3rd ed.). New York: Columbia University Press.

Gagliese, L., & Melzack, R. (1997). Chronic pain in elderly people. *Pain, 70*(1), 3–14.

Gallagher, D., Rose, J., Rivera, P., Lovett, S., & Thompson, L. W. (1989). Prevalence of depression in family caregivers. *Gerontologist, 24*(4), 449–456.

German, P. S., Rovner, B. W., & Burton, L. C. (1992). The role of mental morbidity in the nursing home experience. *Gerontologist, 32*(2), 152–158.

Goldman, L. S., & Luchins, D. J. (1984). Depression in the spouses of demented patients. *American Journal of Psychiatry, 141,* 1467–1468.

Haley, W. E., LaMonde, L. A., Han, B., Burton, A. M., & Schonwetter, R. (2003). Predictors of depression and life satisfaction among spousal caregivers in hospice: Application of a stress process model. *Journal of Palliative Medicine, 6*(2), 215–224.

Hanrahan, P., & Luchins, D. J. (1995a). Access to hospice care for end-stage dementia patients: A national survey of hospice programs. *Journal of the American Geriatrics Society, 42*(1), 56–59.

Hanrahan, P., & Luchins, D. J. (1995b). Feasible criteria for enrolling end-stage dementia patients in home hospice care. *The Hospice Journal, 10*(3), 47–54.

Hanrahan, P., Luchins, D. J., & Osview, F. (1999). Dementia in the public mental health settings. In F. Osview (Ed.), *Neuropsychiatry and mental health services* (69–104). Washington, DC: American Psychiatric Association.

Hanrahan P., Murphy, K., Luchins. D. J., Patrick, G., Johnson, S., Hougham, G., et al. (2002). Palliative care for dementia: Clinical choice points. *Journal of the American Geriatrics Society, 50*(4), P84.

Hanrahan, P., Raymond, M., McGowan, E., & Luchins, D. J. (1999). Criteria for enrolling dementia patients in hospice: A replication. *American Journal of Hospice and Palliative Care, 16*(1), 395–409.

Hazzard, W. R., Bierman, E. L., & Blass, J. P. (Eds.). (1994). *Principles of geriatric medicine and gerontology* (3rd ed.). New York: McGraw-Hill.

Herr, K. A., & Mobily, P. R. (1996). Pain management for the elderly in alternate care settings. In B. R. Ferrell & B. A. Ferrell (Eds.), *Pain in the elderly* (pp. 101–109). Seattle: IASP Press.

Hougham, G. W., Stocking, C. B., & Sachs, G. A. (2002, October). *Burdens on family caregivers of persons with Alzheimer's disease.* Paper presented at the Best Practices Conference, Northwestern University, Chicago.

Hoyert, D. L. (1996). Mortality trends for Alzheimer's disease: 1979–1991. *Vital Health Stat 20, 28,* 1–23.

Kleinfeld, N. R. (2003, July 19). Elderly patients whose final wishes go unsaid put many doctors in a bind. *New York Times,* p. A12.

Linsk, N., Hanrahan, P., & Pinkston, E. M. (1991). Teaching older people and their families to use community resources. In P. A. Wisocki (Ed.), *Clinical behavior therapy for the elderly client* (479–504). New York: Plenum Press.

Luchins, D. J., & Hanrahan, P. (1993). What is the appropriate level of health care for end-stage dementia patients? *Journal of the American Geriatrics Society, 41*(9), 25–30.

Luchins, D. J., Hanrahan, P., & Litzenberg, K. (1998). Acceptance of hospice care for dementia patients by health care professionals and family members. In L. Volicer & A. Hurley (Eds.), *Hospice care for patients with advanced progressive dementia* (pp. 207–230). New York: Springer.

Luchins, D. J., Hanrahan, P., Murphy, K. (1997). Criteria for enrolling dementia patients in hospice. *Journal of the American Geriatrics Society, 45*(9), 1054–1059.

Lynn, J. (1996). Caring at the end of our lives. *Journal of the American Medical Association, 335*(3), 172–178.

McCarthy, M., Addington-Hall, J., & Altmann, D. (1997). The experience of dying with dementia: A retrospective study. *International Journal of Geriatric Psychiatry, 12,* 404–409.

Meco, G., Alessandria, A., Bonifati, V., & Giustini, P. (1994). Risperidone for hallucinations in levo-dopa treated Parkinson's disease patients. *Lancet, 343,* 1320–1371.

Mega, M. S., Cummings, J. L., Fiorello, T., & Gornbein, J. (1996). The spectrum of behavioral changes in Alzheimer's disease. *Neurology, 46*(1), 130–135.

Michelson, C., Mulvihill, M., Hsu, M. A., & Olson , E. (1991). Eliciting medical care preferences from nursing home residents. *Gerontologist, 31*(3), 358–363.

Moak, G. S., & Fisher, W. H. (1990). Alzheimer's disease and related disorders in state mental hospitals: Data from a nationwide survey. *Gerontologist, 30*(6), 798–802.

Morrison, R. S., & Siu, A. L. (2000). Survival in end-stage dementia following acute illness. *Journal of the American Medical Association, 284*(1), 47–52.

Murphy K. (2002). Personal communication.

Murphy, K., Hanrahan, P., Hougham, G. W., Luchins, D. J., Johnson, S., & Sachs, G. A. (2000). The use of clinical choice points in shaping end-of-life care for patients with advanced dementia. Washington, DC: Gerontological Society of America.

Murphy, K., Hanrahan, P., & Luchins, D. J. (1997). A survey of grief and bereavement in nursing homes: The importance of hospice grief and bereavement for the end-stage Alzheimer's disease patient and family. *Journal of the American Geriatrics Society, 45*(9), 1104–1107.

Naleppa, M., & Reid, W. J. (2003). *Gerontological social work : A task-centered approach.* New York: Columbia University Press.

Nasman, F., Bucht, G., & Eriksson, S. (1993). Behavioural symptoms in the institutionalized elderly: Relationship to dementia. *International Journal of Geriatrics Psychiatry, 8,* 843–849.

Ogle, K, Mavis, B., & Wang, T. (2003). Hospice and primary care physicians: Attitudes, knowledge and barriers. *American Journal of Hospice and Primary Care, 20*(1), 41–51.

Payne, K., Taylor, R. M., Stocking, C., & Sachs, G. A. (1996). Physicians' attitudes about the care of patients in the persistent vegetative state: A national survey. *Annals of Internal Medicine, 125*(2), 104–10.

Petrisek, A. C., & Mor, V. (1999). Hospice in nursing homes: A facility-level analysis of the distribution of hospice beneficiaries. *Gerontologist, 39*(3), 279–290.

Pinkston, E. M., & Linsk, N. (1984). *Care of the elderly: A family approach.* New York: Pergamon Press.

Pruchno, R. A., & Resch, N. L. (1989). Aberrant behaviors and Alzheimer's disease: Mental health effects on spouse caregivers. *Journal of Gerontology, 44*(5), S177–S182.

Reisberg, B. (1988). Functional assessment staging (FAST). *Psychopharmacology Bulletin, 24*(4), 653–659.

Reisberg, B., Ferris, S. H., DeLeon, M. J., & Crook, T. (1982). The Global Deterioration Scale for assessment of primary degenerative dementia. *American Journal of Psychiatry, 139*(9), 1136–1139.

Rice, D. P., Fox, P. J., & Max, W. (1993). The economic burden of Alzheimer's disease care. *Health Affairs, 12,* 164–176.

Sachs, G. A. (1994). Flu shots, mammograms, and Alzheimer's disease: Ethics of preventative medicine and dementia. *Alzheimer's Disease and Associated Disorders, 8*(1), 8–14.

Sachs, G. A. (2003). Research at the interface of palliative care and geriatrics. *Journal of Palliative Care, 19*(1), 5–6.

Schneider, L. S., Pollack, V. E., & Lyness, S. A. (1990). A meta-analysis of controlled trials of neuroleptic treatment in dementia. *Journal of the American Geriatrics Society, 38*(5), 553–563.

Sengstaken, E. A., & King S. A. (1993). The problems of pain and its detection among geriatric nursing home residents. *Journal of the American Geriatrics Society, 41*(5), 541–544.

Schulz, R., & Beach, S. (1999). Caregiving as a risk factor for mortality: The Caregiver Health Effects Study. *Journal of the American Medical Association, 282,* 2215–2219.

Shega, J. W., Levin, A., Hougham, G. W., Cox-Haley, D., Luchins, D. J., Hanrahan, P., et al. (2003). Palliative Excellence in Alzheimer's Care Efforts (PEACE). *Journal of Palliative Medicine, 6*(2), 315–320.

Skoog, I., Nielson, L., Palmertz, B., Andreasson, L. A., & Svanborg, A. (1993). A population based study of dementia in 85 year olds. *New England Journal of Medicine, 328*(3), 153–158.

Strahan, G., & Burns, B. J. (1991). *Mental illness in nursing homes: United States, 1985 (DHHS Publication No. PHS 91-1766).* Washington, DC: U.S. Government Printing Office.

Stuart, B., Herbst, L., Kinzbrunner, B., Alexander, C., Arenella, C., Connor, S. (1996). Medical guidelines for determining prognosis in selected non-cancer diseases. *Hospice Journal, 11,* 47–63.

Teri, L., Larson, E. B., & Reifler, B. V. (1988). Behavioral disturbance in dementia of the Alzheimer's type. *Journal of the American Geriatrics Society, 36*(1), 1–6.

Teri, L., & Uomoto, J. M. (1991). Reducing excess disability in dementia patients: Training caregivers to manage patient depression. *Clinical Gerontologist, 10,* 49–63.

Volicer, L., Collard, A., Hurley, A., Bishop, C. Kern, D., & Karon, S. (1994). Impact of special care unit for patients with advanced Alzheimer's disease on patients' discomfort and costs. *Journal of the American Geriatrics Society, 42*(6), 597–603.

Volicer, B. J., Hurley, A., Fabiszewski, K. J., Montgomery, P., & Volicer, L. (1993). Predicting short-term survival for patients with advanced Alzheimer's disease. *Journal of the American Geriatrics Society, 41*(5), 535–540.

Volicer, L., Rheaume, Y., Brown, J., Fabiszewski, K., & Brady, R. (1986). Hospice approach to the treatment of patients with advanced dementia of the Alzheimer's type. *Journal of the American Medical Association, 256*(16), 2210–2213.

Welch, H. G., Walsh, J. S., & Larson, E. B. (1992). The cost of institutional care in Alzheimer's disease: nursing home and hospital use in a prospective cohort. *Journal of the American Geriatrics Society, 40*(3), 221–224.

Wernicke, T. F., & Reisches, F. M. (1994). Prevalence of dementia in old age: Clinical diagnoses in subjects ages 95 years and older. *Neurology, 44*(2), 250–253.

Wilson, G. R., & Reisfield, G. M. (2003). More patients served by hospice, but still a last resort. *American Journal of Hospice and Palliative Care, 20*(3), 173–174.

Zerzan, J., Stearns, S., & Hanson, L. (2000). Access to palliative care and hospice in nursing homes. *Journal of the American Medical Association, 284*(19), 2489–2494.

CHAPTER 13

BEHAVIORAL INTERVENTIONS FOR SEVERE AND PERSISTENT MENTAL DISORDERS

Stephen E. Wong, David A. Wilder,
Keven Schock, and Cris Clay

This chapter outlines a behavioral approach to the conceptualization and treatment of severe and persistent mental disorders. Behavioral interventions are derived from operant and social learning principles that analyze the effects of the environment on human behavior. This approach has been fruitful in expanding the understanding of human activity and in designing interventions for a wide range of social and clinical problems (Barlow, 1993; Bellack, Hersen, & Kazdin, 1990; Mattaini & Thyer, 1996; Van Houten & Axelrod, 1993). In this chapter, the term *severe and persistent mental disorders* refers to the emergence of behavioral and emotional problems that significantly interfere with clients' adaptive functioning, such as their ability to relate to others, to work, or to live on their own. The term is used herein as a general label synonymous with psychosis (Wong, 1996). Clients with these problems may have been given diagnoses of schizophrenic disorder, schizoaffective disorders, paranoid disorders, mood disorders, organic mental disorders, or other diagnoses. For reasons to be explained shortly, we will focus on clients' behavioral problems rather than on their psychiatric diagnoses.

THE HIDDEN CONTROVERSY IN EVIDENCE-BASED TREATMENTS FOR SEVERE AND PERSISTENT MENTAL DISORDERS

Given the theoretical perspective of this chapter, a review of evidence-based treatments for severe and persistent mental disorders is a challenge, because biomedical concepts completely dominate current thinking about mental disorders and existing treatment approaches. The prevailing belief about mental disorders is that they are brain diseases that must be treated with psychotropic medication. Despite the institutional authority and popular acceptance of the biomedical model, the evidence in support of this position has been weak and inconsistent (Pam, 1990; Ross & Pam, 1995; Seibert, 1999; Shean, 2001; Valenstein, 1998).

Citations from a variety of authoritative sources suggest that data underpinning biomedical models of mental disorders are inconclusive or lacking. Describing the quintessential psychotic syndrome, the fourth edition of the Diagnostic and Statistical Manual of Mental Disorders (DSM–IV) stated: "No laboratory findings have been identified that are diagnostic of schizophrenia" (American Psychiatric Association, 19994, p. 280). Similarly, the *Surgeon General's Report on Mental Health* (U.S. Department of Health and Human Services, 1999) noted, "The precise causes (etiology) of most mental disorders are not known." Most recently, an official statement issued by the American Psychiatric Association (APA, 2003) conceded, "Brain science has not advanced to the point where scientists or clinicians can point to readily discernable pathological lesions or genetic abnormalities that in and of themselves serve as reliable or predictive biomarkers of a given mental disorder or mental disorders."

The DSM diagnostic categories and specific diagnoses may even be viewed as arbitrary classifications and reifications. Close examination of DSM diagnoses and their origins reveals that these categories are based on many unsubstantiated assumptions and circular reasoning (Boyle, 1990). They were composed by committees responding to political and economic concerns (Kutchins & Kirk, 1997; Brown, 1990), and their validity was never established. Moreover, major field trials evaluating the psychiatric nosology showed that many DSM diagnoses, including those for severe mental disorders, have low reliability (Kirk & Kutchins, 1992, 1994), casting further doubt on their validity.

For nearly half a century, neuroleptic medication (e.g., chlorpromazine, the trade name of which is Thorazine) has been the backbone of biomedical treatment for severe and persistent mental disorders. Although neuroleptic medication has been evaluated in numerous studies, until recently it has eluded critical inquiry. Results of more than thirteen hundred outcome studies published since the mid-1950s reveal that neuroleptic medications may be expected to prevent exacerbation of symptoms or rehospitalization in one of three patients who receive them (Cohen, 1997). Although not insignificant, this is hardly the success rate one would expect from interventions that are considered indispensable and universally applied. Furthermore, reliance on symptom suppression as an outcome measure may be misleading because there is practically no research showing that neuroleptic medication improves clients' social relationships or ability to work (Cohen, 1997; Gelman, 1999).

Neuroleptics are well known for their ability to make patients less agitated, uncooperative, and combative, but this ability is part of a general enervation that consists of extreme weakness and fatigue, blunting of affect, and interference with higher thought processes (e.g., planning and speaking) (Breggin, 1991, 1997; Cohen, 1997). These effects are clinically nonspecific and are observed in persons both who do and who do not have mental disorders. One psychiatrist who took a neuroleptic drug described how it made her feel very "tired" and "weak" as though she were "dying;" yet "indifferent," so as not to care that she was dying (Cohen, 1997; p. 180).

Neuroleptic drugs also produce a host of adverse effects, many that are unpleasant and disturbing to the client and some that are severely debilitating and irreversible. *Extrapyramidal symptoms* are movement disorders, including a masklike facial expression, muscle rigidity, strange uncoordinated movements and muscular spasms, and an inability to sit still, which is produced in 62 percent of patients receiving neuroleptic medications (Cohen, 1997). *Tardive dyskinesia* is another neurological disorder manifested in uncontrolled movements such as blinking; tongue curling and thrusting; contortions of the neck, torso, and pelvis; and an abnormal gait. These symptoms are often visible only after the medication is withdrawn and are usually irreversible (Brown & Funk, 1986). The risk of developing tardive dyskinesia after exposure to neuroleptics is cumulative over time and is estimated to increase from 32 percent after five years to 65 percent after twenty years (Breggin, 1997). Neuroleptic drugs are also associated with less common but more perilous disorders such as the *malignant neuroleptic syndrome*. Between 1.4 percent and 2.4 percent of the patients receiving neuroleptic drugs may be expected to develop this problem, and up to 20 percent of those afflicted with this iatrogenic disorder will die from it (Breggin, 1997).

New medications, called atypical antipsychotics, have been promoted as effective with many clients who do not respond to older neuroleptics and as having a lower risk of extrapyramidal symptoms and tardive dyskinesia. On closer inspection, however, these drugs can present the same hazards as their predecessors and additional ones as well (Cohen, 2002; Wahlbeck, Hamann, & Kissling, 2003). One of the drugs, Clozaril, recently has been reported to produce various movement disorders and tardive dyskinesia (Cohen, 1994). Clozaril suppresses white cell production and leaves the client susceptible to lethal infections, and for this reason it was banned in European countries in the mid-1970s. Clozaril is also associated with *gran mal* seizures (Breggin, 1997) and the insidious neuroleptic malignant syndrome (Breggin, 1997; Cohen, 1994).

In summary, despite psychiatry's hegemony over mental health services, its reductionist biological theories, its questionable diagnoses, and its chemical treatments for severe and persistent mental disorders leave much to be desired. In light of the apparent need to explore and develop alternative approaches, we offer a framework for behavioral interventions with severe and persistent mental disorders. This model conceptualizes these disorders within the framework of the client's learning processes and current environment, and it offers humane, empirically validated treatments to remediate the problems.

GUIDES AND PRINCIPLES FOR PRACTICE: BEHAVIORAL INTERVENTIONS FOR SEVERE AND PERSISTENT MENTAL DISORDERS

Constellations of behavioral disorders exhibited by persons with severe and persistent mental disorders vary greatly, but all interfere with clients' functioning as adults in society. Focusing on the frequency of observable behavior, behavioral clinicians often categorize problems in terms of behavioral excess and deficits.

Behavioral excesses are responses occurring at unusually high rates that disrupt social relations, occupational activities, or activities of daily living. Interventions for behavioral excesses typically remove or lessen reinforcement for these responses and concurrently teach and reinforce appropriate responses that can replace the inappropriate behavior. Behavioral deficits are responses occurring at rates too low to sustain satisfactory social relations, employment, or independent living. Interventions for behavioral deficits usually teach and reinforce the specific skills or responses needed for that particular context.

Behavioral Excesses

In this chapter we will describe three behavioral excesses and learning-based interventions for them: bizarre behavior, oppositional behavior, and stereotypic behavior. Bizarre behavior will be discussed first and in greater depth because of its complex and puzzling nature.

Bizarre behavior.   Odd or strange behavior is a distinguishing feature of severe and persistent mental disorders or psychosis. The Time Sample Behavioral Checklist (Paul, 1987) describes myriad forms of bizarre behavior (e.g., unrealistic statements, inappropriate laughing, peculiar mannerisms) that have been observed in chronic mental patients. Bizarre behavior can be disorganized and incoherent, or it can revolve around grotesque religious, somatic, grandiose, or persecutory themes. Unfortunately, fascination with the physical form of bizarre behavior has kept clinical researchers from examining the causal relationships between environmental events and this behavior, and from recognizing that bizarre behavior, like ordinary behavior, is affected by environmental stimuli that precede and follow it.

Antecedent stimuli—such as commands or questions from others, or the presence of particular people and objects in the setting—can control behavior by signaling that specific responses will have certain consequences. A growing body of evidence that antecedent stimuli affect bizarre behavior comes from research on cognitive-behavioral therapies. These investigations (Alford, 1986; Bentall, Haddock, & Slade, 1994; Chadwick & Lowe, 1990, 1994; Chadwick, Lowe, Horne, & Higson, 1994; Haddock et al., 1999; Himadi & Kaiser, 1992; Lowe & Chadwick, 1990; Siddle, Turkington, & Dudley, 1997; Velligan et al., 2000; Wykes, Parr, & Landau, 1999) have shown that delusional verbalizations of patients with schizophrenia can be altered with a combination of tactful suggestions and leading questions. The original procedure for modifying delusions, proposed by Watts, Powell, and Austin (1973), consisted of (1) beginning treatment by modifying the belief least strongly held, (2) asking clients to merely consider an alternative to their belief, (3) challenging evidence for the belief (rather than the belief itself), and (4) asking clients to present arguments contrary to their own beliefs. Social reinforcement probably also plays a role in this intervention because a sizable number of therapy sessions (six to twelve) are devoted to establishing a therapeutic relationship before challenging clients' delusional beliefs (Chadwick & Lowe, 1994). However cognitive-behavioral therapy operates, it is a promising psychosocial intervention that has been used to reverse long-standing delusional verbalizations in many clients (Bouchard, Vallieres, Roy, & Maziade, 1996; Dickerson, 2000; Glaser, Kazantzis, Deane, & Oades, 2000; Kingdon, Turkington, & John, 1994).

Antecedent stimuli arising from physical ailments can also affect bizarre and delusional statements (Schock, Clay, & Cipani, 1998). In such cases, relieving the physical ailment often eliminates the delusional behavior. For example, a forty-two-year-old female client reported that she could not get out of bed because she was dying or dead. A physical examination determined that she in fact had extremely low blood pressure (i.e., 60/40). After teaching the client a series of simple movements to increase her blood pressure prior to standing up, the delusional statements disappeared. Another case involved a client with a history of screaming "at demons who were spitting fire on her genital region." Upon examination by a gynecologist, it was determined that she had several sexually transmitted diseases. After receiving antibiotics to treat her condition, the screaming ceased (Schock, Browning, Clay, & Gipson, 1996). These reports reveal that bizarre, irrational-sounding speech may actually be metaphorical and that it is important to undercover the variables controlling these communicative acts.

Consequent stimuli can also give rise to and maintain psychotic behavior through the process of *positive reinforcement*. Positively reinforcing consequences might be attention from others, preferred activities, consumables (e.g., food), or desired objects. In a landmark study, Ayllon and Haughton (1964) modified consequent stimuli to treat the speech of a forty-seven-year-old woman who, for fourteen years, had claimed to be Queen Elizabeth. The procedure involved having nursing staff ignore delusional statements and concurrently reinforce appropriate speech with consumables and attention. The rate of delusional statements dropped to roughly one-quarter of the baseline level, and the frequency of appropriate speech quadrupled relative to the rates observed in the preceding phase. Ayllon, Haughton, and Hughes (1965) also demonstrated that positive reinforcement, in the form of attention and consumables delivered contingently by nursing staff, could be used both to create and to eliminate a strange broom-holding behavior in a woman with chronic schizophrenia. Following the lead of Ayllon and Haughton (1964), clinical researchers have modified bizarre speech by ignoring inappropriate verbalizations and by prompting and positively reinforcing appropriate verbalizations with parent attention (Pinkston & Herbert-Jackson, 1975); therapist attention (Moss & Liberman, 1975); staff attention, coffee, and snacks (Himadi, Osteen, & Crawford, 1993; Himadi, Osteen, Kaiser, & Daniel, 1991; Liberman, Teigen, Patterson, & Baker, 1973); access to a preferred work assignment (Anderson & Alpert, 1974); and tokens (Jimenez, Todman, Perez, Godoy, & Landon-Jimenez, 1996; Patterson & Teigen, 1973; Wincze, Leitenberg, & Agras, 1972).

Recently, several studies have illustrated the use of a preintervention, *func-*

tional analysis to select a treatment for individuals with severe and persistent mental disorders exhibiting bizarre speech. In contrast with previous reports on the treatment of bizarre behavior, these recent studies have determined the "reason(s)" for the specific reinforcing consequences maintaining the behavioral excess. A treatment procedure that targets this reason or uses this consequence is then implemented. In the first published study that employed a functional analysis and function-based intervention with bizarre speech, Mace and Lalli (1991) collected observations indicating that their client's bizarre verbalization was related to escape from household tasks or attention from staff at the board-and-care home. These investigators then performed a functional (i.e., experimental) analysis involving different sessions in which the client could obtain one of these two consequences by speaking bizarrely. Results of the functional analysis showed that bizarre speech occurred predominately in sessions during which this behavior produced attention. The investigators then evaluated two function-based treatments, one that provided the client with noncontingent attention and one that taught the participant more appropriate verbal behavior to obtain attention. Both of these treatments were successful in reducing bizarre speech to low rates.

Wilder, Masuda, O'Connor, and Baham (2001) employed a brief functional analysis to assess the bizarre speech of a forty-three-year-old man with schizophrenia. These authors used ten-minute exposures to various reinforcement contingencies to determine the environmental conditions that maintained bizarre speech. They found that the client's bizarre speech occurred most frequently when it was followed by therapist attention. A treatment consisting of differential reinforcement of appropriate speech and extinction (i.e., planned ignoring) of bizarre speech was then applied and found to be effective in reducing the occurrence of the bizarre speech and increasing appropriate verbal behavior. This study is notable in that it was the first to use a functional analysis with an individual diagnosed with schizophrenia who did not also have a diagnosis of mental retardation.

Dixon, Benedict, and Larson (2001) assessed the bizarre speech of a man with moderate mental retardation and severe and persistent mental disorders. After determining that the client's bizarre speech was maintained by attention for the peculiar topics being discussed, an intervention consisting of differential reinforcement and extinction was employed. The intervention was successful in decreasing bizarre speech and increasing appropriate speech.

Finally, Wilder, White, and Yu (2003) employed an extended functional analysis to assess the occurrence of bizarre speech and inappropriate laughter exhibited by a woman with schizophrenia. After determining that the behaviors were reinforced by therapist attention, the authors employed a three-step procedure similar to simplified habit reversal (Rapp, Miltenberger, Long, Elliott, & Lumley, 1998) to reduce the occurrence of the target behaviors. First, they used awareness training, by allowing the client to view a videotape of herself engaging in the bizarre behaviors to see the impropriety of her conduct. Then they taught the participant phrases (e.g., "Oh, that didn't make sense, we were talking about . . .") that correct for inappropriate verbalizations. Finally, the therapist delivered social praise contingent on the use of any of the phrases taught. The client's bizarre behavior was substantially reduced with the use of this procedure.

All the previously discussed functional analyses determined that the bizarre behavior was maintained by positive reinforcement in the form of attention from others. Consequent stimuli can also operate as *negative reinforcement* when bizarre behavior prevents or terminates certain stimuli. Grotesque speech and actions can be confusing and even frightening to the onlooker. Bizarre behavior will be negatively reinforced and occur more frequently if it heads off or stops demands, criticism, reprimands, or other aversive stimulation. Bizarre behavior motivated by escape or avoidance must be treated differently from similar behavior motivated by positive reinforcement. Ignoring inappropriate verbalizations and attending to appropriate verbalizations is likely to be an effective intervention for bizarre statements (e.g., claiming one is God) if attention is maintaining these statements. However, if a client makes bizarre statements to get other people to leave him or her alone, then ignoring the client or withdrawing is likely to negatively reinforce this inappropriate behavior and increase the frequency of psychotic verbalizations.

Unfortunately, the technology for treating inappropriate behavior that is negatively reinforced (Iwata, 1987; Iwata, Vollmer, Zarcone, & Rodgers, 1993) has seldom been applied in clinical studies with psychotic individuals. Only one study has employed a functional analysis and subsequent function-based intervention to analyze and treat bizarre behavior maintained by negative reinforcement in an individual with psychosis. Mace, Webb, Sharkey, Mattson, and Rosen (1988) determined that the bizarre verbalizations of a woman with schizophrenia occurred at the highest rate when such behavior gained experimenter attention and a temporary escape from staff demands. A treatment consisting of guided compliance with task demands, extinction, and social attention contingent on task completion reduced bizarre vocalizations and increased her task completion.

Without the benefit of a functional analysis, Wong et al. (1987) successfully treated a woman with paranoid delusional statements (e.g., saying that she was being held in the hospital illegally). These investigators speculated that this woman's bizarre verbalizations were negatively reinforced because they effectively put off staff requests to get up in the morning and groom. Schock et al. (1996) recount an analogous behavior of a client who claimed that he was made of dirt and would dissolve in water, which he presented as a rationale for not bathing. Previous attempts to force compliance had resulted in the client becoming assaultive. To address the noncompliance and delusional behavior, the amount and quality of reinforcement associated with bathing was increased, and the participant was taught a verbal response that enabled him to postpone taking a bath. This procedure was successful at getting the client to bathe regularly. In addition, no incidents of assault occurred during the client's treatment.

Oppositional behavior.   If persons with severe and persistent mental disorders or psychosis would act appropriately whenever they were asked to do so, this disorder would not be a serious problem. The term severe and persistent mental disorder implies conduct that is not amenable to instructions and other means of social influence. Oppositional behavior among people with severe and persistent mental disorders can vary in form, ranging from refusing to answer a question, to becoming loud and disruptive during a gathering, to punching a family member after repeatedly being asked to do a household chore. Mixed with other acts and justified with fantastical explanations, oppositional behavior may not be recognized as such even by the trained clinician.

A variety of contingency-management and skills-training procedures have been used to treat oppositional and aggressive behavior in persons with severe and persistent mental disorders in psychiatric hospitals (Wong, Slama, & Liberman, 1985; Wong, Woolsey, Innocent, & Liberman, 1988). Token economies have used written descriptions to make task expectations explicit and have delivered tangible reinforcement to motivate task performance (Atthowe & Krasner, 1968; Ayllon & Azrin, 1965). Therapists have taught social skills to instill acceptable response patterns and to replace disruptive and aggressive behavior (Frederiksen, Jenkins, Foy, & Eisler, 1976; Matson & Stephens, 1978). Individual programs, behavioral contracts, and differential reinforcement schedules have been instituted to make praise, tangible items, and privileges contingent on pro-social behavior. Concurrently, point fines, privilege loss, time out from reinforcement, or some combination of these procedures have been applied as reductive consequences for noncompliant and aggressive behaviors (Wong et al., 1988).

A limitation of the aforementioned contingency management programs is that they imposed arbitrary reinforcers and reductive consequences to override inappropriate responses, without first identifying variables that were causing the problem behavior. Lacking information on the purpose or motivation underlying the problem behavior, the previous interventions were not designed to help clients satisfy their personal motives in more socially acceptable ways. Conducting a functional analysis and then teaching skills that allow clients to appropriately satisfy their specific needs is more likely to promote generalization and maintenance of the desired behavior change (Mace, Lalli, Lalli, & Shea, 1993; Mace & Roberts, 1993).

Determining the function of oppositional behavior can sometimes lead to simple and swift solutions. For example, Schock et al. (1998) report the case of a client who was placed in a locked institution because he refused to shower independently. When asked why he refused to shower, the client stated that he often lost his balance while standing in the shower. When asked if he would bathe while seated in the bathtub, he responded affirmatively and proceeded to do so at a rate of three times a week without need for incentives. A more knotty issue related to oppositional behavior is psychotropic medication. Nearly all persons with severe and persistent mental disorders are prescribed psychotropic medication, and many clients find these drugs to have disagreeable effects, so "medication noncompliance" is a frequent source of conflict. However, such noncompliance is understandable because it allows for escape from and avoidance of disagreeable sensations (Schock et al., 1996). Given our previous discussion about psychotropic medication, such conflicts present dilemmas because they question psychiatric authority and suggest the need for individualized, objective evaluation of the cost-benefit ratio of psychotropic drug treatment for that client—something rarely done in this zeitgeist of universal drug treatment. The rational (though certainly not politically expedient) course of action would be to advocate for individualized evaluations of drug efficacy and treatment acceptability comparable to those required of behavioral and other psychosocial interventions.

Other promising strategies for facilitating compliance increase the likelihood of instruction following by establishing a pattern of compliance or by gradually shaping desired behavior. Procedures for enhancing compliance can involve giving clients a sequence of requests that they typically comply with before giving them a request that they typically refuse (Mace & Belfiore, 1990; Mace et al., 1988) or by presenting a graduated series of requests beginning with ones most likely to be followed and ending with those least likely to be followed (Ducharme & Popynick, 1993). However, these more sophisticated compliance-promoting strategies have yet to be applied with persons with severe and persistent mental disorders, so research on nonaversive compliance training with this population is sorely needed.

Stereotypic behavior. Individuals with psychotic disorders often engage in repetitive behaviors such as rituals, pacing, posturing, and self-talk (Alevizos, DeRisi, Liberman, Eckman, & Callahan, 1978; Luchins, Goldman, Lieb, & Hanrahan, 1992; Paul, 1987). These strange responses can occur for lengthy periods without any noticeable social or environmental consequences that might serve as positive reinforcement. Although stereotypical behaviors may appear odd to the onlooker, they are not unique to individuals with severe and persistent mental disorders or inherently pathological. People commonly display repetitive behavior (e.g., finger twiddling, doodling, playing with one's hair) in situations in which more reinforcing activities are unavailable (e.g., when forced to sit through a boring lecture).

One treatment for stereotypic behavior restructures the client's environment to promote alternative appropriate responses. Early token economy programs accomplished this by scheduling an adequate number of self-care, work, and leisure activities in clients' daily routine. Ayllon and Azrin (1968) anecdotally reported that many bizarre behaviors of chronic psychiatric patients vanished when they were engaged in such productive tasks. Paul and Lentz (1977) conducted intensive behavioral observations of the chronic psychiatric patients under their care and quantified sizable, long-term reductions of bizarre behavior with enriched schedules of self-care, social, and educational activities.

In a series of studies, the first author and his colleagues demonstrated that providing activities reduced a variety of bizarre, repetitive behavior in persons with severe and persistent mental disorders. Wong et al. (1987) found that psychotic self-talk and mumbling in two patients diagnosed as schizophrenic decreased 60 percent to 70 percent when the patients were engaged in preferred recreational activities (e.g., reading, handicrafts, assembling models). Similar clinical improvements were obtained for ruminating (e.g., searching for dirt and feces) by a patient with obsessive-compulsive disorder and for grotesque posturing by another patient diagnosed as schizophrenic (Corrigan, Liberman, & Wong, 1993). Another study (Wong, Wright, Terranova, Bowen, & Zarate, 1988) showed a 70 percent reduction in bizarre behaviors in ten chronic psychiatric patients when they were engaged in structured leisure and work activities (e.g., team sports, art projects, housework). More recent investigations (Morris, Card, & Menditto, 1999; Pestle, Card, & Menditto, 1998) have replicated these findings. These studies outlined a simple and efficient treatment for stereotypy and highlighted the need for ecological analyses of psychotic behavior. Future research can advance on this work by incorporating pretreatment functional analyses to determine the specific causes for individual stereotypic behavior.

Behavioral Deficits

The adaptive skills and work performance of persons with severe and persistent mental disorders often diminish, sometimes to markedly low levels. In the following sections we review four functional domains that may be impaired in persons with severe and persistent mental disorders—social skills, self-care, vocational skills, and recreational behavior—and behavioral interventions that have been used to remediate these deficiencies.

Social skills. Persons with severe and persistent mental disorders often used desired interactive behavior at lower rates than ordinary people. Because these social responses have a large impact in many important realms of life, behavioral researchers have taught social skills to persons with schizophrenia and severe and persistent mental disorders (Bellack & Mueser, 1990; Halford & Hayes, 1991; Hayes, Halford, & Varghese, 1995). Component skills that have been successfully trained include eye contact and facial expression (Eisler, Blanchard, Fitts, & Williams, 1978; Hersen, Eisler, & Miller, 1974; Silverstein et al., 1998), simple greetings (Kale, Kaye, Whelan, & Hopkins, 1968; Wong & Woolsey, 1989), conversational skills (Holmes, Hansen, & St. Lawrence, 1984; Kelly, Urey, & Patterson, 1980; Wilder, Masuda, Baham, & O'Connor, 2002; Wong et al., 1993), and assertive responses (Frederiksen, Jenkins, Foy, & Eisler, 1976; Hersen & Bellack, 1976; Hersen, Turner, Edelstein, & Pinkston, 1975).

Social skills training typically occurs in a therapy room with the client and the therapist role-playing relevant encounters. The therapist gives a rationale for teaching the targeted skill, describes it, demonstrates it, asks the client to rehearse it in a role play, praises or gives the client corrective feedback, and repeats the process as necessary. Numerous studies have shown that these procedures are effective in teaching important interactive behaviors and that trained skills carry over to novel role-plays with novel conversants. There is, however, little data showing that these trained skills generalize to real-life encounters outside of the therapy situation (Donahoe & Driesenga, 1988; Halford & Hayes, 1991). This lack of carryover might have been anticipated, given the knowledge that generalization rarely occurs after training in circumscribed conditions that do not resemble the natural setting (Stokes & Baer, 1977; Stokes & Osnes, 1989).

The first author and several of his colleagues taught conversational skills to persons diagnosed with schizophrenia and applied procedures to promote generalization of those skills to situations outside of the therapy room (Wong et al., 1993). After teaching conversational skills in an office and observing inconsistent spontaneous generalization to extratherapy settings and novel conversants, intermittent prompts and positive reinforcement were applied in the unit dayroom to encourage clients to use trained skills in settings outside of the office. An analogous training procedure has been instituted at University of the Pacific's Transitional Residential Facility Program, which provides short-term treatment for persons with chronic mental disorders. Clients were first taught social skills during fifteen-minute classes at the community care center. The clients were then instructed to use these skills in their daily interactions with other clients and staff in and around the center. Clients who were observed not to display the targeted skills were again prompted to use and to rehearse the appropriate social skills. Multiple staff assisted with the training process throughout the day and in a wide variety of situations, producing a minimum of 80 percent mastery of targeted skills in all participants (Schock et al., 1996).

Personal hygiene and self-care.   The most basic of self-care routines, including bathing, grooming, and dressing, can deteriorate in persons with severe and persistent mental disorders. The breakdown of these personal habits can adversely affect social relations, jeopardize employment, and increase health risks. Behavioral programs have successfully restored self-care skills by arranging for the systematic administration of prompts and positive reinforcement for desired responses.

Token economies have been implemented in hospitals (Ayllon & Azrin, 1968; Liberman, Wallace, Teigen, & Davis, 1974; Paul & Lentz, 1977) and community mental health centers (Liberman, King, & De Risi, 1976) to improve clients' grooming and housekeeping performance. Within these programs, staff dispensed tokens or points (exchangeable for tangible items or privileges) to clients after they completed self-care tasks or on the basis of clients' appearance during periodic inspections. Working in a psychiatric hospital unit with a token economy, Nelson and Cone (1979) reported significant improvements in patients' grooming skills after the introduction of a training program including verbal instructions, modeling, posters, and token reinforcement. Consulting with a hospital unit that lacked a token economy, Wong, et al. (1988) successfully taught chronic psychiatric patients hand and face washing, hair cleaning, tooth brushing, and proper dressing using a systematic training protocol resembling that of Nelson and Cone (1979). These two studies showed that systematic behavioral training can improve grooming and self-care skills even in severely regressed clients.

Vocational skills.   Work is another critical area of human functioning in which persons with severe and persistent mental disorders need assistance. Unemployment among persons with "severe mental illness" has been reported to be as high as 80 percent (Bond & McDonel, 1991). Behavioral interventions address this problem by prompting and reinforcing successive approximations to standard work performance (Ayllon & Azrin, 1968). The first token economy provided a continuum of well-defined hospital jobs, such as kitchen, personal care, clerical, and housekeeping aides, which required from ten minutes to six hours of work per day (Ayllon & Azrin, 1965). As clients showed better responsiveness to instructions and greater work tolerance, they were assigned more demanding and better paying tasks.

After the client's discharge from the hospital, vocational training can proceed to supported employment or participation in a community-based work program for disabled persons. Rise and Shine Industries (Ruiz, 1992) is one such program affiliated with the University of the Pacific. It offers supervised employment for clients with chronic mentally disorders who wash cars using high-pressure cleaning equipment. The program is a commercial enterprise that gives clients twenty to twenty-eight hours of work per week at or slightly above minimum wage. Rise and Shine Industries is part of a community reentry program that furnishes congregate housing and teaches independent living skills (e.g., money management, cooking, shopping, apartment cleaning, recreation).

Focusing on clients who were ready to join the regular workforce, investigators have used social skills training techniques to improve clients' job interviewing skills (Furman, Geller, Simon, & Kelly, 1979; Kelly, Laughlin, Claiborne, & Patterson, 1979). Clients were taught to give positive information about their education and previous work experience, to ask questions, to use gestures, and to express enthusiasm during interviews. Training incorporated exposure to videotaped models, behavioral rehearsal during simulated interviews, coaching to improve performance, and praise or corrective feedback. Data from the two studies showed that training increased participants' skills and raised employability ratings given by an actual personnel manager.

One behavioral program that assists clients in all of the steps required to obtain employment is the "job club" (Azrin & Besalel, 1980; Azrin, Flores, & Kaplan, 1975). A job club provides social support groups and guidance in preparing a résumé, conducting a systematic job search, proper dressing and grooming, job interviewing, and following up on job leads. Jacobs, Kardashian, Kreinbring, Ponder, and Simpson (1984) modified the job club for clients with severe and persistent mental disorders by adding instruction in community survival skills of personal goal setting, problem solving, coping with daily problems, and maintaining one's employment. Job seeking and community survival skills were taught through lecture, programmed reading materials, role-playing, and in vivo exercises. Evaluations of this expanded job club showed that 76 percent of the participants found jobs or started full-time vocational training by the end of the program and that 67 percent were still employed six months after completing the program.

Recreational behavior. Recreation can be an avenue for pursuing diverse personal goals, including socialization, physical fitness, creative fulfillment, amusement, and relaxation (Nesbitt, 1970). Individuals with severe and persistent mental disorders often appear to lack productive and socially acceptable leisure pastimes and this may predispose them to engage in socially unacceptable diversions.

Two studies cited previously in this chapter provided sedentary recreational activities to reduce bizarre behavior (Corrigan et al., 1993; Wong, et al., 1987). An outcome not reported in these articles was the large increase in socially appropriate behavior during recreation sessions—rising from less than 15 percent in the baseline sessions to more than 80 percent in the recreation sessions. Patients' outward demeanor changed dramatically during recreational activities, and in these sessions they were indistinguishable from nonpatients. Relevant to this, Skinner, Skinner, and Armstrong (2000) demonstrated how to lengthen the duration of a sedentary activity using shaping procedures. These investigators increase a client's reading persistence of from one page per day during baseline to six to eight pages per day during treatment. Follow-up data indicated that increased reading persistence maintained after treatment ended.

In a study evaluating the effect of various group activities requiring gross body movement, Wong et al., (1988) showed that these activities increased socially appropriate and productive behavior 400 percent to 500 percent over that recorded during unstructured free time. A recent study by Finnell, Card, and Menditto (1997) clarified these findings by showing that engagement in therapeutic recreation produced greater decreases in bizarre and stereotypic behavior among individuals with schizophrenia than did engagement in vocational rehabilitation.

A few clinical researchers have attempted to increase clients' daily exercise and physical fitness. Nelson and Cone (1979) increased physical activity among a group of psychiatric inpatients through scheduled exercise sessions and token reinforcement. Working in a community group home, Thyer, Irvine, and Santa (1984) used consumable reinforcement to motivate two former mental patients to exercise longer and more frequently on a stationary bicycle. In a similar fashion, Mills, Gipson, and Schock (1992) increased the frequency and duration of physical exercise in chronically mentally disabled adults at a drop-in socialization center by using a combination of token and social reinforcement. Finally, Faulkner and Sparkes (1999) also showed that a program of exercise improved psychotic symptoms, affect, and behavior in three participants with schizophrenia.

DISCUSSION AND IMPLICATIONS: CHALLENGES TO BEHAVIORAL INTERVENTIONS FOR SEVERE AND PERSISTENT MENTAL DISORDERS

As we revealed in the varied interventions described in this chapter, the behavioral approach has much to offer in the treatment of severe and persistent mental disorders. This approach teaches clients skills and motivates appropriate behavior with the ultimate goal of client self-sufficiency and independence from all therapies. The behavioral focus on environmental stimuli that influence significant responses is a relatively benign technology that lacks the grave hazards of biomedical interventions. Most important, this is an ecological approach that seeks to identify and correct harsh or impoverished environments or living conditions that do not adequately guide or reward desired conduct. This emphasis on optimizing environments to advance clients' welfare and functioning is central to the profession for which this book was written.

Progress in developing and disseminating behavioral treatment programs for severe and persistent mental disorders has been slow compared with other problem areas, such as developmental disabilities. There are at least two reasons for this delay. The first is the national policy of deinstitutionalization started in the 1950s (Keisler & Sibulkin, 1987) that has reorganized or closed many of the state mental hospitals that were the staging grounds for innovative behavioral programs. Several of the facilities that served as sites for the early research reported in this chapter no longer exist or no longer serve the same population. Thus, the failure to use behavioral interventions to their fullest potential is part of a larger contemporary trend in which persons with severe and persistent mental disorders have been cast out of discredited institutions, but then often left without needed rehabilitation programs or community supports.

The second reason is an alliance between psychiatry and the pharmaceutical industry that has developed into an immense hegemony. In this country, billions of public and private dollars are spent on mental health services and research that centers on psychotropic drugs. Although the outcome for persons with severe and persistent mental disorders receiving this advanced biomedical treatment is poorer than for persons in developing nations that have limited access to this technology (de Girolamo, 1996; Jablensky, 1992), the biomedical establishment has been highly successful in eliminating competition and consideration of alternative treatment approaches. Behavioral programs must compete for recognition and funding within bureaucracies that accept the legitimacy of medical interventions without question but that respond to positive outcome data on alternative treatments with mild curiosity. These are huge obstacles that can be overcome only gradually by exposing the faulty premises and poor results of biomedical treatments while calling attention to the untapped potential of social and educative interventions.

REFERENCES

Alevizos, P., DeRisi, W., Liberman, R., Eckman, T., & Callahan, E. (1978). The behavior observation instrument: A method of direct observation for program evaluation. *Journal of Applied Behavior Analysis, 11,* 243–257.

Alford, B. A. (1986). Behavioral treatment of schizophrenic delusions: A single case experimental analysis. *Behavior Therapy, 17,* 637–644.

American Psychiatric Association. (2003, September 25). *American Psychiatric*

Association statement on diagnosis and treatment of mental disorders (Release No. 03-39). Washington, DC: Author.

American Psychiatric Association. (1994). *Diagnostic and statistical manual of mental disorders* (4th ed.). Washington, DC: Author.

Anderson, L. T., & Alpert, M. (1974). Operant analysis of hallucination frequency in a hospitalized schizophrenic. *Journal of Behavior Therapy and Experimental Psychiatry, 5,* 13–18.

Atthowe, J. M., & Krasner, L. (1968). Preliminary report on the application of contingent reinforcement procedures (token economy) on a "chronic" psychiatric ward. *Journal of Abnormal Psychology, 73,* 37–43.

Ayllon, T., & Azrin, N. H. (1965). The measurement and reinforcement of behavior of psychotics. *Journal of the Experimental Analysis of Behavior, 8,* 357–383.

Ayllon, T., & Azrin, N. H. (1968). *The token economy: A motivational system for therapy and rehabilitation.* Englewood Cliffs, NJ: Prentice Hall.

Ayllon, T., & Haughton, E. (1964). Modification of symptomatic verbal behavior of mental patients. *Behavior Research and Therapy, 2,* 87–97.

Ayllon, T., Haughton, E., & Hughes, H. B. (1965). Interpretation of symptoms: Fact or fiction? *Behaviour Research Therapy, 3,* 1–7.

Azrin, N. H., & Besalel, V. A. (1980). *Job-club counselors manual: A behavioral approach to vocational counseling.* Baltimore: University Park Press.

Azrin, N. H., Flores, T., & Kaplan, S. J. (1975). Job-finding club: A group-assisted program for obtaining employment. *Behaviour Research and Therapy, 13,* 17–27.

Barlow, D. H. (Ed.). (1993). *Clinical handbook of psychological disorders* (2nd ed.). New York: Guilford Press.

Bellack, A. S., Hersen, M., & Kazdin, A. E. (Eds.). (1990). *International handbook of behavior modification and therapy* (2nd ed.). New York: Plenum Press.

Bellack, A. S., & Mueser, K. T. (1990). Schizophrenia. In A. S. Bellack, M. Hersen, & A. E. Kazdin (Eds.), *International handbook of behavior modification and therapy* (2nd ed., pp. 353–369). New York: Plenum Press.

Bentall, R. P., Haddock, G., Slade, P. (1994). Cognitive behavior therapy for persistent auditory hallucinations: From theory to therapy. *Behavior Therapy, 25,* 51–66.

Bond, G. R., & McDonel, E. C. (1991). Vocational rehabilitation outcomes for persons with psychiatric disabilities: An update. *Journal of Vocational Rehabilitation, 1,* 9–20.

Bouchard, S., Vallieres, A., Roy, M., & Maziade, M. (1996). Cognitive restructuring in the treatment of psychotic symptoms in schizophrenia: A critical analysis. *Behavior Therapy, 27,* 257–277.

Boyle, M. (1990). *Schizophrenia: A scientific delusion?* London: Routledge.

Breggin, P. R. (1991). *Toxic psychiatry.* New York: St. Martin's Press.

Breggin, P. R. (1997). *Brain disabling treatments in psychiatry: Drugs, electroshock, and the role of the FDA.* New York: Springer.

Brown, P. (1990). The name game: Toward a sociology of diagnosis. *The Journal of Mind and Behavior, 11,* 385–406.

Brown, P., & Funk, S. C. (1986). Tardive dyskinesia: Barriers to the professional recognition of an iatrogenic disease. *Journal of Health and Social Behavior, 27,* 116–132.

Chadwick, P. D. J., & Lowe, C. F. (1990). Measurement and modification of delusional beliefs. *Journal of Consulting and Clinical Psychology, 58,* 225–232.

Chadwick, P. D. J., & Lowe, C. F. (1994). A cognitive approach to measuring and modifying delusions. *Behavior Research and Therapy, 32,* 353–367.

Chadwick, P. D. J., Lowe, C. F., Horne, P. J., & Higson, P. J. (1994). Modifying delusions: The role of empirical testing. *Behavior Therapy, 25,* 35–49.

Cohen, D. (1994). Neuroleptic drug treatment of schizophrenia: State of the confusion. *The Journal of Mind and Behavior, 15,* 139–156.

Cohen, D. (1997). A critique of the use of neuroleptic drugs in psychiatry. In S. Fisher & R. G. Greenberg (Eds.), *From placebo to panacea: Putting psychiatric drugs to the test* (pp. 173–228). New York: John Wiley & Sons.

Cohen, D. (2002). Research on the drug treatment of schizophrenia: Critical appraisal and implications for social work education. *Journal of Social Work Education, 38*(2), 217–239.

Corrigan, P. W., Liberman, R. P., & Wong, S. E. (1993). Recreational therapy and behavior management on inpatient units: Is recreational therapy therapeutic? *Journal of Nervous and Mental Disease, 181,* 644–646.

De Girolamo, G. (1996). WHO studies on schizophrenia: An overview of the results and their implications for the understanding of the disorder. In P. R. Breggin & E. M. Stern (Eds.), *Psychosocial approaches to deeply disturbed persons* (pp. 213–231). New York: Haworth Press.

Dickerson, F. B. (2000). Cognitive behavioral psychotherapy for schizophrenia: A review of recent empirical studies. *Schizophrenia Research, 43,* 71–90.

Dixon, M., Benedict, H., & Larson, T. (2001). Functional analysis and treatment of inappropriate verbal behavior. *Journal of Applied Behavior Analysis, 34,* 361–363.

Donahoe, C. P., & Driesenga, S. A. (1988). A review of social skills training with chronic mental patients. In M. Hersen, R. M. Eisler, & P. M. Miller (Eds.), *Progress in behavior modification* (Vol. 23, pp. 131–164). Newbury Park, CA: Sage.

Ducharme, J. M., & Popynick, M. (1993). Errorless compliance to parental request: Treatment effects and generalization. *Behavior Therapy, 24,* 209–226.

Eisler, R. M., Blanchard, E. B., Fitts, H., & Williams, J. G. (1978). Social skills training with and without modeling for schizophrenic and non-psychotic hospitalized psychiatric patients. *Behavior Modification, 2,* 147–172.

Faulkner, G., & Sparkes, A. (1999). Exercise as therapy for schizophrenia: An ethnographic study. *Journal of Sport and Exercise Physiology, 21,* 52–69.

Finnell, A., Card, J., & Menditto, A. (1997). A comparison of appropriate behavior scores of residents with chronic schizophrenia participating in therapeutic recreation services and vocational rehabilitation services. *Therapeutic Recreation Journal, 31,* 10–21.

Frederiksen, L. W., Jenkins, J. O., Foy, D. W., & Eisler, R. M. (1976). Social skills training to modify abusive verbal outbursts in adults. *Journal of Applied Behavior Analysis, 9,* 117–125.

Furman, W., Geller, M., Simon, S. J., & Kelly, J. A. (1979). The use of a behavioral rehearsal procedure for teaching job-interviewing skills to psychiatric patients. *Behavior Therapy, 10,* 157–167.

Gelman, S. (1999). *Medicating schizophrenia: A history.* New Brunswick, NJ: Rutgers University Press.

Glaser, N. M., Kazantzis, N., Deane, F. P., & Oades, L. (2000). Critical issues in using homework assignments within cognitive-behavioral therapy for schizophrenia. *Journal of Rational Emotive and Cognitive Behavior Therapy, 18,* 247–261.

Haddock, G., Tarrier, N., Morrison, A., Hopkins, R., Drake, R., & Lewis, S. (1999). A pilot study evaluating the effectiveness of individual inpatient cognitive-behavioral therapy in early psychosis. *Social Psychiatry and Psychiatric Epidemiology, 34,* 254–258.

Halford, W. K., & Hayes, R. (1991). Psychological rehabilitation of chronic schizophrenic patients: Recent findings on social skills training and family psycho-education. *Clinical Psychology Review, 11,* 23–44.

Hayes, R. L., Halford, W. K., & Varghese, F. T. (1995). Social skills training with chronic schizophrenic patients: Effects on negative symptoms and community functioning. *Behavior Therapy, 26,* 433–449.

Hersen, M., & Bellack, A. S. (1976). A multiple-baseline analysis of social-skills training in chronic schizophrenics. *Journal of Applied Behavior Analysis, 9,* 239–245.

Hersen, M., Eisler, R. M., & Miller, P. M. (1974). An experimental analysis of generalization in assertive training. *Behavior Research and Therapy, 12,* 295–310.

Hersen, M., Turner, S. M., Edelstein, B. A., & Pinkston, S. G. (1975). Effects of phenothiazines and social skills training in a withdrawn schizophrenic. *Journal of Clinical Psychology, 34,* 588–594.

Himadi, B., & Kaiser, A. J. (1992). The modification of delusional beliefs: A single-subject evaluation. *Behavioral Residential Treatment, 7,* 1–14.

Himadi, B., Osteen, E., & Crawford, E. (1993). Delusional verbalizations and beliefs. *Behavioral Residential Treatment, 8,* 229–242.

Himadi, B., Osteen, F., Kaiser, A. J., & Daniel, K. (1991). Assessment of delusional beliefs during the modification of delusional verbalizations. *Behavioral Residential Treatment, 6,* 355–366.

Holmes, M. R., Hansen, D. J., & St. Lawrence, J. S. (1984). Conversational skills training with aftercare patients in the community: Social validation and generalization. *Behavior Therapy, 15,* 84–100.

Iwata, B. A. (1987). Negative reinforcement in applied behavior analysis: An emerging technology. *Journal of Applied Behavior Analysis, 20,* 361–378.

Iwata, B. A., Vollmer, T. R., Zarcone, J. R., & Rodgers, T. A. (1993). Treatment classification and selection based on behavioral function. In R. Van Houten & S. Axelrod (Eds.), *Behavior analysis and treatment* (pp. 101–125). New York: Plenum Press.

Jablensky, A., Sartorius, N., Ernberg, G., Anker, M., Korten, A., Cooper, J. E., Day, R., et al. (1992). Schizophrenia: Manifestations, incidence, and course in different cultures: A World Health Organization ten-country study. *Psychological Medicine,* (Mon. Suppl. 20), 1–97.

Jacobs, H. E., Kardashian, S., Kreinbring, R. K., Ponder, R., & Simpson, A. R. (1984). A skills-oriented model for facilitating employment among psychiatrically disabled persons. *Rehabilitation Counseling Bulletin, 28,* 87–96.

Jimenez, J. M., Todman, M., Perez, M., Godoy, J. F., & Landon-Jimenez, D. V. (1996). The behavioral treatment of auditory hallucinatory responding of a schizophrenic patient. *Journal of Behavior Therapy and Experimental Psychiatry, 27,* 299–310.

Kale, R. J., Kaye, J. H., Whelan, P. A., & Hopkins, B. L. (1968). The effects of reinforcement on the modification, maintenance, and generalization of social responses of mental patients. *Journal of Applied Behavior Analysis, 1,* 307–314.

Kelly, J. A., Laughlin, C., Claiborne, M., & Patterson, J. T. (1979). A group procedure for teaching job interviewing skills to formerly hospitalized psychiatric patients. *Behavior Therapy, 10,* 299–310.

Kelly, J. A., Urey, F. R., & Patterson, J. T. (1980). Improving heterosocial conversational skills of male psychiatric patients through a small group training procedure. *Behavior Therapy, 11,* 179–188.

Kiesler, C. A., & Sibulkin, A. E. (1987). *Mental hospitalization: Myths and facts about a national crisis.* Newbury Park, CA: Sage.

Kingdon, D., Turkington, D., & John, C. (1994). Cognitive behavior therapy of schizophrenia: The amenability of delusions and hallucinations to reasoning. *British Journal of Psychiatry, 164,* 581–587.

Kirk, S. A., & Kutchins, H. (1992). *The selling of the DSM: The rhetoric of science in psychiatry.* New York: Aldine De Gruyter.

Kirk, S. A., & Kutchins, H. (1994). The myth of the reliability of the DSM. *The Journal of Mind and Behavior, 15,* 71–86.

Kutchins, H., & Kirk, S. A. (1997). *Making us crazy: DSM: The psychiatric bible and the creation of mental disorders.* New York: Free Press.

Leucht, S., Wahlbeck, K., Hamann, J., & Kissling, W. (2003). New generation antipsychotics versus low-potency conventional antipsychotics: A systemic review and meta-analysis. *Lancet, 361,* 1581–1589.

Liberman, R. P., King, L. W., & De Risi, W. J. (1976). Behavior analysis and therapy in community mental health. In H. Leitenberg (Ed.), *Handbook of behavior modification and behavior therapy* (pp. 566–603). Englewood Cliffs, NJ: Prentice Hall.

Liberman, R. P., Teigen, J., Patterson, R., & Baker, V. (1973). Reducing delusional speech in chronic paranoid schizophrenics. *Journal of Applied Behavior Analysis, 6,* 57–64.

Liberman, R. P., Wallace, C., Teigen, J., & Davis, J. (1974). Interventions with psychotic behaviors. In K. S. Calhoun, H. E. Adams, & K. M. Mitchell (Eds.), *Innovative treatment methods in psychopathology* (pp. 232–412). New York: Wiley.

Lowe, C. F., & Chadwick, P. D. J. (1990). Verbal control of delusions. *Behavior Therapy, 21,* 461–479.

Luchins, D. J., Goldman, M. B., Lieb, M., & Hanrahan, P. (1992). Repetitive behaviors in chronically institutionalized schizophrenic patients. *Schizophrenia Research, 8,* 119–123.

Mace, F. C., & Belfiore, P. (1990). Behavioral momentum in the treatment of escape-motivated stereotypy. *Journal of Applied Behavior Analysis, 23,* 507–514.

Mace, F. C., Hock, M. L., Lalli, J. S., West, B. J., Belfiore, P., Pinter, E., et al. (1988). Behavioral momentum in the treatment of noncompliance. *Journal of Applied Behavior Analysis, 21,* 123–141.

Mace, F. C., & Lalli, J. (1991). Linking descriptive and experimental analyses in the treatment of bizarre speech. *Journal of Applied Behavior Analysis, 24,* 553–562.

Mace, F. C., Lalli, J. S., Lalli, E. P., & Shea, M. C. (1993). Functional analysis and treatment of aberrant behavior. In R. Van Houten & S. Axelrod (Eds.), *Behavior analysis and treatment* (pp. 75–99). New York: Plenum Press.

Mace, F. C., & Roberts, M. L. (1993). Factors affecting selection of behavioral interventions. In J. Reichle & D. P. Wacker (Eds.), *Communicative alternatives to challenging behavior: Integrating functional assessment and intervention strategies* (pp. 113–133). Baltimore: Paul H. Brooks.

Mace, F. C., Webb, M. E., Sharkey, R. W., Mattson, D. M., & Rosen, H. S. (1988). Functional analysis and treatment of bizarre speech. *Journal of Behavior Therapy and Experimental Psychiatry, 19,* 289–296.

Matson, J. L., & Stephens, R. M. (1978). Increasing appropriate behavior of explosive chronic psychiatric patients with a social-skills training package. *Behavior Modification, 2,* 61–76.

Mattaini, M., & Thyer, B. A. (Eds.). (1996). *Finding solutions to social problems: Behavioral strategies for change.* Washington, DC: American Psychological Association.

Mills, K., Gipson, M., & Schock, K. (1992, May). *Increasing weekly exercise among outpatient chronic mentally disabled adults.* Paper presented at the 15th annual convention of the Association for Behavioral Analysis, San Francisco, CA.

Morris, D., Card, J., & Menditto, A. (1999). Active and passive therapeutic recreation activities: A comparison of appropriate behaviors of individuals with schizophrenia. *Therapeutic Recreation Journal, 33,* 275–286.

Moss, G. R., & Liberman, R. P. (1975). Empiricism in psychotherapy: Behavioral specification and measurement. *The British Journal of Psychiatry, 126,* 73–80.

Nelson, G. L., & Cone, J. D. (1979). Multiple-baseline analysis of a token economy for psychiatric inpatients. *Journal of Applied Behavior Analysis, 12,* 255–271.

Pam, A. (1990). A critique of the scientific status of biological psychiatry. *Acta Psychiatrica Scandinavica, 82*(Suppl. 362), 1–35.

Patterson, R. L., & Teigen, J. R. (1973). Conditioning and post-hospital generalization of nondelusional responses in a chronic psychotic patient. *Journal of Applied Behavior Analysis, 6,* 65–70.

Paul, G. L. (1987). *The time-sample behavioral checklist: Observational assessment instrumentation for service and research.* Champaign, IL: Research Press.

Paul, G. L., & Lentz, R. J. (1977). *Psychosocial treatment of chronic mental patients.* Cambridge, MA: Harvard University Press.

Pestle, K., Card, J., & Menditto, A. (1998). Therapeutic recreation in a social-learning program: Effect over time on appropriate behaviors of residents with schizophrenia. *Therapeutic Recreation Journal, 32,* 28–41.

Pinkston, E. M., & Herbert-Jackson, E. W. (1975). Modification of irrelevant and bizarre verbal behavior using parents as therapists. *Social Service Review, 49,* 46–63.

Rapp, J., Miltenberger, R., Long, E., Elliott, A., & Lumley, V. (1998). Simplified habit reversal treatment for chronic hair pulling in three adolescents: A clinical replication with direct observation. *Journal of Applied Behavior Analysis, 31,* 299–302.

Ross, C. A., & Pam, A. (1995). *Pseudoscience in biological psychiatry.* New York: John Wiley & Sons.

Ruiz, A. (1992, May). *Rise and shine industries: A model of enclave employment for the mentally disabled.* Paper presented at the 18th annual convention of the Association for Behavior Analysis, San Francisco, CA.

Schock, K., Browning, H., Clay, C., & Gipson, M. (1996, May). *Treating the untreatable: An applied behavioral approach to the treatment of resistive schizophrenia.* Symposium conducted at the 22nd annual convention of the Association for Behavior Analysis, San Francisco, CA.

Schock, K., Clay, C., & Cipani, E. (1998). Making sense of schizophrenic symptoms: Delusional statements and behavior may be functional in purpose. *Journal of Behavior Therapy and Experimental Psychiatry, 29,* 131–141.

Shean, G. (2001). A critical look at some assumptions of biopsychiatry. *Ethical Human Sciences and Services, 3*(2), 77–96.

Siddle, R., Turkington, D., & Dudley, R. (1997). Cognitive behavior therapy in a case of organic hallucinosis. *Behavioral and Cognitive Psychotherapy, 25,* 371–379.

Siebert, A. (1999). Brain disease hypothesis for schizophrenia disconfirmed by all evidence. *Ethical Human Sciences and Services, 1*(2), 179–189.

Skinner, C., Skinner, A., & Armstrong, K. J. (2000). Analysis of a client-staff-developed program designed to enhance reading persistence in an adult diagnosed with schizophrenia. *Psychiatric Rehabilitation Journal, 24,* 52–57.

Stokes, T. F., & Baer, D. M. (1977). An implicit technology of generalization. *Journal of Applied Behavior Analysis, 10,* 349–367.

Stokes, T. F., & Osnes, P. G. (1989). An operant pursuit of generalization. *Behavior Therapy, 20,* 337–355.

Thyer, B. A., Irvine, S., & Santa, C. A. (1984). Contingency management of exercise by chronic schizophrenics. *Perceptual and Motor Skills, 58,* 419–425.

U.S. Department of Health and Human Services. (1999). Overview of etiology. In *Mental Health: A Report of the Surgeon General*. Retrieved January 26, 2004, from http://www.mentalhealth.org/features/surgeongeneralreport/chapter2/sec3.asp#biosocial

Valenstein, E. S. (1998). *Blaming the brain: The truth about drugs and mental health.* New York: Free Press.

Van Houten, R., & Axelrod, S. (Eds.). (1993). *Behavior analysis and treatment.* New York: Plenum Press.

Velligan, D. I., Bow, T. C., Huntzinger, C., Ritch, J., Ledbetter, N., Prihoda, T. J., et al. (2000). Randomized controlled trial of the use of compensatory strategies to enhance adaptive functioning in outpatients with schizophrenia. *American Journal of Psychiatry, 157,* 1317–1323.

Watts, F. N., Powell, E. G., & Austin, S. V. (1973). The modification of abnormal beliefs. *British Journal of Medical Psychology, 46,* 359–363.

Wilder, D. A., Masuda, A., Baham, M., & O'Connor, C. (2002). An analysis of the training level necessary to increase independent question asking in an adult with schizophrenia. *Psychiatric Rehabilitation Skills, 6*(1), 32–43.

Wilder, D. A., Masuda, A., O'Connor, C., & Baham, M. (2001). Brief functional analysis and treatment of bizarre vocalizations in an adult with schizophrenia. *Journal of Applied Behavior Analysis, 34,* 65–68.

Wilder, D. A., White, H., & Yu, M. (2003). Functional analysis and treatment of bizarre vocalizations exhibited by an adult with schizophrenia: Replication and extension. *Behavioral Interventions, 18,* 43–52.

Wincze, J. P., Leitenberg, H., & Agras, W. S. (1972). The effects of token reinforcement and feedback on the delusional verbal behavior of chronic paranoid schizophrenics. *Journal of Applied Behavior Analysis, 5,* 247–262.

Wong, S. E. (1996). Psychosis. In M. Mattaini & B. A. Thyer (Eds.), *Finding solutions to social problems: Behavioral strategies for change* (pp. 319–343). Washington, DC: American Psychological Association.

Wong, S. E., Flanagan, S. G., Kuehnel, T. G., Liberman, R. P., Hunnicutt, R., & Adams-Badgett, J. (1988). Training chronic mental patients to independently practice personal grooming skills. *Hospital and Community Psychiatry, 39,* 874–879.

Wong, S. E., Martinez-Diaz, J. A., Massel, H. K., Edelstein, B. A., Wiegand, W., Bowen, L., et al. (1993). Conversational skills training with schizophrenic inpatients: A study of generalization across settings and conversants. *Behavior Therapy, 24,* 285–304.

Wong, S. E., Slama, K. M., & Liberman, R. P. (1985). Behavioral analysis and therapy for aggressive psychiatric and developmentally disabled patients. In L. H. Roth (Ed.), *Clinical treatment of the violent person* (pp. 22–56). New York: Plenum Press.

Wong, S. E., Terranova, M. D., Bowen, L., Zarate, R., Massel, H. K., & Liberman, R. P. (1987). Providing independent recreational activities to reduce stereotypic vocalizations in chronic schizophrenics. *Journal of Applied Behavior Analysis, 20,* 77–81.

Wong, S. E., & Woolsey, J. E. (1989). Re-establishing conversational skills in overtly psychotic, chronic schizophrenic patients: Discrete trials training on the psychiatric ward. *Behavior Modification, 13,* 415–430.

Wong, S. E., Woolsey, J. E., & Gallegos, E. (1987). Behavioral treatment of chronic psychiatric patients. *Journal of Social Service Research, 10*(2/3/4), 7–35.

Wong, S. E., Woolsey, J. E., Innocent, A. J., & Liberman, R. P. (1988). Behavioral treatment of violent psychiatric patients. *Psychiatric Clinics of North America, 11,* 569–580.

Wong, S. E., Wright, J., Terranova, M. D., Bowen, L., & Zarate, R. (1988). Effects of structured ward activities on appropriate and psychotic behavior of chronic psychiatric patients. *Behavioral Residential Treatment, 3,* 41–50.

Wykes, T., Parr, A., & Landau, S. (1999). Group treatment of auditory hallucinations: Exploratory study of effectiveness. *British Journal of Psychiatry, 175,* 180–185.

PART THREE

SELECTED ISSUES

The third and final section of the book examines selected issues that affect practice. Six core issues have been chosen as representative of the commitment to the use of critical thinking and best evidence in social work practice. In chapter 14, McCracken and Corrigan address barriers to the adoption of evidence-based interventions in psychiatry. They also present educational and organizational strategies for staff development that maximize the potential for successful dissemination of innovative practices. Christine Marlow (chapter 15) offers a cogent discussion of the cultural responsiveness of social science research on which evidence-based practice depends. She emphasizes the role of the social worker as a consumer of social research and discusses factors to be considered in determining the cultural relevance of research findings and their implications for practice. Next, Tina Rzepnicki (chapter 16) discusses issues of obtaining informed consent with an emphasis on strategies for effective communication. She highlights the extra care that must be taken to avoid placing clients at greater risk than they already are as a result of their life circumstances. Practitioners seeking practical guides on ethical ways to involve clients in treatment evaluation and intervention decision making will find this chapter especially useful. Karen Budd (chapter 17) describes a project that illustrates both the benefits and the challenges of collaborative ventures in social service settings. In this case, the project was to develop a comprehensive assessment of service needs of teenage parents in foster care. The assessment model was based on the empirical literature on risks and protective factors affecting teenage parents and on the practical experiences of public child-welfare service workers who collaborated with Budd on design and application. A detailed discussion by Donald Baer on program evaluation (chapter 18) informs readers of the realities of evaluating social work programs by highlighting the threats, challenges, and politics involved, along with the benefits. In the final chapter, Harold Briggs, William Feyerherm, and Wallace Gingerich (chapter 19) provide a review of the distinctions among research, practice, and evaluation. Using a case example, they describe the role of research methods in the practice of social work as well as the benefits and challenges of practice derived from the incorporation of research tools.

CHAPTER 14

STAFF DEVELOPMENT IN MENTAL HEALTH

Stanley G. McCracken and
Patrick W. Corrigan

"Build it, and they will come." "Build a better mousetrap, and the world will beat a path to your door." The figurative language of success is seductive, nowhere more so than among evidence-based practice innovators. Unfortunately, what may be true of baseball and rodent control is not true of evidence-based practice in mental health. There has long been research demonstrating the effectiveness of behavioral treatment for individuals with severe and persistent mental illnesses. Approaches with demonstrated effectiveness include the token economy, with more than thirty years of empirical support (Atthowe & Krasner, 1968; Ayllon & Azrin, 1968, Paul & Lentz, 1977), psychoeducational and social skills training (Bellack, Hersen, & Turner, 1976; Hogarty et al., 1986; Liberman, Mueser, & Wallace, 1986), and behavioral family management (Anderson, Reiss, & Hogarty, 1986; Falloon, Boyd, & McGill, 1984). More recently, the American Psychiatric Association reprinted a series of articles, initially published in *Psychiatric Services,* on evidence-based practices for individuals with severe and persistent mental illnesses (American Psychiatric Association, 2003). Practice innovators have learned, however, that having a good product does not mean that people will use it. A decline in both clinical use and research interest has been noted for token economies and other behavioral interventions (Bellack, 1986; Boudewyns, Fry, & Nightengale, 1986; Corrigan, 1991; Glynn, 1990). Similarly, the data suggest that people with severe and persistent mental illnesses do not receive the evidence-based practices that have been found effective in addressing their disabilities (Department of Health and Human Services, 1999; Kuipers, 2000; Lehman, Steinwachs, & associates, 1998). The primary reason for this breakdown is not lack of effective teaching methods; several strategies have been identified to help students and staff acquire new skills in evidence-based practices (Berryman, Evans, & Kalbag, 1994; Nemec & Pratt, 2001; Paul, McInnis, & Mariotto, 1973; Sackett, Straus, Richardson, Rosenberg, & Haynes, 2000; Wallace, Liberman, MacKain, Blackwell, & Eckman, 1992). Rather, the primary problem has been that staff may not implement their newly learned skills, or not implement them correctly, when they return from training to their home programs (Corrigan & McCracken, 1995a; Corrigan, Steiner, McCracken, Blaser, & Barr, 2001; Liberman & Eckman, 1989; Milne, 1986). In addition, there are data showing that graduates of university-based training programs do not keep up with current literature in psychosocial services for this population (Casper, 2001). Because there is a long history of evidence supporting effectiveness, and a similarly long history of difficulty implementing and maintaining programs, staff development in mental health will be discussed with respect to the use of evidence-based psychiatric rehabilitation and behavioral interventions in psychiatric hospitals and community programs. Many of the problems in psychiatric hospitals are analogous to difficulties encountered in other settings, particularly those in which therapists are outside the traditional power hierarchy or those in which the therapist may design the intervention but may not have primary responsibility for implementing the program, such as in schools, nursing homes, day care centers, and families (Milne, 1985, 1986). Many of the lessons learned in psychiatric settings can also be applied to other service environments in which the practitioner is required to provide training to staff who have little formal education or who have training in disciplines and methods other than that of the practitioner.

Two models have influenced approaches to training staff in use of evidence-based practices: the educational model and the organizational model (Corrigan & McCracken, 1995a). The educational model focuses on imparting knowledge to individual staff members through use of didactic and experiential teaching methods such as lecture, demonstration or modeling, role-playing and feedback, on-the-job training, professionally prepared manuals and treatment modules with instruments to assess staff fidelity in conducting the intervention, and trainer apprentices. Training methods based on the educational model—virtually the only ones used in preservice training programs for mental health professionals—have been demonstrated to be effective in training existing staff to use newly developed methods (Backs Edwards, Giffort, McCracken, & Corrigan, 2002; Liberman, Eckman, Kuehnel, Rosenstein, & Kuehnel, 1982; Paul & Lentz, 1977; Rogers, Cohen, Danley, Hutchinson, & Anthony, 1986; Wallace et al., 1992). The organizational model, drawing heavily on strategies from organizational psychology, focuses on identifying job competencies and evaluating job performance, addressing the needs of the treatment team, and maintaining the program through quality improvement methods (Corrigan & McCracken, 1995b, 1997a; Corrigan, Steiner, McCracken, Blaser, & Barr, 2001; Giffort, 1998; Sluyter & Mukherjee, 1993). Although there is a smaller body of literature investigating the effects of training methods of the organizational model, there are studies demonstrating its effectiveness in reducing aggression on inpatient psychiatric units, reducing staff burnout and improving staff satisfaction, and improving staff attitudes about using behavioral interventions (Barnett & Clendenen, 1996; Corrigan et al., 1995; Corrigan et al., 1998; Corrigan, McCracken, Edwards, Brunner, et al. 1997; Corrigan, McCracken, Edwards, Kommana, & Simpatico, 1997; Corrigan, McCracken, Kommana, Edwards, & Simpatico, 1996; Hunter & Love, 1996).

Training approaches based on the educational model may be sufficient for disseminating innovative intervention methods to individual practitioners. However, studies investigating barriers to implementing and maintaining behavioral interventions in mental health programs suggest that these training methods need to be augmented by consideration of organizational factors when the goal is implementation of newly developed interventions.[1]

LITERATURE REVIEW: BARRIERS TO IMPLEMENTING AND TECHNIQUES FOR TRAINING AND DISSEMINATING BEHAVIORAL INTERVENTIONS

It has been suggested that behavior changes when intention to change is combined with the necessary skill and the absence of environmental constraint (Fishbein, 1995). Investigators have identified several factors that may impede the implementation of behavioral interventions in psychiatric inpatient and outpatient programs (Backer, Liberman, & Kuehnel, 1986; Corrigan, MacKain, & Liberman, 1994; Dickerson, 1993; Franco & Kelly, 1994; Hersen, Bellack, & Harris, 1993). Corrigan and associates (Corrigan, Kwartarini, and Pramana, 1992; Corrigan, MacKain, & Liberman, 1994) proposed that these barriers are clustered into three groups: characteristics of the interventions themselves, institutional constraints, and staff-related barriers.

Barriers Related to the Intervention Itself

Behavioral interventions may be described in language that is overly technical and unfamiliar to staff who are not trained in behavior therapy (Barlow, 1981; Garfield & Kurtz, 1976). The scientific community has often been criticized for its inattention to the need to develop materials that are more accessible to practitioners who are, presumably, the ultimate customers of these innovative practices. The need for materials that are more useful for practitioners has fostered the development of a number of highly structured treatment manuals and training modules (Bellack, Mueser, Gingerich, & Agresta, 1997; Jewell, Silverstein, & Stewart, 2001; Liberman, DeRisi, & Mueser, 1989; Mueser, Noordsy, Drake, & Fox, 2003). Although development of user-friendly, structured manuals and modules has reduced some of the barriers to disseminating innovative interventions, it has been found that use of these materials should be combined with some method to insure practitioner fidelity to the intervention. Research has found that the quality of implementation of evidence-based practices strongly influences the outcome (Bond et al., 2000; McHugo, Drake, Teague, & Xie, 1999). Wallace and associates (1992) found, for example, that deviation from the specified procedures had a deleterious effect on the ability of patients to learn the material

---

1. We will examine two types of evidence-based interventions for individuals with severe and persistent mental illnesses: behavioral interventions and psychiatric rehabilitation approaches. It should be noted that in some situations a particular intervention, such as skills training, may be described by some authors as a behavioral intervention and by others as a psychiatric rehabilitation intervention. When reviewing the literature, we will use the term used by the authors.

presented in the skills-training modules. Practice innovations, which are typically developed in academic settings, may need to be modified for use in settings that have fewer resources, such as availability of staff with training and intellectual commitment to the innovation (Corrigan & McCracken, 1997b, Morisse, Batra, Hess, Silverman, & Corrigan, 1996).

There is considerable disagreement, however, about the degree to which evidence-based practices should be modified to fit the practice setting instead of modifying the practice setting to facilitate implementation of the practice (Backer et al., 1986; Paul, Stuve, & Cross, 1997). Some authors believe that modification of empirically validated procedures to fit the needs of real-world settings runs the risk of diluting effective interventions and producing mediocre programs (Paul et al., 1997). Others argue that staff members have opinions and attitudes about these innovations and that their opinions must be considered. Furthermore, dissemination research offers ways to shape innovations into user-friendly programs without sacrificing the innovation's potency (Corrigan & McCracken, 1997b). The reality, of course, is that both fidelity to the evidence-based practices and flexibility in adapting the intervention to the realities of practice in the real world are necessary. Regardless of whether the intervention or the setting is modified, all would agree about the need to gather outcome data to ensure the effectiveness of the intervention in that setting (Rosenheck, 2001; Torrey et al., 2001).

Institutional Constraints

Institutional constraints are among the most difficult to address. First, the organizational structure of the typical psychiatric unit is based on a medical power structure of physician/psychiatrist, nurse, and mental health technician, and the behavioral practitioner is external to this structure (Dickerson, 1993; Hersen et al, 1993). Furthermore, it is the nursing or direct care staff (nurses and mental health technicians) who have the most frequent contact with the patient,[2] compared with psychology and social work staff who may spend more time in meetings and doing paperwork (Hess, Corrigan, & Buican, 1994). As a result, nursing staff may have the burden of implementing a behavioral program written by a behavior therapist who is outside the nursing supervisory structure. In addition, behavioral programming may have a low priority compared with other interventions, such as medication management (Dickerson, 1993; Franco & Kelly, 1994). When staff are occupied with other duties, such as observing individuals placed in restraints, or when there are staff shortages on the unit, behavioral programming activities, such as running skills groups or opening the token store, may be

---

2. There are several terms used to refer to individuals who receive psychiatric rehabilitation services. For purposes of clarity when discussing the research, we will use the term *patient* when referring to recipients of inpatient services and *client* when referring to recipients of outpatient services.

cancelled. In addition, financial pressures that may lead to a high unit census, to staffing vacancies resulting in high patient to staff ratios, and to inability to purchase supplies, such as patient workbooks or token store items, needed to run the program (Franco & Kelly, 1994). Finally, large human-services organizations are characterized by multiple (and sometimes conflicting) goals, unclear or uncertain technologies for attaining these goals, and inconsistent participation and attentiveness of the most important players. In contrast, the environment in which research interventions are studied and introduced are characterized by clear, well-defined goals; explicitly defined technologies; and consistent leadership from a committed principal investigator (Rosenheck, 2001). Institutional constraints may result in a catch-22 situation in which evidence-based practice therapists have little influence over the institutional constraints because these factors place them outside the power structure needed to influence the institutional factors.

Staff-Related Barriers

The most obvious of the staff-related barriers is lack of knowledge, particularly among direct-care staff, of evidence-based interventions for individuals with severe and persistent mental illnesses (Blair & Eldridge, 1997; Corrigan et al., 2001; Donat & McKeegan, 1990; Milne, 1986; St. Lawrence, Hansen, & Steele, 1985). These interventions may require knowledge that differs from what they already know from biological or psychodynamic approaches (Backer et al. 1986; Hersen et al., 1993). Staff attitudes may also constitute barriers to learning and implementing evidence-based interventions; these approaches may require skills that are considered contrary to some very basic tenets of prior training. For example, a fairly common intervention on inpatient psychiatric units is contingent attention or ignoring, depending on whether an individual's behavior is appropriate or inappropriate. Contingent attention may be fundamentally opposed to some nurses' training, in which they learned that one should respond positively to all patient communications, regardless of content (Hersen et al., 1993). Similarly, the idea of quantifying behavior and measuring outcomes may be unacceptable to nursing staff and some physicians (Hersen et al., 1993; Silverstein, Bowman, & McHugh, 1997). Some providers may believe that measurement is contrary to caregiving. Others may fear accountability, such as assessing fidelity to an evidence-based practice model; this is particularly a problem when there is worry over the possibility of layoffs or program closing. Finally, evidence-based practice programming may be perceived as undermining the control exerted by supervisory staff, because some decisions formerly made by nursing staff may be made more or less automatically along programmatic lines (Hersen et al., 1993).

Training Approaches Based on an Educational Model

Several approaches have been developed for teaching knowledge and skills to mental health staff at all levels. Liberman and associates at University of California, Los Angeles (Liberman & Eckman, 1989; Liberman, Eckman, Kuehnel,

Rosenstein, & Kuehnel, 1982) developed a staff-training package consisting of instructional manual, learning exercises, and videotapes that demonstrated the techniques. The skills were typically presented during a two-day workshop, followed by in-service training sessions over several months. They also identified a training coordinator at each participating program. The results of this package were reported for eighteen community mental health centers (Liberman & Eckman, 1989). Learning was assessed by means of a sixty-item multiple-choice test administered before and after fourteen weeks of training and by assessing whether participants were using the techniques in their practice. The authors found that 26 percent of the staff completed the workshop and in-service training for all six training modules; 66 percent completed the workshop and four or more modules. Subjects who completed at least four sessions showed a significant increase in their knowledge on the multiple-choice test and a concurrent increase in favorable attitudes about behavior therapy. More important, two-thirds of the community mental health centers reported using one or more of the modules one year later.

The effects of a similar training program were investigated by researchers from Boston University (Rogers et al., 1986). Thirty trainer apprentices from ten mental health centers participated in several weeks of intensive training that incorporated many of the elements used by the group from University of California, Los Angeles (introduction, modeling, behavioral rehearsal) with homework at their home clinics. Staff participating in this training demonstrated significant gains in skills related to rehabilitation diagnosis, planning, and intervention. Furthermore, trainer apprentices rated psychiatric rehabilitation interventions as more essential to comprehensive treatment after the training.

Paul and associates developed a comprehensive behavioral training program for staff at a psychiatric hospital (Paul & Lentz, 1977; Paul et al., 1973). This program included intensive academic training that staff completed before they began work on the behavioral unit, followed by on-unit training and supervision. The academic training included elements similar to the University of California program, such as modeling, role-play, feedback, group discussion, and use of a manual that described targeted procedures and strategies. Staff who completed the academic training showed a significant increase in knowledge of behavioral principles and severe and persistent mental illnesses. Following successful completion of their training, staff began on-unit training in which they were provided with structured situations to practice their newly learned skills and with supervision and feedback from senior staff members. Supervision and feedback faded as staff competence increased. On-unit training was found to produce increased quantity and quality of staff and patient interactions (Paul et al., 1973).

Delamater, Conners, and Wells (1984) used single-case methodology to investigate training of six staff to use behavioral procedures with children in a psychiatric hospital. They examined the independent effects of three training procedures: multimedia presentations and in-class exercises, direct feedback to staff about the appropriateness of their attention to and rewarding of child behavior during structured observation sessions, and role-playing. Evaluation of training consisted of direct observations of the staff during a free play period. Although the results must be interpreted cautiously, it appeared that staff skills improved most during the role-play condition (Delamater et al., 1984).

Taken together, these studies suggest that structured training methods can be used to teach behavioral principles and intervention skills. There is support for the use of many of the same methods used to teach skills to clients, such as introduction of the material, modeling, role play, in vivo observation and feedback, and the use of training manuals and workbooks. There is also evidence of the need for on-site experts or champions to provide supervision and consultation (Corrigan, 1995; Silverstein & Jewell, 2002, Torrey et al., 2001).

Training Approaches Based on an Organizational Model

Organizational models of training recognize that improvement of knowledge and skills is necessary but not sufficient for establishing and maintaining behavioral programming (Corrigan & McCracken, 1995a; Milne, Gorenski, Westerman, Leck, & Keegan, 2000; Sluyter, 1998b). Both institutional constraints and staff variables can impede implementation of evidence-based practice innovations. For example, although it is necessary to improve staff knowledge and skills, staff attitudes can either facilitate or impede the implementation of evidence-based interventions. Both the University of California (Liberman & Eckman, 1989) and the Boston University (Rogers et al., 1986) groups noted that staff attitudes improved concurrently with increased knowledge and skills. This improvement in attitudes is supported by the results of a pilot study, by Jewell and associates (2001), of a structured manual for training staff from community programs to use therapeutic contracting. These investigators found that, in addition to improving learning, staff reported that they expected that the course would help them in their future work with clients (Jewell et al., 2001). Studies examining interactive staff training, a training method based on an organizational model, have found similar improvements in staff attitudes about behavior therapy (Corrigan et al., 1998).

Interactive staff training (Corrigan & McCracken, 1995b, 1997a), which focuses on the treatment team rather than the individual staff person, consists of four stages: introduction to the system, program development, program implementation, and program maintenance (see figure 14.1). In the first stage, introduction to the system, training facilitators obtain support of program administrators and explore/establish the fit between existing organizational goals and goals of the intervention, conduct a staff needs assessment to identify program-development priorities, and identify a program committee and champion who represent their colleagues and have responsibility for developing the program. During the program-development stage, the training facilitator meets monthly with the program committee and champion to assign a series of homework assignments that require the committee to make decisions about their program. These homework assignments are based on a framework that is grounded in the literature, although

FIGURE 14.1   The Four Stages of Interactive Staff Training

Introduction to the system ➡	Program development ➡	Program implementation ➡	Program maintenance
1. Secure administrative support 2. Conduct staff-needs assessment 3. Identify program committee and champions	4. Participative decision making 5. Socratic questions about drafts 6. Augment knowledge with learning opportunities	7. Pilot the program 8. Problem solve program shortfalls	9. User-friendly and controlled continuous quality improvement 10. Train organizational champion and leave the system

SOURCE: Adapted from Corrigan, McCracken, Edwards, Brunner, et al. (1997).

the committee is not required to produce an intervention that adheres strictly to research. The training facilitator uses Socratic questioning techniques to assist the program committee in evaluating their programmatic decisions. The more traditional staff training methods noted previously are used here to teach staff knowledge and skills needed to implement intervention strategies with which they are unfamiliar.

Program implementation begins with a pilot test in which program limitations are identified and resolved using problem-solving techniques. After the pilot test, the program is implemented throughout the unit or agency. In the final stage, program maintenance, the program committee is taught user-friendly continuous quality improvement methods to identify relevant process and outcome measures, collect data, and use these data to modify the program as needed (Corrigan, Luchins, Malan, & Harris, 1994). Interactive staff training has been evaluated in several studies in both hospital and community settings and has been found to decrease patient aggression, increase both patient and staff participation in rehabilitation programming, decrease staff emotional exhaustion, improve staff attitudes about behavioral interventions, and increase staff perceptions of collegial support (Corrigan et al., 1995; Corrigan, McCracken, Edwards, Brunner, et al., 1997; Corrigan, McCracken, Edwards, Kommana, et al., 1997).

As can be seen from this brief review, there are data to support several staff training strategies based on both educational and organizational models (for reviews of additional studies based on both educational and organizational models, see Corrigan & Giffort, 1998; Corrigan & McCracken, 1995a; Hersen et al., 1993; Milne, 1986) Several authors have reviewed these data and have extracted principles for staff training and for dissemination and adoption of evidence-based practice innovations.

APPROACH: RECOMMENDATIONS FOR DISSEMINATION AND ADOPTION OF EVIDENCE-BASED PRACTICE INNOVATIONS

Reviews of the staff training, consultation, and intervention dissemination literature have led to a number of recommendations for practice (see table 14.1). Backer and associates (1986) identified six factors in their review of three large-scale studies of dissemination of psychosocial interventions in community settings; they then made six practice generalizations and four supporting recommendations based on the factors. They also related these factors to the larger literature on utilization and noted that their generalizations were relevant to adoption of psychosocial interventions by individual psychotherapists and by programs or agencies (Backer et al., 1986). The authors found that interpersonal contact between the credible professional peers and recipient staff was important in most studies of successful innovation adoption. This recommendation suggests that whereas professional conferences might be useful as a vehicle for presenting outcome data or alerting professionals to the development of innovations, conference presentations and workshops are not likely to be a productive method for large-scale dissemination and adoption of practice innovations. Not least among the reasons for this is that many of the staff who need to be trained do not attend the conferences at which innovations are presented.

The second and third points ("outside consultation on the adoption process and especially on the psychological and administrative ramifications of the change," and "organizational support for the innovation . . . consistent with . . . support from the top," p. 115) are closely related. The authors found that senior administration's support for change is essential. Without the support of senior administrators, the efforts of the consultant to engage staff in developing innovative interventions are an intellectual exercise, since the innovation is unlikely to be adopted. However, it is also necessary that the consultant provide technical support to the senior and midlevel administrators on the process and implications of change. The traditional practice of providing staff training focused only on the technical aspects of the innovation is doomed to failure without attention to the impact that this training will make on the organization. Fourth, in addition to outside consultation by credible professional peers, there must be an internal champion of the innovation. There must be a member of the recipient organization who takes ownership for innovation and who provides ongoing support for adoption of the practice. The authors recommend providing evidence of success of the innovative program. Staff need to be reminded that their efforts have had favorable results, and public recognition in the form of publications and conference presentations may be a potent reinforcer for their efforts at adopting the innovation. Innovators would do well to heed the advice, "spread credit widely." The final recommendations of Backer and associates (1986) address the need to develop a network of professionals interested in the innovation and the usefulness of technical supports such as videotapes, online information clearinghouses, and publications.

TABLE 14.1   Recommendations for Disseminating and Adopting Evidence-Based Practice Innovations

Source	Recommendations
Backer, Liberman, & Kuehnel (1986)	1. Provide interpersonal contact between staff and credible professional peers. 2. Provide outside consultation on the adoption process and technical assistance on the process of change. 3. Ensure organizational support for the innovation and support for the innovation from senior administrators. 4. Ensure persistent championship of the innovation by one or more agency staff. 5. Ensure adaptability of the innovation by separating the innovation into component parts and promoting only those elements that fit with the adopting agency. 6. Provide credible evidence of success for the innovative program. 7. Network with other professionals interested in innovation; provide videotapes to convey information on innovation; use technological innovations such as computer (Internet) clearinghouse for information on the innovation; provide publications on innovations.
Hersen, Bellack, & Harris (1993)	1. Apprise hospital administration of all of the consequences and implications of having a behavioral program. 2. Ensure full cooperation of unit administrator and head nurse. (Ideally, the program director should be a behavior therapist.) 3. Include both practical application and some theory in staff training. "On-the-spot" teaching should have precedence supplemented by additional classroom role playing. 4. Use behavioral techniques systematically to promote maintenance of staff performance. For example, reward staff with advancement and raises (if possible), public feedback, social reinforcement, and modeling. 5. Ensure that the behavioral program director has visibility on the unit to reinforce and model appropriate interactions with the patients. 6. Examine the political and interpersonal atmosphere before and during implementation of program.
Milne, Gorenski, Westerman, Leck, & Keegan (2000)	1. Select training sites carefully. 2. Train key staff from these sites to train their colleagues in situ. 3. Provide extensive consultant support. 4. Prepare staff for the tribulations of innovation. 5. Form a working alliance with the providers. 6. Provide a therapy manual. 7. Arrange for staff to collaborate with a colleague (co-therapy). 8. Ensure administrative and supervisory support. 9. Integrate the training with the caseload, available time, and other responsibilities. 10. Assess learning needs of the staff.

continued

TABLE 14.1 (*continued*)

Source	Recommendations
	11. Develop user-friendly interventions.
	12. Organize staff into an effective treatment team.
	13. Obtain administrative support.
	14. Form a program committee that includes innovation champions.
	15. Implement continuous quality improvement.
	16. Maximize support from managers.
	17. Develop relevant skills and knowledge.
	18. Set specific goals.
	19. Enhance recognition from colleagues.
	20. Arrange for consultant support.
Rosenheck (2001)	1. Construct a leadership coalition that favors implantation and that can provide ongoing support.
	2. Link initiatives to legitimated organizational goals and values.
	3. Implement quantitative monitoring of fidelity to the model and ongoing program performance.
	4. Develop a self-sustaining subculture or community of practice that both perpetuates and modifies program procedures and values.

Hersen and associates (1993) provided a number of recommendations from their extensive review of the training and consultation literature addressing implementation of behavioral programs in psychiatric hospitals. Their first recommendation was that hospital administrators should be apprised of all the consequences and implications, both on the units and hospital-wide, of having a behavioral program. The authors cautioned behavior therapists not to overlook or underemphasize the issue of middle managers' (e.g., unit directors and nursing supervisors) losing administrative power to "more automatically carried-out dictates of the behavioral program" (p. 161). Although the authors stated their preference that a behavior therapist has administrative authority, such as being the program director or unit administrator, Hersen and colleagues believed it was essential that he or she have the full cooperation of the unit director and head nurse. Without such support, behavioral program development will fail and be no more than an academic exercise.

The authors recommended combining theory and practical application, with priority given to on-the-spot training supported by role-playing in the classroom. Their emphasis on hands-on training echoes the previous recommendation that skills are best taught by interactive training methods and the principle that generalization is enhanced by training in the environment in which the skill will ultimately be used. Their fourth recommendation emphasizes the necessity of using well-established behavioral techniques in training, such as tangible reinforcers when possible (e.g., promotions, raises, other monetary reinforcers), direct and public feedback, social reinforcement, and modeling by professional and (particularly) nursing staff. On-unit feedback, reinforcement, and modeling require that the behavioral program director be present and visible on the unit. Finally, the authors note that the political and interpersonal climate should be examined both before and during development and implementation of any program (Hersen et al., 1993). They acknowledge that this practice, though important, is not characteristic of usual behavioral analysis.

Milne and colleagues (2000) identified several contextual factors that contribute to training effectiveness in both hospital and community settings. They found twenty characteristics of successful transfer of training programs in psychiatric rehabilitation. Since most of their recommendations have already been addressed previously in this chapter, we will focus on two recommendations that have not been mentioned. Their first recommendation—careful selection of training sites—echoes a priority identified by Corrigan and McCracken (1997a); trainers of interactive staff training should begin working with units or programs that are interested in developing innovative services. Selection of units that are more interested in developing innovative programs may produce initial results that can be used to engage more resistant units. This is particularly true if the initial results reduce problems experienced by other units in the hospital.

Milne and colleagues' (2000) ninth recommendation (integrate training with the caseload, available time, and other responsibilities) also is a wise suggestion. A primary difficulty of introducing evidence-based practice innovations into real-world settings is staff who are overwhelmed by current responsibilities. A primary staff concern is that new practice will result in an even greater burden of time and work. Although trainers should acknowledge that learning new skills will require additional time and effort (the fourth recommendation), integration of the training with current responsibilities may reduce this burden somewhat.

Rosenheck (2001)—in his discussion of organizational factors in adoption of evidence-based practices in large, complex organizations—identified four strategies important in promoting the transition from research to practice. These strategies were derived from his work promoting the development of programs for homeless, mentally ill veterans and for veterans with posttraumatic stress disorder served by the Veterans' Administration. The first strategy is construction of leadership coalitions that favor implementation and that can provide ongoing support. This step is necessary because, in most situations, a single proponent of an intervention is unable to affect his or her own adoption, even if this person has the formal authority to do so. In most cases, a coalition of advocates is needed to argue, through formal and informal channels, for establishment of the new practice. The second strategy is to link the new initiative with legitimated organizational goals and values, since a principal factor influencing the decision to implement a new practice is its relationship to larger organizational objectives. The third strategy is quantitative monitoring of fidelity to the model and ongoing program performance. The results of this monitoring should be compiled and circulated to both staff and administrators. The fourth strategy is the development of self-sustaining subcultures or communities of practice that both perpetuate and modify program procedures and values. The key to developing this community is frequent interaction to enable members to share common experiences and to codify their knowledge in catchphrases, symbols, and stories (Rosenheck, 2001). Taken together, the recommendations from these four articles reflect the need both to base training on sound educational and organization practices and to combine attention to evidence-based practice with user-friendliness.

GUIDES AND PRINCIPLES FOR PRACTICE: TRAINING METHODS FOR DISSEMINATION AND IMPLEMENTATION OF EVIDENCE-BASED PRACTICE INNOVATIONS

Table 14.2 lists several practice principles and options derived from the literature on staff training and intervention dissemination. The practice principles constitute general themes that frequently recur in the literature; the practice options are specific tasks that operationalize these principles. The practice options should be modified to fit the service setting. The principles and options include both educational and organizational techniques and roughly reflect the chronological sequence of training and dissemination activities.

Engage and Prepare the Organization for the Innovation

The first step in dissemination of an innovation is to engage and prepare the organization for the innovation. One of the first tasks for the trainer or innovation specialist (consultant) is to meet with and secure public support from the senior administrators and middle managers, such as program directors, unit directors, and nurse supervisors. Even when the senior administrator has invited the consultant to work with his or her staff, the administrator's support should be solicited and proclaimed publicly to middle managers and line-level staff. The consultant should discuss the administrator's vision and goals for the organization and for the innovation and make clear how the innovation fits with established organizational goals and values. These goals should be kept in mind throughout the consultation and training, and the consultant should make frequent contact with the administrator to ensure that program development and training efforts continue to be consistent with these goals. One should not presume support of middle managers naturally follows from the endorsement of senior administrators. As we noted previously, innovation may potentially be threatening to all levels of administration, particularly to middle-level managers and direct supervisors of line staff. Part of the engagement process is advising administrators and middle managers of the consequences and implications of implementing the practice innovation and assuring them that consultation will be provided on both the content and the process of change.

Concurrent with engaging the administration and middle managers, the consultant must begin to evaluate the political and interpersonal atmosphere of the

TABLE 14.2 Guidelines for Disseminating and Adopting Evidence-Based Practice Innovations

Practice Principle	Practice Options
Engage and prepare the organization.	1. Obtain public support of senior administration and middle management, such as unit administrators and nursing supervisors. 2. Advise senior administration and middle management on the consequences and implications of implementing the practice innovation. 3. Elicit the vision and goals of the administration and maintain frequent contact with administrators to ensure that innovation remains consistent with the stated vision and goals. 4. Evaluate the political and interpersonal atmosphere of the organization before and during implementation of the program. 5. Provide consultation on the adoption process and the process of change. 6. Select training sites carefully; start with the most receptive units or programs. 7. Identify a facility champion of the innovation.
Engage and form a working alliance with the treatment team.	8. Provide an overview of the process of change and program innovation. 9. Conduct a staff needs assessment to identify program development priorities and learning needs. 10. Identify a program champion and program committee.
Develop a user-friendly program based on identified program-development priorities and the innovation.	11. Ensure adaptability of the innovation by separating the innovation into component parts and promoting only those elements that fit with the adopting agency. 12. Develop an adoption "frame" based on a sequential arrangement of these component parts. 13. Use interactive methods, such as participative decision making and Socratic questioning, to assist the champion and program committee in identifying which components should be adopted and which should be changed to develop the program. 14. Provide frequent (monthly) consultation to the staff and program committee.
Use established educational principles in training.	15. Base training on skills that are identified by the staff and that are needed to implement the program. 16. Integrate training with caseload, available time, and staff responsibilities. 17. Integrate theory and practical application; emphasize on-the-spot training.

continued

TABLE 14.2   (*continued*)

Practice Principle	Practice Options
	18. Train the staff as a team.
	19. Model the skills, by the consultant and by key staff, such as nursing supervisors and other unit professionals in on-the-spot demonstrations.
	20. Provide opportunities to role-play skills off unit.
	21. Set performance goals and provide opportunities for in situ skill performance and feedback.
	22. Develop and use an intervention fidelity measure.
	23. Provide a manual for the innovation.
Implement the program in a stepwise manner; plan for maintenance.	24. Conduct a pilot test of the innovation; identify specific questions to be answered by the pilot test; problem solve identified deficiencies.
	25. Implement the innovation throughout the unit.
	26. Set up continuous quality improvement process based on process and outcome measures identified by staff.
	27. Gather data and disseminate findings to the staff, to the organization, and in regional or national professional conferences.
	28. Provide incentives to staff for implementing the innovations, such as, tangible incentives (where possible), social reinforcement, public recognition, letters of commendation.
	29. Establish a consultation and support network of supervisors and staff involved in implementing the innovation.
	30. Provide technical supports such as videotapes demonstrating the innovative technique, computer-based supports (Web sites, databases, computer-based learning), and relevant publications.

organization. This evaluation will continue throughout adoption of the innovation. Among the elements to consider are both official and unofficial power structures, relationships between disciplines and shifts, and the organization communication patterns. Consultants should also consider the presence of major stressful events, such as staff or client injuries, visits by surveyors, changes in the client population or nature of work, and major staffing changes (particularly job losses). Information can be gathered by listening, observing, questioning tactfully, and reviewing an organizational chart. One of the most valuable methods of gathering and sharing information is conducting focus groups and informational seminars with administrators, staff, clients, and other stakeholders. Information provided by this organizational assessment is useful in a number of ways, such as identification of individuals whose support is necessary in adopting the innovation and who should be included, or at least represented, on the program committee.

During the securing of administrative support, a facility champion and the initial units or programs for innovation should be identified. In addition to identifying an individual to champion adoption of the new program, the consultant should identify several other individuals at the facility who are enthusiastic about the new intervention so that there is a coalition to provide vocal support for the innovation and to serve as models for other staff. The facility champion accompanies the consultant and represents the senior administrator. Presence of the facility champion at program-development and innovation activities underscores the seriousness of the activity and the support of the senior administrator. The facility champion provides a means of communication with management, both to articulate and to clarify relevant policy about programmatic decisions and to provide ongoing information to management about the progress of consultation.

The organizational engagement process should also result in identification of the initial units or programs for training and program development. Ideally, the first units should be those units whose staff are most interested in developing innovative programs or those who recognize a need for change. The task of adopting innovation is considerably more difficult and time consuming, perhaps even impossible, if the staff do not buy into system change. Starting with a unit whose staff accept the idea of change increases the chance that these individuals will adopt new ways of doing business and subsequently that these changes will produce favorable results. These favorable results can then be used to increase interest or acceptance of innovation among other units.

Engage and Form a Working Alliance with the Treatment Team

The second step in innovation is engaging and forming of a working alliance with the treatment team; one of the most important components in the dissemination effort is a strong relationship between the consultant and the agency personnel. If the consultant has not already done so, he or she should meet with and solicit support of unit and program administrators, such as the unit director, program director, and nursing supervisors. The consultant should provide a realistic overview of the process and benefits of change and should elicit and address fears of change. Examples from other similar programs should be provided along with the opportunity to observe programs at other facilities and talk with staff who have made similar changes. The consultant should disseminate a needs assessment to all staff in order to identify program-development and learning needs. After this information is gathered and analyzed, results should be discussed with the administrators and unit staff, and program-development and learning needs should be prioritized.

The final task in this phase is identification of a unit or program champion and a corresponding program committee (for a more detailed description of the role and function of champions and program committees, see Corrigan & Mc-Cracken, 1997a; for a discussion of quality-improvement teams, see Sluyter, 1998a). The champion should be an energetic and enthusiastic individual who is interested in program development and innovation. It is desirable, but not essential, that the individual is knowledgeable about the innovation; knowledge is easier to augment than interest. The natural choice for the program champion is the clinical director, unit director, or chief nurse. If, however, none of these individuals has the time or interest, they must be willing to delegate authority for program development and innovation to the individual who will be champion. When the champion is not the clinical supervisor, unit administrator, or chief nurse, these individuals should still be members of the program committee. The danger is, of course, that competing power structures may be established to the detriment of both the unit and the innovation efforts. In larger units or programs, the program committee should consist of representatives of the various professional disciplines and shifts. In smaller programs, the program committee may be the entire treatment team. Ideally, the program committee should include client, and in some cases family, representation. The program committee oversees and has responsibility for the development and implementation of the program or innovative practice. The program committee provides both leadership for and ownership of the program or innovation. If either of these is lacking, it is unlikely that the innovation will be adopted, implemented, or maintained.

Develop a User-Friendly Program Based on Identified Program Development Priorities and on the Innovation

The consultant works with the program committee and champion to develop a user-friendly program based on the identified program development and learning priorities and the evidence-based practice (for a detailed description of this process, see Corrigan & McCracken, 1997a). Prior to beginning work with the organization, the consultant should have separated the evidence-based practice into component elements and constructed a development frame consisting of a sequential arrangement of these components. Both the components and the frame are based on the research literature and on the consultant's experience with development of the innovation on similar units. The consultant meets regularly with the program committee and uses participative decision making and Socratic questioning to assist the committee in deciding which components of the innovative practice fit best with the unit and which need to be modified to be feasible. The goal of this process is to involve the program committee, and by extension all the staff, in developing user-friendly programs for the unit. In addition, it is at this stage, as well as in the needs assessment, that the program committee and the consultant identify specific skills and knowledge that staff must learn to implement the program. Successful identification of the staff-training needs at this stage ensures that the skills are relevant and will be used immediately.

Use Established Educational Principles in Training

Considerable training occurs adventitiously during the course of program development and Socratic questioning, but skill and knowledge deficits also are addressed by formal training and established educational methods based on principles of adult learning, such as modeling, role-playing, goal setting, and providing feedback on performance. If a user-friendly training or intervention manual exists, it should be made available to all staff. Training should integrate theory and practical application, with emphasis on the latter. To the degree possible, staff should be trained as a team, and training should be integrated into the ongoing work of the unit and staff responsibilities. It also is advisable that the consultant train unit professionals and supervisory personnel to provide on-unit modeling and feedback. Although it is often useful for the consultant to demonstrate skills, it is equally important that staff have someone consistently available and visible on the unit to observe using the skills. After staff have learned targeted skills, a performance measure should be obtained or developed to ensure that staff maintain fidelity to those components identified by the program committee. Staff and supervisors should be evaluated regularly with the fidelity measure, and results of the evaluation should be used to provide immediate feedback to individuals.

It is important that this activity be framed as a learning activity rather than a performance-evaluation activity, since performance-evaluation activities have been used in many settings to punish staff for their inadequacies. This and the previous step will be enhanced by increasing availability of evidence-based practice toolkits that contain, among other things, detailed training manuals, Web site information, fidelity measures, and other written materials that can be used to introduce staff to the intervention, to form the basis for training, and to assess fidelity to the innovation (Torrey et al., 2001).

Implement the Program in a Stepwise Manner: Plan for Maintenance

After a working draft of the program has been developed, a pilot test of the intervention should be conducted, concurrent with formal training. In many ways, the process of program maintenance begins with the pilot test, since this is the point at which the program committee establishes the practice of gathering and using data to make decisions. Specific programmatic questions should be identified, such as whether it is necessary to identify more than one staff person to be responsible for running a skills group. The pilot test gives staff and clients the opportunity to gain some initial experience with the program, to identify deficiencies in the program, and to use problem solving to modify the program as needed. The pilot test can also be used to generate interest in the innovation among both clients and staff and to provide a mind-set that the program can and should be modified. After the pilot test, the program or innovation is implemented throughout the unit and the program committee shifts a greater portion of its attention to program maintenance. When the program is implemented throughout the unit, consideration should be given to restructuring the flow of work on the unit so that routine procedures make it natural for staff to provide care in the new way.

The process of data collection, begun during the pilot test, continues as unit-based continuous quality improvement. The program committee identifies relevant process measures, such as program implementation fidelity by staff and participation by clients, and outcome measures, such as effect on client functioning and quality of life and on staff job satisfaction (for a more detailed discussion of continuous quality improvement, see Corrigan et al., 1994; for a discussion of total quality management, see Sluyter & Mukherjee, 1993). Staff use these data to monitor progress and to assist them in making decisions about the program. It is important that a mechanism be identified for disseminating data about the program to unit staff, to the facility, and even in conferences or publications. The opportunity to share success is one of several potential incentives that can be provided to staff for their work in learning and using the practice innovation. Other incentives might include public recognition of their efforts; letters of commendation; and even tangible incentives, where allowed by collective bargaining and organizational policies. Ongoing support for the innovation can take several forms, including continuing contact with the consultant, professional networks, and technical supports. The consultant may continue to provide ongoing consultation and training at a reduced frequency, or the consultant may maintain regular telephone or e-mail contact with the facility and/or program champion. As more programs in the organization or geographic region begin to use the innovation, the consultant may choose to facilitate the establishment of a professional network or consultation group (Linehan, 1993, Rosenheck, 2001). This professional network can be used for peer consultation and problem solving, as a vehicle for sharing data, and as a means of maintaining interest in the practice innovation.

DISCUSSION AND IMPLICATIONS FOR STAFF TRAINING AND DISSEMINATION OF EVIDENCE-BASED PRACTICE INNOVATIONS

In a 1997 book, we coined the term *interactive staff training* (Corrigan & McCracken, 1997a). The term has a double meaning. First, we mean that comprehensive training to yield regular use of evidence-based innovations by real-world staff requires an interaction of *educational* and *organizational* approaches to staff training. Educational approaches rest on learning theory and help individual staff members acquire the necessary principles and skills of evidence-based practice. Organizational approaches teach individual staff members how to work as a team and develop evidence-based treatment programs that are user-friendly and meet consumer needs.

Second, interactive staff training emerges when educational and organizational approaches are integrated. Namely, the consultant who is assisting the program team in development of user-friendly and effective treatments must interact with that team. The consultant must listen to the needs of local staff members and their clientele so that he or she can help the team develop relevant programs. The resultant development strategy needs to reflect this information. Consultants need to avoid being wedded to specific treatments in a doctrinaire method. Rigid consultants succeed by building programs that represent the state of the art but fail by setting up treatment systems that do not meet local goals. As a result, these formal systems fail to endure.

These interactive processes describe an interesting tension for the research enterprise related to evidence-based practices. On the one hand, practice innovations need to be transferred to real-world settings in a manner that corresponds with the research in which the specific practice was empirically supported. Only in this manner can a treatment team assume that it is providing a service with supportive evidence. On the other hand, an interactive approach to staff training and program development suggests that treatment teams need to adjust components of evidence-based interventions to meet the local needs of staff and consumers. In the process, some empirically based elements of an intervention may be deleted or modified. Basic clinical scientists who develop the evidence-based practice frequently gasp at this effort.

The distinction described herein parallels the difference in agendas of efficacy and effectiveness research. Much of what we call research on efficacy is what has been reviewed throughout this book; namely, in carefully controlled clinical settings, what evidence emerges that a specific intervention leads to significant changes in outcome variables compared to control conditions? Effectiveness studies begin where efficacy research stops. How effective is an evidence-based intervention in meeting real-world problems of service consumers in real-world treatment settings? Education and organizational models must be combined to achieve the effectiveness research agenda. In this chapter, we have reviewed recommendations that authors have gleaned from studies of educationally based and organizationally based training approaches. From these recommendations, we have identified several practice principles and options from both educational and organizational models to provide guidance to trainers and consultants who attempt to "build it" in the real world.

REFERENCES

American Psychiatric Association. (2003). *Evidence-based practices in mental health*. Washington, DC: Author.

Anderson, C. M., Reiss, D. J., & Hogarty, G. E. (1986). *Schizophrenia and the family*. New York: Guilford Press.

Atthowe, J. M., & Krasner, L. (1968). Preliminary report on the application of contingent reinforcement procedures (token economy) on a "chronic" psychiatric ward. *Journal of Abnormal Psychology, 73*, 37–43.

Ayllon, T., & Azrin, N. (1968). *The token economy: A motivational system for therapy and rehabilitation.* New York: Appleton-Century-Crofts.

Backer, T. E., Liberman, R. P., & Kuehnel, T. G. (1986). Dissemination and adoption of innovative psychosocial interventions. *Journal of Consulting and Clinical Psychology, 54,* 111–118.

Backs Edwards, A., Giffort, D. W., McCracken, S. G., & Corrigan, P. W. (2002). Public academic training partnerships for paraprofessionals who provide psychiatric rehabilitation. *Psychiatric Rehabilitation Skills, 5,* 437–454.

Barlow, D. H. (1981). On the relation of clinical research to clinical practice: Current issues, new directions. *Journal of Consulting and Clinical Psychology, 49,* 147–155.

Barnett, J. E., & Clendenen, F. (1996). The quality journey in a comprehensive mental health center. *JCAHO Journal on Quality Improvement, 22,* 8–17.

Bellack, A. S. (1986). Schizophrenia: Behavioral therapy's forgotten child. *Behavior Therapy, 17,* 199–214.

Bellack, A. S., Hersen, M., & Turner, S. M. (1976). Generalization effects of social skills training with chronic schizophrenics: An experimental analysis. *Behavioral Research and Therapy, 14,* 391–398.

Bellack, A. S., Mueser, K. T., Gingerich, S., & Agresta, J. (1997). *Social skills training for schizophrenia: A step-by-step guide.* New York: Guilford Press.

Berryman, J., Evans, I. M., & Kalbag, A. (1994). The effects of training in nonaversive behavior management on the attitudes and understanding of direct care staff. *Journal of Behavior Therapy and Experimental Psychiatry, 25,* 241–250.

Blair, C. E., & Eldridge, E. F. (1997). An instrument for measuring staff's knowledge of behavior management principles (KBMQ) as applied to geropsychiatric clients in long-term care settings. *Journal of Behavior Therapy and Experimental Psychiatry, 28,* 213–220.

Bond, G., Williams, J., Evans, L., Salyers, M., Kim, H.-W., Sharpe, H., et al. (2000). *Psychiatric rehabilitation fidelity tool kit.* The Evaluation Center@HSRI. Available from materials@tecathsri.org

Boudewyns, P., Fry, T., & Nightengale, E. (1986). Token economy programs in VA medical centers: Where are they today? *Behavior Therapist, 6,* 126–127.

Casper, E. S. (2001). Psychiatric rehabilitation degree-granting programs and practitioners' knowledge and practice patterns. *Psychiatric Rehabilitation Skills, 5,* 534–547.

Corrigan, P. W. (1991). Strategies that overcome barriers to token economies in community programs for severe mentally ill adults. *Community Mental Health Journal, 27,* 17–30.

Corrigan, P. W. (1995). Wanted: Champions of rehabilitation for psychiatric hospitals. *American Psychologist, 50,* 514–521.

Corrigan, P. W. (1998). Building teams and programs for effective psychiatric rehabilitation. *Psychiatric Quarterly, 69,* 193–209.

Corrigan, P. W., & Giffort, D. W. (Eds.) (1998). *Building teams and programs for effective psychiatric rehabilitation: New directions for mental health services.* San Francisco: Jossey-Bass.

Corrigan, P. W., Holmes, E. P., Luchins, D., Basit, A., Delaney, E., Gleason, W., et al. (1995). The effects of interactive staff training on staff programming and patient aggression in a psychiatric inpatient ward. *Behavioral Interventions, 10,* 17–32.

Corrigan, P. W., Kwartarini, W. Y., & Pramana, W. (1992). Staff perception of barriers to behavior therapy at a psychiatric hospital. *Behavior Modification, 16,* 132–144.

Corrigan, P. W., Luchins, D. J., Malan, R. D., & Harris, J. (1994). User-friendly continuous quality improvement for the mental health team. *Medical Interface, 7,* 89–95.

Corrigan, P. W., MacKain, S. J., & Liberman, R. P. (1994). Skills training modules: A strategy for dissemination and utilization of a rehabilitation innovation. In J. Rothman & E. Thomas (Eds.), *Intervention research* (pp. 317–352). Chicago: Haworth Press.

Corrigan, P. W., & McCracken, S. G. (1995a). Psychiatric rehabilitation and staff development: Educational and organizational models. *Clinical Psychology Review, 15,* 699–719.

Corrigan, P. W., & McCracken, S. G. (1995b). Refocusing the training of psychiatric rehabilitation staff. *Psychiatric Services, 46,* 1172–1177.

Corrigan, P. W., & McCracken, S. G. (1997a). *Interactive staff training: Rehabilitation teams that work.* New York: Plenum Press.

Corrigan, P. W., & McCracken, S. G. (1997b). Intervention research: Integrating practice guidelines with dissemination strategies: A rejoinder to Paul, Stuve, and Cross. *Applied and Preventive Psychology, 6,* 205–209.

Corrigan, P. W., McCracken, S. G., Edwards, M., Brunner, J., Garman, A., Nelson, D., et al. (1997). Collegial support and barriers to behavioral programs for severe mental illness. *Journal of Behavior Therapy and Experimental Psychiatry, 28,* 193–202.

Corrigan, P. W., McCracken, S. G., Edwards, M., Kommana, S., & Simpatico, T. (1997). Staff training to improve implementation and impact of behavioral rehabilitation programs. *Psychiatric Services, 48,* 1336–1338.

Corrigan, P. W., McCracken, S. G., Kommana, S., Edwards, M., & Simpatico, T. (1996). Staff perceptions about barriers to innovative behavioral rehabilitation programs. *Cognitive Therapy and Research, 20,* 541–551.

Corrigan, P. W., Steiner, L., McCracken, S. G., Blaser, B., & Barr, M. (2001). Strategies for disseminating evidence-based practices to staff who treat people with serious mental illness. *Psychiatric Services, 52,* 1598–1606.

Corrigan, P. W., Williams, O. B., McCracken, S. G., Kommana, S., Edwards, M., & Brunner, J. (1998). Staff attitudes that impede the implementation of behavioral treatment programs. *Behavior Modification, 22,* 548–562.

Delamater, A. M., Conners, C. K., & Wells, K. C. (1984). A comparison of staff training procedures: Behavioral applications in the child psychiatric inpatient setting. *Behavior Modification, 8,* 39–58.

Department of Health and Human Services. (1999). *Mental health: A report of the surgeon general.* Rockville, MD: U.S. Department of Health and Human Services, Center for Mental Health Services.

Dickerson, F. B. (1993). Hospital structure and professional roles. In A. S. Bellack & M. Hersen (Eds.), *Handbook of behavior therapy in the psychiatric setting* (pp. 133–141). New York: Plenum Press.

Donat, D. C. & McKeegan, G. F. (1990). Behavioral knowledge among direct care staff in an inpatient psychiatric setting. *Behavioral Residential Treatment, 5,* 95–103.

Falloon, I. R. H., Boyd, J. L., & McGill, C. W. (1984). *Family care of schizophrenia.* New York: Guilford Press.

Fishbein, M. (1995). Developing effective behavioral change interventions: Some lessons learned from behavioral research. In T. E. Backer, S. L. David, & G. Soucy (Eds.), *Reviewing the behavioral science knowledge base on technology transfer.*

(NIDA Research Monograph No. 155, NIH Publication No. 95-4035, 246–261). Washington, DC: U.S. Government Printing Office.

Franco, H., & Kelly, T. H. (1994). Obstacles in the implementation of a behavior therapy ward in a state psychiatric hospital. In P. W. Corrigan & R. P. Liberman (Eds.), *Behavior therapy in psychiatric hospitals* (pp. 167–178). New York: Springer.

Garfield, S. L., & Kurtz, R. (1976). Clinical psychologists in the 1970s. *American Psychologist, 31,* 1–9.

Giffort, D. W. (1998). A systems approach to developing staff training. In P. W. Corrigan & D. W. Giffort (Eds.), *Building teams and programs for effective psychiatric rehabilitation: New directions for mental health services* (pp. 25–33). San Francisco: Jossey-Bass.

Glynn, S. (1990). The token economy: Progress and pitfalls over 25 years. *Behavior Modification, 14,* 383–407.

Hersen, M., Bellack, A. S., & Harris, F. (1993). Staff training and consultation. In A. S. Bellack & M. Hersen (Eds.), *Handbook of behavior therapy in the psychiatric setting* (pp. 143–164). New York: Plenum Press.

Hess, L. E., Corrigan, P. W., & Buican, B. J. (1994). *What psychologists working at state hospitals do.* Paper presented at the annual convention of the American Psychological Association, Los Angeles, CA.

Hogarty, G. E., Anderson, C. M., Reiss, D. J., Kornblith, S. J., Greenwald, D. P., Javna, C. D., et al. (1986). Family psychoeducation, social skills training, and maintenance chemotherapy in the aftercare treatment of schizophrenia. *Archives of General Psychiatry, 43,* 633–642.

Hunter, M. E., & Love, C. C. (1996). Total quality management and the reduction of inpatient violence and costs in a forensic psychiatric hospital. *Psychiatric Services, 47,* 751–754.

Jewell, T. C., Silverstein, S. M., & Stewart, D. A. (2001). Development and evaluation of a treatment manual and course for writing behavior contracts for people with severe mental illness. *Psychiatric Rehabilitation Skills, 5,* 255–271.

Kuipers, E. (2000). Psychological treatments for psychosis: Evidence based but unavailable? *Psychiatric Rehabilitation Skills, 4,* 249–258.

Lehman, A. F., Steinwachs, D. M., & associates. (1998). Patterns of usual care for schizophrenia: Initial results from the schizophrenia patient outcomes research team (PORT) client survey. *Schizophrenia Bulletin, 24,* 11–19.

Liberman, R. P., DeRisi, W. J., & Mueser, K. T. (1989). *Social skills training for psychiatric patients.* Boston: Allyn & Bacon.

Liberman, R. P., & Eckman, T. A. (1989). Dissemination of skills training modules to psychiatric facilities: Overcoming obstacles to the utilization of a rehabilitation innovation, *British Journal of Psychiatry, 155*(Suppl. 5), 117–122.

Liberman, R. P., Eckman, T., Kuehnel, T., Rosenstein, J., & Kuehnel, J. (1982). Dissemination of new behavior therapy programs to community mental health programs. *American Journal of Psychiatry, 139,* 224–226.

Liberman, R. P., Mueser, K. T., & Wallace, C. J. (1986). Social skills training for schizophrenic individuals at risk for relapse. *American Journal of Psychiatry, 143,* 523–526.

Linehan, M. M. (1993). *Cognitive-behavioral treatment of borderline personality disorder.* New York: Guilford Press.

McHugo, G. J., Drake, R. E., Teague, G. B., & Xie, H. (1999). Fidelity to assertive community treatment and client outcomes in the New Hampshire dual disorders study. *Psychiatric Services, 50,* 818–824.

Milne, D. (1985). An observational evaluation of the effects of nurse training in behaviour therapy on unstructured ward activities. *British Journal of Clinical Psychology, 24,* 149–158.

Milne, D. (1986). *Training behaviour therapists: Methods, evaluation, and implementation with parents, nurses, and teachers.* Cambridge, MA: Brookline.

Milne, D., Gorenski, O., Westerman, C., Leck, C., & Keegan, D. (2000). What does it take to transfer training? *Psychiatric Rehabilitation Skills, 4,* 259–281.

Morisse, D., Batra, L., Hess, L., Silverman, R., & Corrigan, P. (1996). A demonstration of a token economy for the real world. *Applied and Preventive Psychology, 5,* 41–46.

Mueser, K. T., Noordsy, D. L., Drake, R. E., & Fox, L. (2003). *Integrated treatment for dual disorders: A guide to effective practice.* New York: Guilford Press.

Nemec, P. B., & Pratt, C. W. (2001). Graduate education in psychiatric rehabilitation. *Psychiatric Rehabilitation Skills, 5,* 477–494.

Paul, G. L., & Lentz, R. J. (1977). *Psychosocial treatment of chronic mental patients: Milieu versus social learning programs.* Cambridge, MA: Harvard University Press.

Paul, G. L., McInnis, T., & Mariotto, M. J. (1973). Objective performance outcomes associated with two approaches to training mental health technicians in milieu and social learning programs. *Journal of Abnormal Psychology, 82,* 523–532.

Paul, G. L., Stuve, P., & Cross, J. V. (1997). Real-world inpatient programs: Shedding some light: A critique. *Applied and Preventive Psychology, 6,* 193–204.

Rogers, E. S., Cohen, B. F., Danley, K. S., Hutchinson, D., & Anthony, W. A. (1986). Training mental health workers in psychiatric rehabilitation. *Schizophrenia Bulletin, 12,* 709–719.

Rosenheck, R. A. (2001). Organizational process: A missing link between research and practice. *Psychiatric Services, 52,* 1607–1612.

Sackett, D. L., Straus, S. E., Richardson, W. S., Rosenberg, W., & Haynes, R. B. (2000). *Evidence-based medicine: How to practice and teach EBM.* Edinburgh, Scotland: Churchill Livingstone.

Silverstein, S. M., Bowman, J., & McHugh, D. (1997). Strategies for hospital-wide dissemination of psychiatric rehabilitation interventions. *Psychiatric Rehabilitation Skills, 2,* 1–24.

Silverstein, S. M., & Jewell, T. C. (2002). Effectiveness of a psychiatric rehabilitation training program for community services staff. *Psychiatric Rehabilitation Skills, 6,* 53–61.

Sluyter, G. V. (1998a). *Improving organizational performance: A practical guidebook for the human services field.* Thousand Oaks, CA: Sage.

Sluyter, G. V. (1998b). Total quality management in behavioral health care. In P. W. Corrigan & D. W. Giffort (Eds.), *Building teams and programs for effective psychiatric rehabilitation: New directions for mental health services* (pp. 35–43). San Francisco: Jossey-Bass.

Sluyter, G. V., & Mukherjee, A. K. (1993). *Total quality management for mental health and mental retardation services: A paradigm for the '90s.* Annandale, VA: American Network of Community Options and Resources.

St. Lawrence, J. S., Hansen, D. J., & Steele, C. (1985). An inventory to measure staff knowledge of behavioral methods with inpatient children and adolescents. *Journal of Behavior Therapy and Experimental Psychiatry, 16,* 317–323.

Torrey, W. C., Drake, R. E., Dixon, L., Burns, B. J., Flynn, L., Rush, A. J., et al. (2001). Implementing evidence-based practices for persons with severe mental illnesses. *Psychiatric Services, 52,* 45–50.

Wallace, C. J., Liberman, R. P., MacKain, S. J., Blackwell, G., & Eckman, T. A. (1992). Effectiveness and replicability of modules for teaching social and instrumental skills to the severely mentally ill. *American Journal of Psychiatry, 149,* 654–658.

CHAPTER 15

THE EVIDENCE-BASED PRACTITIONER: ASSESSING THE CULTURAL RESPONSIVENESS OF RESEARCH

Christine Marlow

The underlying premise of evidence-based practice is that interventions are based on knowledge accrued from systematic empirical research in the form of large-scale outcome studies or multiple single-system studies. The evidence-based literature has been dominated by discussions about how knowledge should be produced, many concluding that significantly more evaluation outcome studies, rather than descriptive and exploratory studies, need to be undertaken (Fortune, 1999; Thyer, 2001). Criticism has also surrounded single-system studies and their ability to produce new knowledge (Wakefield & Kirk, 1997); reasons for this include a lack of agency support; intrusiveness of the designs (Gorey, 1996), and unrealistic expectations for social work practitioners (Marlow, 2003).

Although these discussions about the production of empirically based research are critical for the success of evidence-based practice, they tend to overshadow another important aspect, namely, that the practitioner must serve as an informed "consumer" of research. As consumers, practitioners are required to extract the newly generated knowledge from the research and apply this information to their practice (Gambrill, 2003). The consumer aspect of evidence-based practice has been embraced by medicine—"the conscientious, explicit, and judicious use of current best evidence in making decisions about the care of individual patients" (Sackett, Rosenberg, Gray, Haynes, & Richardson, 1996, p.17)—but less so in other professions, including social work. There was an indication that, in the past, social work practitioners rarely read and applied the results of research studies to their practice (Kirk, 1991). With the growth of evidence-based practice combined with an explosion of information access, the potential for "consumption" increases exponentially. Complex and rich databases now are available. Today a social worker can readily access and search databases across disciplines using sophisticated search engines. Some databases even include critical reviews of the research, such as the Cochrane Collection Database (Bero & Rennie, 1995), providing an important resource for evidence-based practice (Gambrill, 1999). Other databases, such as the Sociometric Program Archives (Card, 2001) further enhance opportunities for research utilization.

As these databases grow and access to them increases, a new need emerges—

the need for instruction in their use and an awareness of their complexities. Research consumption or use can be overwhelming (Reid & Fortune, 1992), which provides difficult challenges for the evidence-based practitioner. Research use involves consideration of the complexity of the entire practice environment in combination with the characteristics of the knowledge or research itself (Staller & Kirk, 1998). Add to this the difficulties in actual interpretation and understanding of the research, and the task confronting the researcher/practitioner can be daunting. With respect to the rehabilitation counseling field, Olney (2002) states the following: "understanding theoretical analyses, complex statistics, or sometimes ambiguous findings has not been the highlight of most rehabilitation counseling programs. Former students, now enmeshed in the day to day struggle to provide services . . . are understandably unenthusiastic about maintaining such reading efforts" (p. 1)—a sentiment shared across many of the human service–related disciplines and professions. Few resources exist to guide the practitioner, though Katzer, Cook, and Crouch (1991) provide one example. Even social science research textbooks, including those in social work, seem to ignore or treat very superficially research use and consumption.

An entire aspect of research use, the cultural responsiveness of research, is almost completely ignored. This is not surprising given the overall paucity of information on research use overall but nevertheless interesting because cultural responsiveness is central to social work practice (Laird, 1995). Culturally responsive interventions and practices are developed for a wide variety of contexts and with several different populations. Some of this literature is empirically based and may even assess the cultural appropriateness or relevance of a specific intervention, which provides rich resources for evidence-based practice. For example, Kruzich, Friesen, Williams-Murphy, and Longley (2002) examined African Americans' perspectives on residential treatment and compared them with those of European Americans, noting that the values associated with the different groups could affect treatment outcomes. Acevado (2000) examined the perspectives of battered immigrant Mexican women on abuse and help-seeking; the findings indicated that participants' attitudes about seeking help were influenced more by cultural factors (e.g., gender role expectations) than psychosocial stressors such as financial dependency or immigration status. Herek, Cogan, and Gillis (2002) examined the effect of sexual orientation on victims' experience of hate crimes; they note variations among experiences of lesbian, gay, and bisexual participants in the study.

Another aspect of cultural responsiveness, and the one of concern in this chapter, is the extent to which research methods themselves are culturally responsive. If evidence-based practitioners are to use research effectively, they must not only be aware of empirical studies assessing the cultural appropriateness of certain interventions but also understand the cultural biases that can permeate the research studies.

Cultural bias in the research context includes a wide range of distortions that may characterize the research in favor of certain groups, whether these groups are based on sex, ethnicity, race, socioeconomic status, age, or sexual orientation, among others. Regardless of the research paradigm adopted, whether it is logical positivism or heuristics, all are subject to biases throughout the research process (Heineman-Pieper, Tyson, & Heineman-Pieper, 2002). Sometimes the researcher makes the biases explicit and discusses them frankly, customarily in the limitations section of a research report or article; such biases include those introduced through purposeful sampling or the lack of a comparison group or a measuring instrument of questionable validity. However, other cultural biases may not be so explicit and, in fact, may not be discussed at all if they are so deeply embedded in the research method or the assumptions underlying the research. Both types of biases, whether explicit or hidden, present challenges to evidence-based practitioners who seek to understand how they can apply the research findings to their practice.

This chapter will assess each stage of the research process for its potential cultural "pitfalls" and identify some strategies to overcome them. The chapter will conclude with a summary of the issues in the form of a culturally responsive guide that evidence-based practitioners can use as an aid in navigating the research literature.

CULTURAL RESPONSIVENESS THROUGHOUT THE RESEARCH PROCESS

Many people claim that the characteristics of the researcher are primary in conducting culturally responsive research. In the past, a fairly homogeneous group conducted most social work research, which resulted in an inherent bias in the types of questions asked and the research methods used (Davis, 1986). Now there is greater diversity among those undertaking research and a corresponding diversity of topics and methods. However, it is important to note that the problem of researcher identity bias still can exist. The discussion of the characteristics of researchers tends to focus on either ethnic or racial diversity or sex diversity, relatively ignoring another important source of researcher bias: socioeconomic status. Hodge (2003) points out this potential discrepancy between client and social worker, but a similar social class and subsequent value disparity can also exist between researcher and subject; after all, graduate students are more likely to be from the upper socioeconomic classes (Mullen, Goyette, & Soares, 2003). Although socioeconomic status is related to other aspects of diversity, particularly race and ethnicity, almost certainly the researcher will be well educated and middle class, which introduces a whole set of socioeconomic values that drive the research from the initial question to the interpretation of the findings.

A strategy to address this issue is for the researcher to undertake a participatory approach. If the research participants are directly involved in planning, designing, implementing, and disseminating the results of the research, the researcher's identity and associated biases become less influential in the research itself. Instead, it is the "subjects" who drive the direction of the research, a philosophy that is directly compatible with the empowering approach of social work in general. This research participation can occur in various ways and along different continua. Hick (1997) suggests two ways for researchers to understand and guide participatory research: a role in which the researcher has direct control over decision making about the research and a role in which the researcher actively conducts the research activities. One or both approaches can be adopted. Participatory research can also be conducted at the individual, program, or community level (Altpeter, Schopler, Galinsky, & Pennell, 1999). On the basis of Lykes's (1997) work in Guatemala, he has generated some criteria for evaluating the adequacy of participatory methods, focusing on adapting the methodology to local realities.

Participatory research has been conducted extensively throughout the world, and in developing countries, for many years. Just a few of many examples are Mwansa, Mufune, and Osei Hwedie's (1994) study of youth programs in Botswana, Swaziland, and Zambia, where the youths, officials, and academics were all involved in assessing income-generating projects; Coughlan and Collins's (2001) study in a children's home in South Africa, in which they proposed a model for the implementation of participatory research; and Crabtree, Wong, and Mas'ud's (2001) study of dengue fever prevention in Malaysia.

This wider adoption of participatory research in developing countries may be due in part to the wider use of community-based practice in these areas; participant involvement in the research can positively affect practice by serving as an entry point for community organization and development (Sohng, 1996).

However, in the United States, the majority of published research does not follow the participatory research model, with a few exceptions, including Stevens's (1999) study of adolescent developmental issues, in which teenage parents were actively involved in designing the research in addition to serving as respondents, and Reese, Ahern, Nair, O'Faire, and Warren's (1999) study of African Americans' hospice use and access. In the United States, studies instead are portrayed as involving a practitioner-researcher collaboration or partnership rather than following a participatory research model as such. Again, this may be a reflection of a greater emphasis on individual rather than community practice. An example of this is Galinsky, Turnbull, Meglin, and Wilner's (1993) description of the collaboration between researcher and practitioner in the evaluation of single-session groups of families of psychiatric patients, which includes a discussion of the issues that can arise from this type of collaboration. Similarly, Carise, Cornely, and Gurel (2002) describe a successful researcher-practitioner collaboration in substance abuse treatment and suggest multiple benefits of adopting this approach. For the clinician, these benefits include developing biopsychosocial assessment tools that are clinician friendly and research reports, written in an accessible way, that allow for the development of research-based interventions. Benefits for researchers include minimizing barriers to the implementation of research, which often occur when researchers undertake agency-based research.

Another variation of a participatory method, though it is not usually labeled as such, is the feminist approach to research. Here, the validation and acknowl-edgement of women's voices takes place, with the recognition that the research process involves a relationship between the researcher and participant that informs and directs the research rather than denying the presence of the relationship under the cloak of "objectivity" (Davis, 1986). For example, Drumm, Pittman, and Perry (2001) use a feminist approach to understand the emotional needs of ethnic Albanians in refugee camps. Emerging common themes included trauma, anxiety, boredom, and maintaining hope that they can return home. Using a similar approach, Barrios and Egan (2002) explore the experiences of Native American women living in the majority culture.

THE FORMULATION OF THE RESEARCH QUESTION

Research questions derive from several different sources, including direct practice issues, the research and conceptual literature, and personal experience. All bring their own type of cultural bias. Personal experience is grounded in a cultural context; thus, whenever possible, assumptions associated with that context should be presented clearly, but often they are not. Although the social work literature is becoming more diverse—with an increasing number of texts, articles, and journals devoted exclusively to diversity issues—there still remains an over-representation of studies that do not address cultural issues at all, either substantively or in the research methodology. For example, Low and Organista's (2000) review of the literature on sexual assault among Latinas disclosed a lack of attention paid to this population; they commented that the cultural and social characteristics contextualize this trauma in specific ways, which practitioners need to understand. Even if the focus of the research is specifically on intercultural issues, the tendency is to focus on differences rather than similarities, which results in biases. Ofori-Dankwa and Tierman (2002) suggest that this emphasis on differences "may reinforce stereotypes about ethnic groups because of the nature of the research process and the continued preference among researchers for the publication of any data that show statistically significant findings" (p. 1). They strongly advocate that researchers specifically look for both cultural similarities and differences.

Sex is one type of stereotype often perpetuated in research questions: in studies of caretakers, there is an assumption that they are females; in assessing child sexual abuse, there is an assumption that perpetrators are males and victims are females. Strug, Rabb, and Nantos (2002) studied the needs of male primary caretakers of children affected or infected by HIV/AIDS and, in doing so, stepped away from researchers' often-gender-biased lens. Although a strength of social work as a profession is to counter these stereotypes both in practice and in research, this is not consistently the case.

There is also a tendency to perpetuate stereotypes in the undertaking of needs assessments. This is because the purpose of this type of research often is to identify deficits or problems so they can be addressed through new programs or program changes. Identification of needs, though a necessary step in program development, can lead to the stigmatization and stereotyping of certain groups, including the extant examples of inner-city African American youth and crime, adolescent parents and inadequate parenting skills, and refugee groups and acculturation problems. Marin and Vacha (1994) provide an alternative approach to needs assessment by examining self-help strategies and resources available to people at risk for homelessness. They studied the practice of doubling up with friends and relatives and examined the participants' relationships with those who housed them. Recommendations were made to enhance the living conditions in these types of households in order to enable them to continue serving as a foundation in the prevention of homelessness.

THE DEFINITION OF VARIABLES

The most challenging aspect of avoiding cultural bias in research is definition of the research variables. Cultural bias is almost inherent in the way variables are defined, and the definitions need to be viewed with caution. For example, in some cultures, *independent living* may involve, for example, living with the family but being employed outside of the family setting, living with the family and being married, or being single and living alone. Cultural meanings pertaining to variables can be extremely complex. For example, Lowery (1998) describes how Native American perspectives on addiction and recovery are vastly different from standard U.S. views. They also go beyond the notion of "healing the spirit"—they conceptualize addiction as a crisis of the spirit with respect to the Native American colonization experience—to include such notions as balance and wellness. At first it may appear that mental health terms, such as *schizophrenia* and *depression,* have commonalities across cultures, but when examined from a worldwide cultural perspective, it is clear this is not the case. Vranckx's (1999) study of mental illness in Namibia pointed out that certain symptoms commonly experienced in schizophrenia among the OvaHimba were more congruent with ordinary experience, including hearing voices and seeing people who had died. Thus, the definition of these experiences as mental illness was problematic. This is not to say that, as a mental illness, schizophrenia cannot be universal in some ways, but perhaps it is so with more limited parameters. The conceptual spectrum is broad; the key is accurate identification of concepts within their specific cultural settings.

Some of these challenges of definition have been specifically addressed in social work and related disciplines. Researchers have undertaken exploratory studies seeking to describe the nature of a concept or behavior. Collier, McClure, Collier, Otto, and Polloi (1999) studied child abuse, investigating teachers' perceptions of child abuse in the Republic of Palau. They found that some cultures did not consider abusive, some traditional parenting practices that other cultures might perceive as maltreatment. Similarly, Negroni-Rodriguez's (1998) study of Puerto Rican mothers' thoughts and attitudes about child discipline provide some interesting insights into how social work concepts are culturally embedded. Patterson and Marsiglia (2000) examined the concept of natural helping among Mexican Americans and suggest that a full understanding of natural helping is essential before it is possible to compare the concept among groups.

Some research studies take the definition of concepts further and adopt a preliminary definition of a concept to be used in the research; they then test the definition in the study itself. This is a useful approach when there is reason to suspect that the concept is open to cultural misinterpretations. For example, Savaya and Cohen (1998) used both qualitative and qualitative methods to provide a preliminary definition of the reasons for divorce among Israeli Arab women. The findings support the authors' hypotheses that the reasons for divorce among Israeli Arab women—which include physical violence, emotional abuse, mental illness or addiction of the spouse, and active intervention of in-laws—are different from those for Western women, who are motivated more by emotional reasons, poor communication, and lack of self-fulfillment. Such factors were then included in a culturally responsive research instrument to assess Israeli Arab women's risk of divorce.

In definition of variables, it is better to err on the side of caution. For example, in Finch, Hummer, Kolody, and Vega's (2001) study of the role of discrimination and acculturative stress in the physical health of Mexican-origin adults, the authors understood that discrimination can take on multiple dimensions. They used a perceived discrimination measure that consisted of a four-point scale and included answers to the following questions: (1) how often do people dislike you because you are Mexican or of Mexican origin? (2) How often do people treat you unfairly because you are Mexican or of Mexican origin? and (3) How often have you seen friends treated unfairly because they are Mexican or of Mexican origin?

THE METHOD OF DATA-COLLECTION

Often researchers select a particular data-collection method because it seems to be appropriate for the topic under investigation. For example, a structured mailed questionnaire to parents might seem to be the best data-collection instrument for assessing the need for after-school programming in middle schools. However, this might be an inappropriate method for certain cultural groups in which the oral tradition is dominant. Other options that involve face-to-face interactions, such as focus groups or personal interviews, might be more appropriate and yield more valid data. Voss, Douville, Little Soldier, and White Hat (1999) studied Lakota healing traditions and examined their potential contributions to U.S. social work theory and practice. The authors recognized the challenge of collecting data with this cultural group and used a log of their observations and conversations.

Incorporation of participatory or collaborative approaches can yield appropriate data collection in specific groups. For example, Gibbs and Bankhead-Greene

(1997) discuss the methodological issues involved in conducting research with inner-city African American youth. The study investigated the impact of the verdict and the subsequent civil disturbances in Los Angeles's Rodney King police brutality case. The authors contacted several civic, religious, and professional leaders in an African American community in Los Angeles for suggestions on how to proceed with the study. After consultation, researchers decided to use focus groups and personal interviews with community leaders and youth to collect both qualitative and quantitative data.

Some researchers specifically examine certain measuring instruments to assess their validity with diverse populations; knowledge of the characteristics of populations with which the instruments have been validated become important for evidence-based practitioners. For example, Fries, Simon, Morris, Flodstrom, and Bookstein (2001) validated a pain scale in nursing home subpopulations; Gupta (1999) evaluated the validity of a caregiver burden scale with a number of different populations; and McCoach (2002) validated a school-attitude assessment survey with middle and high school students.

In addition to ensuring that the data-collection method is appropriate, the researcher should also determine whether the way in which it is administered is culturally responsive. In carrying out a needs assessment for socially isolated, recently immigrated Asian women, for example, not only should questions be relevant to the population, but also interviews should be conducted in a culturally appropriate manner. Ideally, to successfully engage participants in interviews and to obtain valid and reliable data, interviewers should be, at a minimum, familiar with participants' language and social and cultural mores, such as gender roles and role expectations.

Many groups have expected protocols for interaction between strangers (i.e., the researcher and the participant), particularly when the topic of discussion is sensitive, in which case more traditional data-collection methods may need to be modified. Kesby (2000) explored the use of visual diagramming as a means of facilitating rural Zimbabweans' communication about sexual health. He suggests that the use of visual diagramming in the context of a focus group provides richer and more-nuanced data about sexual activity than does dialogue alone.

POPULATION AND SAMPLE

There are well-known examples in the social science research literature of researchers using very selective samples and applying the results to broad populations. The classic example is Kohlberg's (1969) study of the development of morality; his sample consisted of male Harvard graduates, and he used the resultant model of moral development as a template to assess moral development of all individuals. Gilligan (1977) challenged Kohlberg's findings in her now-famous feminist version of his study. Today this is acknowledged as a fairly obvious example of cultural bias. Other examples are more subtle and can be difficult for evidence-based practitioners to identify, such as identification of the family as a unit of analysis but failure to include lesbian and gay families in the sample, which introduces the assumption that the unit is heterosexual. Other situations present even greater challenges to researchers, such as when some Native Americans speak, in the traditional way, about "all my relations" and refer to everyone and everything (Silko, 1996) including men and women, plants and animals, water and stones. Clearly, cultural concepts such as the previous example also have an impact on the measurement of variables and sampling.

If sampling is to be carried out systematically and in a way that will yield generalizable results, there needs to be a recognition of the complexity of demographic profiles and the subgroups that exist within certain populations. Flores, Bauchner, and Feinstein (1999) examined the impact of ethnicity, family income, and parents' level of education on children's health and use of health services and necessarily included a large, ethnically diverse national sample of children that included several ethnic subgroups. Similarly, Clark and Mendoza (2002) recognized that use of monocultural or bicultural subgroups in studies of Native Americans is problematic and ineffective; because of the complex history of Native Americans, researchers must use an approach that considers the equally complex Native American experience.

Of course, beyond gender and ethnicity, there are multiple dimensions to populations. One such dimension that is gaining increasing recognition for its importance, both in the United States and internationally, is the distinction between rural and urban. Many aspects of rural and urban lives differ dramatically, and not all of these are readily apparent. For example, Quandt and Rao (1999) studied food security among older adults, pointing out how urban and rural populations experience this very differently. They identified predictors of food security in rural Appalachia, including taking three or more prescription drugs, eating alone, and having an income of less than 150 percent of poverty level.

The standard texts in social science research methods often claim that, with certain groups, particularly the disenfranchised and marginalized, it is difficult if not impossible to construct sampling frames that allow for probability sampling. However, it would be a mistake to dismiss these groups as not researchable in terms of generalizing the findings. For example, Acosta and Toro (2000) included a probability sample of 301 homeless adults in their study, and Nam and Tolman (2002) selected a random sample of low-income African American women and Latinas from a Chicago neighborhood.

RESEARCH DESIGN

Research design also must be examined for indications of cultural bias. This issue is not as problematic in recent years as it was in the past, when comparison groups (usually those not receiving treatment or intervention) were selected from disadvantaged groups, as in the now classic Tuskegee experiment, well documented by Jones (1981), when researchers told several hundred poor African American men suffering from syphilis that they would receive free treatment even though there was no intention to give it. Ideally, randomly assigned groups ensure the comparability of the experimental and control groups; however, this is often difficult, if not impossible, to accomplish. If decisions must be made about participants in the comparison group, they are often made at a more subtle level and may still include biases. Parlee (1981) argues that in psychology research (and, in general, social science research), the choice of a particular comparison group demonstrates the scientist's implicit theoretical framework. She suggests that many of these frameworks are biased against women and that this bias can become a problem, particularly in the construction of "matching" comparison groups. Knowledge of the variables to include entails biases that might favor certain groups over others, or the variables may not be known at all. The choice of the comparison group defines the perspective that will dominate the research and, in turn, affect the findings.

As with sampling, part of the issue is understanding the characteristics of the various population subgroups and the relative complexities in seemingly similar groups. Guillette, Meza, Aguilar, Soto, and Garcia (1998) undertook an evaluation of preschool children who had been exposed to pesticides. They recognized the difficulty of establishing comparison groups in such a study, aware that there are many variables that influence children's growth and development. Subsequently, they selected two groups of Yaqui children who resided in the same area of northwest Mexico and who shared similar genetic backgrounds, diets, water mineral contents, cultural patterns, and social behavior but varied in their exposure to pesticides.

DATA ANALYSIS

Data analysis can also disclose cultural biases. The response rates from many surveys are low, not unusually around 20 percent, and when the characteristics of the respondents are examined, it is important to examine how the respondents differ from the original sample along various cultural dimensions. Subsequent analysis of survey and other quantitative data by means of statistical techniques is also subject to bias; texts on statistics and research methods describe potential problems with specific tests and approaches (Rubin & Babbie, 2001) and an occasional discrepancy between the research question and the reported data. A common source of bias is in the visual representation of data, in which the researcher's cultural biases may result in tables and charts that are misleading (Marlow, 2001). In addition, subgroups recognized when the variables were defined and the sample selected become "absorbed" and lost in the data analysis, often because of their low populations.

For qualitative data, data can be analyzed and hypotheses generated that directly reflect researchers' biases, which may negatively affect certain groups. Validation becomes particularly important, and evidence of the use of techniques such as posing alternative or rival hypotheses, examining negative cases, and using triangulation methods can help eliminate this bias. In Gregg's (1994) study of how women make choices about genetic and prenatal diagnoses, she suggested that women use a rational, cost-benefit approach, which her research confirmed. However, the research also provided unanticipated answers: she found that women also experienced pregnancy as a risk-laden path and experienced a state defined as "a little bit pregnant," two rival hypotheses that may not have emerged had she not explored a "cultural alternative" to her original hypothesis.

Triangulation involves the use of different research approaches to study the same research question. Researchers can achieve triangulation in several ways: by collecting different types of data, by having different people collect or analyze the data, by using different theories to interpret the data, or by comparing data from different sources. Varga (2002) used multiple data types in a study of pregnancy termination among South African adolescents, including focus groups, narrative workshops, role playing, surveys, and in-depth interviews. She suggests that the use of a single method to study dynamics of pregnancy termination may not be appropriate in the study of "clandestine or illegal behavior." Gutiérrez, DeLois, and GlenMaye (1995) examined the concept of empowerment from the perspective of human services workers. They state the following: "The data were independently analyzed by three readers. The three readers then met to discuss their findings and to work toward a common understanding. Areas of agreement and disagreement were noted during each meeting and became the focus for discussion. When the readers were satisfied that all themes from an interview had been identified they moved on to the next transcript" (p. 516).

REPORTING THE RESEARCH LIMITATIONS

As I mentioned previously in this chapter, researchers are sometimes explicit about the cultural limitations of their research. For example, in Pettys and Balgopal's (1998) study of the multigenerational conflicts of Indian American immigrants, they concluded that some of the study's limitations were that the findings had limited generalizability because the sample included only people from the middle and upper-middle classes; participants were not of the Brahman caste; and the families were from South India, which tends to be more conservative than other regions of India. Similarly, in Saewyc, Skay, Bearinger, Blum, and Resnick's (1998) study of sexual behavior and sexual orientation of Native American and Anglo-American adolescents, the authors found a significantly higher prevalence of homosexual, bisexual, and unsure responses among Native Americans; however, the authors stated that the large nonresponse rate for Native American adolescents raised questions about the cultural relevance of the survey method and underscored the need for more culturally relevant research tools and methods.

Thus, evidence-based practitioners, apart from needing to stay alert to subtle biases in the research literature, should carefully examine the research limitations as discussed by the researchers themselves.

CULTURAL RESPONSIVENESS RESEARCH GUIDE

The following questions can serve as a guide and review of the cultural responsiveness of research articles and studies for evidence-based practitioners.

- Who is involved in each aspect of the research decision making?
- Who actually conducts the research?
- To what extent are diversity issues a part of the research question?
- How are diversity issues included in the research question or topic?
- Are the variables defined within a cultural context?
- Is the measurement instrument validated for the population under study?
- Is the manner in which the data are collected appropriate for the study population?
- Is the sample representative of a specific population or subgroup?
- Are adequate procedures undertaken to validate qualitative findings?
- Does the quantitative analysis fully reflect the initial research question?
- Does the data analysis preserve the integrity of the original sample?
- Are the research limitations presented, and do they include any discussion of diversity issues?

Clearly, this is not a fully comprehensive list of methodological questions; however, it is intended as a starting point for evidence-based practitioners as they examine the research literature in the search for empirical evidence to support their practice.

REFERENCES

Acevado, M. J. (2000). Battered immigrant Mexican women's perspectives regarding abuse and help-seeking. *Journal of Multicultural Social Work, 8*(3/4), 243–281.

Acosta, O., & Toro, P. A. (2000). Let's ask the homeless people themselves: A needs assessment based on a probability sample of adults. *American Journal of Community Psychology, 28*(3), 251–273.

Altpeter, M., Schopler, J. H., Galinsky, M. J., & Pennell, J. (1999). Participatory research as social work practice: When is it viable? *Journal of Progressive Human Services, 10*(2), 31–53.

Barrios, P. G., & Egan, M. (2002). Living in a bicultural world and finding the way home: Native women's stories. *Affilia, 17*(2), 206–228.

Beccerra, R. M., & Tambrana, R. E. (1985). Methodological approaches to research on Hispanics. *Social Work Research and Abstracts, 21*(2), 42–49.

Benbenishty, R. (1996). Integrating research and practice: Time for a new agenda. *Research on Social Work Practice, 6*(1), 77–82.

Bero, L., & Rennie, D. (1995). The Cochrane collaboration: Preparing, maintaining, and disseminating systematic reviews of the effects of health care. *Journal of the American Medical Association, 274*(24), 1935–1938.

Card, J. J. (2001). The Sociometrics Program archives: Promoting the dissemination of evidence based practices through replication kits. *Research on Social Work Practice, 11*(4), 521–526.

Carise, D., Cornely, W., & Gurel, O. (2002). A successful researcher-practitioner collaboration in substance abuse treatment. *Journal of Substance Abuse Treatment, 23,* 157–162.

Clark, R. L., & Mendoza, R. H. (2002). Assessing cultural lifestyles of urban American Indians. *American Indian Culture and Research Journal, 26*(1), 1–13.

Collier, A. F., McClure, F. H., Collier, J., Otto, C., & Polloi, A. (1999). Culture-specific views of child maltreatment and parenting styles in a Pacific Island community. *Child Abuse & Neglect, 23*(3), 229–244.

Coughlan, F. J., & Collins, K. J. (2001). Participatory developmental research: A working model. *International Social Work, 44*(4), 505–518.

Crabtree, S. A., Wong, C. M., & Mas'ud, F. (2001). Community participatory approaches to dengue prevention in Sarawak, Malaysia. *Human Organization, 60*(3), 281–287.

Davis, L. (1986). A feminist approach to social work research. *Affilia, 1*(3), 32–47.

DeSchmidt, A., & Gorey, K. M. (1997). Unpublished social work research: Systemic replication of a recent meta analysis of published intervention effectiveness research. *Social Work Research, 21*(1), 58–62.

Drumm, R., Pittman, S., & Perry, S. (2001). Women of war: Emotional needs of ethnic Albanians in refugee camps. *Affilia, 16*(4), 467–487.

Finch, B. K., Hummer, R. A., Kolody, B., & Vega, W. A. (2001). The role of discrimination and acculturative stress in the physical health of Mexican-origin adults. *Hispanic Journal of Behavioral Sciences, 23*(4), 399–429.

Flores, G., Bauchner, H., & Feinstein, A. R. (1999). The impact of ethnicity, family income, and parental education on children's health and use of health services. *American Journal of Public Health, 89*(7), 1066–1071.

Fortune, A. (1999). Intervention research editorial. *Social Work Research, 23*(2), 2–3.

Fries, B. E., Simon, S. E., Morris, J. N., Flodstrum, C., & Bookstein, F. L. (2001). Pain in U.S. nursing homes: Validating a pain scale for the minimum data set. *The Gerontologist, 41*(2), 99–120.

Frisby, C. (1996). The use of multidimensional scaling in the cognitive mapping of cultural difference judgments. *The School Psychology Review, 25*(1), 77–93.

Galinsky, M. J., Turnbull, J. E., Meglin, D. E., & Wilner, M. E. (1993). Confronting the reality of collaborative practice research: Issues of practice, design, measurement, and team development. *Social Work, 38*(4), 440–449.

Gambrill, E. (1999). Evidence based practice: An alternative to authority based practice. *Families in Society, 80*(4), 341–50.

Gambrill, E. (2003). Evidence based practice: Sea change or the emperor's new clothes? *Journal of Social Work Education, 39*(1), 3–23.

Gibbs, J. Y., & Bankhead-Greene, T. (1997). Issues of conducting qualitative research in an inner-city community: A case study of black youth in post–Rodney King Los Angeles. *Journal of Multicultural Social Work, 61*(2), 41–57.

Gilligan, C. (1977). In a different voice: Women's conceptions of self and of morality. *Harvard Educational Review, 47,* 481–512.

Gregg, R. (1994). Explorations of pregnancy and choice in a high-tech age. In C. K. Reisman (Ed.), *Qualitative studies in social work research* (pp. 49–66). Thousand Oaks, CA: Sage.

Gorey, K. M. (1996). Effectiveness of social work intervention research: Internal versus external evaluations. *Social Work Research, 20*(2), 119–128.

Guillette, E. A., Meza, M. M., Aguilar, M. G., Soto, A. D., & Garcia, I. E. (1998). An anthropological approach to the evaluation of preschool children exposed to pesticides in Mexico. *Environmental Health Perspectives, 106*(6), 347–353.

Gupta, R. (1999). The revised caregiver burden scale: A preliminary evaluation. *Research on Social Work Practice, 9*(4), 508–520.

Gutiérrez, L. M., DeLois, K. A., & GlenMaye, L. (1995). Understanding empowerment practice: Building on practitioner based knowledge. *Families in Society, 76*(9), 534–542.

Heineman-Pieper, B., Tyson, K., & Heineman-Pieper, M. (2002). Doing good science without sacrificing good values: Why the heuristic paradigm is the best choice for social work. *Families in Society: The Journal of Contemporary Human Services, 83*(1), 15–35.

Herek, G., Cogan, J. C, & Gillis, R. (2002). Victim experience in hate crimes based on sexual orientation. *Journal of Social Issues, 58*(2), 319–340.

Hick, S. (1997). Participatory research: An approach for structural social workers. *Journal of Progressive Human Services, 8*(2), 63–78.

Hodge, D. R. (2003). Value differences between social workers and members of the working and middle classes. *Social Work, 48*(1), 107–120.

Hodge, D. R., & Williams, T. R. (2002). Assessing African American spirituality with spiritual ecomaps. *Families in Society, 83*(5/6), 585–595.

Jones, J. (1981). *Bad blood*. New York: Free Press.

Katzer, J., Cook, K. H., & Crouch, W. W. (1991). *Evaluating information* (3rd ed.). New York: McGraw-Hill.

Kesby, M. (2000). Participatory diagramming as a means to improve communication about sex in rural Zimbabwe: A pilot study. *Social Science & Medicine, 50,* 1723–1741.

Kirk, S. A. (1991). Research utilization: The substructure of belief. In L. Videka-Sherman & W. J. Reid (Eds.), *Advances in clinical social work research* (pp. 45–68). Washington, DC: NASW Press.

Kohlberg, L. (1969). *Stages in the development of moral thought and action*. New York: Holt, Rinehart and Winston.

Kruzich, J. M., Friesen, B. J., Williams-Murphy, T., & Longley, M. J. (2002). Voices of African American families: Perspectives on residential treatment. *Social Work, 47*(4), 461–471.

Laird, J. (1995). Cultural diversity in clinical practice. *Psychotherapy in Practice, 1*(4), 1–7.

Lifanu-Likotola, N. (1978). Community self-reliance and rural social development in Zambia's western province. Unpublished doctoral dissertation, Brandeis University, Waltham, MA.

Low, G., & Organista, K. C. (2000). Latinas and sexual assault: Towards culturally sensitive assessment and intervention. *Journal of Multicultural Social Work, 8*(1/2), 131–157.

Lowery, C. T. (1998). Social justice and international human rights. In M. A. Mattaini, C. T. Lowery, & C. H. Meyer (Eds.), *The foundations of social work practice: A graduate text* (2nd ed., pp. 20–42). Washington, DC: NASW Press.

Lykes, M. B. (1997). Activist participatory research among the Maya of Guatemala:

Constructing meanings from situated language. *Journal of Social Issues, 53*(4), 203–221.

Marin, M. V., & Vacha, E. F. (1994). Self help strategies and resources among people at risk of homelessness: Empirical findings and social service policy. *Social Work, 39*(6), 649–657.

Marlow, C. (2001). *Research methods for generalist social work.* Belmont, CA: Wadsworth.

Marlow, C. (2003, March). Evaluating the cultural responsiveness of social work research for evidence-based practice. Paper presented at the symposium conducted in honor of Elsie Pinkston, School of Social Service Administration, University of Chicago.

McCoach, D. B. (2002). A validation study of the school attitude assessment survey. *Measurement and Evaluation in Counseling and Development, 35*(2), 66–77.

Mullen, E. J. (1978). The construction of personal models for effective practice: A method for utilizing research findings to guide social interventions. *Journal of Social Service Research, 2*(1), 45–63.

Mullen, A. L., Goyette, K. A., & Soares, J. A. (2003, April). Who goes to graduate school?: Social and academic correlates of educational continuation after college. *Sociology of Education, 76,* 143–169.

Mwansa, L., Mufune, P., & Osei Hwedie, K. (1994). Youth policy and programmes in the SADC countries of Botswana, Swaziland, and Zambia: A comparative assessment. *International Social Work, 37*(3), 329–263.

Nam, Y., & Tolman, R. (2002). Partner abuse and welfare receipt among African American and Latino women living in low-income neighborhoods. *Social Work Research, 26*(4), 241–253.

Negroni-Rodriguez, L. K. (1998). Puerto Rican mothers' thoughts and attitudes about child discipline and child abuse: Their attributions toward and expectations of children. Unpublished doctoral dissertation, Boston College.

Ofori-Dankwa, K., & Tierman, A. (2002). The effect of researchers' focus on interpretation of diversity data. *The Journal of Social Psychology, 142*(3), 277–293.

Olney, M. (2002). Why research matters: Forging a reciprocal relationship between the researcher and the practitioner. *Rehabilitation Counseling Bulletin, 46*(1), 2–4.

Parlee, M. B. (1981). Appropriate control groups in feminist research. *Psychology of Women Quarterly, 5,* 637–644.

Patterson, S. L., & Marsiglia, F. F. (2000). Mi casa es su casa: Beginning exploration of Mexican Americans' natural helping. *Families in Society, 81*(1), 22–31.

Pettys, G. L., & Balgopal, P. R. (1998). Multigenerational conflicts and new immigrants: An Indo American experience. *Families in Society, 79*(1), 410–432.

Quandt, S. A., & Rao, P. (1999). Hunger and food security among older adults in a rural community. *Human Organization, 58*(1), 28–35.

Reese, D. J., Ahern, R. E., Nair, S., O'Faire, D., & Warren, C. (1999). Hospice access and use by African Americans: Addressing cultural and institutional barriers through participatory action research. *Social Work, 44*(6), 549–559.

Reid, W. J. (2001). The scientific and empirical foundations of clinical practice. In H. E. Briggs & K. Corcoran (Eds.), *Social work practice.* Chicago: Lyceum Books.

Reid, W., & Fortune, A. (1992). Research utilization in direct social work practice. In T. Grasso & E. Epstein (Eds.), *Research utilization in social work.* New York: Haworth Press.

Rubin, A., & Babbie, E. (2001) *Research methods for social work.* Pacific Grove, CA: Brooks/Cole.

Sackett, D. L., Rosenberg, W. M. C., Gray, A. M., Haynes, R. B., & Richardson, W. S. (1996). Evidence based medicine: What it is and what it isn't [Editorial]. *British Medical Journal, 312*(1), 71–72.

Saewyc, E. M., Skay, C. L., Bearinger, L. H., Blum, R. W., & Resnick, M. D. (1998). Demographics of sexual orientation among American Indian adolescents. *American Journal of Orthopsychiatry, 68*(4), 590–600.

Savaya, R., & Cohen, O. (1998). A qualitative cum quantitative approach to construct definition in a minority population: Reasons for divorce among Israeli Arab women. *Journal of Sociology and Social Welfare, 25*(4), 157–179.

Silko, L. M. (1996). *Yellow woman and the beauty of the spirit.* New York: Simon & Schuster.

Sohng, S. S. L. (1996). Participatory research and community organizing. *Journal of Sociology and Social Welfare, 23*(4), 77–97.

Staller, K. M., & Kirk, S. A. (1998). Knowledge utilization in social work and legal practice. *Journal of Sociology and Social Welfare, 25*(3), 91–113.

Stevens, J. W. (1999). Creating collaborative partnerships: Clinical intervention research in an inner-city middle school. *Social Work in Education, 21*(3), 151–162.

Strug, D., Rabb, L., & Nanton, R. (2002). Provider views of the support service needs of male primary caretakers of HIV/AIDs infected and affected children: A needs assessment. *Families in Society, 83*(3), 303–314.

Thyer, B. (2001). What is the role of theory in research on social work practice? *Journal of Social Work Education, 37*(1), 9–25.

Tierney, L. (1993). Practice research and social work education. *Australian Social Work, 46*(2), 9–22.

Varga, C. A. (2002). Pregnancy termination among South African adolescents. *Studies in Family Planning, 33*(4), 283–299.

Videka-Sherman, L. (1988). Meta analysis of research on social work practice in mental health. *Social Work, 33*(2), 325–338.

Voss, R. W., Douville, V., Little Soldier, A., & White Hat, A. (1999). Wo'Lakol Kiciyapi: Traditional philosophies of helping and healing among the Lakotas: Towards a Lakota-centric practice of social work. *Journal of Multicultural Social Work, 7*(1/2), 73–93.

Vranckx, C. (1999). Notes from Namibia: Assessing mental illness in a multicultural developing country. *International Journal of Mental Health, 28*(3), 38–43.

Wakefield, J. C., & Kirk, S. A. (1997). Science, dogma, and the scientist-practitioner model. *Social Work Research, 21*(3), 201–205.

CHAPTER 16

INFORMED CONSENT AND PRACTICE EVALUATION: MAKING THE DECISION TO PARTICIPATE MEANINGFUL

Tina L. Rzepnicki

Because social work practice is increasingly undertaken in environments governed by managed care organizations and with clients who have multiple vulnerabilities, evidence-based practice may be critical to the successful management and survival of social programs. In fact, it is likely that the demands of managed care will have a greater impact on the development of evidence-based practice than will "decades of social work education, paradigmatic squabbling, or academic dreaming" (Epstein, 1996, p. 99). In support of this movement, the National Association of Social Workers' Code of Ethics requires social workers to make practice decisions based on the best available evidence and to actively evaluate their practice interventions (National Association of Social Workers, 1997). However, the combination of social work practice and evaluation poses ethical challenges to the clinician. These challenges are due to the particular vulnerabilities of social work clients and the conflicts inherent in attempts to combine practice and evaluation goals (Bloom, Fischer, & Orme, 1999; Gambrill, 1997; Gambrill & Barth, 1980; Nugent, Sieppert, & Hudson, 2001; Proctor, 1990; Thomas, 1978; Wakefield & Kirk, 1997). Undoubtedly, these challenges have contributed to the reluctance of social workers to make use of single-subject designs in practice. Still, many practitioners engage in some form of structured data collection and analysis of change, even if they do not go so far as to apply single-subject evaluation methods. Increasingly, these activities will be viewed as an important part of direct service and management decisionmaking. Responsibility for the conduct of ethical practice and evaluation rests on the clinician's integrity; thus, it is important for practitioners to understand the legal, ethical, and procedural standards that serve to protect their clients from harm.

This chapter addresses issues of obtaining informed consent and emphasizes effective communication to enhance client understanding of how changes in their problems will be evaluated. For the members of society who are most at risk, extra care must be taken to avoid placing clients at greater risk than they already face as a result of their life circumstances. The process of informed consent is a vehicle for achieving this protection. Major goals of informed consent are to ensure (1) that clients understand what is being asked; (2) that clients can make knowledgeable decisions regarding their participation in service; and (3) that consent is given voluntarily, with no coercion and no negative repercussions for refusal. Social work practitioners need to be mindful of issues pertaining to obtaining informed consent not only for intervention but also for the explicit purpose of case evaluation.

Although it is understood that intervention and evaluation strategies may be inextricably linked in practice, this chapter attempts to distinguish them and to focus primarily on informed consent for the evaluation components. The distinction is important because of two common omissions in practice. First, when the social worker obtains agreement from a client to engage in a particular set of services or intervention, discussion of data collection and evaluation procedures, the rationale for their use, and related risks and benefits are not likely to receive the same careful attention. For example, the practitioner may discuss data-collection strategies but fail to carefully consider their social and psychological risks as well as benefits of the information they provide. Second, assessment of client progress at the individual level is not typically considered research. Structured evaluation methods, including systematic data-collection strategies (e.g., rapid assessment instruments, repeated observations) and single-subject designs, are taught to professionals to encourage a more objective basis for making practice decisions, not to publish or to contribute to general social work knowledge. Their application also benefits the social worker by building knowledge for his or her own practice, which encourages the development of a personal repertoire of effective strategies. In some cases, these efforts may lead to generalized knowledge through replication and publication, even though their primary purpose was to examine the impact of a social intervention for a particular client system.

ETHICAL EVALUATION STRATEGIES: A PRECURSOR TO INFORMED CONSENT

Practice evaluation requires balancing the goal of obtaining knowledge with the risks and benefits to individual clients. Tensions arising out of efforts to balance these goals have led to ongoing debate about the feasibility of using single-subject designs for case evaluation in the professional social work literature (Blythe, 1990; Corcoran, 1990; Dangel & Bronson, 1994; Downs & Rubin, 1994; Gambrill & Barth, 1980; Gingerich, 1990; Heineman-Pieper, 1985; Jayaratne & Kagle, 1994; Kagle, 1982; Nelson, 1990; Reinherz, 1990; *Social Work Research,* 1996; Thomas, 1978; Thyer, 1990; Tolson, 1990; Wakefield & Kirk, 1997). The traditional social work position has been that postponement of intervention to establish a baseline conflicts with a service orientation and jeopardizes the client's welfare. However, as Gambrill (1997) points out, to engage a client in change efforts without the ability to draw data-based conclusions regarding intervention effects is increasingly recognized as unethical—it subjects the client to risks without an ability to measure or verify the benefits. Emerging from applied behavior analysis, single-subject designs have made it possible to link changes in client functioning to the application of a specific intervention by reducing or eliminating alternative explanations in a structured and systematic way. Elsie Pinkston's mentoring, teaching, and scholarship have brought these scientific methods to many generations of social work professionals in the field and at both the master's and the doctoral levels. She has been a leader in adapting rigorous data-collection and analytical methods to the complexities of social work practice and in their dissemination (e.g., Pinkston, 1997; Pinkston, Howe, & Blackman, 1987; Pinkston, Levitt, Green, Linsk, & Rzepnicki, 1982; Pinkston & Linsk, 1984).

It must be acknowledged, however, that even though many practitioners do not implement single-subject design methods routinely, they still evaluate case progress (Blythe & Rodgers, 1993; Penka & Kirk, 1991). Evaluation methods may involve no more than the tracking of clear progress indicators. At a minimum, the strategies chosen must be capable of showing changes in client functioning. This means that measurements are sensitive to changes in the targeted areas of client functioning and that change is monitored over time, so that adjustments in treatment can be made when necessary. As social service agencies encounter renewed pressure to produce evidence of effectiveness and as the evidence-based practice movement gains momentum, there is likely to be less debate over this issue.

A sound approach to evaluation takes into account several considerations. Principles described subsequently are based, in part, on Lieberman et al. (1999). Their application increases the likelihood that intervention and evaluation strategies are implemented in a thoughtful and ethical way. More specifically, they maximize opportunities for knowledgeable decision making by the client as to whether to participate in intervention and evaluation activities.

Select an Approach That Is as Informative as Possible and Within the Agency's Program Context and the Client's Needs

Social workers need to be knowledgeable of the range of designs and data-collection strategies as well as their strengths and limitations, especially with regard to the kinds of information they can provide and their fit with individual client needs and in real practice settings. Practitioners should use the most rigorous but feasible evaluation designs. Although it is widely recognized that many social workers operate under conditions of limited resources, intense time pressure, and minimal administrative support, this may mean applying reliable and valid data-collection methods but not conducting a baseline.

Minimize Risks to the Client

Risks to clients are minimized when two conditions are met. First, the practitioner is bound to select the most effective intervention available. Second, selection of an appropriate approach to evaluation is then based on an analysis of risks balanced with the benefits of the alternatives. For example, single-subject methods offer options, such as multiple baseline designs to avoid a lengthy post-ponement of intervention. Risks to the client of withholding intervention are balanced with the benefit of being able to demonstrate the relationship between problem change and intervention. More than an academic exercise, this demonstration can provide powerful evidence that a client has control over the problem and/or can attribute improvements to his or her own behavior. In situations in which collection of prospective baseline data is not defensible (e.g., in serious abuse cases), a retrospective baseline may be most appropriate. Furthermore, a good evaluation design will provide timely information to the practitioner and client when services are not beneficial and when the client's problems are worsening.

Describe in Detail the Intervention/Evaluation Strategies and Modifications Made along the Way

Although detailed description of intervention/evaluation strategies and modification may be self-evident, it serves at least three purposes: (1) to accurately document intervention strategies, resources provided, and data-collection strategies; (2) to aid in the replication of successful interventions, which perhaps is most important for this discussion; (3) to help ensure that the client is knowledgeable about services and evaluation strategies implemented.

Engage in Discussion with the Client that Draws Links Between Intervention and Outcome and Encourages Transfer of Change

Visual inspection and discussion of data, graphs, and charts depicting changes in client functioning can be extremely useful in establishing attributions of change required for successful long-term outcomes, identifying points at which intervention failed, and providing opportunities for timely adjustments to problem-solving strategies. Interventions that produce initial improvements, however, may not lead to lasting change. Empirical evidence suggests that unless the practitioner plans for maintenance of effects, most problems are likely to revert to preintervention levels (Rzepnicki, 1991).

Conduct Postintervention Follow-up to Determine Durability of Effects and Transfer of Learning

It is important to discuss with the client plans to continue monitoring activities after termination, whether and under what circumstances follow-up contacts by the practitioner are likely. A poorly timed follow-up will lead to inaccurate evaluation and conclusions. Timing of follow-up is based on several factors, including the nature of the original problem, ongoing development and changing life circumstances of the client, and agency policy. It is most likely to yield useful information if it occurs when circumstances that previously led to the problem are present. Again, the client's participation in determining when and how data collection is to take place is crucial to its completion and informed consent is required for this aspect of practice as well.

VOLUNTARY INFORMED CONSENT

Informed consent is the application of self-determination. It indicates not only that the client freely consents to intervention and evaluation procedures (as intertwined yet distinct entities) but also that he or she is informed about options and about their relative advantages and disadvantages. It is a process, not a piece of paper, although elements of the agreement may be represented in a written document. In *A History and Theory of Informed Consent,* Faden and Beauchamp (1986) describe how informed consent entails more than the client's agreement with, submission to, or compliance with an arrangement. It is the authorization of a plan. It is also an ongoing process that requires revisiting at every decision point. Informed consent requires substantial autonomy on the part of the client: substantial understanding, substantial absence of control by others, and intentional authorization of a professional to intervene and/or evaluate progress.

Elements of Consent

An adequate consent statement, whether in written or oral form, incorporates considerations pertaining to both intervention and case evaluation. These elements explicitly recognize the client's right to make a voluntary and knowledgeable decision to participate by clearly establishing probable risks, benefits, and rights to which he or she is entitled as well as obligations to which he or she is bound. Table 16.1 outlines a sequence of steps offered as a possible approach to linking the two in discussion. The sequence is derived from the Code of Federal Regulations (45 CFR 46.116[a]), which governs the consent to participate in research, and from Bloom, Fischer, and Orme (2003), who also offer a model consent form.

Underlying informed consent is the assumption that the client understands the information disclosed by the practitioner. Research is lacking that examines the informed-consent process in social work practice. However, empirical studies of informed consent to participate in research show that patients and other human subjects often have little understanding of the purpose and procedures and risks and benefits of the protocols in which they participate (Benson et al., 1988; Irwin et al., 1985). Subgroups of psychiatric patients have even more difficulty comprehending clinical vocabulary used with them, but improving the quality of the information given to them improves their understanding of it (Benson et al., 1988; Meisel & Roth, 1983). Although clear and simple language is necessary, it is not enough to ensure informed consent. The practitioner must be certain that the information has been received and understood as well. In the case

TABLE 16.1   Elements of Informed Consent

Elements	*Basic actions*
1. Explanation of purpose and general procedures	Explain the purpose of your work together, specific problems and goals, expected duration of intervention, description of assessment, and intervention procedures. State that you will monitor case progress; explain the purpose of evaluation and general procedures.
2. Permission requested for voluntary participation	The client is asked if he or she is willing to participate in intervention and data-collection/evaluation activities. In general, clients should be told that they have the right to participate voluntarily and are free to refuse service or withdraw at any time without penalty. Some clients, however, may be required to participate by the court or some other authority. Perceptions of coerciveness can be diminished by providing service and data-collection options, within a more limited range, from which to choose.
3. Discussion of intervention alternatives, known risks and benefits	Disclose intervention alternatives and known effectiveness. Present a balanced view including all information, both positive and negative, likely to affect the client's decision to participate.
	Discuss reasonably foreseeable risks or discomforts of intervention—physical, social, psychological, financial—and their likelihood of occurring. Included should be the possibility of waiting lists, fees for service, and hidden costs (e.g., transportation, child care).
	Describe likely benefits of services (e.g., as specific improvements in functioning, return of children from foster care, termination of state agency involvement). Intervention and evaluation must have a favorable balance of risks to benefits for the client. Persuasive arguments for participation are acceptable, provided that the client is free of coercion and can balance known risks against benefits of participating.
4. Discussion of data-collection procedures, alternatives, risks, and benefits	Select data-collection and evaluation strategies. Decision will be governed by agency/program requirements in addition to client and practitioner interests. Recognize that the practitioner has access to a range of strategies requiring different levels of active participation by the client, with different risks and different benefits. Discuss alternative approaches to data collection and evaluation (for a good discussion, see Wakefield and Kirk, 1997). Include a description of potential evaluation designs and what can be learned from each (e.g., AB, ABAB, multiple baseline), pros and cons of collecting alternative forms of data (e.g., validity, reliability), use of data for ongoing modification of intervention, and implications for decision making by others (e.g., judges, protective services staff, psychiatrists, school personnel). Address potential risks and benefits with particular attention to the potential for serious deterioration of problems, relapse, and after-effects.

TABLE 16.1   *(continued)*

Elements	Basic actions
5. Discussion of confidentiality of records and possible risks to confidentiality	Discuss confidentiality of records and possible risks to confidentiality, including reportable conditions (e.g., evidence of child maltreatment, intentions to inflict harm on oneself or another). Describe how data are stored. Acknowledge that data collected for monitoring and evaluation purposes may be subject to unintentional breaches of confidentiality if they will be stored in unsecured computer files, transferred through fax machines, or other technological devices that may be subject to tampering or misdirected communications (Reamer, 1997). Promise to disguise information that could be used to identify client if case data will be used for purposes other than service decisionmaking (see #6).
6. Discussion and permission requested to disseminate service and/or outcome information	Identify other people who are involved in service decisionmaking and have access to service and outcome data (e.g., supervisor, judge). If further dissemination of case data is a reasonable possibility, request client permission for the specific use (e.g., conference presentation, publication).
7. Identification of whom to contact for answers to questions about client rights or for help	Give client a name and contact information for answers to questions about client rights or for help.

of children and other clients with limited cognitive functioning, a third party responsible for safeguarding their welfare must provide consent. I next address obstacles to meeting the requirements of true informed consent that arise from the unique features of social work practice, the settings in which practice often occurs, and the particular vulnerabilities of clients.

BARRIERS TO MEANINGFUL CONSENT AND STRATEGIES TO ADDRESS THEM

Capacity to Consent

For clients with cognitive or emotional impairments, determination of capacity to give informed consent may not be straightforward. Conditions such as schizophrenia, bipolar disorder, major depressive disorder, and anxiety disorder, for example, involve episodic psychosis or mood disorders, the effects of which may be subtle (Wolpe, Moreno, & Caplan, 1999). The presence of impairment, however, does not necessarily mean that a person is not capable of making particular decisions with respect to his or her participation in an intervention protocol or evaluation. A client may be capable of making some decisions or taking some actions but not others. An assessment must be made of the client's capacity to make a knowledgeable judgment to participate in treatment and evaluation tasks. Little guidance for this assessment is available in the literature.

Most of the medical, psychological, and bioethical literature does not distinguish between competence for intervention and research decision making. Not surprisingly, case evaluation, as a related set of activities, is not addressed at all, yet decisions regarding data collection, analysis, and documentation are likely to have significant repercussions for the client's (and sometimes the family's) further involvement with the clinician, agency, and judicial system. Major life situations may change as a result of findings from a case evaluation, including the temporary or permanent removal of children from their parents or their return home. Applebaum and colleagues (Appelbaum, 1997; Appelbaum & Grisso, 1995; Appelbaum & Roth, 1982) have identified criteria for assessing decision-making competence that are consistent with those commonly used by the courts:

1. The individual is able to communicate a choice. This requires that he or she be able to express their wishes in some way.

2. The individual is able to understand relevant information. This ability is decreased by impairments of intelligence, attention, and memory.

3. The individual is able to appreciate the nature of the situation and its likely consequences. This criterion differs from the criterion of understanding in that it requires the person to apply the information to his or her own situation.

4. The individual is able to manipulate information rationally by applying logic to compare the risks and benefits of their participation and weighing alternatives.

Appelbaum and Grisso (1995) review a large body of research examining each of these standards and have found that persons with psychiatric disorders, particularly schizophrenia, frequently exhibit impairments of one or more criterion ability (although in the MacArthur Treatment Competence Study, patients with schizophrenia and depression performed no different from the controls). It is worth noting, however, that the most dysfunctional patients were usually excluded from participation in research on decision-making abilities, which has resulted in samples biased toward healthier functioning.

Voluntary and informed client consent can be particularly difficult to achieve in situations in which lucidity and reason are intermittent. The frequency and duration of such periods and the corresponding quality of clients' decision-making competence are likely to vary depending on the severity and type of mental disorder experienced (Arboleda-Florez & Weisstub, 1998). These circumstances make it all the more important to frequently revisit and reestablish consent for all procedures, interventional and evaluative. In cases in which decision capacity declines over time (e.g., with Alzheimer's patients), it may be necessary to eventually obtain consent from a surrogate (someone who can, on behalf of the client, confirm that he or she would consent to participate if capable of doing so). This surrogate may be someone chosen by the potential participant or a family member appointed by the physician. Thomasma (1997) cautions that a substituted decision based totally on another's judgment of what is best for the client increases risk that the values applied are not shared by the person for whom the decision is being made. In fact, two medical studies found that surrogate decisions often reflected preferences of the substitute decision maker rather than of the patient (Muncie, Magaziner, Hebel, & Warren, 1997; and Warren et al., 1986, cited in Nelson & Merz, 2002). Thus, the decision maker should be someone who can determine the prior wishes of the person who becomes unable to make the decision or someone who can otherwise be trusted to act in the client's best interest (Chen, Miller, & Rosenstein, 2002).

The Communication Process

A variety of factors other than cognitive capacity also influence the client's understanding of consent information (Brody, 2001; McEvoy & Keefe, 1999). Barriers to accurate understanding include information overload, stress and illness, and language differences. The presence of these barriers results in clients comprehending only some of what is communicated and leads to deficits in knowledge that is important for full informed consent. When the client receives new information about the problem, services, or intervention or measurement strategies to be considered, new pieces of information must be processed with respect to previous knowledge before the information can be retained. This process requires that the practitioner place limits on the amount communicated. The literature on cognition suggests that people can only retain about seven new "chunks" of information at any one time (Klatzky, 1980). Social workers need to be sensitive to information overload and to communicate as clearly and simply as possible, without sacrificing accuracy or completeness.

So, how can the practitioner ascertain that information communicated is understood? Most practitioners simply ask, "Do you understand?" or "Do you have any questions?" to which clients quickly affirm their understanding without providing any real evidence of it. Using this strategy, the practitioner is likely to move on to the next item. In some instances, however, clients may be communicating their acceptance of the information rather than a real understanding of it (Faden & Beauchamp, 1986). A more reliable strategy to elicit understanding is to incorporate a feedback loop into the presentation of the new information, that is, encouraging the client to summarize, interpret, or engage in discussion about the information provided by the practitioner. The goal is to invite active participation in the communication by the client. This approach permits the practitioner to correct misunderstandings and to provide additional details in the context of a natural interaction. It enhances both understanding and effective communication more generally. Consequently, the process of informed consent takes place over time. Because humans are unable to accurately process and retain large amounts of new information, periodic review of the intervention and evaluation strategies and the particular agreements made as well as reestablishment of the client's commitment and consent to continue is essential.

Arboleda-Florez and Weisstub (1998) suggest that even though the practitioner may be able to determine whether the client understands the information, it is more difficult to establish the extent to which he or she understands the implications of participation at a more emotional level. For example, it is one thing to cognitively understand that monitoring progress requires that the client record negative thoughts in a daily journal. It may be more difficult for the client to appreciate the effort it takes to pull out a journal numerous times a day to record the necessary information or how to respond to someone who observes this activity. The ability to fully appreciate the consequences of evaluative activities in one's life may also be affected by factors beyond pure cognitive ability, such as level of stress, depression, or anxiety (Brody, 2001).

The practitioner and client may need to periodically revisit discussion of the data-collection activity to ensure that the client has the requisite knowledge and skill and is not feeling coerced in any way. Ongoing discussion of data-collection strategies, especially when the client is responsible for them, ensures that important data are obtained consistently and as planned.

If monitoring has provided evidence of improvement, this information can be incorporated into the discussion and is likely to reinforce continuation. If data show that the client's situation has not improved or has worsened, then review of the data creates an opportunity to modify the intervention or the evaluation strategy.

Problems of language and inference are barriers when the practitioner and client do not share a language or background knowledge (Faden & Beauchamp, 1986; Kuczewski & Marshall, 2002). Words may be unfamiliar to the client or have different meanings. Inferences may be incorrect as a result of a different knowledge base. Understanding and communication are impeded, and neither participant may be aware of it without efforts by one of them to elicit feedback. When the clinician and client share the same language, cultural differences can result in different meanings attributed to particular words. Even when client and social worker are from similar backgrounds, the use of jargon and scientific language may pose a substantial obstacle.

Strategies to improve communication beyond those described previously include use of multiple methods to provide information (e.g., other individuals who may be able to better communicate information, presentation of sample data-collection instruments, examples of graphs, video illustration, articles, hypothetical case examples), involvement of family members or other client advocates to address questions of participation on behalf of the client, and the encouraging of clients to audiotape during the presentation of information. At this point, studies have not been published that investigate the relative efficacy of these approaches (Wolpe, Moreno, & Caplan, 1999).

Role Constraints

Situational factors may compromise the ability of a client to provide informed consent freely. A common example is in child protective services, when families are under threat of court action, child placement into substitute care, or termination of parental rights, for noncompliant behavior. Even in cases when the practitioner holds no objective authority, the client may not feel free to refuse or propose alternatives because of the perceived status or power differences in their relationship (Faden & Beauchamp, 1986; Kuczewski & Marshall, 2002; Nelson & Merz, 2002; Rooney, 1992).

Lidz and Meisel (1982) point out that, in health care settings, the choice often made is one of passive acceptance rather than resistance. Institutionalized patients, for example, might be highly susceptible to the social work practitioner's recommendations. Institutionalization contributes to one's vulnerability by increasing dependency and cultivating peer pressure and a desire to please caregivers. Physical confinement and its consequences—whether in a health care setting, institution, or prison—reduce confidence in the voluntary nature of a resident's consent (Keyserlingk et al., 1995). In many other settings, too, a person's role can still carry with it certain expectations for behavior, as happens in some social institutions when there are particular expectations assigned to the staff and others assigned to the recipients/consumers of the service. For the practitioner wishing to elicit voluntary consent, the situation is made more difficult because individuals respond to similar situations quite differently. Objective criteria, then, cannot yet be established to determine which situations produce such patterns of behavior.

Measures can be taken to counter obstacles raised by role constraints. Relationships that are expected to encourage client role passivity can be identified and the conscientious application of all elements of informed consent reinforced in these situations. For example, Faden and Beauchamp (1986) suggest that explicit discussion of the purpose and importance of informed consent may help a client overcome the tendency to passively yield to an authority figure. In addition, the practitioner can encourage discussion of strategies and intervention and evaluation decisions and promote an environment in which the client is encouraged to raise objections about anything related to treatment or evaluation procedures. Another approach is to ask an objective third party, supervisor, or client advocate to monitor the informed-consent procedure. There are, of course, certain situations in which families may be concerned that refusal to consent to intervention and/or evaluation will result in a loss of service, benefits, or custody of their child. The social work practitioner must be especially sensitive to these possibilities and make certain that these risks are addressed as necessary. In some situations (e.g., protective service investigations), negative consequences of nonparticipation may be a real possibility and need to be communicated. In these cases, client autonomy can be preserved by offering choices, within a limited range, on service decisions, monitoring, and evaluation procedures.

Children and Youth

Children are defined as persons between birth and the age of majority (a determination set by state statutes). Their rights and responsibilities differ from those of adults. Weisstub, Verdun-Jones, and Walker (1998) identify two factors that make children unique as a vulnerable population. First, their dependency and legally recognized lack of competency is applied universally—that is, all children and all adults, at one time or another, share or have shared this status. Second, children are the only vulnerable population to have legally designated for them the persons responsible for making decisions on their behalf. Their dependency and statutory incompetence require that their legal guardian, most often their parents, must provide consent for their participation in intervention and evaluation efforts. Passive consent is not sufficient (i.e., leaving a message for a parent to call only if they are not consenting for their child to participate).

Because practitioners are necessarily concerned with the child's developmental needs and growing autonomy, children are also asked for their assent to participate in intervention and evaluation protocols, taking into account their age, cognitive abilities, maturity, unique strengths and vulnerabilities, and context in which the decision making is taking place (Jensen, Fisher, & Hoagwood, 1999).

Weisstub et al. (1998) conducted a comprehensive review of international research ethics codes and issues surrounding biomedical research on children and adolescents. Out of this review, common practices emerged pertaining to informed consent. These are useful for considering both the right of children to express their preferences and parental obligation to fulfill their duties with respect to social intervention and evaluation decisions. For example, children and their parents are encouraged to make joint decisions about participation. Children are given as much information as possible for them to understand and are also given the right to refuse or withdraw participation at any time. When a child is incapable of making a decision, the parent may provide consent, provided that the child does not object. However, objection by the child may be overridden by the child's legal guardian when the intervention or evaluation promises significant benefits.

Children should never be subjected to more than minimal risk as a result of intervention and evaluation activities.[1] As discussed previously, level of risk is assessed when selecting from among several interventions and evaluation approaches, some of which may result in greater likelihood of harm than others. Children may be particularly vulnerable to trauma that is typically less distressful to adults, such as social or psychological harm resulting from harassment by peers when observed collecting self-report data in school. In general, older children are more able to anticipate harms than are younger children. The practitioner should always seriously consider the possibility of such harms and take the necessary precautions.

---

1. Minimal risk is defined as the amount of risk faced in normal daily activities.

THE ETHICS REVIEW BOARD AND CASE EVALUATION

When should an ethics review board be involved in the consideration and implementation of practice evaluation procedures? Should it ever be involved? In general, ethics boards exist in settings in which risk management is an ongoing concern (e.g., hospitals, other health care settings) and in settings that undertake federally supported research on human subjects. They tend to include representatives from various disciplines and professions, including social work. There are two types of ethics review boards: the first often provides case consultation and nonbinding advice about ethical dilemmas in patient/client care and case decision making, including on informed consent issues (Reamer, 2000). The second type of ethics board, institutional review boards (also known as IRBs or human subjects committees), were mandated by the National Research Act of 1974 (Public Law Number 93-348) to be established in universities and other organizations that conduct federally funded research involving human participants. Institutional review boards review research projects before they are undertaken and annually thereafter until data analyses have been completed. Their purpose is to ensure that research is conducted in an ethically responsible way. Research ethics, originally set forth in the Belmont Report (National Commission for Protection of Human Subjects of Biomedical and Behavioral Research, 1978), are embodied in a comprehensive regulatory framework that institutional review boards apply to their research reviews, known as The Common Rule or Title 45 CFR Part 46. A major focus of the regulatory framework and the review process is the voluntary informed-consent procedure. Particular attention is paid to ensure that subjects are adequately informed of and protected from physical, social, and psychological harms as a consequence of participating in the research. For practice situations in which there are questions regarding level of risk to a client or the client's ability to understand and enter into a voluntary agreement, the practitioner may be able to get some help from an ethics board on how to present information or reduce risk. Ethics review boards can be useful for both case consultation and educational purposes.

Although the matter of taking intervention and evaluation questions to an ethics board has received little attention in the social work literature, it is addressed in the medical research literature. Verdun-Jones and Weisstub (1998) describe how applications of innovative therapy[2] and situations in which it is likely that patients do not fully understand the significance of the treatment and the alternatives are treated as experiments and submitted to the ethics committee for review. Ideally, the ethics committee measures the strength of the expected benefits against the sum of the assessment, measurement, and intervention procedures

---

2. *Innovative therapy* is defined as medical procedures that are administered for the benefit of a specific patient but that have uncertain outcomes or the application of tested procedures in novel contexts.

in the protocol. Focus on the interrelationship among the assessment, diagnostic, and measurement procedures on the one hand and the therapeutic procedure on the other hand ensures that the measures are all necessary and that the client is not subjected to extra, nonessential procedures. In addition, the board considers the immediacy of therapeutic benefit. How long will it be before the client is likely to experience benefits of the intervention? How does this weigh in the risk-benefit analysis? Finally, the committee considers the risks involved in the evaluative design as measured against the potential benefits to be gained. If the conclusion drawn is that the intervention is primarily experimental and that there is more than minimal risk of harm likely to result from application of the particular intervention, evaluation design, or measurement strategy, then the intervention or evaluation procedures are expected to be reconsidered.

Little has been written specifically on this issue as applied to social work practice, but I cannot think of a good reason why such an approach should not be extended to social work practice situations. Bruce Thyer (1993) has suggested that institutional review boards be avoided whenever possible because they represent "a major impediment to the timely completion of evaluative research projects" (p. 140). He makes this recommendation in the context of evaluating routine practice, with an emphasis on evaluation as an essential component of intervention, and thus would probably not disagree with the approach described previously. He goes on to say, however, that other common criteria for a review by institutional review boards, including intention to publish the evaluation, "have little bearing on the protection of human subjects and should not be determinants of whether a given project should be subject to [institutional review board] approval" (p. 141). His position ignores potentially serious risks to confidentiality of data and client anonymity that extend beyond social or psychological risks customarily found in practice.

Nonetheless, barriers to practitioners' use of ethics review boards must be acknowledged. Many agencies do not have their own ethics committees, and the logistics of submitting a protocol for review and obtaining approval may require an unreasonable delay in services for clients with urgent problems (the obstacle to which Thyer alludes). In these cases, the practitioner is wise to scale back the experimental aspects of intervention and search existing knowledge for a more evidenced-based approach. Public dissemination through publication or conference presentation, if desired, can be pursued with client permission and after disguising identifying case information.

CONCLUSION

Individual case study methods and single-subject designs are taught to social work students with the hope that they will be used to assess whether client functioning improves or deteriorates and to make timely midcourse corrections in helping strategies. At this point in time, few social workers actually conduct formal evaluations of practice. The managed care environment, renewed calls to demonstrate effectiveness, and the push for evidence-based practice all require a renewed commitment to systematic data collection for case decision making and ethically sound practice evaluations. An important component of this commitment is reexamination of the informed-consent process and its relation to data-collection activities.

In response to the changing practice environment, this chapter addressed several issues that pertain to obtaining meaningful informed consent for evidence-based practice. Principles for selecting appropriate evaluation strategies were presented as an antecedent to informed consent. Elements of the consent process were considered along with communication issues and other obstacles to obtaining voluntary informed consent. Finally, the potential for ethics boards to play a role in helping social work practitioners protect their clients was described.

Extra vigilance is required because social work clients are increasingly members of vulnerable populations, the oppressed, and the disenfranchised. Many clients are involuntary service recipients as a result of legal mandate or informal pressure applied by other professionals and service providers or family members. Regardless of the situation, full and consensual understanding of the nature of intervention and evaluation procedures forms the basis of a trusting and respectful relationship between the social worker and client. Practitioners are advised to always make sure that clients have provided voluntary informed consent and are well informed about the treatment options, strategies for monitoring progress, and risks and benefits of service and evaluation strategies. Meaningful informed consent begins with the initial session and is revisited in each subsequent encounter. In the end, the best protection is that provided by a practitioner who has the client's interests at heart.

REFERENCES

Appelbaum, P. S. (1997). Patients' competence to consent to neurobiological research. In A. E. Shamoo (Ed.), *Ethics in neurobiological research with human subjects: The Baltimore Conference on Ethics* (pp. 253–264). Amsterdam, The Netherlands: Gordon and Breach.

Appelbaum, P. S., & Grisso, T. (1995). The MacArthur Treatment Competence Study, I: Mental illness and competence to consent to treatment. *Law and Human Behavior, 19,* 105–126.

Appelbaum, P. S., & Roth, L. H. (1982). Competency to consent to research: A psychiatric overview. *Archives of General Psychiatry, 39,* 951–958.

Arboleda-Florez, J., & Weisstub, D. N. (1998). Ethical research with vulnerable populations: The mentally disordered. In D. N. Weisstub (Ed.), *Research on human subjects: Ethics, law, and social policy* (pp. 433–450). Kidlington, Oxford, UK: Elsevier Science.

Benson, P., Roth, L. H., Appelbaum, P. S., Lidz, C. W., & Winslade, W. (1988). Information disclosure, subject understanding, and informed consent in psychiatric research. *Law and Human Behavior, 12,* 455–475.

Bloom, M., Fischer, J., & Orme, J. (2003). *Evaluating practice: Guidelines for the accountable professional* (4th ed.). Boston: Allyn & Bacon.

Blythe, B. J. (1990). Improving the fit between single-subject designs and practice. In L. Videka-Sherman & W. J. Reid (Eds.), *Advances in clinical social work research* (pp. 29–34). Silver Spring, MD: NASW Press.

Blythe, B. J., & Rodgers, A. Y. (1993). Evaluating our own practice: Past, present, and future trends. *Journal of Social Service Research, 18*(1/2), 101–119.

Brody, B. A. (2001). Making informed consent meaningful. *IRB Ethics and Human Research, 23*(5), 1–5.

Chen, D. T., Miller, F. G., & Rosenstein, D. L. (2002). Enrolling decisionally impaired adults in clinical research. *Medical Care, 40*(9), 20–29.

Corcoran, K. J. (1990). Illustrating the value of practice wisdom. In L. Videka-Sherman & W. J. Reid (Eds.), *Advances in clinical social work research* (pp. 55–57). Silver Spring, MD: NASW Press.

Dangel, R. F., & Bronson, D. E. (1994). Is a scientist-practitioner model appropriate for direct social work practice? In W. W. Hudson & P. S. Nurius (Eds.), *Controversial issues in social work research* (pp. 75–87). Boston: Allyn & Bacon.

Downs, W. R., & Rubin, A. (1994). Should single-case evaluation techniques be encouraged? In W. W. Hudson & P. S. Nurius (Eds.), *Controversial issues in social work research* (pp. 113–127). Boston: Allyn & Bacon.

Epstein, I. (1996). In quest of a research-based model for clinical practice: Or, why can't a social worker be more like a researcher? *Social Work Research, 20*(2), 97–106.

Faden, R. R., & Beauchamp, T. L. (1986). *A history and theory of informed consent.* New York: Oxford University Press.

Gambrill, E. D. (1997). *Social work practice: A critical thinker's guide.* New York: Oxford University Press.

Gambrill, E., & Barth, R. (1980). Single-case study designs revisited. *Social Work Research and Abstracts, 16*(3), 15–20.

Gingerich, W. J. (1990). Re-thinking single-case evaluation. In L. Videka-Sherman & W. J. Reid (Eds.), *Advances in clinical social work research* (pp. 11–24). Silver Spring, MD: NASW Press.

Heineman-Pieper, M. (1985). The future of social work research. *Social Work Research and Abstracts, 21*(4), 3–11.

Irwin, J., Lovitz, A. A., Marderm S. R., Mintz, J., Winslade, W. J., Van Putten, T., et al. (1985). Psychotic patients' understanding of informed consent. *American Journal of Psychiatry, 142*(11), 1351–1354.

Jayaratne, S., & Kagle, J. D. (1994). Should systematic assessment, monitoring, and evaluation tools be used as empowerment aids for clients? In W. W. Hudson & P. S. Nurius (Eds.), *Controversial issues in social work research* (pp. 88–99). Boston: Allyn & Bacon.

Jensen, P. S., Fisher, C. B., & Hoagwood, K. (1999). Special issues in mental health/illness research with children and adolescents. In H. A. Pincus, J. A. Lieberman, & S. Ferris (Eds.), *Ethics in psychiatric research* (pp. 159–175). Washington, DC: American Psychiatric Association.

Kagle, J. D. (1982). Using single-subject measures in practice decisions: Systematic documentation or distortion? *Arete, 7,* 1–9.

Keyserlingk, E. W., et al. (1995). Proposed guidelines for the participation of persons with dementia as research subjects. *Perspectives in Biology and Medicine, 38,* 319.

Klatzky, R. L. (1980). *Human memory: Structures and processes* (2nd ed.). San Francisco: Freeman.

Kuczewski, M. G., & Marshall, P. (2002). The decision dynamics of clinical research: The context and process of informed consent. *Medical Care, 40*(9), 45–54.

Lidz, C. W.., & Meisel, A. (1982). Informed consent and the structure of medical care. In President's Commission for the Study of Ethical Problems in Medicine and Biomedical and Behavioral Research (Ed.), *Making health care decisions: A report on the ethical and legal implications of informed consent in the patient-practitioner relationship* (Vol. 2, pp. 391–392). Washington, DC: Government Printing Office.

Lieberman, J. A., Stroup, S., Laska, E., Volavka, J., Gelenberg, A., Rush, A. J., et al. (1999). Issues in clinical research design: Principles, practices, and controversies. In H. A. Pincus, J. A. Lieberman, & S. Ferris (Eds.), *Ethics in psychiatric research* (pp. 23–60). Washington, DC: American Psychiatric Association.

McEvoy, J. P., & Keefe, R. S. (1999). Informing subjects of risks and benefits. In H. A. Pincus, J. A. Lieberman, & S. Ferris (Eds.), *Ethics in psychiatric research* (pp. 129–157). Washington, DC: American Psychiatric Association.

Meisel, A., & Roth, L. (1983). Toward an informed discussion of informed consent: A review and critique of empirical studies. *Arizona Law Review, 15,* 265–346.

Muncie, H. L., Jr., Magaziner, J., Hebel, J. R., & Warren, J. W. (1997). Proxies' decisions about clinical research participation for their charges. *Journal of the American Geriatric Society, 45,* 929–933.

National Association of Social Workers. (1997). *Code of ethics.* Silver Spring, MD: NASW Press.

National Commission for Protection of Human Subjects of Biomedical and Behavioral Research. (1978). *The Belmont Report: Ethical principles and guidelines for the protection of human subjects of research* (DHEW Publication No. OS 78-0012). Washington, DC: U.S. Government Printing Office.

Nelson, J. C. (1990). Single-case research and traditional practice: Issues and possibilities. In L. Videka-Sherman & W. J. Reid (Eds.), *Advances in clinical social work research* (pp. 37–47). Silver Spring, MD: NASW Press.

Nelson, R. M., & Merz, J. F. (2002). Voluntariness of consent for research: An empirical and conceptual review. *Medical Care, 40*(9), 69–80.

Nugent, W. R., Sieppert, J. D., & Hudson, W. W. (2001). *Practice evaluation for the 21st century.* Belmont, CA: Wadsworth-Brooks/Cole.

Penka, C. E., & Kirk, S. A. (1991). Practitioner involvement in clinical evaluation. *Social Work, 36*(6), 513–518.

Pinkston, E. M. (1997). A supportive environment for old age. In D. M. Baer & E. M. Pinkston (Eds.), *Environment and behavior* (pp. 258–268). Boulder, CO: Westview Press.

Pinkston, E. M., Howe, M. W., & Blackman, D. K. (1987). Medical social work management of urinary incontinence in the elderly: A behavioral approach. *Journal of Social Service Research, 10*(2/3/4), 179–194.

Pinkston, E. M., Levitt, J. L., Green, G. R., Linsk, N. L., & Rzepnicki, T. L. (1982). *Effective social work practice: Advanced techniques for behavioral intervention with individuals, families, and institutional staff.* San Francisco: Jossey-Bass.

Pinkston, E. M., & Linsk, N. L. (1984). *Care of the elderly: A family approach.* New York: Pergamon Press.

Proctor, E. K. (1990). Evaluating clinical practice: Issues of purpose and design. *Social Work Research and Abstracts, 26*(1), 32–40.

Reamer, F. G. (2000). Ethical issues in direct practice. In P. Allen-Meares & C. Garvin

(Eds.), *The handbook of social work direct practice* (pp. 589–610). Thousand Oaks, CA: Sage.

Reinherz, H. (1990). Beyond regret: Single-case evaluations and their place in social work education and practice. In L. Videka-Sherman & W. J. Reid (Eds.), *Advances in clinical social work research* (pp. 25–28). Silver Spring, MD: NASW Press.

Rooney, R. H. (1992). *Strategies for work with involuntary clients*. New York: Columbia University Press.

Rzepnicki, T. L. (1991). Enhancing the durability of intervention gains: A challenge for the 1990s. *Social Service Review, 65*(1), 92–111.

Social Work Research. (1996). Book forum on the scientist-practitioner [Special issue]. *Social Work Research, 20*(2).

Thomas, E. (1978). Research and service in single-case experimentation: Conflicts and choices. *Social Work Research and Abstracts, 14*(4), 20–31.

Thomasma, D. C. (1997). A communal model for presumed consent for research on the neurologically vulnerable. In A. E. Shamoo (Ed.), *Ethics in neurobiological research with human subjects: The Baltimore Conference on Ethics* (pp. 239–251). Amsterdam, The Netherlands: Gordon and Breach.

Thyer, B. A. (1990). Single-system research designs in social work practice. In L. Videka-Sherman & W. J. Reid (Eds.), *Advances in clinical social work research* (pp. 34–36). Silver Spring, MD: NASW Press.

Thyer, B. A. (1993). Promoting evaluation research in the field of family preservation. In E. S. Morton & R. K. Grigsby (Eds.), *Advancing family preservation practice* (pp. 131–149). Newbury Park, CA: Sage.

Tolson, E. R. (1990). Why don't practitioners use single-subject designs? In L. Videka-Sherman & W. J. Reid (Eds.), *Advances in clinical social work research* (pp. 58–66). Silver Spring, MD: NASW Press.

Verdun-Jones, S. N., & Weisstub, D. N. (1998). Drawing the distinction between therapeutic research and non-therapeutic experimentation: Clearing a way through the definitional thicket. In D. N. Weisstub (Ed.), *Research on human subjects: Ethics, law, and social policy* (pp. 88–110). Kidlington, Oxford, UK: Elsevier Science.

Wakefield, J., & Kirk, S. (1997). What the practitioner knows versus what the client is told: Neglected dilemmas of informed consent in an account of single-system experimental designs. *Journal of Social Work Education, 33*(2), 275–291.

Warren, J. W., Sobal, J., Tenney, J. H., Hoopes, J. M., Damron, D., Levenson, S. (1986). Informed consent by proxy: An issue in research with elderly patients. *New England Journal of Medicine, 315*(18), 1124–1128.

Weisstub, D. N., Verdun-Jones, S. N., & Walker, J. (1998). Biomedical experimentation with children: Balancing the need for protective measures with the need to respect children's developing ability to make significant life decisions for themselves. In D. N. Weisstub (Ed.), *Research on human subjects: Ethics, law, and social policy* (pp. 380–404). Kidlington, Oxford, UK: Elsevier Science.

Wolpe, P. R., Moreno, J., & Caplan, A. L. (1999). Ethical principles and history. In H. A. Pincus, J. A. Lieberman, & S. Ferris (Eds.), *Ethics in psychiatric research* (pp. 1–21). Washington, DC: American Psychiatric Association.

CHAPTER 17

Psychosocial Assessment of Teenage Parents: Lessons Learned in Its Application to Child Welfare

Karen S. Budd

Adolescent parenthood is associated with a host of risks and disadvantages that has been well documented by researchers (e.g., Brooks-Gunn & Chase-Landsdale, 1995; Furstenberg, Brooks-Gunn, & Chase-Landsdale, 1989; Hayes, 1987; Rosenheim & Testa, 1992). For example, teenage mothers are less likely than older mothers of similar backgrounds to complete their education, obtain marketable job skills, enter into stable marriages, have realistic expectations of children's development, and interact verbally with their children. Much less is known about adolescent fathers, but they also are subject to some of the same disadvantages as their female counterparts (Elster & Lamb, 1985).

The current chapter deals with a subgroup of teen parents who, by virtue of their life circumstances and background, are at elevated risk of difficulties in both personal adjustment and parenting: These young parents are in state foster care because of abuse or neglect in their families of origin. The term *foster care,* as it is used in this chapter, includes a variety of out-of-home placements, such as relative or nonrelative homes, group homes, independent or cooperative living arrangements, and institutional facilities.

Adolescent parents who choose to keep and care for their children present unique challenges to the child-welfare system beyond those normally associated with serving adolescents in foster care (Children's Defense Fund, 1987; National Research Council, 1993). Living arrangements for a parenting teen need to accommodate both the teen and the child(ren), and they must provide appropriate childcare supervision. Adolescent parents need access to daycare and health care services for their children. Because teenage parents are at high risk of school dropout and its associated negative consequences (Card & Wise, 1981), supportive services are needed to facilitate educational achievement. Many young parents are unprepared for the responsibilities of parenting and require training in basic child-rearing skills (Panzarine, 1988). Many need counseling to address emotional difficulties that are exacerbated by neglect, abuse, and/or family disruption, coupled with the stresses of early parenting. A frequent concern that service providers express informally is that teenage parents in foster care are unreceptive to services, with the result that many adolescents fail to receive attention except when crises occur (Stockman & Budd, 1997).

This chapter describes a comprehensive approach for assessing the service needs of adolescent parents in foster care. The model was developed on the basis of evidence in the empirical literature regarding risks and protective factors affecting teenage parents and on the practical experiences of social service workers who collaborated with the author in its design and application. Initial and periodic assessments of youth are integral to providing adequate services. Assessment should focus on the identification of the presence and severity of personal and parenting problems in need of intervention and the identification of compensating strengths that may serve as protective factors. The assessment model described herein consists of a two-tier approach: (1) initial screening of all adolescents who are pregnant or have given birth to a child and (2) more in-depth psychosocial assessment of adolescent parents who are identified as being at clinical risk or having special needs. The model is an outgrowth of a joint project between the Illinois Department of Children and Family Services (DCFS) and DePaul University that was conducted over a five-year period from 1991 to 1996. Although the project dealt only with adolescent mothers, the assessment model can be applied to both male and female youth. Limited aspects of this model have been applied in subsequent DCFS services for teenage parents.

This chapter discusses the rationale, method, and the potential benefits and challenges of implementing a comprehensive assessment model tailored to adolescent parents in the child protection system. The literature review that follows highlights findings of research relevant to adolescent parents in foster care and introduces the Department of Children and Family Services–DePaul project. Subsequent sections provide a description of the screening and psychosocial assessment approach, findings from use of the psychosocial assessment protocol with teenage mothers in Illinois wardship, and systemwide issues involved in implementing such an assessment approach.

LITERATURE REVIEW

There is a large literature on the prevalence of adolescent motherhood, the consequences of teenage childbearing for mothers and their children, and youth in foster care. In contrast, little research has focused specifically on teenage fathers or on adolescents in foster care who are parents. Nevertheless, the available literature is useful for identifying aspects of assessment relevant to teenage parents in wardship.

Prevalence and Antecedents of Adolescent Motherhood

The topic of teenage pregnancy evokes different reactions depending on one's perspective. An adolescent mother interviewed as part of the DCFS-DePaul project (Budd & Kane, 1992) described becoming pregnant as a prized achieve-ment—"My friends had a party for me when I found out because they didn't think it would happen to me." More often, teens report pregnancy as an unplanned and unwelcome event but one to which they become increasingly committed as the pregnancy proceeds, if they decide to bring their child to term (Furstenberg et al., 1989).

In contrast, social, health, and policy analysts have viewed teenage preg-nancy as a serious public concern since the early 1960s (Alan Guttmacher Insti-tute, 1981; Furstenberg et al., 1989; Hayes, 1987; Hofferth & Hayes, 1987). Two demographic changes that thrust teenage pregnancy and childbearing into na-tional visibility were increasing rates of sexual activity among teenagers and de-creasing rates of teen marriage. These two factors resulted in an increased preva-lence of single teen mothers. Despite that the annual rate of teen births has declined from more than ninety births per one thousand females in the 1950s to fewer than fifty births per one thousand females by the early 2000s (Children's Defense Fund, 1996; Child Trends, 2002), an increasing proportion of teens give birth out of wedlock and choose to keep their children rather than place them for adoption. The proportion of all births to teenage unmarried women has climbed from 18 percent in 1963 to 79 percent in 2001 (Children's Defense Fund, 1996; Child Trends, 2002). According to the Institute of Medicine (Brown & Eisen-berg, 1995), 82 percent of pregnancies to teenagers are unintended, compared with 57 percent of all pregnancies to U.S. women.

The persistence of unplanned pregnancy and parenthood among unmarried U.S. adolescents has been attributed to many factors, including changing moral values in society, limited sex education in schools, teens' distortion or misjudg-ment about the likelihood of becoming pregnant, limited access to birth control, and proliferation of positive images of sex in the media (Adler, 1995; Brown & Eisenberg, 1995; Furstenberg, 1991). Furstenberg (1991) describes unplanned teenage pregnancy (and parenthood) as a "default option" for youth who have sex and then fail to take active steps toward abortion or adoption.

A different perspective suggests that adolescent parenthood is a reasonable, adaptive response to social and cultural realities, particularly for poor African American teenage females. Williams (1991) conducted detailed interviews with African American teen mothers in Boston. Her findings indicate that early, out-of-wedlock births mirrored the experiences of the teens' own mothers, peers, and female relatives. Most of the women had poor academic records at inner-city schools, slim hopes for educational or vocational success, and little exposure to employable African American men whom they viewed as likely marriage part-ners. Thus, instead of representing a default option, early childbearing appears to be an accepted "career" option. This rationale reflects the views of other schol-ars from sociological, child welfare, and public policy perspectives (Hamburg & Dixon, 1992; Ladner, 1987; Wilson, 1987).

Consequences of Adolescent Childbearing

Whether teenage childbearing is perceived as a regrettable mistake or as a normative response to social realities, there is reason for concern. Consistent evidence indicates negative effects of early childbearing on women and their children. However, it is difficult to separate the effects of early childbearing from the factors that lead some youth to become teen parents (Furstenberg et al., 1989).

Adolescent mothers are more likely to experience health, emotional, relationship, educational, and economic difficulties than are older mothers and their children. Health risks of pregnancy are greatest for teens sixteen years old and younger (Black & DeBlassie, 1985), whereas health problems for pregnant teens ages sixteen to nineteen appear to be associated with lower socioeconomic status (Barnett, 1991). Given the combined demands of parenthood and adolescence, it is not surprising to find that teenage mothers are at greater risk for psychological difficulties than are other adolescents (Taylor, 1991). Adolescent mothers frequently report anxiety, depression, and hostility and are at greater risk of suicide than are other adolescents (Foster & Miller, 1980). Social relationships are likely to change as a result of pregnancy and childbirth. Teenage mothers often have restricted time to socialize with peers, experience difficulties dating, and experience stress from relationships with friends and relatives. From her clinical interviews with African American adolescent mothers, Boxill (1987) notes that teen parenting often results in loneliness and frustration for the teen mother. Former teenage mothers are less likely to enter into stable marriages than are peers who delayed childbearing (McCarthy & Menken, 1979).

Research has consistently associated teenage parenting with reduced educational, occupational, and socioeconomic attainment, even after controlling for socioeconomic status and academic aptitude (Card & Wise, 1981; Mott & Marsiglio, 1985). Teenage mothers are highly likely to drop out of school as a result of pregnancy (Hechtman, 1989) and to complete fewer years of school than their peers who postpone childbearing (Taylor, 1991). Lower educational attainment is linked to less stable and lucrative employment (Furstenberg, Brooks-Gunn, & Morgan, 1987; Scott-Jones, Rowland, & White, 1989). The negative effects of early parenthood appear to be lessened for teen mothers who complete high school. In a seventeen-year follow-up study of African American teenage mothers, Furstenberg et al. (1987) found that two-thirds of the mothers had completed high school and one-third had some postsecondary education. Many of these mothers were able to "stage a recovery" in later life.

The risk of negative outcomes extends to the children of adolescent mothers as well. Although less is known about the effects of adolescent parenthood on children than on mothers, deleterious effects have been found in children's cognitive and academic development (Brooks-Gunn & Furstenberg, 1986). Children of teenage parents also have been shown to be at higher risk of health, behavioral, and emotional problems; however, many of these effects may be attributable to lower socioeconomic status and inadequate health care rather than to the mother's young age (Brooks-Gunn & Chase-Landsdale, 1995; Scott-Jones et al., 1989).

Another serious potential outcome of adolescent parenthood is increased risk for child maltreatment. Some research has found a correlation between the mother's age and child maltreatment, although the findings are mixed and complicated by methodological difficulties (Klerman, 1993; Massat, 1995). Stier, Leventhal, Berg, Johnson, and Mezger (1993) found that maltreatment and change of primary caregivers occurred more often with the children of adolescent mothers than with children of older mothers. However, an important consideration is that the mother was rarely considered the perpetrator. Therefore, the heightened risk of child maltreatment and change of primary caregivers may be associated with poor choices of the adolescent mother about who becomes involved in the lives of her children.

Researchers postulate that an explanation for the negative effects of teenage parenting on children is the quality of parenting exhibited by mothers. Younger teen mothers have been found to be less knowledgeable about child development and more punitive in their attitudes toward their children than older mothers (Reis, 1989). Panzarine's (1988) literature review found that, compared with older mothers, adolescent mothers provide lower levels of verbal stimulation, which can be detrimental to cognitive, language, and social development. Compared with older mothers, teenage mothers have been shown to have more unrealistic expectations around children's developmental progress (Field, 1981; Karraker & Evans, 1996). In one study, half of adolescent mothers surveyed were considered at significant risk of child maltreatment (Haskett, Johnson, & Miller, 1994). These adolescents were considered at risk because they showed distress, rigid parenting attitudes, and inappropriate expectations of children. Younger adolescents and those with limited social support were at greater risk of maltreatment.

Little research has been conducted on the consequences of parenting on teenage fathers, in part because of traditional views discouraging paternal involvement for young, unmarried men and because half or more children born to teenage mothers are fathered by men older than age twenty (Furstenberg et al., 1989). However, high school dropout rates have been shown to be higher for teenage fathers, whether or not they marry their pregnant partner (Marsiglio, 1986). Many male partners of adolescent mothers report that they do not believe that they are prepared to take on the role of caregiver or provider for their children (Furstenberg et al., 1989).

Consequences of Foster Care

The child-welfare system was established to provide a safety net for children and adolescents who encounter developmental risks due to child maltreatment, dysfunctional families, and other serious problems (National Research Council, 1993). However, the evidence suggests that this net has failed, because the disadvantages already encountered by youth are too numerous and costly to overcome, because the state is an inadequate parent, or both. Many youth who leave foster care are unprepared to make the transition to productive, independent adulthood (Barth, 1990; Cook, 1994). Studies report adverse outcomes for adolescents who are wards over those who are not wards (Oz & Fine, 1988; Yancey, 1992). Furthermore, the experience of foster care can compound the problems, leaving the youth at risk for emotional and social isolation, educational underachievement, substance abuse, unintended pregnancy, and early childbearing (Barth, 1990; Cook, 1994; Yancey, 1992).

Girls with a history of foster care have been shown to be more likely to become adolescent mothers than those without foster care experience (Oz & Fine, 1988; Quinton, Rutter, & Liddle, 1985; Wolkind, 1977). Young mothers with prior experience in foster care are more likely than young mothers without this experience to demonstrate serious parenting problems (Quinton et al., 1985). In addition, adolescent girls in foster care who become parents have been shown to have worse educational and employment outcomes than other adolescent girls in foster care who do not become parents (Cook, 1994).

Considering the combined vulnerabilities of a history of child maltreatment, foster care experience, and early childbearing, teenage parents in foster care are among the most at-risk groups. However, it is important to note that, among every study reviewed, there are youth who did succeed despite the many obstacles in their lives. There were adolescents who graduated from high school or went on to college, found stable employment, formed successful interpersonal relationships, and were good parents to their own children. Longitudinal research on adolescent mothers found that those who avoided repeat childbirths as teens, completed high school, and entered into stable marriages were found to be indistinguishable from their counterparts who were not adolescent parents (Furstenberg et al., 1989). These findings underscore the importance of individual differences in adolescents' needs and outcomes, even among at-risk populations.

Rationale for the DCFS-DePaul Project

Given the numerous disadvantages associated with adolescent parenthood and foster care, it makes sense to focus special attention on youth contending with both of these conditions. In Illinois, the impetus for this attention was a class-action lawsuit, *Hill v. Erickson* (1988), which was brought against DCFS on behalf of pregnant and parenting adolescent wards. The suit alleged that teen wards had been subjected to multiple violations of their rights and failed to receive treatment and services consistent with their needs. As part of a preliminary consent decree in 1991, DCFS agreed to collect descriptive data on the wards to inform service planning. DCFS contracted with the author at DePaul University to gather systematic information on the psychosocial functioning, parenting strengths and weaknesses, and service needs of a sample of adolescent mothers residing in Cook County, which covers much of metropolitan Chicago. In subsequent years, DCFS contracted with DePaul to conduct additional psychosocial assessments, to carry out a follow-up study on previously assessed teens, to survey caseworkers on needs of adolescent parents, to pilot test a program for training selected service providers to conduct the psychosocial assessments, to work collaboratively with DCFS on developing a screening protocol, and to perform other activities. The findings of these activities are summarized in five annual reports (Budd, 1994, 1995, 1996, 1997; Budd & Kane, 1992) and in related publications (Budd, Heilman, & Kane, 2000; Budd, Stockman, & Miller, 1998; Felix Kelly, Poindexter, & Budd, 2003; Stockman & Budd, 1997).

APPROACH

A standardized system of initial and periodic assessment provides a mechanism for determining what services teens need and reviewing whether they benefit from services. The approach we developed in the context of the DCFS-DePaul project is a two-tier assessment: (1) universal screening of all adolescents in state care who are pregnant or have given birth to a child and (2) in-depth, psychosocial assessment of a select subgroup of adolescent parents who are identified as having special needs or clinical concerns. The next sections describe the initial screening form, the psychosocial assessment protocol, and criteria for determining which teens are referred for psychosocial assessment.

Initial Screening Form

All service programs need to obtain some initial information on the adolescents in their care. For programs serving pregnant or parenting teens, this information typically includes basic demographic data, educational status, number and age of the adolescent's children, major medical conditions, prior placements, and so on. However, in a statewide survey of service providers, we learned that many programs did not gather systematic information on background variables, mental health conditions, or other behavior patterns that indicate risks (e.g., history of sexual abuse, young age at first pregnancy) or current areas of functioning (e.g., substance abuse, depressed mood, parenting knowledge) (Stockman & Budd, 1997). Even when programs did gather this information, they had no organized system for using the information to guide case planning.

In response to these concerns, the DCFS-DePaul project worked jointly with a subgroup of caseworkers in teen parent programs to develop the Pregnant and/or Parenting Wards Screening Information Form (Budd, 1997). This form was designed to highlight basic demographic information, conditions that may signify risk, the reports in the ward's file most relevant to current service planning, the most recent placements, information regarding the child(ren) of the teen, and the location and status of the teen's receipt of services. The screening form was designed to be used at initial entry and at each placement change. We formulated items for the screening form on the basis of input from service providers and the research literature on teenage parenting. To make the screening form comprehensive, it was designed to fit pregnant adolescents as well as both female and male teenage parents. Several caseworkers volunteered to use the form informally with teens, and we revised it on the basis of their feedback to enhance the form's usefulness and applicability.

Exhibit 17.1 displays the sections covered in the screening form and selected topics in each section. It contains the complete list of items included in the section titled "Possible Risk Factors," which is organized into subsections on stable factors and factors subject to change.

The screening form alone is not sufficient to determine an adolescent's service needs. Other information is needed about the teen's functioning in everyday life skills and parenting skills, and more detail is needed on many items covered in the screening form. Often, information available at initial screening relies on prior records, which may be erroneous or outdated, so periodic review and update of the information is necessary. Instead of serving as a sole source of documentation, the screening form was designed to provide a wide-ranging but concise summary of key areas for consideration in planning services.

Psychosocial Assessment Protocol

When clinical concerns arise about adolescents' chronic behavior problems, mental health difficulties, or parenting adequacy, individualized assessment may be needed. The psychosocial assessment model presented herein was designed to gather clinical information on the functioning of teenage parents in areas empirically identified as indicative of risk and in adaptive competence. The assessment protocol includes measures of parenting functioning, such as child-rearing beliefs, child abuse potential, and quality of parent-child interactions. It also addresses domains such as emotional adjustment, academic achievement, social support, and adaptive living skills that relate to the teen's ability to fulfill the normal expectations of adolescence. Finally, there is a provision for screening the developmental status of the adolescent's child(ren) to determine whether the child is progressing as expected.

Psychosocial assessments differ from traditional psychological or other mental health evaluations in several important ways:

1. They focus on *functional competencies* of parents (i.e., what parents believe, understand, do, and are capable of doing with respect to child rearing) and *adaptive behaviors* (e.g., academic achievement, emotional and social adjustment);

2. They screen both strengths and weaknesses in teens' functioning to provide useful guidelines for treatment planning;

3. They emphasize adolescents' current functioning as most relevant to behavioral competence;

4. They occur in familiar surroundings (usually the home or facility at which the teen resides), in order to take into account the natural childcare environment;

EXHIBIT 17.1   Sections and Selected Topics Covered in the Pregnant and/or Parenting Wards Screening Information Form

---

I. Teen's identifying information
   A. Demographic data (age, sex, race/ethnicity)
   B. Education (years of school completed, special education needs)
   C. Health (major health problems or conditions, pregnancy/childbirth status)

II. Child's information (for each child)
   A. Demographic data (name, age, sex)
   B. Living arrangement and wardship status
   C. Father (name, age)
   D. Health or developmental problems

III. Possible risk factors (entire list provided below; form asks respondent to identify documentation and source for each entry)
   A. Stable factors
      1. Teen was/is younger than sixteen at the time of her first pregnancy.
      2. Teen has a history of sexual abuse.
      3. Teen has a history of school failure, truancy, or school dropout.
      4. Teen has a history of arrests or juvenile court involvement.
      5. Teen has a history of substance abuse (e.g., alcohol, street drugs).
      6. Teen has a history of suicidal behaviors.
      7. Teen has a history of running away from placements.
      8. Teen has a history of violent behaviors.
      9. Teen has known developmental disabilities (e.g., mental retardation, significant language disorder).
      10. Teen has more than one child in his/her care or is pregnant with a subsequent child.
      11. Teen has one or more indicated incidents of abuse and/or neglect toward a child.
      12. Teen has a history of sexual offense.
   B. Factors subject to change
      1. Teen is currently in contact with an individual who has physically/sexually abused or neglected him/her.
      2. Teen is currently abusing a substance (e.g., alcohol, street drugs).
      3. Teen has health problems that need current or regular medical attention (e.g., sexually transmitted disease, asthma).

continued

EXHIBIT 17.1   (*continued*)

4. Teen has trouble maintaining placements as a result of behavior problems or rule violations.
5. Teen is currently involved with a gang.
6. Teen is currently involved with the court system regarding criminal or delinquent behavior.
7. Teen has known emotional problems (e.g., depression, anxiety disorders, schizophrenia, aggression).
8. Other current concerns (describe).

IV. Key reports/activities in teen's file (list most recent date of each type of report)
   A. Child-welfare service reports
   B. Court records
   C. Mental health evaluations
   D. Health records
   E. School records

V. Placement and services update
   A. Three most recent, approved placements (date, site, type of placement)
   B. Unofficial placements (e.g., on run, living with boyfriend)
   C. Significant placement history (e.g., frequent placement disruptions, began ward status as young child)

VI. Services client is receiving (as per DCFS Rules and Regulations for Pregnant and Parenting Wards)
   A. Specific services (e.g., counseling, pre/postnatal health care, parent training)
   B. Topics covered in parent training (e.g., nurturance and stimulation needs of child, proper nutrition)
   C. Other rights and obligations (e.g., efforts made to include father in services, efforts to assist teen in completing schooling, day care services for child)

NOTE: A complete copy of the form is in the Appendix of the Year 5 annual report of the DCFS-DePaul project (Budd, 1997).

---

5. They occur with the child present, in order to allow for observation of parent-child interactions;

6. They employ methodologically sound procedures (e.g., standardized instruments, multiple measures and sessions, trained evaluators) to obtain comprehensive information; and

7. They follow a systematic assessment protocol tailored to adolescent parents to allow for comparison of findings across adolescents.

The measures chosen for inclusion in the psychosocial assessment protocol are listed in exhibit 17.2 in the order they are typically administered with adolescents. These measures have evidence of reliability and validity, most provide normative comparison levels, and together they yield practical findings for the development service recommendations. Psychosocial assessments are completed during two home visits that last approximately one-and-a-half hours each with the parent and child(ren). Written measures are administered orally to control for differences in adolescents' reading proficiency. Evaluation findings are discussed individually with the teen in a feedback session to provide information and to correct misunderstandings. An individualized written report of the results is provided to the DCFS caseworker and to other key service providers and is used in planning services. In the DCFS-DePaul project, teens that completed the psychosocial assessment received a check for twenty-five dollars and a toy for their child in appreciation of their cooperation. In addition, the adolescents received a summary of their child's current developmental performance, along with suggestions for promoting the child's development.

Psychosocial assessments require evaluators to have advanced training in test construction and interpretation, psychometrics, and clinical assessment procedures. Thus, they were designed to be conducted by professionals with advanced training (e.g., psychologists, social workers), not caseworkers. As part of the project, we developed a training guide (Budd & Smith, 1995) for conducting psychosocial assessments, and we pilot tested the feasibility of training a small group of community professionals (predominantly master's-level social workers) (Budd, 1997). This dissemination pilot implied that the training was successful in preparing professionals to responsibly use the psychosocial assessment protocol.

As is true of any assessment method, the psychosocial assessment protocol is subject to limitations in its applicability. First, it is essentially an overview of parental and personal functioning. For pragmatic reasons, the evaluation does not include a review of prior records or collateral contacts; rather, it was designed to sample several relevant domains of adolescent functioning with a standardized approach. Second, adolescents in acute distress or with severe mental health problems would be better served by more specialized evaluation procedures (e.g., psychiatric or multidisciplinary assessment). Third, despite attempts to tailor the assessment content to teens in foster care, caution must be exercised in interpreting the findings with minority individuals. Research on culture and testing (e.g., Miller-Jones, 1989) reveals that cultural differences can produce relevant differences in test performance that are not accounted for by norms based on majority populations. Fourth, no mental health evaluation can predict future behavior with certainty, and thus the results of psychosocial assessments must be interpreted conservatively at the level of the individual case.

EXHIBIT 17.2 Measures and Selected Topics Included in the Psychosocial Assessment Protocol, in the Order Typically Administered

I. Session 1
   A. Demographics questionnaire—items for gathering basic information, such as age, ethnicity, years of education, relationship status, and child's names and ages.
   B. Clinical interview—structured questions inquiring about personal background and current functioning on topics including history of involvement with DCFS; family of origin; school, health, and employment history; typical day; and services received and needed.
   C. Child-abuse-potential inventory (Milner, 1986)—a 160-item screening device for identifying physical child abusers as well as those who may be at risk of becoming abusers.
   D. Wide Range Achievement Test 3 (Wilkinson, 1993)—a screening measure of fundamental skills required for reading, spelling, and arithmetic.
   E. Minnesota Infant Development Inventory (Ireton & Thwing, 1980) or Denver Developmental Screening Test II (Frankenburg et al., 1992)—screening instruments for assessing the developmental status of infants and young children.

II. Session 2
   A. Parent opinion questionnaire (Azar, Robinson, Hekimian, & Twentyman, 1984; Azar & Rohrbeck, 1986)—an eighty-item questionnaire assessing the extent to which parents endorse unrealistic expectations for children's behavior.
   B. Home observation for the measurement of the environment (Caldwell & Bradley, 1984)—an interview and observational instrument for evaluating the quality of stimulation present in a young child's environment by measuring aspects of parent-child interactions, the child's activities and routines, and the physical environment.
   C. Arizona Social Support Interview Schedule (Barrera, 1981, as modified by Mitchell, 1989)—a structured set of questions for assessing the makeup of an individual's social support network with regard to sharing private feelings, obtaining material aid, receiving positive feedback, participating in social or leisure activities, and experiencing negative interactions.
   D. Symptom Checklist-90-Revised (Derogatis, 1983) or Brief Symptom Inventory (Derogatis, 1993)—a rating scale of ninety or fifty-three items, respectively, assessing the current level of psychological or emotional symptoms of distress in areas such as depression, anxiety, and somatic complaints.

> **EXHIBIT 17.2** (*continued*)
>
> III. Possible supplemental measure
>   A. Vineland Adaptive Behavior Scales—Survey Form (Sparrow, Balla, & Cicchetti, 1984)—a structured interview instrument examining the extent to which an individual takes responsibility for himself/herself in several aspects of everyday functioning, including daily living skills, socialization, and communication.

GUIDES AND PRINCIPLES FOR PRACTICE

Two ways of considering the usefulness of the psychosocial assessment model are to examine what we have learned from its implementation with teenage mothers during the project and to examine how the model influenced DCFS services since the project ended.

Lessons Learned from Psychosocial Assessment Findings

The psychosocial assessment protocol was administered to more than 150 adolescent mothers as a means of providing directions for service planning during the DCFS-DePaul project. Findings from research (Budd, 1994, 1995; Budd et al., 2000; Budd & Kane, 1992) on seventy-five primarily African American adolescent mothers, ages fourteen to eighteen years, with infants ages two months to twenty months, revealed the following patterns:

First, teenage mothers as a group were functioning approximately three years below grade level in reading and math. Compared with the normative sample, the teens had mean reading scores at the twelfth percentile and arithmetic scores at the seventh percentile.

Second, despite low academic achievement, 89 percent of the teens reported being enrolled in high school or, if evaluated in the summer, planning to return to school during the next academic year.

Third, on a standardized measure of child abuse potential, 56 percent of young mothers responded in a manner similar to the response patterns of known physical child abusers. Another 19 percent had invalid scores on this measure due to socially desirable responding, and the remaining 25 percent had scores in the normal range, suggesting low likelihood of abuse.

Fourth, approximately 33 percent of adolescents appeared to have unrealistic expectations of the developmental abilities and limitations of young children. Inaccurate beliefs were most common about children's ability to care for younger siblings and children's role as emotional supports to parents.

Fifth, most mothers displayed some adequate interactions with their babies, suggesting emotional attachments on which to build stronger parenting skills.

However, about 33 percent of mothers scored in the lowest quartile of the observational measure of parent-child interactions, which indicates at-risk status.

Sixth, only 9 percent of the teens acknowledged clinically elevated levels of emotional distress on a standardized measure; however, several other teens displayed difficulties (e.g., anger, family conflict, persistent sadness, suicidal thoughts) severe enough to warrant therapeutic services. Individual psychosocial assessment reports prepared for clinical purposes contained recommendations to initiate individual therapy or counseling on 25 percent of the teens and advised continuation of ongoing counseling for another 20 percent of the cases. Other recommendations for specific teens included peer support groups, further mental health evaluation, or sexual abuse counseling.

Seventh, about 71 percent of the adolescent mothers were involved in a relationship with a male who typically was not their child's father. Teen mothers typically identified their current dating partner as part of their social support network.

Last, the five areas in which mothers most frequently identified a need for additional assistance were parenting skills, child care, material resources, instrumental support, and emotional support.

Our findings confirm impressions from the research literature that teenage parents in foster care have multiple service needs. Many of the mothers assessed showed substantial educational, emotional, and parenting skills deficits. Nevertheless, despite their disadvantaged backgrounds, several of the young mothers evidenced relatively few risk factors and were strongly motivated to become successful caregivers. The individual variation among the mothers underscores the importance of approaching each adolescent parent as a unique case.

Application of Psychosocial Assessment Model to Child-Welfare Services

Shortly after the DCFS-DePaul project concluded in 1996, DCFS began contracting with a community service organization to coordinate service provision for all pregnant and parenting teens in foster care. As part of the agency's responsibilities, it set up a uniform data information system for tracking youth. It developed a comprehensive assessment form, to be completed by caseworkers, that includes many of the items covered in the initial screening form developed previously as part of the project. We were not directly involved in developing the comprehensive assessment form, and it is unclear whether the form was modeled on our project's work. Nevertheless, the comprehensive assessment form is similar in purpose to the initial screening form: it is a uniform, organized means of gathering and updating information on individual pregnant and parenting teens, and it contains a wealth of information relevant to planning services. Thus, although the initial screening protocol was never formally adopted after the DCFS-DePaul project ended, this goal appears to have been met by subsequent activities of DCFS and its selected coordinating agency.

In contrast, the psychosocial assessment protocol developed in the DCFS-

DePaul project was not incorporated into clinical practice for pregnant and parenting wards, nor has another assessment protocol emerged to serve its functions. Despite positive consumer evaluations of the psychosocial assessment model and DCFS support for conducting the dissemination study, no provisions were made to fund or train persons to carry out psychosocial assessments of adolescent parents after the contract period. The primary option available for assessing these individuals remains the traditional psychological evaluation. Unfortunately, traditional cognitive and personality assessments are, at best, indirectly related to parenting and daily living concerns of adolescents (Budd & Holdsworth, 1996). Thus, they are not well suited to informing caseworkers as to how to plan services for pregnant and parenting teens and their children.

Because DCFS did not adopt the psychosocial assessment model, no system exists for individualized assessment of parenting and personal functioning on pregnant or parenting adolescents. Two likely factors in this outcome are the DCFS-DePaul project's stakeholders and existing DCFS precedents. The major stakeholders of the project were the legal team that successfully initiated the class-action law suit and advocated for improved services to teens in foster care, the judge who carefully supervised and enforced the reforms within DCFS, and selected administrators and caseworkers who recognized the need for more professional services to adolescents. However, not all DCFS administrators and workers supported the project or the reasons for its initiation. The executive leadership of DCFS changed three times during the five-year contract period, and each new director brought new administrators into key positions, new political realities, and new economic pressures.

The second likely reason that the psychosocial assessment model was not adopted into DCFS practice is that no structure existed to sustain it. DCFS had an established practice of hiring psychologists to conduct traditional assessments and caseworkers who are acquainted with making referrals for psychological evaluations. No similar precedent existed for psychosocial assessments. Our experience in the dissemination project suggested that master's-level social workers could be trained to conduct the psychosocial assessments and that they were interested in doing so. However, the use of social workers as mental health evaluators (beyond social assessments conducted on clients) departs from typical child-welfare practice. In hindsight, it was probably unrealistic to envision DCFS initiating a system for hiring, training, and paying social workers in assessment activities. Thus, we were faced with a mismatch between our model of practice and existing systemwide supports.

DISCUSSION AND IMPLICATIONS

The experiences of the DCFS-DePaul project illustrate both the benefits and the challenges of collaborative ventures in social service settings. The project came about as a result of political realities that exposed inadequate services and functioned as a catalyst for change. The lessons learned from five years of conducting psychosocial assessments, along with other applied research and service activities, are valuable, and they are available to others through reports and publications (Budd, 1994, 1995, 1996, 1997; Budd et al., 1998, 2000; Budd & Kane, 1992; Felix et al., 2003; Stockman & Budd, 1997). The findings have informed caseworkers, administrators, and other professionals working with pregnant and parenting teens in Illinois foster care. However, the project did not achieve its desired service outcome—an established system of psychosocial assessment for pregnant and parenting adolescents about whom service providers have clinical concerns.

The adequacy of assessment information available to inform service planning for this population remains unclear, given the absence of a model tailored to the needs and risk of young parents. By documenting the potential value of the psychosocial assessment model, this project has contributed to increased knowledge about assessments relevant to teenage parents. Perhaps others will use the experiences of the DCFS-DePaul project to establish a model that becomes part of DCFS practice.

REFERENCES

Adler, N. (1995, July). *Adolescent sexual behavior looks irrational—but looks are deceiving*. Address presented at the Federation of Behavioral, Psychological and Cognitive Sciences, Washington, DC.

Alan Guttmacher Institute. (1981). *Teenage pregnancy: The problem that hasn't gone away*. New York: Author.

Azar, S. T., Robinson, D. R., Hekimian, E., & Twentyman, C. T. (1984). Unrealistic expectations and problem-solving ability in maltreating and comparison mothers. *Journal of Consulting and Clinical Psychology, 52,* 687–691.

Azar, S. T., & Rohrbeck, C. A. (1986). Child abuse and unrealistic expectations: Further validation of the Parent Opinion Questionnaire. *Journal of Consulting and Clinical Psychology, 54,* 867–868.

Barnett, A. P. (1991). Sociocultural influences on adolescent mothers. In R. Staples (Ed.), *The Black family: Essays and studies* (4th ed., pp. 160–169). Belmont, CA: Wadsworth.

Barrera, M. (1981). Social support in the adjustment of pregnant adolescents: Assessment issues. In B. H. Gottlieb (Ed.), *Social networks and social support* (pp. 69–96). Beverly Hills, CA: Sage.

Barth, R. P. (1990). On their own: The experiences of youth after foster care. *Child and Adolescent Social Work, 7,* 419–440.

Black, C., & DeBlassie, E. R. (1985). Adolescent pregnancy: Contributing factors: Consequences, treatment and plausible solutions. *Adolescence, 20,* 281–290.

Boxill, N. (1987). "How would you feel . . . ?" Clinical interviews with Black adolescent mothers. *Child and Youth Services, 9,* 41–51.

Brooks-Gunn, J., & Chase-Lansdale, P. L. (1995). Adolescent parenthood. In M. H. Bornstein (Ed.), *Handbook of parenting: Status and social conditions of parenting* (pp. 113–149). Mahwah, NJ: Erlbaum.

Brooks-Gunn, J., & Furstenberg, F. F. (1986). The children of adolescent mothers:

Physical, academic, and psychological outcomes. *Developmental Review, 6,* 224–251.

Brown, S. S., & Eisenberg, L. (1995). *The best intentions: Unintended pregnancy and the well-being of children and families.* Washington, DC: National Academy Press.

Budd, K. S. (1994). *Psychosocial assessment and follow-up of teenage parents—Year 2: 1992–93. A report to the Illinois Department of Children and Family Services.* Chicago: DePaul University, Department of Psychology.

Budd, K. S. (1995). *Psychosocial assessment and follow-up of teenage parents—Year 3: 1993–94. A report to the Illinois Department of Children and Family Services.* Chicago: DePaul University, Department of Psychology.

Budd, K. S. (1996). *Psychosocial assessment and follow-up of teenage parents—Year 4: 1994–95. A report to the Illinois Department of Children and Family Services.* Chicago: DePaul University, Department of Psychology.

Budd, K. S. (1997). *Psychosocial assessment and follow-up of teenage parents—Year 5: 1995–96. A report to the Illinois Department of Children and Family Services.* Chicago: DePaul University, Department of Psychology.

Budd, K. S., Heilman, N. E., & Kane, D. (2000). Psychosocial correlates of child abuse potential in multiply disadvantaged adolescent mothers. *Child Abuse & Neglect, 24,* 611–625.

Budd, K. S., & Holdsworth, M. J. (1996). Issues in clinical assessment of minimal parenting competence. *Journal of Clinical Child Psychology, 25,* 1–14.

Budd, K. S., & Kane, D. (1992). *Psychosocial assessment and follow-up of teenage parents—A report to the Illinois Department of Children and Family Services.* Chicago: DePaul University, Department of Psychology.

Budd, K. S., & Smith, S. (1995). *Training guide for psychosocial assessment of teenage mothers.* Chicago: DePaul University, Department of Psychology.

Budd, K. S., Stockman, K. D., & Miller, E. M. (1998). Parenting issues and interventions with adolescent mothers. In J. Lutzker (Ed.), *Handbook of child abuse research and treatment* (pp. 357–376). New York: Plenum Press.

Caldwell, B. M., & Bradley, R. H. (1984). *Home observation for the measurement of the environment: Administration manual* (Rev. ed.). Little Rock: University of Arkansas.

Card, J. J., & Wise, L. L. (1981). Teenage mothers and teenage fathers: The impact of early childbearing on the parents' personal and professional lives. In F. F. Furstenberg, Jr., R. Lincoln, & J. Menken (Eds.), *Teenage sexuality, pregnancy and childbearing* (pp. 211–222). Philadelphia: University of Pennsylvania Press.

Child Trends. (2002, September). *Facts at a glance.* Retrieved from http://www.childtrends.org/PDF/FAAG2002.pdf.

Children's Defense Fund. (1987). *Teens in foster care: Preventing pregnancy and building self-sufficiency.* Washington, DC: Author.

Children's Defense Fund. (1996). *The state of America's children: Yearbook 1996.* Washington, DC: Author.

Cook, R. J. (1994). Are we helping foster care youth prepare for their future? *Children and Youth Services Review, 16,* 213–229.

Derogatis, L. R. (1983). *Symptom Checklist-90 Revised administration, scoring & procedures manual-II.* Towson, MD: Clinical Psychometric Research.

Derogatis, L. R. (1993). *Brief symptom inventory: Administration, scoring and procedures manual.* Minneapolis, MN: National Computer Systems.

Elster, A. B., & Lamb, M. E. (Eds.). (1985). *Adolescent fatherhood*. Hillsdale, NJ: Erlbaum.

Felix, E. D., Kelly, A. O., Poindexter, L. M., & Budd, K. S. (2003). Cross-generational parenting influences on psychosocial functioning of adolescent mothers in substitute care. *Journal of Adolescent Research, 18,* 154–168.

Field, T. (1981). Early development of the preterm offspring of teenage mothers. In K. Scott, T. Field, & E. G. Robertson (Eds.), *Teenage parents and their offspring* (pp.145–175). New York: Grune & Stratton.

Foster, C., & Miller, G. (1980). Adolescent pregnancy: A challenge for counselors. *Personnel and Guidance Journal, 59,* 236–240.

Frankenburg, W. K., Dodds, J., Archer, P., Bresnick, B., Maschka, P., Edelman, N., et al. (1992). *Denver II: Training manual* (2nd ed.). Denver, CO: Denver Developmental Materials.

Furstenberg, F. F., Jr. (1991). As the pendulum swings: Teenage childbearing and social concern. *Family Relations, 40,* 127–138.

Furstenberg, F. F., Jr., Brooks-Gunn, J., & Chase-Lansdale, L. (1989). Teenaged pregnancy and childbearing. *American Psychologist, 44,* 313–320.

Furstenberg, F. F., Jr., Brooks-Gunn, J., & Morgan, S. P. (1987). *Adolescent mothers in later life*. Cambridge, MA: Cambridge University Press.

Hamburg, B. A., & Dixon, S. L. (1992). Adolescent pregnancy and parenthood. In M. K. Rosenheim & M. F. Testa (Eds.), *Early parenthood and coming of age in the 1990s* (pp. 17–33). New Brunswick, NJ: Rutgers University Press.

Haskett, M. E., Johnson, C. A., & Miller, J. W. (1994). Individual differences in risk of child abuse by adolescent mothers: Assessment of the perinatal period. *Journal of Child Psychology and Psychiatry, 35,* 461–476.

Hayes, C.D. (Ed.). (1987). *Risking the future: Adolescent sexuality, pregnancy, and childbearing* (Vol. 1). Washington, DC: National Academy Press.

Hechtman, L. (1989). Teenage mothers and their children: Risks and problems: A review. *Canadian Journal of Psychiatry, 34,* 569–575.

Hill v. Erickson, No. 88 CO 296. (Circuit Court, Cook County, IL, filed November 15, 1988).

Hofferth, S., & Hayes, C. D. (1987). *Risking the future: Adolescent sexuality, pregnancy, and childbearing* (Vol. 2). Washington, DC: National Academy Press.

Ireton, H. R., & Thwing, E. J. (1980). *The Minnesota infant development inventory*. Minneapolis, MN: Behavior Science Systems.

Karraker, K. H., & Evans, S. L. (1996). Adolescent mothers' knowledge of child development and expectations for their own infants. *Journal of Youth and Adolescence, 25,* 651–666.

Klerman, L. V. (1993). The relationship between adolescent parenthood and inadequate parenting. *Children and Youth Services Review, 15,* 309–320.

Ladner, J. A. (1987). *Black teenage pregnancy: The Black woman*. Garden City, NY: Doubleday.

Marsiglio, W. (1986). Teenage fatherhood: High school accreditation and educational attainment. In A. B. Elster & M. E. Lamb (Eds.), *Adolescent fatherhood* (pp. 67–87). Hillsdale, NJ: Erlbaum.

Massat, C. R. (1995). Is older better?: Adolescent parenthood and maltreatment. *Child Welfare, 74,* 325–336.

McCarthy, J., & Menken, J. (1979). Marriage, remarriage, marital disruption and age at first birth. *Family Planning Perspectives, 11,* 21–30.

Miller-Jones, D. (1989). Culture and testing. *American Psychologist, 44,* 360–373.

Milner, J. S. (1986). *The child abuse potential inventory manual* (2nd ed.). DeKalb, IL: Psytec.

Mitchell, M. E. (1989). The relationship between social network variables and the utilization of mental health services. *Journal of Community Psychology, 17,* 258–266.

Mott, F. L., & Marsiglio, W. (1985). Early childbearing and completion of high school. *Family Planning Perspectives, 17,* 234–237.

National Research Council. (1993). *Losing generations: Adolescents in high-risk settings.* Washington, DC: National Academy Press.

Oz, S., & Fine, M. (1988). A comparison of childhood backgrounds of teenage mothers and their non-mother peers: A new formulation. *Journal of Adolescence, 11,* 251–261.

Panzarine, S. (1988). Teen mothering: Behaviors and interventions. *Journal of Adolescent Health Care, 9,* 443–448.

Quinton, D., Rutter, M., & Liddle, C. (1985). Institutional rearing, parenting difficulties, and marital support. In S. Chess & A. Thomas (Eds.), *Annual progress in child psychiatry and child development* (pp. 173–206). New York: Brunner/Mazel.

Reis, J. (1989). A comparison of young teenage, older teenage, and adult mothers on determinants of parenting. *Journal of Psychology, 123,* 141–151.

Rosenheim, M. K., & Testa, M. F. (Eds.). (1992). *Early parenthood and coming of age in the 1990s.* New Brunswick, NJ: Rutgers University Press.

Scott-Jones, D., Rolland, E. J., & White, A. B. (1989). Antecedents and outcomes of pregnancy in Black adolescents. In R. L. Jones (Ed.), *Black adolescents* (pp. 341–371). Berkeley, CA: Cobb & Henry.

Sparrow, S. S., Balla, D. A., & Cicchetti, D. V. (1984). *Vineland adaptive behavior scales.* Circle Pines, MN: American Guidance Services.

Stier, D. M., Leventhal, J. M., Berg, A. T., Johnson, L., & Mezger, J. (1993). Are children born to young mothers at increased risk of maltreatment? *Pediatrics, 91,* 642–648.

Stockman, K. D., & Budd, K. S. (1997). Directions for intervention with adolescent mothers in substitute care. *Families in Society: The Journal of Contemporary Human Services, 78,* 617–623.

Taylor, R. L. (1991). Black youth in crisis. In R. Staples (Ed.), *The Black family: Essays and studies* (4th ed., pp. 211–226). Belmont, CA: Wadsworth.

Wilkinson, G. S. (1993). *The Wide Range achievement test 3.* Wilmington, DE: Wide Range.

Williams, C. W. (1991). *Black teenage mothers: Pregnancy and child rearing from their perspective.* Lexington, MA: Lexington Books.

Wilson, W. J. (1987). *The truly disadvantaged: The inner city, the underclass, and public policy.* Chicago: University of Chicago Press.

Wolkind, S. N. (1977). Women who have been "in care": Psychological and social status during pregnancy. *Journal of Child Psychology and Psychiatry, 18,* 179–182.

Yancey, A. K. (1992). Identity formation and social maladaptation in foster adolescents. *Adolescence, 27,* 819–831.

CHAPTER 18

PROGRAM EVALUATION: ARDUOUS, IMPOSSIBLE, AND POLITICAL

Donald M. Baer

People's problems often seem to require a program; programs require evaluation. However, the analysis of program evaluation first requires a definition of *program,* which in turn requires a definition of *problem.*

In most behavioral contexts, the word *problem* means only an absence of the right behaviors and an abundance of the wrong behaviors, or a lack of the stimulus controls for the right behaviors and an abundance of the stimulus controls for the wrong behaviors. The only thing that is "right" about right behaviors is that they help people have the future they want or the one that others want for them. The only thing that is "wrong" about wrong behaviors is that they bar people from the future they want or the one that others want for them.

Not everything is known about behavior or about the behavior changes that are problematic with social work clients, but it is known that environmental contingencies are powerful in changing behavior and thereafter maintaining it, and that individual differences do not alter that behavior. So, if a problem is an absence of the right behaviors and an abundance of the wrong behaviors, or of their stimulus controls, the cause might be an absence of the right contingencies and an abundance of the wrong ones. If the contingencies are changed, the right behaviors and their controls might appear, and the wrong behaviors and their controls might disappear.

The contingencies are changed to determine how often doing so is correct, but sometimes there are many of them to change, and sometimes they need to be changed in just the right order. This calls for a lot of carefully planned work over a long time.

So, a program is a large recipe for solving a large problem. It explains how to decide who receives the program, who applies the program, and what they should do, and in what order they should do it.

Usually, social workers can imagine many different programs that might solve the same problem. So it becomes crucial to ask how well any particular program solves the problem. If a program does not do well, an alternative can be tried, which should occur because programs are expensive. To pursue a bad program is to waste a lot of time and resources. Thus, program evaluation is required. This chapter will sketch the general form of behavioral program evaluation to determine how it should be performed, how it is performed, and when it cannot be performed.

Modern Program Evaluation

Modern program evaluation has six steps, or at least it should. Not one of them is simple.

Step 1: Measure the Program's Effect.   A program is intended to solve a problem. If the problem can be measured, then it should be measured at least once just before the program is applied and at least once after the program is completed. The difference between the two measures is the first evaluation of the program. The difference shows what the program has done and what type of difference the program has made. The postprogram measure, no matter how impressively different from the preprogram measure, reveals something else: Is the problem solved now? If the answer is "yes," then celebrate; if it is "no," then more of the program, and perhaps some additional program, is required; all that extra work needs to be evaluated too.

Incidentally, if the answer is "yes," before you celebrate, remember that whoever funded the problem solving will now stop funding. It is always prudent to have a second, even more urgent problem with a priority that becomes clear when the first problem has been solved—a problem that another program can probably solve.

Step 2: Evaluate Program Fidelity.   How much of the prescribed program was actually performed? Was anything else done, anything not prescribed? If the program did not do well, it would seem to be a bad program, but if not much of it was actually done, or done correctly, it may not be a bad program. It might be a good program if it were done correctly and thoroughly. However, this cannot be determined until the program is done correctly and thoroughly, which brings about an additional problem: How can the program be properly carried out?

Step 3: Show Cause and Effect.   It is essential to determine that a program was carried out correctly, and it is good when it is determined that the problem has been solved. It is also essential to be sure that the problem was solved as a result of the program being run correctly. It is necessary to know whether something else solved the problem, because programs are expensive.

Step 4: Check Generalization.   If the appropriate and desired generalization has not occurred, a program is needed that makes it happen. Many programs change their target behaviors at the time and place of the program. However, programs often are run when and where it is convenient; and when and where it is convenient is not always when and where behavior changes are most useful. Behaviors changed at one time and place do not always change at other times and places. A successful program makes its behavior changes appear when and where they are most needed and are most valuable. This is usually in the social mainstream, which is also where generalized changes last longest. The social mainstream is also one of the most difficult places in which to perform measurement.

Step 5: Measure the Costs and Benefits of the Program and Its Outcome. Do the programs benefits justify its cost? There are many audiences. Some of them believe that the solution to a problem must cost less than the problem costs. Otherwise, they believe that the solution is a bigger problem than the problem itself. To answer to this audience, the program's costs and benefits need to be measured in the same units. The audience usually wants the measurement units to be dollars.

Step 6: Assess the Social Validity of the Program. Determine who has power over the future of this program. Ask them how much they like its goals, procedures, costs, benefits, and personnel. It is easy to like some of those things and dislike others, and any dislike can be fatal to program survival. The people with power over a program can be the program's consumers and their families and advocates. Sometimes the professionals who design and use the program have some power over its future. The people who maintain the program's setting and who pay for it certainly have some power over the future of any programs done there, but so do a lot of other people, if they wish (Schwartz & Baer, 1991). The most difficult part about social validity is the brute fact of sociology: The people who can maintain or end a program can do so whether the program is effective or ineffective, whether it was performed faithfully or not, whether it caused its apparent outcomes, and whether it was cheap or expensive. The evaluation of a program's effectiveness depends on its measures, its generalization, the fidelity of its execution, the proof that it was the cause of what happened, and its cost-benefit ratio. In contrast, the evaluation of a program's future hinges only on its social validity. There is a need for effective programs that are also liked by the people who can determine their future. If those people do not like the programs, they need to at least dislike them less than any of the alternatives. In other words, if you like a program or dislike a program, you had better be sure you have enough power over its future.

Difficulties in Implementing Program Evaluation

None of the previous six steps is easy; each has its problems and requires discussion. To begin, these days, many agencies, especially public agencies, claim to evaluate their programs. On close examination it is clear that all they do is create paper-and-pencil forms for their employees to fill out. The forms ask the employees whether they carried out the program's procedures. Sometimes, the real point of the forms is to allow the employees to say that they could not carry out the program because of a lack of sufficient funding. Sometimes, the program receives more funding, but when funding is sufficient, the forms have a different purpose. At this point, the agencies allow the employees to say that they *did* carry out the program. The employees know that it is customary to say so. Thus, many programs fail until they are well funded; until they are well funded their forms are full of responses about program failures. After funding improves, many programs succeed because their forms are filled with stories about success. That is often referred to as accountability, but responses about success mean only that the employees claim that the program was carried out. Responses that claim success do not mean that the program succeeded. So many agencies cannot imagine that their programs could fail or do poorly if they are executed; thus, accountability becomes any documentation that the programs were executed.

For objective program evaluation, it is necessary to know much more than that the personnel say that the program was performed. To begin, how faithfully was the program performed, and what happened as a result of it? There is no point in criticizing agencies for solving their survival problems, but there remains some point in understanding the evaluation of their programs, apart from a program's role in an agency's survival. Evaluation explores how well the programs solve the problems to which they are applied. If the only problem the programs are meant to solve is the survival of the agency, then the length of that survival is the program evaluation. If the programs are also meant to solve some problems of the agency's clients, then it is necessary to know whether the programs induce more of the right behaviors and stimulus controls and fewer of the wrong ones in those clients.

Views of the Problem.   The problems that the program is meant to solve must be measurable. If a problem can be measured, then one can ask how much of a program's changes are measured. Immediately, two different professional views about measuring problems emerge.

First, the traditional view posits that most problems are too large and complex to be measured directly. The problem can only be represented by many various measures, and each measure only "reflects" the problem. People of the traditional view often have favorite measures. Sometimes those measures are so favored that they are used to measure all the programs that their users ever evaluate, no matter how strained their relation is to the problem at hand. In this context, naming a measure becomes crucial. Increase a measure named "prediction of personal outcomes," and very few people will know if the program is a good one or a bad one. Name that same measure "self esteem," and everyone will know that the program is good.

The assumption that measures only reflect a problem immediately generates a difficult question: How do you *know* whether a measure reflects the problem well? Answering that question leads easily to political program evaluation, sometimes consciously and sometimes not. There are two paths that lead to this program evaluation. One way is to assume that the program is good and ask whether it improves the current measure. If it does, then the measure is good, and the assumption that the program is good is proved. If the program does not improve the measure, then the measure is bad and should be replaced by another measure, until some measure is found that shows that the program is good. The found measure is a good measure. The second way is to assume that the program is bad and then ask whether the program worsens the current measure. If it does, then the measure is good and proves the assumption that the program is bad. If the program does not worsen the measure, then the measure is bad and should be replaced by another measure, until some measure is found that shows the program is bad. That found measure is a good measure. People who use this approach do not actually evaluate programs; they evaluate measures until they find one that yields the desired evaluation of their program. Then they announce that their program has been evaluated.

The second view is that of behaviorists, who, of course, hold to a nontraditional view. Behaviorists assume that a measure "reflects" only itself and nothing else. From the behaviorist's perspective, a measure does not represent a problem, either well or badly. The problem *is* its measure. There is no way to know whether there is a problem unless it is measured. If the measure is problematic, then the measure is the problem. Anyone who claims multiple measures of a problem is a person of multiple problems to solve.

Thus, behaviorists do not screen measures; they evaluate programs by asking whether the program changes the measure in the desired direction. If many behaviors are changed in order to program the solution to a problem, the program should be evaluated by just as many measures. Each behavior to change receives its own subprogram, and the subprogram is evaluated by how well it changes its measure. The program is evaluated by how well all its subprograms change their measures.

It follows that if a problem cannot be measured, a program aimed at solving it cannot be evaluated. Politically, that is the best kind of problem to solve. It is necessary, then, only to find out whether the relevant people like the program and if they do not, to find ways to make them like it. However, that is not an evaluation of the program's effectiveness; it is an evaluation of its social validity. It predicts the program's future, not its effectiveness, generality, fidelity, or cost-benefit ratio. There are quite a few ineffective, low-fidelity, ungeneralized, expensive programs that people seem to like. Perhaps that is because many people say that they like some program not because they like it, but because they like it better than no program. Often, the most important evaluation of a politically inspired program is simply that it exists.

Apart from its social validity, there is still a truth about the effectiveness of a program to consider. Suppose that the problem is aging, which is often accompanied by the diminution of many valuable behaviors and the emergence of new challenging behaviors. Sometimes society's methods of addressing aging lead to six classes of behavior change: (1) the recovery and maintenance of communication, (2) social skills, (3) problem-solving skills, (4) self-care, (5) the diminution of self-injury, and (6) the diminution of self-stimulation. Each class has many members; members are measurable, and thus program evaluation is possible.

When a program's subprograms are running, it is possible to determine how much better any participant is at, for example, the three specific language skills, the two particular problem solutions, the one social skill, and the two self-care skills that he or she is learning that month. It is possible to know just how much the one form of self-injury and the two types of self-stimulation that emerged last month have been eliminated. It is possible to know all these things if they are measured every week, every month, for as long as the program exists. If the program is effective, all or most of those measures will improve. The ones that do not improve instantly reveal that more effective subprograms are needed.

Program fidelity.   Next, consider the problems that arise when program fidelity is questioned. Suppose that the program is running, and the measured changes are good and occur just when and where they should. It is still necessary to know *which* program caused them, to know whether the prescribed program is the program that was actually carried out. In modern terms, program fidelity needs to be evaluated. Evaluation of program fidelity requires a program that is written in a wonderfully special way: (1) planning exactly what would be done by whom to whom and when that would happen, where it would happen, and how often it would happen; (2) measuring how often the plan was carried out; and (3) measuring whether anything else was done that was not prescribed.

If an evaluation of program fidelity finds that only a fraction of the prescribed program was actually carried out, and some unprescribed things were done as well, then program evaluation becomes impossible. If the program achieves its goals, then it could mean that the program is so good that even a fraction of it can solve the problem, or it could mean that the program is bad and that the problem was solved by some of the unprescribed things that happened. If the program does not achieve its goals, then it could mean the program is bad. It could also mean that the program really is good; it just looks bad because it was not done thoroughly or because of the nonprescribed things that were done that were bad. So, lacking program fidelity, the program is either good, bad, or a nonevent, and it is not possible to determine among these. In other words, the program has not been evaluated, and program infidelity means that it cannot be evaluated.

Thus, a small program should always be part of the large program to ensure that the program staff perform the large program as exactly as possible. Ideally, it should not be necessary to evaluate program fidelity because it is programmed. If we are programming program fidelity, that is a program that also needs to be evaluated.

A gloomy rule of thumb follows: Do not bother to evaluate programs unless you know the program staff carried out almost all the program and almost nothing but the program. Next, consider the problem of proving that the apparent results of a program were in fact caused by the program. A problem may improve because of the program applied to it, but sometimes a problem improves without a program being applied to it. Improvements in the program should be separated from improvements the program did not make.

Consider a case in point: Suppose that a program aims to recover and maintain the skills that elderly participants need to continue living independently in their own housing. The necessary program has to recover and maintain certain language, social, problem-solving, and self-care skills and to diminish any problematic challenging behaviors. Suppose that the maintenance and changes are observed. How do you evaluate whether that was because of the program?

There are two grand evaluation strategies. The first is quite traditional. In this case, many elderly participants must be found, and they and their families and caretakers must consent to the evaluation. Then half of them must be assigned at random to the program and the other half to something different. The chosen group participates in the program, and the other group participates in something different. As time passes, it is possible to measure how long each participant of each group maintains independent living. The question is whether, on average, the program maintains independent living longer than occurs in its absence. But this is clearly very expensive.

The second evaluation strategy is the single-subject alternative, or allowing single-subject designs to show cause and effect. That is not traditional, but it can work if one assumption is made. This strategy requires only one participant to agree, but it can always be used with each participant who agrees, and if generality is valued in program evaluation, then it should. Set up steady, ongoing measurement of each skill being recovered or maintained and each challenge being decreased as well as steady, ongoing measurement of the prescribed program procedures. This measurement never stops. Suppose that at some moment in this program, three specific skills are being recovered and two particular challenges are being reduced. The most basic skill is recovered; a few days after it is mastered one challenge is reduced if it is still ongoing; a few days after that the next most basic skill is recovered; after it is mastered the second challenge is reduced if it is still ongoing; and a few days after that the third skill is recovered. It is very nearly what would have been done without formal evaluation of cause and effect.

There is steady, ongoing measurement of the skills and challenges and of the program's procedures. Then the evaluation of program effectiveness, fidelity, and cause and effect will emerge; if measurements are graphed and examined every day, it will become clear how perfectly the program personnel proceeded, and if each of the participant's skills emerged and became dependable promptly after it was recovered, but not before. It will become clear whether each of the participant's challenges decreased promptly after the reduction procedures were applied, but not before. The degree of change in each skill and challenge will become clear, repeatedly, and the size and durability of these changes can be evaluated. If size and durability are lacking, program longer, and perhaps better, until they are satisfactory. Many changes occurring just when they should means they are not coincidental; they match too perfectly the recovery, maintenance, or reduction procedures aimed at them. Any one of them might be a coincidental change, but not all five, especially not when those meant to increase actually increase and those meant to decrease actually decrease.

That is program evaluation only—only if one assumption is made. If you know science—that is, if you know that these *are* the changes that, made thoroughly and dependably, will maintain the kind of independent living desired—*then* this program is evaluating itself as it unfolds.

The traditional strategy of group comparison, at great cost and over a long period of time, evaluates the length of independent living that the program typically achieves compared with that achieved in its absence. The nontraditional single-subject design economically and quickly evaluates how well the program makes the behavior changes believed to be crucial to independent living. The single-subject evaluation is only as good as the knowledge that these *are* the crucial behaviors to increase and decrease.

The next problem is to check generalization, which usually seems straightforward. If it is known how to measure program effects when and where the program is running, it is probable that they can be measured at other times and in other places by pretty much the same techniques. The problem is only the remarkable expense of doing so. It is difficult enough to receive program funding; receiving funding for the evaluation of its generalization is even more difficult, especially if the funders do no know that generalization is always problematic.

The evaluation of costs and benefits usually happens late, if at all. The question is whether the benefits are worth the costs. This is an easy question to ask, but not to answer. It is often a matter of political debate to decide whether a cost is a cost rather than a benefit or if a benefit is a benefit rather than a cost. It is often a matter of accountancy debate of whether to include costs that will be paid whether the program proceeds or not.

In some cases, the question is irrelevant. Perhaps the maintenance of independent living by the elderly is a good example. The cost of institutionalizing elderly dependent people in a humane manner for the remainder of their lifetime is extremely high. It would be a rare program aimed at extending their independent living that would come close to those costs. Thus, almost any program that achieves some extension of that independent life will be worth its costs. That is true, even if the only cost calculated is the maintenance costs if independent living is not extended. When the benefits of the program are considered in terms of human joy and the costs of the nonprogram in human anguish, the bargain becomes hugely better, even if incalculable.

Finally, effective programs need social validity. The people with the power to continue or to end any program must want to continue the program. The usual advice is to educate these people in the effectiveness of the program, which I have just described as a six-step process. A program evaluation centering on proven effectiveness confidently attributable to the program is the first ingredient in such education. It allows for a presentation of the various cost-benefit ratios that can be applied: estimates of the money saved or political credits gained by effectiveness compared with the losses of the commodities that come with failure.

All this is fine with a totally rational audience of critical thinkers. With any other audience, show business may be more relevant; it often can obtain good social validity.

Next, note that the social validity of the program should be checked with everyone who has any power over its future. In a free and wealthy society, it is difficult to predict who has or can acquire power over the future of a social program. A mere bystander, if sufficiently distressed simply by the spectacle of a program, can organize a protest against it. That kind of protest sometimes can end the program, especially if the program is publicly funded, no matter its effectiveness, ease of faithful performance, social validity with its direct consumers, generalization costs, or benefits. The biggest problem with social validity is the need to know how power over a program's future is distributed in society. That is not easy knowledge to acquire.

SUMMARY

This discussion makes behavioral program evaluation seem formidable, tedious, prone to lengthy detours, and very expensive, yet possible, if program fidelity can be achieved. But there is another view of behavior that makes program evaluation impossible.

To establish the appropriate context for this other view, remember the usual assumption that interventions will change the targeted behaviors and not others. The intent to change any other behaviors requires special programming. If that assumption were always true, program evaluation would be the simply expensive, tedious, and frequently frustrating but nonetheless possible process just described.

In 1974, Willems argued the contrary. His thesis was based on a collection of facts and an "ecological" logic. It might also have been labeled "systems theory" (see Huse, 1975; Nichols & Everett, 1986; Weinberg, 1975). The basic idea of systems theory is that most of the events in physical and behavioral domains systematically interact, such that changing any one of them always changes others, and sometimes many others. Conversely, changing any one event often requires changing many others. Willem's thesis was and still is arguable, but the facts alone were sufficient to provoke ongoing debate (e.g., Evans, Meyers, Kurkjian, & Kishi, 1988) and a certain prudence among program appliers (see Rogers-Warren & Warren, 1977).

The facts that Willem cited were many examples of programs that had achieved their intended effects but had also achieved unintended effects, some of them intensely undesirable. Not all these cases can be dismissed as poor initial planning; some showed that even sophisticated planners did not always know enough about the problem and the program to predict all the outcomes, no matter how careful their initial analysis. Thus, ecological prudence suggests that programs should be applied only when the programmer can predict and measure all likely consequences. But how can programmers ever learn to predict all of what will happen, if not from experiments done in ignorance?

Even so, ecological prudence is increasing. Programmers have begun to measure more outcomes than the targeted ones. They also have begun to use global subjective measures such as social validity. They do so to predict program survival, of course, and because they assume that any unexpected, unmeasured bad outcomes of a program may escape programmers' attention but are not lost on the consumers: Unexpected, unmeasured bad outcomes should lower consumer satisfaction. Only uniformly high social-desirability ratings should imply no unexpected, unmeasured bad outcomes.

The imprecision of this logic is obvious: global, subjective ratings of events such as satisfaction certainly can reflect unexpected bad outcomes, but they may not always do so. They can reflect many other processes as well. So, they have no systematic relation to unpredicted consequences, good or bad.

Ecological and systems-analytical logics make program construction problematic and program evaluation impossible. If a program typically can have many costs and many benefits, they all must be measured to evaluate the program. That necessity is fatal: if some outcomes of any program are unpredictable and can be bad, then program evaluation requires measurement of every possible outcome, not just the targeted outcome. But that is obviously an impossible prescription: People do not know enough, they are not rich enough, and they do not live long enough to measure every side effect that a program could have. To measure some possible outcomes but not others is arbitrary, often yields an incorrect program evaluation, and is dangerous. If evaluation programs are insisted on nonetheless, it seems that it is necessary to proceed as if ecological, systems-analytical logic did not exist, existed but had no merit, had merit but in contexts other than program evaluation, or had merit for some programs' evaluations but not the particular program's evaluation.

Before agreeing that only close-minded program evaluation is possible, since unselectively open-minded program evaluation is impossible, perhaps the usual case should be considered, not the scientific ones. I begin with an anecdote from an educational psychologist in a certain developing country. She had spent her professional life urging her government to provide a free, public education to the children of the countryside, just as it did to the children of the cities. Her government always refused on grounds of inadequate public funds. Then, a turn in world markets made the government suddenly much richer than ever before. The government commissioned her to develop its new rural-education program. Overjoyed, she designed the program of her dreams. It included a very thorough program evaluation. The government agreed to fund every part of her expensive proposal—except the relatively cheap program evaluation. Astounded, she asked why. A patient politician undertook her education: the government would receive great credit for spending so much money to educate rural children. If an evaluation showed that the program was good, the government would gain no additional credit; in political logic, expensive programs are supposed to do well. If the evaluation showed the program was bad, then the government would lose all the credit it had just gained. In the next election, it would be accused accurately of having wasted a great deal of money. Surely, the politician suggested, even a Ph.D. could understand when there is no more to gain and everything to lose?

This anecdote suggests that program evaluation can be intensely political, and everyday experience suggests that it often is. Allow the decision to be made politically and, quite rationally, little program evaluation will get done. When it is done, it very rarely will include the six components that modern behavioral science prescribes. Instead, it probably will emphasize whatever worked and ignore whatever failed. An alternative political strategy, as in the ongoing governmentally funded evaluation of day care, is to use a measurement system so complex that no outsider will understand it. That enables the evaluators to put good labels on what increases and bad labels on what decreases, with fear of rational contradiction.

There is one form of political program evaluation that often seems appealing to people who would like an objective program evaluation. It is the concurrent schedule of operant psychology. It asks the organism under study to demonstrate which of two environments, and thereby which of two programs, it prefers. Applied to humans, this is a form of social validity applied to the program's target participants. It does not ask them to talk about the programs; instead, it watches them to determine whether they would rather leave Program A to enter Program B or leave Program B to enter Program A. Laboratory versions of the concurrent schedule can be quite complex (Catania, 1985, pp. 182–187), but its applied, human versions are simple enough to state, though tedious and expensive to do. The process involves five basic steps:

1. Create two concurrent environments, one of them characterized by the program and its outcomes and the other similar in all respects but those. In other words, the difference between these two environments is Program A versus no program or Program A versus Program B.

2. Ensure that the participant has extensive, repetitively alternating experience in both environments.

3. Create a very-easy-entry response to each environment, and teach these entry responses to the participant.

4. Create a very-easy-exit response from each environment, and teach these exit responses to the participant.

5. Allow the participant to enter and exit from either environment at any time, and watch that for a long enough time to determine the participant's preferences for the two environments.

This leads, very expensively, to the participant's evaluation of the program or programs. It may be a different evaluation from that which the participant would give verbally; for participants who cannot or do not speak well, it may be the only evaluation of the programs that can be obtained from them.

In some politics, the participant's evaluation may be the only truly relevant evaluation. This is sometimes the case for professionals who believe that their only politics are their participants' politics; they want for their participants as much as possible of what their participants want for themselves. Their problem is to know what their participants want for themselves (Evans et al., 1988; *Journal of the Association for Persons with Severe Handicaps,* 1998). In that case, effectiveness, program fidelity, generalization, proof of cause and effect, cost-benefit ratios, and other people's ideas of social validity are far less relevant to program evaluation.

The concurrent schedule can be a heartbreaking event for nearly selfless professionals, because it can show them that sometimes their participants want distressingly different things for themselves than the relevant professional wants for them. However, those times can also be the occasion for a complex, good-hearted negotiation among all concerned parties (cf. Bannerman, Sheldon, Sherman, & Harchik, 1990). That negotiation should be at least better informed by the results of a concurrent-schedule evaluation.

Thus, from a political point of view, program evaluation is always the outcome of an often unspoken debate and an art. It is the four skills of (1) knowing what to measure for a program to look good, (2) knowing what to measure for a program to look bad, (3) knowing what to measure for no one to know clearly what the program did, and (4) knowing how to avoid measuring anything while still drawing the desired conclusion.

From a basic-science point of view, of course, program evaluation is simply knowing as much of the truth about what a program accomplishes as is possible. That is a constantly fruitful yet never-ending venture. From an applied-science point of view, program evaluation is simply knowing as much of the truth about what a program accomplishes as is justified by the relevant costs and benefits. The end of that venture presumably depends on the resultant cost-benefit ratio. However, because calculation of cost-benefit ratios is such an uncertain process, it too may be a never-ending venture.

REFERENCES

Bannerman, D. J., Sheldon, J. B., Sherman, J. A., & Harchik, A. E. (1990). Balancing the right to habilitation with the right to personal liberties: The rights of people with developmental disabilities to eat too many doughnuts and take a nap. *Journal of Applied Behavior Analysis, 23,* 79–89.

Catania, A. C. (1985). *Learning.* Englewood Cliffs, NJ: Prentice Hall.

Evans, I. M., Meyer, L. H., Kurkjian, J., & Kishi, G. S. (1988). An evaluation of behavioral interrelationships in child behavior therapy. In J. C. Wit, S. N. Elliot, & F. N. Gresham (Eds.), *Handbook of behavior therapy in education* (pp. 189–215). New York: Plenum Press.

Huse, E. F. (1975). *Organization, development, and change.* St. Paul: West.

Journal of the Association for Persons with Severe Handicaps. (1998). Special series on participatory action research, *23*(3).

Nichols, W. C., & Everett, C. A. (1986). *Systematic family therapy.* New York: Guilford Press.

Rogers-Warren, A., & Warren, S. F. (Eds.). (1977). *Ecological perspectives in behavior analysis.* Baltimore: University Park Press.

Schwartz, I. S., & Baer, D. M. (1991). Social validity. *Journal of Applied Behavior Analysis, 24,* 189–204.

Weinberg, G. (1975). *Introduction to general systems thinking.* New York: John Wiley & Sons.

Willems, E. P. (1974). Behavioral technology and behavioral ecology. *Journal of Applied Behavior Analysis, 7,* 151–165.

CHAPTER 19

EVALUATING SCIENCE-BASED PRACTICE WITH SINGLE SYSTEMS

Harold E. Briggs,
William Feyerherm, and
Wallace Gingerich

Direct-service social workers provide support services to a wide variety of clients, such as the mentally ill, the physically disabled, the homeless, the chemically dependent, and persons suffering from poverty. Common to all of these types of services is a fundamental goal: to help those who are suffering to relieve their conditions and improve their overall functioning. Practice is inherently goal oriented—it needs to be guided by a sense of progress toward (or away from) these broad goals. The fundamental question is: How do social workers know that they have helped clients? This question is of paramount importance to at least three groups—the recipients (clients) of service, those that provide support for the social work services (sponsors), and social workers themselves. As early as the work of Mary Richmond and others in the 1800s, social work adapted the tools, language, and conceptual approaches of the research world to the amelioration of social problems. Although social work practice is different from scientific research, the tools of the scientific process have important applications in the development, delivery, and assessment of practice. Our objective in this chapter is to explore this relationship by working through the following topics:

1. The conceptual overlap and distinctions between research, practice, and practice evaluation;

2. Current controversies about the role of research methods in the practice of social work;

3. Anticipated benefits for practice that may be derived from incorporation of research tools;

4. An example of the use of a single-subject design approach and the benefit that may be derived from the approach for practice; and

5. Limitations and challenges of the single-subject and celeration line approaches for practice.

In developing these objectives, we must be mindful of the excellent historical narrative and interpretation provided by others in this volume (especially

Thyer, Reid, and Gambrill). Our goal is not to repeat their arguments, but to illustrate the application of single-subject design activities for the improvement of practice.

DISTINGUISHING AMONG RESEARCH, PRACTICE, AND PRACTICE EVALUATION

Lundy, Massat, Smith, and Bhasin (1996) offer a distinction between research and social work practice. They conclude that practitioners in private and public agencies share common values that place more emphasis on priorities that involve client focus, diversity, and service-delivery aspects of research partnerships, whereas university researchers hold a greater interest in and place more emphasis on priorities such as "high research expertise . . . methodological rigor, objectivity and abstract theory development than do agencies" (p. 170) To more fully understand the roles of research, evaluation, and practice in the overall development of evidence-based practice in social work, we offer the following discussion of their relative attributes.

Research is based on the use of systematic observations, assessed through the scientific method, to develop and test theories. It emphasizes elements of control over the data-collection processes and environment to achieve the parsimony of theory, and it emphasizes an effort to move toward certainty in establishing cause-and-effect relationships. Beyond that is a concern with generalization—the development of principles that will apply in a wide variety of settings and selections of client populations.

In contrast, practice is the process of selecting goals appropriate to specific clients or client systems. It is driven by problems rather than theory testing, but it represents the application of theory in specific situations. Rather than attempt to remove (control) the complexities in a setting to establish cause and effect, the practitioner must understand those complexities, contingencies, and idiosyncrasies—they may drive the results that are achievable in the unique situation that the client presents. From such a perspective, the agendas of practice and the research community seem far apart, connected only by the tenuous strands of theory. The question "How do we know that we have helped clients?" is difficult to address in each unique setting with research tools that aim toward the generalized setting and the development of theory. In our mind, bridging this gap is the role of practice evaluation and represents a special contribution of single-subject design.

Evaluation is characterized by the application of research tools to the assessment of practice. Although evaluation is critical to identify goals and means of measuring those goals, the focus is more on problem solving than on theory testing. Moreover, the elements of experimental control and rigor, so critical to establishing the internal validity of theory testing, are typically unattainable in practice evaluation. The effort to attain confidence in results (to eliminate all plausible rival explanations for a set of observations) is replaced by an effort to reduce uncertainty—for social workers to believe that they probably are helping their clients but cannot control all aspects of their lives with such a degree of tyranny that no other explanations for their behavior are possible. Evaluation as an approach has primarily focused not on the impact of individual efforts with specific clients, but on the impact of programs and policies (see, e.g., chapter 18 in this volume).

What we propose as a useful distinction is the field of practice evaluation, which has three important attributes: (1) it involves goal setting (as with practice), (2) it involves monitoring or tracking of behavior (using research tools), and (3) it involves a systematic, analytical process of developing insights into the applicability of the specific intervention with the specific client (rather than the generalized program clientele of the evaluator). In this sense, this is a bridge that brings the tools of research and evaluation into the world of practice.

GENERAL CHARACTERISTICS OF PRACTICE EVALUATION IN SOCIAL WORK

In general, practice evaluation is accompanied by its own distinct challenges. As the primary function of practice evaluation, the practitioner seeks to assess "progress toward the goal . . . [and to] monitor [it] continually throughout the intervention to determine whether its is working and to decide when services should change or are no longer needed" (Corcoran, Gingerich, & Briggs, p. 66). This goal is similar for service-delivery research involving developmental and exploratory research methods.

Although practice evaluation is often confused with research, which may be a reason why some practitioners avoid it, the solution to that dilemma for social work practitioners has been addressed by Corcoran, Gingerich, and Briggs (2001): "Although social work interventions incorporate evaluation implicitly, its is important for several reasons to make evaluation an intentional and systematic part of practice" (p. 66). They caution that "it is important to remember that evaluation is a practice activity, done to provide feedback on your works with your client" (p. 67). Other reasons for practice evaluation are to provide a status report on the health of the treatment goal at the end of practice and a report of the usefulness of the intervention in achieving desired results (Corcoran, Gingerich, & Briggs, 2001).

PRACTICE EVALUATION VERSUS CLINICAL RESEARCH

It is our opinion that social work practice, practice evaluation, and research share many common (but not all) implicit functions. They share common scientific bases and ascribe to similar functions, such as hunches, questions, hypotheses, exploration, data gathering, and analysis. The distinction between practice evaluation and research for social work practice is described best by Corcoran, Gingerich, and Briggs: "Although practice evaluation uses research methods and procedures, its primary goals are to provide feedback about client change and enhance the client's outcome" (p. 67). They go on to say about clinical research that "in contrast, clinical research uses rigorous research procedures to develop scientific knowledge" (p. 67), and they believe that the distinctions between them are a matter of "purpose, rigor, and emphasis" (p. 67).

A GENERIC OUTLINE OF PRACTICE EVALUATION

At the most general level in any intervention process, the basic question that we need to address is whether the interventions are changing the targeted systems. Our sense of the word *change* must be probabilistic—that is, we need to understand whether the evidence demonstrates that there is a likely change in the systems. We use the word *systems* to generically include a host of intervention targets, ranging from organizations and groups of clients that may be affected by broad social policies, through families, to the level of individual clients. In each instance, we are looking for evidence that something that matters has changed (we hope for the better). In that search, practice evaluation follows a general method that has at least the following elements:

- Conceptual targets for change—things that can be measured that matter and that are theoretically, logically, and reasonably related to the interventions we implement

- Specification of the systems that are the target of change efforts, whether those systems are individual clients, agencies, and organizations or classes of persons (e.g., Temporary Assistance for Needy Families clients)

- Methods for measuring our conceptual targets within the targeted systems

- The consideration of other possible influences on the systems and other possible explanations for any changes or differences that occur—in essence, that we are not arrogant enough to believe that only our own efforts can change the world

As a field, we have well-developed methodologies for implementing this approach in examining groups of clients, groups of organizations, and so on, but we have less well developed methods for applying this same logic to situations in which we are interested only in a single system—"did the client change?" The paradox is that much of our work, whether clinical or administrative, is aimed at changing the conditions of single systems—we work with each unique client, we administer an agency, we are concerned with the conditions in the community in which we reside. We need to apply the method of science to the operation of our own practice—working within single systems.

This chapter is designed to revisit one such method of examining single systems, the celeration line method. As with all methodologies, it has its unique requirements, limits, and flaws. No method is foolproof and applicable to all situations. The methods of group analysis and experimental design have their place in the analysis of changes in systems, but often we are concerned about change in settings which those more usual methods are not easily applied. Before we introduce the method, we turn to the relevant literature on evaluation of practice with single-subject methods.

THE RELEVANCE OF EVALUATION FOR SOCIAL WORK PRACTICE

The arguments for why social workers should evaluate the practice they provide have already been given by several noted scholars and practitioners (see Bailey-Dempsey & Reid, 1996; Fischer, 1973; Pinskton et al., 1982). Mary Richmond gave the most fundamental reason for accountability to clients. Historically, she recognized the need to collect evidence to fashion treatment development and subsequent implementation and evaluation to determine whether human suffering had been lessened. Although built into the very fabric of a social workers toolkit, the profession abandoned its emphasis on science much later (as previously described by Thyer in this volume). Clearly, if social workers engage in direct or administrative practices that are not empirically derived, they are probably not managing their clients care with the best available science. Second, from its inception, social work has wanted to use properties of science, including measurement, observations, and critical thinking in the delivery of social work services.

Another reason for the use of evaluation methods in social work practice of any form (direct or administrative) is that it corresponds with the profession's emphasis on accountability. To aid a client through treatment in the absence of data, such as clients' self-report and other means of determining client response to intervention, is difficult to justify. It begs the question as to whether the practitioner's self-awareness is the driving force or whether the client's self-determination is the deciding impetus and foundation for the treatment provided.

Yet another major reason for the use of evaluation methods in practice is the need to communicate with the sponsor of the programs and agencies through which people receive services from social workers. Now that managed care is the funding mechanism that defines the cost and duration of social work services, the need for quality assurance has gone from a professional value and ideal to one of survival.

Beyond the mandate that managed care provides, there are sound practical reasons for the use of science in practice. These reasons become obvious to any social worker with a graduate education from an accredited school of social work. Some say that having an inquiry-based perspective in practice can influence the treatment-planning process as a scientific rather than a prophylactic experience. We know from Marsh (in this volume) that case studies based on a scientific process aimed at achieving some treatment outcome or some assessment objective can also contribute to the development of theory (both human behavior and practice) in social work.

The consequences of continued use of data-based interventions are expected to add to an existing arsenal of innovative evidence-based treatment techniques (Thyer, 2001). As these innovations become available, social workers need to know about them and are expected to try them. Gambrill, Reid, Thyer, Rzepnicki, and countless others in this volume believe that social workers should be directed by the profession's code of ethics in more direct ways than before, particularly regarding the issues of using evidence-based methods in direct practice. They believe that social workers need to cautiously use nontested treatment approaches because these approaches may not be the best course of treatment available. As long ago as 1981, the president of the National Association of Social Workers made an urgent call to social workers to carefully and methodologically evaluate their practice, which seems ironic in the face of current indifference and reluctance in social work to do practice evaluations. We therefore need to attend to some of the rationale for the lack of evaluation in practice.

PERSPECTIVES ON LIMITATIONS OF USING SINGLE-SUBJECT METHODS

Research data show that social workers would evaluate their practice only if it was required (Gerdes, Edmonds, Haslam, & McCartney, 1996). In that study, social workers reported using preferred pragmatic and intuitive self-evaluation methods over empirical approaches (Gerdes, Edmonds, Haslam, & McCartney, 1996). Clearly, practice evaluation is not a popular activity among clinicians. Many reasons for that failure exist. Kazi and Wilson (1996) discuss the lack of single-subject methods as practice evaluation as stemming from three points: (1) difficulty in implementation without organizational and information supports, (2) few useful examples as guides for teaching people ways of linking single-subject methods to practice, (3) few studies that show the relative usefulness in increasing practitioner effectiveness.

Gerdes, Edmonds, Haslam, and McCartney (1996) also cite the lack of time to perform evaluation. In their study, 70 percent of the respondents indicated that they would rather use a pragmatic self-evaluation than empirical methods. Most of the respondents said that lack of time was the reason for not using more formal methods of evaluation. Few of them were trained in single-case methods and few reported actual use of empirical procedures. Although most of the respondents reported the nonuse of empirical methods, most reported that they monitor client change.

Rubin and Knox (1996) argue for a lesser emphasis on the use of single-system methods for clinical practice evaluation and urge that schools of social work deemphasize its use in educating graduates. Their points, as Levy (1996) emphasized but later refuted, are that single-system designs used in actual practice yield ambiguous data patterns. These ambiguities discourage clinicians from using single-design methods. Consequently, the emphasis of these methods needs to cease in social work curricula, and significance test and single-subject designs should not be taught in a simplistic fashion.

In the related field of counseling psychology, indifference to the use of single-subject methods has also been noted. Galassi and Gersh (1993) found that the reasons for the nonuse of single-subject methods involves many factors, such as (1) that many university programs did not include sufficient instruction in use of these methods; (2) that, all in all, the faculty lacked expertise in these methods; (3) that single-subject methods were believed to be limited in applicability; (4) that student exposure to these methods came from faculty whose allegiance to other methods and their dislike for single-subject methods would result in competition for instructional time; and (5) that most believe that single-subject methods are only suited for behavioral approaches.

PERSPECTIVES ON THE PRACTICAL USES AND ADVANTAGES OF SINGLE-SUBJECT METHODS

Moving away from such skepticism, there are many people in social work and counseling psychology who do not assess single-subject methodology as ineffectual for practice or research purposes. They perceive the nonuse of single-subject methods as missed opportunities for the use of routine measurement and case-monitoring methods in direct practice. For example, Galassi and Gersh (1993) point out that single-subject methods exist that are nonbehavioral in nature, and they name a few such as the stage-process design (compatible with cognitive approaches) and the research case-representative method (involves the deconstruction of the person and the meanings attached to functioning). Furthermore, they show that there is no evidence that single-subject methods are less valid than group methods. Galassi and Gersh also show that single-subject methods can be used for hypothesis generation. They demonstrate using the AB design applied in nonbehavioral counseling intervention approaches to generate hypotheses. They describe other capacities of multiple baseline and reversal designs as useful for practice research in confirming clinical hypothesis. They describe the linkage of stages of single-subject research to counseling practices and outcomes.

Getting to the heart of the matter, so far as we are concerned, Galassi and Gersh say that single-subject methods not only help as research tools but also are useful for quality assurance in practice by helping categorize and track client change. They further urged that more accountability in counseling practice would occur if more practitioners use simple AB designs in their work. They concluded that "single-subject designs are extremely flexible and can help provide answers to questions about process, outcome, and accountability in clinical practice and supervision" (p. 530).

As a demonstration of that accountability, Kazi and Wilson (1996) show that, in most of their cases, the practitioner effectiveness was increased by using single-subject methods. They did caution, though, that training, agency support, and administrative sanction were key in using single-subject designs as a routine approach for practice evaluation.

In defense of single-subject methods in social work, Levy (1996) points to

Rubin and Knox's (1996) criticism of ambiguous data as a reason to abandon use of these methods as a nonissue that, in general, people do not evaluate their practice because of agency and time constraints. She indicated that the ambiguous data was useful for engaging the practitioner. This engagement includes critical thinking about the possibility of alternative treatment influences or other possible scenarios that were occurring during treatment phases. She said that there are no data to support the claim that practitioners avoid using single-subject methods because of ambiguous data-related issues. Furthermore, she indicated that it is a myth that schools place emphasis on single-subject methods in their curriculum.

Wong (1996) states that Rubin and Knox (1996) scapegoat single-subject designs and use misleading and ambiguous claims to discredit single-subject methods. Wong fears that because the arguments are coming from well-respected researchers in social work, readers may believe them on the basis of who is making the criticism. Wong believes that Rubin and Knox's example was incomplete and left more questions about their intervention and measures. Instead, they spent much of the time reflecting on the fact that their intervention failed and on the limits of single-subject design methods Wong (1996) illustrates that, from its very beginning, single-subject methods have been helpful to practitioners seeking ways to operationalize independent and dependent variables and measures of individual client behaviors. He says that the methodology was later applied successfully to social problems and clinical disorders. Moreover, he notes that most general research texts offer single-subject methods very sparse coverage and that there exist few opportunities for learning from experts in this area. The result is too few practitioners sufficiently trained to use single-subject methods.

Rubin and Knox (1996), Rubin (1996), and Knox (1996), however, are less optimistic that practitioners are adequately taught or prepared to use single-case methods appropriately in practice. They raise caution about a major data-analysis problem that accompanies single-case evaluation methods. They define this as the ambiguity in graphing fluctuating data patterns, which leaves too much room for error in predicting cause and effect. They recommend replication intervention designs, including multiple baseline single-case methods as a basis for correcting the interpretation problem produced when there are coincidences or other external threats that lessen the ability to draw cause-and-effect inferences about the effectiveness of the intervention. Levy (1996), in response to their caution, critically examines the data-analysis issue they discuss but does not have the same level of concern or frustration.

Wong (1996) and Mattaini (1996) agree with Levy (1996) that Rubin and Knox (1996) are far too critical of single-case evaluations as not being useful for practice evaluations. Both Wong and Mattaini agree that Rubin and Knox misrepresent the state of affairs regarding single-case study methods. They believe that Rubin and Knox are unfairly confusing the complications of data analysis associated with using single-case evaluation methods for research with those associated with day-to-day data-analysis issues that are common frustrations of single-case practice evaluations.

Mattaini (1996) argues that single-case methods are useful for both research and practice and that the relative advantages and limitations involved with the methodology are expected to differ across purposes. For research, the degree of methodological rigor and experimental control necessary to render cause-and-effect conclusions are, in general, not possible in actual real-life practice situations. In actual case situations that are amendable to systematic replication of intervention, it is possible for practitioners to feasibly use single-case methods with the intention of judging intervention effectiveness in their social work practice with individuals and agencies.

Although the single-case methodology is not error free, it must still be preferable in the same settings to group designs for evaluating social work practice. Group designs require the use of more than one individual, which may not fit with many practice settings, in which individuals are helped with their individual sets of issues rather than treated as members of a group who can be viewed interchangeably. Moreover, group designs often require the application and ensuring of client matching and sample-selection procedures to generate control or comparison groups. These procedures are critical because they ensure compatibility of client subjects for aggregate analysis and group comparisons. The use of such control groups adds time and expense for locating and matching individuals for a control-group experience. In addition, unknown differences between the groups or differential rates of dropout may skew the results in a way that confounds the data, making it difficult to adequately judge the usefulness of the intervention under investigation.

CELERATION LINE METHOD

What we describe here is an alternative to be used in the study of single systems over time, an approach that may be termed an *experimental clinical method*. It is a situation in which we seek to determine whether there is likelihood that a single system has changed over time, concurrent (or subsequent) with interventions that have been implemented. The essential elements of the setting are that one system (e.g., client, agency) is studied rather than groups, that outcome data (or data of interest) is collected repeatedly about the system, and that there is an intervention or treatment that is applied at some point in time during the evaluation period. These elements lead us to the following seven procedural steps:

1. Identify the system to be studied;
2. Describe the changes that are expected and the basis for the expectation;
3. Select suitable measures of the anticipated change;
4. Record baseline information;
5. Implement and monitor the intervention (treatment);
6. Collect follow-up data;
7. Assess whether the data shows a likely change in the system behavior.

The first six steps are relatively commonly described, and advice regarding their implementation may be obtained in a variety of standard research and theory texts (Briggs & Corcoran, 2001; Corcoran, 1992). What we wish to explore in greater detail here is the last step—the assessment of whether a change has likely occurred. Our intent is to describe methods suitable for the situation in which a few points of data are available but in which an elaborate set of observations spanning hundreds of time periods is not appropriate or practical. We are concerned with a fairly common set of situations in which time may not be available to establish the baseline measures, in which an indication of whether change has occurred is needed in a reasonable practical (and short) period of time, but in which we need to provide some basis other than intuition.

For that situation, we describe a process that we termed the *celeration line*, a six-step analytic sequence as follows:

1. Collect and plot (graph) the baseline data (we suggest that a minimum of ten time periods be included. For the example that follows, we have retrospectively created the early parts of that baseline period).

2. Divide the baseline period into two equal segments so that direction of movement (celeration) may be estimated.

3. Calculate and plot the mean level of behavior or outcome variables for each of the segments (plotted at the midpoint of each segment).

4. Using the two points, plot the celeration line. Determine the number of baseline observations that are in the desired direction (e.g., above the line if improvement is desired).

5. Extend the line into the treatment period. Determine the number of post intervention observations that are in the desired direction.

6. Compare the proportions in the baseline and intervention portions that are in the desired direction to determine whether there is a sufficiently large change to conclude that the difference is greater than might occur by chance. For this we have used a binomial test, tabled in an earlier article (Gingerich & Feyerherm, 1979).

At times, the change in the client is so dramatic and clear that no formal analysis is needed: the graphic display is sufficient. Such visual analysis techniques are more likely to be used by social work practitioners to evaluate client change and may be a practical alternative to highly sophisticated statistical techniques in certain circumstances. However, the advanced methods are needed because of the serial autocorrelation effects that occur in the daily time-series events of client behavior change. For several technical and practical reasons, this kind of inquiry into practice (time-series analysis) may take too much time and money. Moreover, the results from such rigorous analytical technology are not necessary to address the typical practice evaluation concerns of the client consumers or funders of social services.

The celeration-line method is a reasonable alternative to complex and costly statistical analysis of direct practice. It is principally useful for assessing single-client behavior change. It is often a preferred method to the use of quasi-experimental group design for evaluating client change. The celeration-line method has been described by Gingerich (1979) as useful for feasibly evaluating direct practice. Four months later, he published similar comments with Feyerherm (Gingerich & Feyerherm, 1979). This article reintroduces that previous discussion and provides examples of applying the technique to a previously published single-case example by Briggs (1996). Using his data set, we will show the advantages, limitations, and key points of interests for practitioners. We conclude this discussion by raising the critical implications for social work practitioners using evaluation data to guide their critical thinking, decision making, and evaluation of client response to treatment.

In the profession of social work, as in others such as medicine and advertising, there is a shift toward the use of data to make life-and-death, cost-saving, and other crucial decisions. The celeration-line method is helpful to practitioners who face similar situations. It is among the many evaluation techniques available in social work that can be used to shape intervention development. Also, it may assist practitioners using data to make clinical decisions to further behavioral progress and to extend client and other treatment gains. There is, however, the problem of some practitioners who ignore the advances in the profession and dangerously rely on methodologies that are no longer practical or necessary, as in the case presented previously in this volume by Thyer.

CASE ILLUSTRATION OF CELERATION LINE

To demonstrate the application of simple procedures for implementing an accountable organization, we have used the process of the celeration line (Gingerich and Feyerherm, 1979) applied to data derived from Briggs's (1996) study of an inner-city community organization. Although the substantive analyses of these data have been presented previously, we herein apply a relatively simple visual technique to assess whether changes have occurred in the client systems under review. We have also selected a subset of the analyses presented by Briggs to focus on the method and the use of the techniques in moving forward the objectives of an accountable organization.[1]

As a brief recap of the method, it is designed to assess trends over time within the baseline and extend those trends into the treatment period. The assessment of trend is based on calculation of the mean values of the criterion variable during the first and second halves of the baseline period. In that respect, it requires no formulaic manipulations beyond calculating an average and simple plotting

---

1. To fully illustrate the technique, the lead author reconstructed elements of the baseline data that were not presented in the 1996 analysis.

and graphing tools. When the trend has been established, the treatment period is examined to determine whether a preponderance of the observations are within the desired range, and if so, whether that preponderance is greater than would be expected by chance alone. The method has an advantage over simple pre-post comparisons in that many social processes have a built-in direction (growth) as a result of naturally occurring processes. To claim that an intervention is successful when it may be the result of such natural processes would be counter to the principle of running an accountable organization, indeed it could amount to an inefficient and potentially ineffective use of resources that might be better employed elsewhere.

In the current context, the client organization (group home) engaged in efforts to improve the social functioning and community adjustment of a set of four clients, for whom the clinical objectives were to improve family-support contacts and to increase community-support contacts for males, with the expectation that increased contacts would lead to a reduction in critical incidents among male clients. Each of the four clients engaged in behavior-management problems and lacked adequate and frequent contact with family members and community resources and supports. The intervention was individually tailored and applied, but it was applied in a consistent manner across the four clients as a group. For this example, we could have provided examination of the individual progress of each client (and indeed this was charted as the practice took place). Here, however, for the sake of brevity, we present the group averages, which may be treated as a single-client system.

Figure 19.1 provides the first test of the change efforts. The first fourteen months are displayed as baseline data, with the celeration line intersecting the data so that six of the observations are above the line and eight below it. The line, which provides a fairly good visual fit to the baseline data, shows a relatively stable and slowly increasing number of family-support contacts. After the fifteenth month, for the next twenty-five months there were only three months in which the number of family contacts fell below the celeration line. One probably does not need to refer to the chart in the 1979 article (p. 109) to reach the conclusion that indeed this is a positive and significant change.

But the area of family contacts is only one of the hypothesized impacts of the planned change; a second is in the number of community contacts. That data is displayed graphically in figure 19.2. In this instance, examination of the baseline period leads us to plot a celeration line in which nine of the baseline observations are above the line, and six are either on the line or below it. The line is clearly moving upward, reflecting an increase in the number of community contacts, even preceding the change effort. Indeed, if we project the celeration line into the treatment period, there are twelve observations above the line and eleven below the line. In other words, the line seems to fit the treatment period nearly as well as the baseline period. Using the chart from the 1979 article, we would have needed to see at least seventeen observations (of twenty-five treatment observations) above the line before concluding that significant change had

FIGURE 19.1 Family-Support Contacts

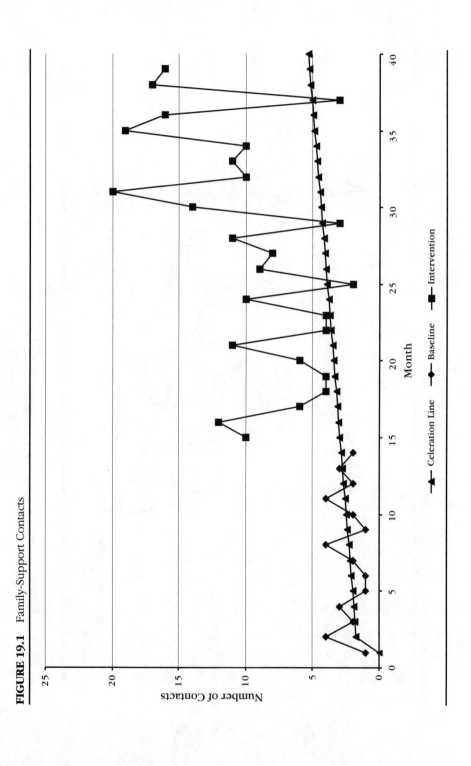

FIGURE 19.2 Community-Support Contacts

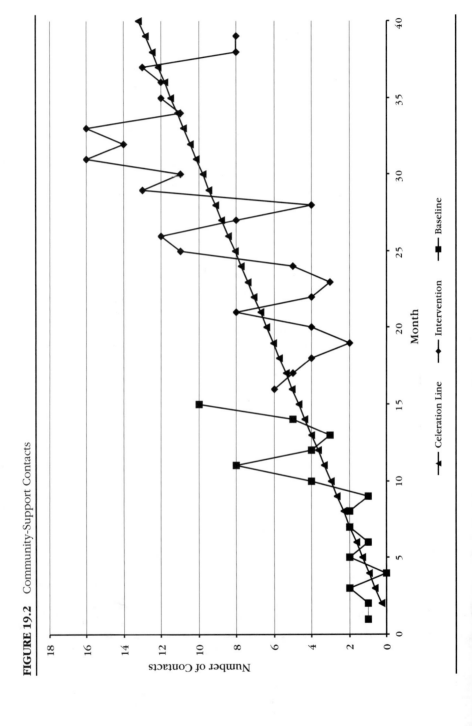

occurred. Although the number of community contacts in the treatment period clearly was higher as an absolute number than those in the baseline period, we cannot conclude that this difference reflects any intentional change process.

Of interest to the organization, however, was not simply changing the number of family and/or community contacts, but using those changes in addition to increasing the number of supportive contacts to reduce the number of critical incidents among male clients. The numbers presented in figure 19.3 give some sense of the reason for this desire—the raw number of critical incidents had been escalating during the baseline period. Indeed, examination of the baseline period led us to chart the celeration line as indicated—it would have suggested that the group home would have reached the point of fifteen incidents per month if the pattern has not been changed. The fit of the line is indicated by the fact that of the fourteen baseline observations, seven fall above and seven below the celeration line—it is designed to reflect the central pattern in the data.

After the treatment period initiated, the number of critical incidents dropped off rather dramatically, with only one intervention period observation even approaching the level of the celeration line. Clearly, there is a significant difference in the numbers of critical incidents before and after the behavior change effort, a difference that cannot be explained by the underlying pattern (represented by the celeration line).

In an effort to put together all of this information, we created a summary score of the total number of contacts, and in figure 19.4 we have graphically displayed that score by month along with the critical incident information. The total number of supportive activities in the baseline period is modeled with the celeration line. Seven of the observations are either on the line or above it, and seven are below the line. Extending that line into the intervention period gives us nineteen observations at or above the line and six below the line. Since our critical value (baseline at 50 percent, twenty-five intervention observations) is seventeen, we have a significant change. Moreover, as is indicated in the graph, that increase in the number of supportive contacts occurred simultaneously with the decrease in critical incidents. The conclusion from the data analysis is that the change in family visits, coupled with the natural growth in community contacts, changed the supportive environment for male clients. This, in turn, occurred at the same time as the decrease in critical incidents. Although this does not establish a causal relationship, it certainly is consistent with the expectation that drove the change effort, and from the vantage point of an accountable group home, it should serve to demonstrate the desired effects.

DISCUSSION

The practicing social worker is faced with a series of immediate tactical decisions that require a sense of whether the intervention is working or needs modification. One such approach, visual analysis of graphical data, may be useful for practitioners seeking handy and easy-to-use procedures for analyzing practice data.

FIGURE 19.3 Male Critical Incidents

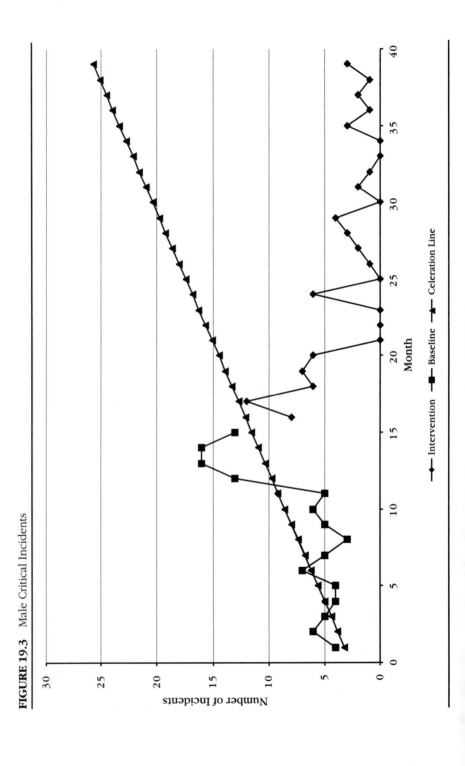

Intervention ◆ Baseline ■ Celeration Line ▲

Number of Incidents

Month

FIGURE 19.4 Support Activities and Critical Incidents: Community Adjustment

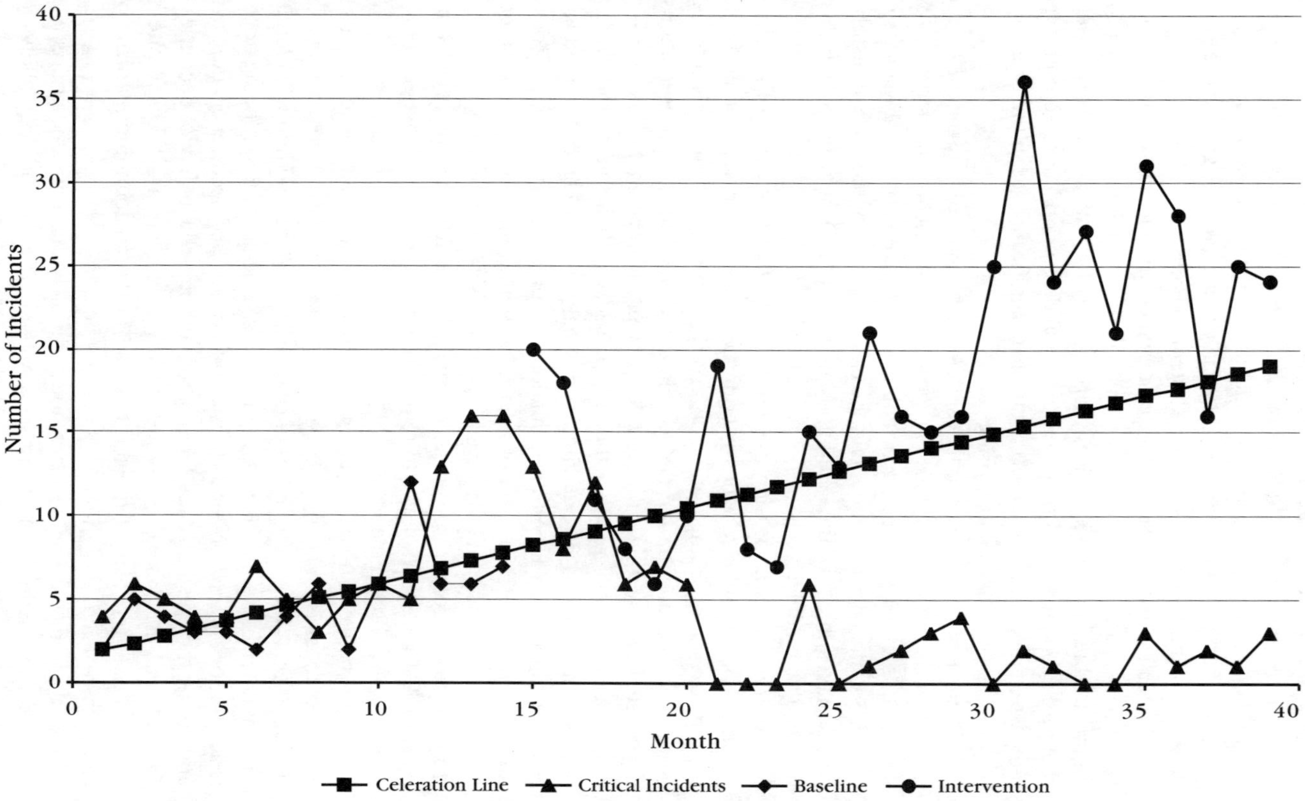

The celeration-line method as an adjunct to such graphing processes is a quasi-statistical method that enables practitioners to assess both therapeutic and statistical significance of change during intervention. Given its connection to probability theory, this approach represents a pragmatic alternative to the expense, time, and methodological rigor required in using group design or more elaborate time-series analysis to assess single-system changes.

We realize that there are situations in which the celeration method is not necessary. First, in those instances in which visual inspection alone clearly provides the method required to establish the presence of a dramatic, clearly observable change. Second is when a predetermined standard or goal has been achieved but the data elements do not support statistical significance, as in the original study of community adjustment by Briggs (1996).

There are several cautions that should be considered in using the celeration-line method. The method does not work well with dichotomous data, in which the client is either succeeding or failing rather than showing gradations of behavior. Such data does not contain the characteristics of the normal distribution, which makes the fit of the celeration line unstable. Data analysis with this type of data also is subject to issues of external validity.

Another caution to using this procedure is that the length of baseline and treatment phases should be nearly equivalent. The assumption is that if the treatment phase is longer, any change observed can be a function of history of maturation toward change in the desired direction. Nonequivalent observations during baseline and treatment phases is less of a problem when the baseline is longer at the outset. This is problematic and presents a challenge to the practitioner working in managed care environments that may not clinically or budgetarily sanction this particular sort of evaluation. For practice-evaluation purposes, this may require the construction of a baseline period retrospectively—either from existing records or from other reliable sources. Although such a practice might be frowned upon from a pure research perspective, from the practice-evaluation perspective, it is a useful tool to reduce the uncertainty about whether an intervention has a discernible impact.

A third area in which the celeration-line method is not particularly useful is when the focus is on change in level and trend because the observations do not distinguish between either types of change. Instead, the method will identify significant change in either aspect. For example, a behavior that is being treated for reduction or elimination tends to rise in frequency of occurrence after baseline and during the initial phases of treatment. Although the behavior decreases gradually toward the desired end—reduction or elimination—its initial rate of expression rises (clinically expected but statistically confounding), which complicates the typical use of the celeration-line method.

Aside from these cautionary notes, the celeration-line method is a useful means for evaluating change in single systems. The methodology allows for the sound detection of behavior change both therapeutically and quantitatively. Moreover, by using relatively intuitive methods to present the possible changes (graphing), the method should enable practitioners to illustrate results to sponsors and other interested parties. As in the Briggs example, the celeration-line method helped us statistically discuss a pattern of observations toward the treatment goal. This was not a pure research function, designed to carefully tease out cause-and-effect relationships over the long run. The use of the celeration-line method enabled us to avoid the alternatives of either engaging in several years of data collection to conduct a time-series analysis or simply stating "I think you are getting better" as a generic bromide of the confident practitioner.

This is one technique for thinking about responsible practice. By this we mean that there are carefully articulated treatment objectives, mechanisms by which to assess attainment of those objectives, a well-reasoned intervention strategy (using any of multiple treatment philosophies), and a consistent examination over time of the progress toward goals. Our hope is that other such techniques will be developed to collectively add to the ability of the profession to engage in responsible practice—which is accountable to the clients, to the funders, and to ourselves for being able to demonstrate the efficacy of our treatment processes as applied in individual client systems.

REFERENCES

Bailey-Dempsey, C. J., & Reid, W. J. (1996). Intervention design and development: A case study. *Research on Social Work Practice, 6*(2), 208–228.

Briggs, H. E. (1996). Enhancing community adjustment of persons with developmental disabilities: Transferring multi level behavioral technology to an inner city community organization. *Journal of Applied Social Sciences, 20*(2), 177–190.

Briggs, H. E., & Corcoran, K. (Eds.). (2001). *Social work practice: Treating common client problems* (2nd ed.). Chicago: Lyceum Books.

Corcoran, K. (1992). *Structuring change: Treating common client problems*. Chicago: Lyceum Books.

Corcoran, K., Gingerich, W. J., & Briggs, H. E. (2001). Practice evaluation: Setting goals and monitoring change. In H. E. Briggs & K. Corcoran (Eds.), *Social work practice: Treating common client problems* (2nd ed.). Chicago: Lyceum Books.

Fischer, J. (1973). Is casework effective? A review. *Social Work, 18*(1), 5–20.

Galassi, J. P., Gersh, T. L. (1993). Myths, misconceptions, and missed opportunity: Single case designs and counseling psychology. *Journal of Counseling Psychology, 40*(4), 525–531.

Gerdes, K. E., Edmonds, R. M., Haslam, D. R., & McCartney, T. L. (1996). Clinical social work use of practice evaluation procedures. *Research on Social Work Practice, 6*(1), 27–39.

Gingerich, W. J. (1979). Procedure for evaluating practice. *Health and Social Work, 4*(2), 105–130.

Gingerich, W. J., & Feyerherm, W. H. (1979). The celeration line technique for assessing client change. *Journal of Social Service Research, 3*(1), 99–113.

Kazi, M. A., & Wilson, J. T. (1996). Applying single-case evaluation methodology in a British social work agency. *Research on Social Work Practice, 6*(1), 5–26.

Knox, K. S. (1996). To graph or not to graph: A clinician's perspective. *Research on Social Work Practice, 6*(1), 100–103.

Levy, R. L. (1996). Data analysis problems in single-case evaluation: Much ado about nothing. *Research on Social Work Practice, 6*(1), 66–71.

Lundy, M., Massat, C. H., Smith, J., & Bhasin, S. (1996). Constructing the research enterprise: Building research bridges between private agencies, public agencies and universities. *The Journal of Applied Social Sciences, 20*(20), 169–176.

Mattaini, M. A. (1996). The abuse and neglect of single case designs. *Research on Social Work Practice, 6*(1), 83–90.

Pinkston, E., Levitt, J., Green, G. L., Linsk, N. L., & Rzepnicki, T. (1982). *Effective social work practice.* San Francisco: Jossey-Bass.

Rubin, A. (1996). The inflaming and defaming of the shrewd. *Research on Social Work Practice, 6*(1), 91–99.

Rubin, A., & Knox, K. S. (1996). Data analysis problems in single case evaluation: Much ado about nothing. *Research on Social Work Practice, 6*(1), 40–65.

Thyer, B. A. (2001). Evidenced-based approaches to community practice. In H. E. Briggs & K. Corcoran (Eds.), *Social work practice: Treating common client problems* (2nd ed., pp. 54–65). Chicago: Lyceum Books.

Wong, S. E. (1996). Single-case evaluation on trial: Broken promise or new scapegoat? *Research on Social Work Practice, 6*(1), 72–76.

CONTRIBUTORS

DONALD M. BAER, Ph.D., died in 2002. He was the Roy A. Roberts Distinguished Professor of Human Development and Family Life (HDFL) and a professor of psychology at the University of Kansas, Lawrence, Kansas.

HAROLD E. BRIGGS, Ph.D., is associate professor in the Graduate School of Social Work at Portland State University, Portland, Oregon.

KAREN S. BUDD, Ph.D., is professor in the Department of Psychology at DePaul University, Chicago, Illinois.

CRIS CLAY, M.A., is the executive director of the Community Re-Entry Program in the Department of Psychology at the University of the Pacific, Stockton, California.

PATRICK W. CORRIGAN, Psy.D., is professor of psychiatry at the University of Chicago and the executive director of the Center for Psychiatric Rehabilitation, Tinley Park, Illinois.

WILLIAM H. FEYERHERM, Ph.D., is a professor in the Graduate School of Social Work at Portland State University, Portland, Oregon.

BEN FRIEDMAN, Ph.D., is home study coordinator at the Family Resource Center, Chicago, Illinois.

EILEEN GAMBRILL, Ph.D., is the Hutto Patterson Professor in the School of Social Welfare at the University of California at Berkeley, Berkeley, California.

WALLACE GINGERICH, Ph.D., is a professor in the Mandel School of Applied Social Sciences at Case Western Reserve University, Cleveland, Ohio.

GLENN R. GREEN, Ph.D., is executive director of the Proviso Council on Aging, Bellwood, Illinois.

PATRICIA HANRAHAN, Ph.D., is a research associate (associate professor) in the Department of Psychiatry at the University of Chicago, Chicago, Illinois.

GAVIN HOUGHAM, M.A., is research director of the Geriatrics Section of the Department of Medicine at the University of Chicago, Chicago, Illinois.

PATRICIA J. KRANTZ, Ph.D., is executive director of the Princeton Child Development Institute, Princeton, New Jersey.

NATHAN L. LINSK, Ph.D., is a professor in the Jane Addams College of Social Work at the University of Illinois at Chicago, Chicago, Illinois.

DANIEL J. LUCHINS, M.D., is chief of clinical services in the Office of Mental Health, Illinois Department of Human Services, and chief of public psychiatry at the University of Chicago, Chicago, Illinois.

CHRISTINE MARLOW, Ph.D., is a professor in the School of Social Work at New Mexico State University, Las Cruces, New Mexico.

JEANNE C. MARSH, Ph.D., is the George Herbert Jones Professor in the School of Social Service Administration at the University of Chicago, Chicago, Illinois.

MARK A. MATTAINI, D.S.W., is an associate professor in the Jane Addams College of Social Work at the University of Illinois at Chicago, Chicago, Illinois.

LYNN E. MCCLANNAHAN, Ph.D., is executive director of the Princeton Child Development Institute, Princeton, New Jersey.

STANLEY MCCRACKEN, Ph.D., is associate professor of clinical psychiatry and senior lecturer in the School of Social Service Administration at the University of Chicago, Chicago, Illinois.

CHRISTOPHER G. MITCHELL is associate professor in the Jane Addams College of Social Work at the University of Illinois at Chicago, Chicago, Illinois.

SARAH K. MOORE, M.S.W., is a doctoral student in the Jane Addams College of Social Work at the University of Illinois at Chicago, Chicago, Illinois.

KATHLEEN MURPHY, M.D., is a clinical assistant professor in the Department of Internal Medicine at Wayne State University, Detroit, Michigan.

GAIL PATRICK, M.P.P., is a research analyst and a medical student in the the Pritzker School of Medicine at the University of Chicago, Chicago, Illinois.

WILLIAM J. REID, D.S.W., died in 2003. He was a Distinguished Professor in the School of Social Welfare at the State University of New York at Albany, Albany, New York.

TINA L. RZEPNICKI, Ph.D., is a professor in the School of Social Service Administration at the University of Chicago, Chicago, Illinois.

GREG SACHS, M.D., is an associate professor, chief of the Geriatrics Section, and co-director of the Memory Center in the Department of Medicine at the University of Chicago, Chicago, Illinois.

KEVEN SCHOCK, M.A., is clinical services director of the Community Re-Entry Program in the Department of Psychology at the University of the Pacific, Stockton, California.

MATSUJIRO SHIBANO, Ph.D., is a professor in the Department of Sociology at Kwansei Gakuin University, Uegahara, Nishinomiya, Hyogo, Japan.

SUSAN B. STERN, Ph.D., is an associate professor in the Faculty of Social Work at the University of Toronto, Toronto, Ontario, Canada.

BRUCE A. THYER, Ph.D., is a professor and dean of the School of Social Work at Florida State University, Tallahassee, Florida.

EARLIE M. WASHINGTON, Ph.D., is a professor and director of the School of Social Work at Western Michigan University, Kalamazoo, Michigan.

DAVID A. WILDER, Ph.D., is an associate professor in the Department of Psychology at Florida Institute of Technology.

STEVEN C. WOLF, Ph.D., is special projects manager in the Office of Quality Management and Training, Division of Health and Quality Care, Virginia Department of Mental Health, Mental Retardation, and Substance Abuse Services, Richmond, Virginia.

STEPHEN E. WONG, Ph.D., is an associate professor in the School of Social Work at Florida International University, Miami, Florida.

INDEX